AN ETHIC OF CARE

Thinking Gender
Edited by Linda J. Nicholson

Also published in the series

AN ETHIC OF CARE

EDITED BY
MARY JEANNE LARRABEE

FEMINIST AND INTERDISCIPLINARY PERSPECTIVES

ROUTLEDGE
NEW YORK AND LONDON

Published in 1993 by

Routledge
An imprint of Routledge, Chapman and Hall, Inc.
29 West 35th Street
New York, NY 10001

Published in Great Britain by

Routledge
11 New Fetter Lane
London EC4P 4EE

Library of Congress Cataloging-in-Publication Data

An Ethic of care: feminist and interdisciplinary perspectives /
   edited by Mary Jeanne Larrabee.
      p.   cm.—(Thinking gender)
   Includes bibliographical references and index.
   ISBN 0–415–90567–2.—ISBN 0–415–90568–0 (pbk.)
   1. Women—Psychology. 2. Moral development. 3. Developmental
psychology. I. Larrabee, Mary Jeanne. II. Series.
   HQ1206.E89 1992
   305.42—dc20   92–13206
                                                                              CIP
ISBN 0–415–90567–2 (HB)
ISBN 0–415–90568–0 (PB)

To David

Contents

Acknowledgments

The preparation of this manuscript was funded in part by the Philosophy Department and the University Research Council of DePaul University. Special thanks go to the university's Wordprocessing Department, which aided in the quick turnaround in the preliminary rounds of preparation, and to Patty Callahan and J. Patrick Hayden, who served as able editorial assistants at different stages of this project—Patrick especially for his careful editing in the last hurried time before submission. And warm appreciation to David, Daniel, and Colin who offered humor as the best form of help.

INTRODUCTION

1

Gender and Moral Development: A Challenge for Feminist Theory

Mary Jeanne Larrabee

I

In the early 1970s, a student at Harvard Graduate School of Education, researching real-life moral conflicts, was preparing a study of Harvard students facing the Vietnam draft. But when Richard Nixon ended both the war and the draft, she had to find alternative situations involving difficult decisions. With the 1973 Supreme Court's legalization of abortion, Carol Gilligan (Gilligan among others 1985, 37) found a rich site to investigate and, with the publication of her research materials in the 1982 work, *In a Different Voice,* initiated a still growing field of study strongly marked by her contributions—the study of an ethic of care.

Gilligan's work is related to that of the first dominant theorist in psychological development, Jean Piaget, who formulated a theory of cognitive growth which posited a series of stages through which infants and children progress during their first years. This process included the development of reasoning, one facet of which is moral reasoning. In the 1960s and 1970s, Lawrence Kohlberg at the Harvard Graduate School of Education expanded Piaget's skeletal theory on moral reasoning through empirical research and conceptual studies. Kohlberg became the major speaker for the importance of understanding moral development in educating children in the moral attitudes necessary for a mature citizenry in a democratic society (Kohlberg 1981, 96). His theory postulates a series of stages, which begins with the self-centered stance of young children, moves through a socially conventional orientation, and ends finally with one based on justice and equality.

Against this background, Carol Gilligan, working with Kohlberg, began her dissertation research at Harvard Graduate School of Education. Many of Kohlberg's conclusions were based on hypothetical dilemmas, i.e., projected situations where a moral judgment had to be made. Those people tested were asked to explain their decision in such situations and their motivating reasons. Gilligan attempted similar research, but in a different way—to find people who faced or had faced a difficult moral decision, a real-life dilemma, in order to compare the results of real life with hypothetical dilemma solutions. Real life steered her into an abortion study, the results of which appeared to her to contest the model of moral reasoning claimed by her mentor, Lawrence Kohlberg. For Gilligan, Kohlberg's results were sex-biased against a moral orientation based on care, in contrast to his positing of a justice orientation as the goal for mature moral development.

The study of an ethic of care, the field of study that developed from Gilligan's *In a Different Voice*, has moved in various directions: some psychologists have taken her conclusions to further their work on the relation between empathy and moral growth, others have reacted against the challenge to Kohlberg (including Kohlberg himself [Kohlberg, Levine & Hauer 1983]) by collecting evidence in support of his stage theory, while feminists either took up with excitement the seemingly new valuation of "feminine" morality or reacted against the gender differentiation and possibly even biological determinism underlying Gilligan's claims. These questions remain: Can a care orientation be distinguished from a justice orientation? To what extent are either of these moral "voices" related to gender? Can the ethic of care based on relatedness and responsiveness to others be considered a truly feminist ethic?

In the decade following the publication of *In a Different Voice*, the study of the ethic of care has become "a minor academic industry," in the words of Alison Jaggar (1990), the first to hold a funded Chair in Women's Studies in the United States (at Rutgers). The deluge of materials from the fields of psychology, philosophy, social theory, history, literature, law and jurisprudence, nursing, professional ethics, therapy and counseling, and pedagogy, to name more than a few, has occurred primarily in the latter half of the 1980s. Almost anyone today who raises some question about moral development, moral reasoning, ethical systems and applications, the nature of care, and related topics will at least mention Gilligan's work, if not deal directly with her claims.

Whence comes the source of Gilligan's influence? The impact of *In a Different Voice* and subsequent works (see References) from Gilligan and her colleagues at Harvard stems in part from her claim that there is a moral orientation, a "different voice," which she discovered in the women she investigated (but, she was careful to note, a voice which could also belong to men). This voice was one of care and responsibility, of concern and connection with other people, and Gilligan claims that it stems from a self which is intrinsically related to other people. It is a voice that, according to Gilligan, Kohlberg consistently underrated because his theory of moral reasoning accentuates, and therefore limits its investigations to, a voice of justice and, by implication, considers a mature self to be autonomous and capable of abstract reasoning. Gilligan thus points to a serious oversight in Kohlberg's paradigm of human development: the failure to take seriously a moral orientation based on care that could display a type of moral reasoning as mature as the one based on the voice of justice. Gilligan did not want to overturn the Kohlberg theory, but rather to supplement it with a theory of moral concern grounded in responsiveness to others that dictates providing care, preventing harm, and maintaining relationships. She also claims that her evidence shows that this mode of moral concern typically dominates the moral reasoning of women, whereas a moral system of rights and formal reasoning that uses a universalizable, abstract, and impersonal style dominates men's moral decision-making and development. With this assertion of gender differences, Gilligan enters the academic debates on gender, debates that demand the inclusion of women's experiences in all areas which traditionally excluded or devalued them, experiences either intrinsic to being a woman or the result of life within patriarchal societies.

Gilligan enthusiasts continue to seek corroboration of her thesis concerning differential moral development and its implications for such phenomena as women's impact on predominately male professions (e.g., lawyering, Menkel-Meadow 1985). Critics have questioned Gilligan's methodology and her conclusions, as much for their lack of "empirical vigor" as for the tenuousness of the evidence. Feminist critics, in particular, have worried about the undesirable implications concerning her focus on the "womanly virtues" that have traditionally been used to keep women in the "private" sphere. But the wide interdisciplinary impact of Gilligan's work is perhaps most interesting, in part due to her claims about the value of women's experience. Her work thus trumpets aspects of women's experience found defective, deficient, or undervalued by the broader culture. This validation could be carried into any field of research on women and gender. The importance of Gilligan's work is particularly obvious in philosophical moral theory, where the abstractions of ethicists have dominated the field, allowing little if any reference to the reality of people's moral lives.

II

It was through my experience in teaching a course on the ethic of care that I recognized the richness of this topic and perhaps also the reason behind the multitudinous responses. In dealing with any ethical theory, a dozen relevant questions are inevitably raised and must be answered, e.g., concerning the reality and nature of human freedom, of individual's responsibility for actions, of what does and does not count as relevant to moral decisions. Such questions move us, particularly many feminists, into even more fundamental issues—the nature of the human person, of human decision-making and action, of the roles of personality and environment, especially social environment, in human behavior, of the developmental aspects of human life, and especially of the specific impact of race/ethnicity, gender, and class. Many of these areas of research have undergone vast changes over the last twenty-five years, whether undertaken in philosophy, psychology, educational theory, religious studies, or applied fields such as management and corporate behavior, the legal arena, social and political action, and environmental problems.

For this volume I have gathered several of the key essays published during the initial decade following the appearance of *In a Different Voice*. There are a number of reasons for my choices. First, it seemed appropriate to bring together a variety of scholars who have engaged their minds and emotions with the question of an ethic of care and of the nature of care itself. Thus we find in this collection voices opposed on one ground or another to Gilligan's central claims or her methodology or the impact of her views on the goals of feminist praxis. But we also find other voices which pick up strands of her concerns and tie them into other relevant topics or attempt to expand and clarify an ethic of care and its implications. There are also both clearly feminist voices and those seemingly neutral to the interests of feminists.

Second, I wished to show by the organization of this collection the manner in which such a rich topic as an ethic of care has its own web of accumulating and interconnected historical sightings/citings, minds of differing occupations pulling in other minds in their contemplation and distillation of a complicated notion. Thus, we can follow these various lines from one text to the other, watching how the debate takes now this turn and now another, elicits new calls for clarification, and continuously points to an even more complicated future.

Part One, "Gilligan's 'Different Voice': Probings," outlines the psychological and philosophical issues for those unfamiliar with the relation between Gilligan's work and that of Kohlberg. Annette Baier's essay situates Gilligan within the wider contexts of women who have provided "what women want" in a moral theory: something that offers a contrast to duty and obligation, the key concept in modern philosophical and psychological moral theory. Women like Gilligan have claimed a need for supplementation to older (largely male-devised) theory; Baier herself has offered trust as one such addition.

Mary Brabeck places Gilligan's work within the broader context of traditional stereotypes of women and men—a tradition asserting women's "superior" morality that, in fact, views females as "deviant" from the better, because more reason-based, male standard. Her essay carefully contrasts Gilligan's and Kohlberg's theories on moral development. Brabeck also gives historical placement for Gilligan's research—within past empirical investigations on empathy, altruism, and other "prosocial" behaviors which may be aspects of Gilligan's notion of care. Brabeck closes with a clear challenge: she calls for an "enlarged conception of morality" that integrates justice and care, a suggestion that will be taken up in Part Four.

Lawrence Blum brings us back to the point of view of the moral philosopher, citing the theory of a care orientation against the network of concepts of increasing importance in discussions of Gilligan: the sense of self, relationships with others, and types of reasoning and standards within morality. He helps to clarify the issues that "impartialists," in whose camp he places Kohlberg, would raise against Gilligan, and then defends Gilligan and the voice of care within moral philosophy (see Adler 1989). Blum too questions the adequacy of the two voices, as well as the possibility that care could actually be considered a universal standard, thus meeting one of Kohlberg's criteria for stage 3 morality.

Part One closes with an essay by Owen Flanagan and Kathryn Jackson, who offer another philosophical perspective by analyzing the conceptual apparatus of Gilligan's "ethic of care," particularly her use of the gestalt metaphor to explain the relation between her theory and Kohlberg's. The authors call for a better understanding of care, hypothesizing possible differences in actual instances of caring, some of which may not be intuitively understood as moral. They then hint at the likelihood that there are a wide variety of good moral personalities, far more than the two postulated by Gilligan, a hint that needs testing by more specific delineation of the experiences underlying the development of any moral personality.

Part Two, *Expanding the Question,* looks beyond the bare bones of the original debate insofar as it centers on delineating the incompatibilities arising from the Gilligan and Kohlberg formulations of moral development. Linda Nicholson argues for expanding the discussion into the Western historical contexts of these theories, noting parallels that could be drawn between Gilligan's separation of her care orientation and Kohlberg's justice orientation, on the one hand, and patriarchal distinctions of private and public spheres, and of desire or emotion ("subjective" caring) and reason ("objective" standards of justice), on the other. She notes the limited cultural parameters of Gilligan's own discussions and the need to listen to other voices than the primarily white, middle-class women interviewed by Gilligan.

Linda Kerber, in the first widely-circulated interdisciplinary forum on Gilligan's work (in *Signs* 1986), extends this historical perspective by linking the "separate spheres" rhetoric of earlier feminist writers with Gilligan's account. Kerber agrees to the possible advantages of a revaluation of "women's sphere" of care, but she also underlines the danger of romantic oversimplication of women's moral personalities (see Lauritzen 1989). Kerber proposes that the antidote to such romanticization of women's caring may be found in accounts of fallibility, imperfection, or even evil in many women (and men). However, many people prefer to avoid this, the darker side of human existence, especially when doing theory (Spelman 1991 particularly notes the history of women mistreating other women, as well as children). A sense of the dangers hidden in the romanticization of women's caring will also encourage a cautious analysis of the implications of studying *women's* caring. One implication is positive, since it allows the revaluation of care; another is negative—socialization into a caring role has frequently fitted the needs of oppressive patriarchal societies (cf. Blum et al. 1976) and the emphasis on care may yield fodder for these needs.

Carol Stack's essay (also in the *Signs* forum) brings light from African-American women's experience, noting the parallels between Gilligan and other Women's Studies writers who cite the male/female difference in a care orientation. Like Nicholson, Stack states clearly that Gilligan's work leaves history and different cultures out of account; from Stack's perspective there is a clear failure to listen to black history and experience. Stack's studies of black migrants returning to the South display a contextual morality that differs from what Gilligan found in her female interviewees and which is in fact shared by both African-American women and men in the social groups that Stack studies, groups which differ from Gilligan's (1982a) samples in at least class and race. Theirs might be yet another voice, close to, but not identical with, the contextuality of the care orientation. What voices remain to be discovered and measured?

Broughton writes a creatively dense essay, bringing to bear a variety of questions about Gilligan's undertaking, yet landing on neither side of the Gilligan-Kohlberg divide. Broughton points out that Kohlberg responded to critics of his theory, including Gilligan, by embracing some notions of care and responsibility and placing them as he saw they fit into the assessment of moral development (see Kohlberg et al. 1984). And, while Broughton takes issue with both Gilligan and Kohlberg for their dualistic psychologies, he particularly takes Gilligan to task for reviving a liberal romantic idealism, as well as a thoroughgoing Cartesianism, and for misinterpreting Nancy Chodorow's view of women. Broughton's reaction to Gilligan's rejection of stage theory for a more cyclical living out of the levels of care orientation leads us to ask a more fundamental question: What is actually meant by human development? Is it linear and fixed, a series of necessarily linked stages, or is it a process with different contours, splitting apart, circling back on itself and reemerging ahead of where it was? This question reappears in our later essays and remains largely unanswered (see Houston 1988).

Part Three, *Checking the Data*, provides opportunity to study some of the empirical data supporting or refuting Gilligan's claim for a sex difference in moral reasoning, a difference that proves the sex bias in Kohlberg's theory. The first essay provides a transition between philosophical and empirical concerns, for Gertrude Nunner-Winkler tries to clarify the place of an ethic of care within the Western ethical tradition. She draws on Immanuel Kant's distinction between perfect and imperfect duties, aligning the Kohlbergian justice view with the former, Gilligan's care orientation with the latter. This configuration then allows her to claim that Kohlberg's interpretation of the choice of life over property in the Heinz dilemma as the best moral choice is actually a preference for a "radical female position." Nunner-Winkler also uses the perfect/imperfect distinction to test Gilligan's claims by means of interviews on hypothetical dilemmas and finds them unsupported. (See Benhabib 1987 for an alternative alignment of Gilligan's and Kohlberg's theories with notions of the "generalized other" in contrast with the "concrete other.")

Lawrence Walker draws upon a wide variety of empirical studies to refute Gilligan's allegations of sex bias in Kohlberg's theory and of sex differences in moral reasoning. Overall his review shows few significant sex differences between the development of moral reasoning throughout childhood and adolescence; those that appear in adult testings are usually correlated with difference in educational levels and occupation (see Walker's later 1989 study). This essay provides the nonexpert with an excellent example of the application of empirical and statistical information interpretation, a methodology that Gilligan both attempts to emulate and remains distinct from (see her reply to critics in this volume).

Diana Baumrind brings her own empirical expertise to a rereading of Walker's study, particularly to his use of the large Family Socialization Project in which she was involved. Her discussion points out by example the "interpretations" that can occur even in the weighing of "facts," in this case, statistical evidence of individuals' experiences. For those of us who are not empirical scientists, it is helpful to be reminded that specific individuals set up hypotheses and devise means of testing them; feminist critics have noted the ramifications of this fact for the status of "objective" science (see, e.g., Harding & Hintikka 1983). In a criticism reminiscent of feminist concerns with looking below the surface of empirical investigations, Baumrind wonders why Kohlberg and Walker take what is measured by their devices as indicating *real* moral development if the people questioned are asked only to *think through* a hypothetical dilemma. Baumrind thinks that Kohlberg's (and thus Walker's) measurement is one of *cognitive* judgments, in contrast to actual decisions that lead to action in the judging person's life. Cognitively one might have a level of sophistication about one's (Western) culture and what is taken therein as moral—this could be displayed in response to a hypothetical dilemma in a way that it might not in a parallel real-life decision on the same matter. We need ask what other factors may be involved in moral reasoning and to what degree any of these can be measured. The cultural bias of Kohlberg's claims about the justice orientation as morally superior seems more evident when we compare them with the measurements of moral reasoning in Eastern and third-world countries, as well as in women. These differences are clearly linked in Baumrind's mind to cultural differences in the social construction of the individual, since the latter groups tend toward strong social connectedness with others and ethical perspectives that share much with Gilligan's care orientation. (Walker responds to Baumrind in his 1986 essay.)

Catherine Greeno and Eleanor Maccoby (from the *Signs* forum) also take up the charge of sex bias against Kohlberg and find it lacking merit, pointing to Lawrence Walker's review for evidence. They also indicate that, while certain findings (e.g., Eisenberg & Lennon 1983) show women to have a greater reputation for altruism and empathy, there is little proof they actually *are* more "caring" in behavior. The warning here is to be wary about quickly accepting our "intuitions" about women's caring nature, a longstanding gender stereotype. Zella Luria (also in *Signs*) questions Gilligan's sample selection and the use of interviews, particularly the methodology of shifting these stories into an objective, measurable, and thus statistical matrix (cf. Nails 1983).

Part Four, "Feminist Ethics and the Future of Care," brings us back to Carol Gilligan's *In a Different Voice*, with a defense by Gilligan—primarily against the writers in the *Signs* forum, but also against the strong criticisms of Lawrence Walker and others in the Kohlberg camp. She tries to steer her theory away from her critics' "central confusion" by emphasizing that she has developed a theory about a different *voice*, i.e., a different way of constituting the self and morality, and thus a way of thinking about moral decisions differently from those articulated in Kohlberg's theory (see Lyons 1989). This is a difference in *theme* from Kohlberg's justice theme; this theme is not identified by gender, even though her empirical observation shows a stronger association of this theme with women than with men. She thus rejects her critics' objections, claiming the very difference of her work and methodology to be justifiable given her intent and the further data generated by the studies of her doctoral students and colleagues in the last few years, studies which, she contends, confirm this different voice (see, e.g., Gilligan & Attanucci 1988; Lyons 1983/1988).

The next three essays move beyond pure criticism, in one way or another playing off Gilligan's claims against the requirements for a feminist ethical theory. Bill Puka separates Gilligan's treatment of care as a moral developmental theme from care as liberation, hoping to maintain the value of Gilligan's account without denying feminist worries over her emphasis on the sex-differentiated orientation toward care. Puka's hypothesis shows the value of care understood as liberation, when care of both self and others allows a freedom from a purely other-centered care. Puka considers Gilligan's description of the latter to be a self-justificatory coping strategy, a "slavish" conventionalism proclaiming the value of self-sacrifice for others (within the patriarchy). Thus, when Gilligan contrasts the mature form of care recognizing both self and other, Puka can celebrate it as a second coping strategy, resulting from reflection and self-choice. We see here two sides of liberation: what the women's movement liberates women *from*, a "slavish" conventionalism, and what it would liberate them *to* (cf. Houston 1989). Yet, Puka nonetheless questions the latter. Since this liberation is accomplished by cognitively revaluating one's role in a sexist society, Puka suggests that Gilligan might be giving a theory of *cognitive*-moral development (an echo of earlier essays in this volume) and providing women with a rationalization, i.e., a cognitive account, for shifting to a more mature form of care which merely adds self to the pot and stirs. For support Puka calls into question Gilligan's readings of the women whose self-concepts changed such that Gilligan placed them at the mature level of care because of their self-reflective responses. In a vein similar to Broughton's recovery of Gilligan's interviews, Puka suggests rethinking the interview data and the processes they express, in order to unravel the strands of thought, judgment and decision, of socialized and individually formed selves, and of development, that are found in the ethic of care (see, e.g., Mullett 1987 concerning the processes from which a mature caring might arise).

Joan Tronto provides a clear summary of Gilligan's work and its claims about bias in Kohlberg's theory, noting that responses supporting Gilligan belong with previous writers who favored a "women's morality." She cites a variety of other voices that point up the Eurocentric bias of current moral theory. Her real concern for feminist ethics, however, has to do with the adequacy of using care in a truly feminist ethics, not just for intellectual interest, but with a serious stance towards the relevance of theory for feminist action within whatever community we find ourselves. Tronto urges the need to understand the broad social contexts from which a theory of care emerges, including that specific social context which is the philosophical culture of academic theory-formation, e.g., the "metaethical question" which asks about the nature of a good moral theory, perhaps even before formulating one. The current "standard" for many moral philosophers is some type of Kantian view, and a strong alternative is contextual moral theory, where an ethic of care would fit. Yet the possibilities of this ethic conserving existing social arrangements, or of being relativistic, show the difficulties of deciding whom should be cared for and when. So how do we move toward this theory of care? Tronto poses many tasks and some hints of directions, some of which she follows elsewhere (see Tronto 1989; Fisher & Tronto 1991).

Marilyn Friedman revisits the question of an empirically evidenced gender difference in moral reasoning, but adds an interesting dimension to the debate, by seeing the social construction of genders to include the "moralization" of individuals along gender lines. In other words, if Gilligan is correct about there being sex differences in moralities, this situation would be due to women and men being differently socialized into such moralities. She begins to move the debate beyond discussion of two distinct moral orientations and toward an understanding of care as involving justice themes, questioning whether the description of these orientations as distinct in theory actually matches a distinction in practice, that is, in actual moral decision-making. The dichotimization of justice and care seems inadequate particularly when we analyze the moral dimensions of close personal relationships (cf. Friedman 1989); Gilligan (and Kohlberg) are thus faulted for a narrow understanding of justice. Justice, and care as well, understood in terms of commitments to individual persons in their particularity, can be integrated on some levels while distinguished on others. Friedman leaves us to deliberate on the variety of moral orientations that such considerations would uncover, a deliberation of value for a feminist ethic that could investigate types of caring and justice-seeking without the narrowness of Gilligan and Kohlberg. Friedman would agree with Tronto (1989) who demands a shift from a feminine to a feminist approach to caring, splitting caring from its linkage with the traditional gender divisions that have historically devalued women and "their" virtues.

III

What in this interplay of issues remains most important to feminist theory as we look for a path outward from Gilligan and either beyond gender difference as she pronounces it or, perhaps, beyond caring itself? And to what extent, if any, must a feminist ethic be an ethic of care, either wholly or in part? The decade has already provided us with a number of trails on this phenomenon called care: Nel Noddings has given us a volume entitled *Caring: A Feminine Approach to Ethics and Moral Education* (1984), and Sarah Ruddick one entitled *Maternal Thinking: Toward a Politics of Peace* (1989), expanding on her well-received (1980) essay. These follow to some extent the path opened by Annette Baier and the women she mentioned in this volume (e.g., Iris Murdoch)—and, I would note, by Simone de Beauvoir (1948/1976), who claimed that an authentic consideration of the freedom of others is integral to any ethical decision. Other scholars reflecting a variety of experiences as women (African-Americans and other women of color, lesbian-feminists, care-workers such as those in the healthcare industry) are expanding upon the points we find in Stack's essay: Toinette Eugene (1989) directly addresses the applicability of Gilligan's findings to African-Americans, Patricia Collins integrates into a black feminist theory African-American women's experiences of an enlarged notion of mothering, and Aída Hurtado (1989) expands on the need to keep class and race or ethnicity in mind as often deleterious parameters of supposed caring relations between women who are connected by work (e.g., the Hispanic or Chicana caring for the privileged white woman and her children) but are never equal (see Moody-Adams 1991).

I think, however, a key to our understanding the notion of care brings us back to one of the original "discoveries" of the earliest women's studies scholars in the 1960s and 1970s: that gender is socioculturally constructed, which means that personality and the self or selves that women exist with and within are also socioculturally constructed (see Ferguson 1987). Further, since society and culture are historically conditioned and culture is various, even in such "smaller" social units as a modern city, then race and ethnicity, class and economic status, and sex are modified and interlaced by these parameters of human life (see Lykes 1989).

And I would add that feminist theorists, even some in this volume, are largely silent about a crucial aspect of this social construction of individual women, that is, the "sociohistorical" dimension that lies between the individual and larger society—I mean the family. Part of Gilligan's alleged romanticism in her assignment of caring attitudes to her interviewees follows from her assumption that caring stems directly from the mother-daughter dyad. Granted, this particular family tie is considered most important, not only by Freud, but also by the feminist psychoanalyst, Nancy Chodorow, from whose (1978) work Gilligan derives her theory concerning the engendering of a morally caring orientation in women (see Chodorow 1986). But we have several writers in this volume who take Gilligan to task for adopting too uncritical a stance towards Chodorow's theory. The widely-known feminist therapy theorist and practitioner Harriet Lerner (1988), while understanding the allure of a revised feminist psychoanalytic theory, notes that a great variety of intrafamilial and intergenerational processes operative in the formation of any individual person are completely disregarded by many feminists. But is history only the history of the largest social groups, a view already criticized by the feminists challenging the valuation of public over private lives as these are approached in traditional academic research? Does the engendering of the socially constructed individual reflect only this macrodimension and a fairly limited microdimension, the mother-daughter relation? Lerner urges that feminists incorporate a broader interactive view from systemic theories, and thus avoid the narrow linear perspective of human development given in a stage theory approach, as well as the polarized dichotomies of personalities it claims, the "different" selves of Gilligan's theory (cf. Bograd 1988). Feminists might also reflect on what recent scholars call "psychohistory," i.e., incorporating intrapsychic developmental issues into the wider cultural-historical scene, particularly in order to understand the fallible or too often evil behavior history has witnessed (see *Journal of Psychohistory*).

This multilevel understanding of the historical processes and societal networks within which we grow into our selfhood and individuality, including gender, needs to be applied to the theory of self, since one of Gilligan's major claims concerns the interconnection of the care orientation and the relational self from which that orientation springs, both in its "feminine" conventional sense and its mature sense (see Card 1990). The recent work of Gilligan and her colleagues accentuates the distinction between the autonomous (separate, objective) self with the justice orientation and the connected (interdependent) self with the care orientation. Lyons (1983/1988) describes these as two types of "self-in-relation": the self using the justice voice speaks of a relation of reciprocity giving rules for roles, the self using the care voice speaks of a relation of response to the other's particular needs (1988, 33; cf. Jordan & Surrey 1986). She concludes, however, that a relations conception of self is in fact found in both sexes at all ages (cf. Gilligan 1986a).

Gilligan (with Attanucci 1988) reiterates the two distinct moral orientations of justice and care, but the fact that many women and men are shown to use now one and now another raises a query about whether a specific "self" is correlated with each orientation. Gilligan defines these two selves dichotomously; if therefore their development underlies either the care or the justice voice, she (and Lyons) must be finding persons with split selves, multiple selves. This curious implication about Gilligan's self theory could actually cohere well with other feminist work on women's experience within patriarchal society and help explain the difficulties of female adolescents studied in Gilligan's most recent work (with Lyons & Hanmer 1989), difficulties in maintaining their *own* voice against the imposition of a socially expected voice to which they must adapt as they move into adulthood. The implication of multiple selves also connects with Morgan's (1988) skillful articulation of women's "moral madness." Such "madness" stems from alienating experiences embedded in patriarchal life; these can split a woman into a variety of voices, if not a variety of selves, so that she can make sense of her experiences while adapting to a patriarchal society undergoing change. The indication of multiple selves also echoes the puzzling complexity often experienced by women moving through important life transitions where the rules provided by roles fail. For instance, some women of color, some double- or triple-marginalized women, speak of the difficulties of remaining rooted in their ethnic identities as they attempt to situate themselves within the dominant society (see Anzaldua 1987).

What of the *development* of self or selves that is claimed to underlie the two voices (cf. Auerbach et al. 1985)? The essays in this volume contain various suggestions for furthering the discussion of care as it relates to this issue: Brabeck's characterization of both Gilligan's and Kohlberg's view of self as "myths"; Flanagan and Jackson's proposal for a wide variety of good moral selves and the experiences leading to these (cf. Blum 1990), and Broughton's criticism of dualistic psychologies (in both Kohlberg and Gilligan) which fracture human qualities between the two types of self. The gaps become clearer. First and foremost in my mind is the question of "development," especially since Broughton sees Gilligan's care orientation view as implying that women do *not* develop, at least in moral reasoning. Rather they shift back and forth between the levels of the care orientation, depending on the context of the decision, and also sometimes between the care and the justice orientation. Although Broughton considers his point a criticism, some feminists could see Gilligan's theory as having the advantage that Lerner (1988) cites of some feminist theories, that is, it avoids straightforward linear thinking and the projection of linearity onto their models of appropriate human experience.

I see a need to open the ground toward a feminist analysis of female development that is rooted, *not* in a Freudian framework, but in women's own experiences articulated and "interpreted" by themselves. Such experiences can be mined for the commonalities of women's development. Ramona Mercer and her colleagues (1989) lay a basis for such work in their study of women over sixty, determining the ways in which various factors had an impact upon these women's development. They use Erikson's developmental theory, which already moves beyond the Gilligan/Chodorow view of development that seems to end with the shift into adult sexuality (and rationality). There are, instead, various transitions from infancy all the way into late adulthood, each stage marked by a new challenge for self-development (e.g., individuation in adolescence, intimate relationships in early adulthood). This sample of eighty women who began life in the first quarter of this century was measured against the stages of Erikson's theory, and also in light of a complex picture of both intrapsychic and extrapsychic influences, including such events as the Depression.

A more original departure comes from Sharon Conarton and Linda Silverman, who derive part of their theory of the earlier phases of female development from the object relations school which is Chodorow's main influence. They propose that women's experiences (again we might need to question which women) move through a multistage developmental process that finds both linear and cyclical movement, as well as concurrent experiences that reflect different stages. The question becomes to what extent can a woman's "self" be considered finalized in early adulthood, particularly given the less constrained models of leading a female life today (compared with Mercer's sample)—both the wider range of employment available in professional, white- and blue-collar areas, and the greater freedom for choosing whether and when to bear children. For example, if children's departure from home provides for some women a transition point demanding a self-examination of their core identity (who am I now?), this reflection will have different determinants and different outcomes depending on whether the women had a well-established "public work-self" before having children, still maintained one while raising children, or never had this sense of self. Development of a *self*-identity might arise differently in such various circumstances (cf. Josselson 1987), and since the demands on each woman's caring would also differ it becomes even more obvious that one simple understanding of the care orientation and the self that it presupposes will not suffice for a feminist theory of care or for a feminist ethic. Even these modest beginnings of a feminist theory of female development point to the need for a variety of theories concerning the different paths of female development, both actual and ideal, and the correlation and possible integration of these with theories of male development. And we would always understand these beginnings to be sensitive to divergences given historical events, changes in cultures and societies, and factors of race, class, and other determinants of women's and men's lives. These divergences will include various positive *and* negative forms of caring, so that a feminist theory of care moves away from a one-sided orientation to care (see Mullett 1988). Finally, as theorists we would be mindful and careful in developing our theories to keep an ear tuned for what we might have missed (see Lugones 1991).

At this point, at this marking of a decade of responses to Gilligan's original *Voice*, we find we have more questions than answers, have moved in more directions than Gilligan could have foretold, and have been stung to further curiosity and concern far beyond the original intent of Gilligan's thesis. Gilligan began with the problem of real-life dilemmas, rather than merely the hypothetical ones studied by Kohlberg. In some ways the question of the place of care within a feminist ethic remains a real-life dilemma for many feminist theorists. We have yet to see the extent to which a study of care will provide further understanding of women's places within the histories, cultures, and societies in which women, each so very different, live their lives. More importantly, we have yet to see the way in which care relates to the broadly-defined feminist agenda of opening up possibilities for the positive development and liberation of individual women from the limitations of these lives; this agenda cannot be accomplished with too much caring for patriarchal life, and cannot be undertaken with too little care for individual women. With more than a quarter of a century behind us in this phase of the Women's Movement, the work for feminists, both in the academic arena and in praxis at large, seems more complex and difficult than ever: the more we learn, the more we realize what we have yet to learn; the more we act the more we find needs changing—and the feistier we must become in order to affect change (see Card 1990). A feminist care, exercised in light of each woman's concrete circumstances, will help us change what needs changing for the better. While we cannot necessarily wait for feminist theories of care or of an ethic of care to be provided to our satisfaction, it appears to me intuitively clear that in some broad sense care will have a place both in our theories and in our activities as feminists.

Part I

GILLIGAN'S "DIFFERENT VOICE": PROBINGS

2

What Do Women Want in a Moral Theory?

Annette C. Baier

When I finished reading Carol Gilligan's *In a Different Voice*, I asked my-self the obvious question for a philosopher reader, namely what differences one should expect in the moral philosophy done by women, supposing Gilligan's sample of women representative, and supposing her analysis of their moral attitudes and moral development to be correct. Should one expect them to want to produce moral theories, and if so, what sort of moral theories? How will any moral theories they produce differ from those produced by men?

Obviously one does not have to make this an entirely a priori and hypo-thetical question. One can look and see what sort of contributions women have made to moral philosophy. Such a look confirms, I think, Gilligan's findings. What one finds *is* a bit different in tone and approach from the standard sort of moral philosophy as done by men following in the footsteps of the great moral philosophers (all men). Generalizations are extremely rash, but when I think of Philippa Foot's work on the moral virtues, of Eliz-abeth Anscombe's work on intention and on modern moral philosophy, of Iris Murdoch's philosophical writings, of Ruth Barcan Marcus' work on moral dilemmas, of the work of the radical feminist moral philosophers who are not content with orthodox Marxist lines of thought, of Jenny Teichman's book on illegitimacy, of Susan Wolf's recent articles, of Claudia Card's essay on mercy, Sabina Lovilbond's recent book, Gabriele Taylor's work on pride, love and on integrity, Cora Diamond's and Mary Midgeley's work on our attitude to animals, Sissela Bok's work on lying and on secrecy, Virginia Held's work, the work of Alison Jaggar, Marilyn Frye, and many others, I

Reprinted by permission from *Nous* 19, no.1: 53–63. Copyright © 1985 by the journal.

seem to hear a different voice from the standard moral philosophers' voice. I hear the voice Gilligan heard, made reflective and philosophical. What women want in moral philosophy is what they are providing. And what they are providing seems to me to confirm Gilligan's theses about women. One has to be careful there, of course, for not all important contributions to moral philosophy by women fall easily into the Gilligan stereotype, or its philosophical extension. Nor has it been only women who recently have been proclaiming discontent with the standard approach in moral philosophy, and trying new approaches. Michael Stocker, Alasdair MacIntyre, and Ian Hacking (1984, when he assesses the game theoretic approach to morality), all should be given the status of honorary women, if we accept the hypothesis that there are some moral insights which for whatever reason women seem to attain more easily or more reliably than men do. Still, exceptions confirm the rule, so I shall proceed undaunted by these important exceptions to my generalizations.

If Hacking is right, preoccupation with prisoner's and prisoners' dilemma is a big boys' game, and a pretty silly one too. It is, I think, significant that women have not rushed into the field of game-theoretic moral philosophy, and that those who have dared enter that male locker room have said distinctive things there. Edna Ullman Margalit's book *The Emergence of Norms* put the prisoner's dilemma in its limited moral place. Supposing that at least part of the explanation for the relatively few women in this field is disinclination rather than disability, one might ask if this disinclination also extends to a disinclination for the construction of moral theories. For although we find out what sort of moral philosophy women want by looking to see what they have provided, if we do that for moral theory, the answer we get seems to be "none." For none of the contributions to moral philosophy by women really count as moral theories, nor are seen as such by their authors.

Is it that reflective women, when they become philosophers, want to do without moral theory, want no part in the construction of such theories? To conclude this at this early stage, when we have only a few generations of women moral philosophers to judge from, would be rash indeed. The term "theory" can be used in wider and narrower ways, and in its widest sense a moral theory is simply an internally consistent, fairly comprehensive account of what morality is and when and why it merits our acceptance and support. In that wide sense, a moral theory is something it would take a skeptic, or one who believes that our intellectual vision is necessarily blurred or distorted when we let it try to take in much, to be an antitheorist. Even if there were some truth in the latter claim, one might compatibly with it still hope to build up a coherent total account by a mosaic method, assembling a lot of smaller-scale works until one had built up a complete account—say taking the virtues or purported virtues one by one until one had a more or less complete account. But would that sort of comprehensiveness in one's moral philosophy entitle one to call the finished work a moral theory? If it does, then many women moral philosophers today can be seen as engaged in moral theory construction. In the weakest sense of "theory," namely a coherent near-comprehensive account, then there are plenty incomplete theories to be found in the works of women moral philosophers. And in *that* sense of theory, most of what are recognized as the current moral theories are also incomplete, since they do not purport to be yet really comprehensive. Wrongs to animals and wrongful destruction of our physical environment are put to one side by Rawls, and in most "liberal" theories there are only hand waves concerning our proper attitude to our children, to the ill, to our relatives, friends, and lovers.

Is comprehensiveness too much to ask of a moral theory? The paradigm examples of moral theories—those that are called by their authors "moral theories," are distinguished not by the comprehensiveness of their internally coherent account, but by the *sort* of coherence which is aimed at over a fairly broad area. Their method is not the mosaic method, but the broad brushstroke method. Moral theories, as we know them, are, to change the art form, vaults rather than walls—they are not built by assembling painstakingly-made brick after brick. In *this* sense of theory, namely, that of a fairly tightly systematic account of a fairly large area of morality, with a key stone supporting all the rest, women moral philosophers have not yet, to my knowledge, produced moral theories, nor claimed that they have.

Leaving to one side the question of what good purpose (other than good clean intellectual fun) is served by such moral theories, and supposing for the sake of argument that women can, if they wish, systematize as well as the next man, and if need be systematize in a mathematical fashion as well as the next mathematically minded moral philosopher, then what key concept, or guiding motif, might hold together the structure of a moral theory hypothetically produced by a reflective woman, Gilligan-style, who has taken up moral theorizing as a calling? What would be a suitable central question, principle, or concept, to structure a moral theory which might accommodate those moral insights women tend to have more readily than men, and to answer those moral questions which, it seems, worry women more than men? I hypothesized that the women's theory, expressive mainly of women's insights and concerns, would be an ethics of love, and this hypothesis seems to be Gilligan's too, since she has gone on from *In a Different Voice* to write about the limitations of Freud's understanding of love as women know it (Gilligan 1984a). But presumably women theorists will be like enough to men to want their moral theory to be acceptable to all, so acceptable both to reflective women and to reflective men. Like any good theory, it will need not to ignore the partial truth of previous theories. So it must accommodate both the insights men have more easily than women, and those women have more easily than men. It should swallow up its predecessor theories. Women moral theorists, if any, will have this very great advantage over the men whose theories theirs supplant, that they can stand on the shoulders of men moral theorists, as no man has yet been able to stand on the shoulders of any woman moral theorist. There can be advantages, as well as handicaps, in being latecomers. So women theorists will need to connect their ethics of love with what has been the men theorists' preoccupation, namely obligation.

The great and influential moral theorists have in the modern era taken *obligation* as the key and the problematic concept, and have asked what justifies treating a person as morally bound or obliged to do a particular thing. Since to be bound is to be unfree, by making obligation central one at the same time makes central the question of the justification of coercion, of forcing or trying to force someone to act in a particular way. The concept of obligation as justified limitation of freedom does just what one wants a good theoretical concept to do—to divide up the field (as one looks at different ways one's freedom may be limited, freedom in different spheres, different sorts and versions and levels of justification) and at the same time hold the subfields together. There must in a theory be some generalization and some specification or diversification, and a good rich key concept guides one both in recognizing the diversity and in recognizing the unity in it. The concept of obligation has served this function very well for the area of morality it covers, and so we have some fine theories about that area. But as Aristotelians and Christians, as well as women, know, there is a lot of morality *not* covered by that concept, a lot of very great importance even for the area where there are obligations.

This is fairly easy to see if we look at what lies behind the perceived obligation to keep promises. Unless there is some good moral reason why someone should assume the responsibility of rearing a child to be *capable* of taking promises seriously, once she understands what a promise is, the obligation to obey promises will not effectively tie her, and any force applied to punish her when she breaks promises or makes fraudulent ones will be of questionable justice. Is there an *obligation* on someone to make the child into a morally competent promisor? If so, on whom? Who has failed in their obligations when, say, war orphans who grew up without parental love or any other love arrive at legal adulthood very willing to be untrue to their word? Who failed in what obligation in all those less extreme cases of attempted but unsuccessful moral education? The parents who didn't produce promise-keeping offspring? Those who failed to educate the parents in how to educate their children (whoever it might be who might plausibly be thought to have the responsibility for training parents to fulfill their obligations)? The liberal version of our basic moral obligations tend to be fairly silent on who has what obligations to new members of the moral community, and it would throw most theories of the justification of obligations into some confusion if the obligation to lovingly rear one's children were added to the list of obligations. Such evidence as we have about the conditions in which children do successfully "learn" the morality of the community of which they are members suggests that we cannot substitute "conscientiously" for "lovingly" in this hypothetically needed obligation. But an obligation to love, in the strong sense needed, would be an embarrassment to the theorist, given most accepted versions of "ought implies can."

It is hard to make fair generalizations here, so I shall content myself with indicating how this charge I am making against the current men's moral theories, that their version of the justified list of obligations does not ensure the proper care of the young, so does nothing to ensure the stability of the morality in question over several generations, can be made against what I regard as the best of the men's recent theories, namely John Rawls' theory of justice. One of the great strengths of Rawls' theory is the careful attention given to the question of how just institutions produce the conditions for their continued support, across generations, and in particular of how the sense of justice will arise in children, once there are minimally just institutions structuring the social world into which they are born. Rawls, more than most moral theorists, has attended to the question of the stability of his just society, given what we know about child development. But Rawls' sensitive account of the conditions for the development of that sense of justice needed for the maintenance of his version of a just society takes it for granted that there will be loving parents rearing the children in whom the sense of justice is to develop. "The parents, we may suppose, love the child, and in time the child comes to love and trust the parents" (Rawls 1971, 463). Why may we suppose this? Not because compliance with Rawls' version of our obligations and duties will ensure it. Rawls' theory, like so many other theories of obligation, in the end must take out a loan not only on the natural duty of parents to care for children (which he will have no trouble including), but on the natural *virtue* of parental love (or even a loan on the maternal instinct?). The virtue of being a *loving* parent must supplement the natural duties and the obligations of justice, if the just society is to last beyond the first generation. And as Nancy Chodorow's work indicates, the loving parents must also accept a certain division of childcare responsibility if their version of the obligations and virtues of men and of women is, along with their version of the division of labor accompanying that allocation of virtues, to be passed on.

Reliance on a recognized obligation to turn oneself into a good parent, or else avoid becoming a parent, would be a problematic solution. Good parents tend to be the children of good parents, so this obligation would collapse into the obligation to avoid parenthood unless one expected to be a good parent. That, given available methods of contraception, may itself convert into the obligation, should one expect not to be a good parent, to sexual abstinence, or sterilization, or resolute resort to abortion when contraception fails. The conditional obligation to abort, and in effect also the conditional obligation to sterilization, falls on the women. There may be conditions in which the rational moral choice is between obligatory sexual abstinence or obligatory sterilization, but obligatory abortion, such as women in China now face, seems to me a moral monster. I do not believe that liberal moral theorists will be able to persuade reflective women that a morality that in any conditions makes abortion obligatory, as distinct from permitted, or advisable, or, on occasion, best, is in their own as well as their men fellows' long-term self-interest. It would be tragic if such moral questions in the end come to the question of whose best interests to sacrifice, men's or women's (and I do not believe they *do* come to this) but, should they come to this, then justice would require that, given the long history of the subordination of women's to men's interests, men's interests be sacrificed. Justice, of course, never decides these issues unless power reinforces justice, so I am not predicting any victory for women, should it ever come to a fight over obligatory abortion, or over who is to face obligatory sterilization.

No liberal moral theorist, as far as I know, is advocating obligatory abortion or obligatory sterilization when necessary to prevent the conception of children whose parents do not expect to love them. My point rather is that they escape this conclusion only by avoiding the issue of what is to ensure that new members of the moral community do get the loving care they need to become morally competent persons. Liberal moral theories assume that women will either provide loving maternal care, or will persuade their mates to provide loving paternal care, or when pregnant will decide for abortion, encouraged by their freedom-loving men. In other words, they exploit the culturally encouraged maternal instinct, and/or the culturally encouraged docility of women. The liberal system would receive a nasty spanner in its works should women use their freedom of choice as regards abortion to choose *not* to abort, and then leave their newborn children on their fathers' doorsteps. That would test liberal morality's ability to provide for its own survival.

At this point it may be objected that every moral theory must make some assumptions about the natural psychology of those on whom obligations are imposed. Why shouldn't the liberal theorist count on a continuing sufficient supply of good loving mothers, as it counts on continuing self-interest, and perhaps on a continuing supply of pugnacious men who are able and willing to become good soldiers, without turning any of these into moral *obligations*? Why waste moral resources recognizing as obligatory or as virtuous what one can count on getting without moral pressure? If one can get enough good mothers and good warriors "for free," in the moral economy, why not gladly exploit what nature and cultural history offer? I cannot answer this question fully here, but my argument does depend upon the assumption that a decent morality will *not* depend for its stability on forces to which it gives no moral recognition. Its account books should be open to scrutiny, and there should be no unpaid debts, no loans with no prospect of repayment. I also assume that once we are clear about these matters, and about the interdependencies involved, we will not, compatibly with our principles of justice, be able to recognize either a special obligation on every woman to initiate the killing of the fetus she has conceived (should she and her mate be, or think they will be, deficient in parental love), or a special obligation on every young man to kill those his elders have labeled enemies of his country. Both such "obligations" are prima facie suspect, and difficult to make consistent with any of the principles supposedly generating obligations in modern moral theories. I also assume that, on reflection, we will not want to recognize as *virtues* the character traits of women and men which lead them to supply such life and death services for free. Neither maternal servitude, nor the resoluteness needed to kill-off one's children to prevent their growing up unloved, nor the easy willingness to go out and kill when ordered to do so by authorities, seem to be character traits a decent morality will encourage by labeling "virtues." But the liberal's morality must somehow encourage them if its stability depends on enough people showing them. There is, then, understandable motive for liberals' avoidance of the question of whether such qualities are or are not morally approved of, and of whether or not there is any obligation to act as one with such character traits would act.

It is symptomatic of the bad faith of liberal morality, as understood by many of those who defend it, that such issues as whether to fight or not to fight, to have or not to have an abortion, to be or not to be an unpaid maternal drudge, are left to individual conscience. Since there is no coherent guidance liberal morality can give on these issues, which clearly are *not* matters of moral indifference, liberal morality tells each of us "the choice is yours," hoping that enough will choose to be self-sacrificial life-providers and self-sacrificial death-dealers to suit the purposes of the rest.

Rawls' theory does explicitly face the question of the moral justification of refusal to bear arms, and of how a just society provides for its own defense. The hardships imposed on conscripted soldiers are, he says, a necessary evil, and the most that just institutions can do is to "make sure that the risks of suffering from those misfortunes are more or less evenly shared by all members of society over the course of their life, and that there is no avoidable class bias in selecting those who are called for duty." What of sex/gender bias? Or is that assumed to be unavoidable? Rawls's principles seem to me to imply that women should be conscripted, if anyone is (and I think that is right), but since he avoids the question of justice between men and women one does not know whether he intended this implication. His suggestion that one argument in favor of a conscripted army is that it is less likely to be an instrument of unjustified foreign adventures will become even stronger, I believe, if half the conscripts are women. Like most male moral theorists, Rawls does not discuss the morality of having children, refusing to have them, refusing to care for them, nor does he discuss how just institutions might equalize the responsibilities involved in ensuring that there be new members of society, and that they become morally competent members of it. Thus, one does not know whether he accepts a gender-based division of social service here, leaving it to the men to do the dangerous defensive destruction of life and cities, while leaving the support of new life, and any costs going or contrived to go with that, to the women. I hope that is not what he meant.

I do not wish, by having spoken of these two traditionally gender-based allocations of responsibility together—namely, producing and caring for new human life, on the one hand, and the destruction of the human lives officially labeled "enemies," on the other—to leave the impression that I see any parallel between them except that they have both been treated as gender-based, and that both present embarrassments for liberal moral theory. Not all allocations of responsibility are allocations of burdens, and parenthood, unlike military life, need not be seen as essentially burden-bearing. Good mothers and good soldiers make contributions of very different sorts of importance to the ongoing life of a moral community, and should not be seen, as they sometimes are, as fair mutual substitutes, as forms of social service. Good mothers will always be needed by a moral community, in the best conditions as well as the worst, while the need for good military men, although foreseeably permanent, is a sign of some failure of our morality, a failure of our moral laws to be valid theorems for the conservation of men in multitudes. Nor do the burdens of soldiering have any real analogue in the case of motherhood, which today *need* not impose real costs on the mother. If there are significant costs—loss of career opportunity, improperly recompensed drudgery in the home, or health risks—this is due to bad but largely remediable social arrangements, as the failure of parents to experience any especially parental satisfactions may be also due to bad but remediable socially-produced attitudes to parental responsibility. We do not, I think, want our military men to enjoy the no doubt humanly possible peculiar satisfactions of killing the enemy and destroying their cities, and any changes we made in social customs and institutions to make such pleasures more likely would be deplorable ones. Military life in wartime should always be seen as a sacrifice, while motherhood should never need to be seen as self-sacrificial service. If it is an honor and a privilege to bear arms for one's country, as we understandably tell our military conscripts and volunteers, part of the honor is being trusted with activities that are a necessary evil, being trusted not to enjoy their evil aspects, trusted to see the evil as well as the necessity. Only if we contrive to make the bringing into the world of new persons as nasty a business as killing already present persons will there be any just reason to exclude young women from conscripted armies, or to exclude men from equal parental responsibility.

Granted that the men's theories of obligation need supplementation, to have much chance of integrity and coherence, and that the women's hypothetical theories will want to cover obligation as well as love, then what concept brings them together? My tentative answer is—the concept of appropriate trust, oddly neglected in moral theory. This concept also nicely mediates between reason and feeling, those tired old candidates for moral authority, since to trust is neither quite to believe something about the trusted, nor necessarily to feel any emotion towards them, but to have a belief-informed and action-influencing attitude. To make it plausible that the neglected concept of appropriate trust is a good one for the enlightened moral theorist to make central, I need to show, or begin to show, how it could include obligation, indeed shed light on obligations and their justification, as well as include love and the other moral concerns of Gilligan's women, and many of the topics women moral philosophers have chosen to address, mosaic fashion. I would also need to show that it could connect all of these in a way which holds out promise both of synthesis and of comprehensive moral coverage. A moral theory which looked at the conditions for proper trust of all the various sorts we show, and at what sorts of reasons justify inviting such trust, giving it, and meeting it, would, I believe, not have to avoid turning its gaze on the conditions for the survival of the practices it endorses, so it could avoid that unpleasant choice many current liberal theories seem to have—between incoherence and bad faith. I do not pretend that we will easily agree once we raise the questions I think we should raise, but at least we may have a language adequate to the expression of both men's and women's moral viewpoints.

My trust in the concept of trust is based in part on my own attempts to restate and consider what was right and what was wrong with men's theories, especially Hume's, which I consider the best of the lot. There I found myself reconstructing his account of the artifices of justice as an account of the progressive enlargement of a climate of trust, and found that a helpful way to see it. It has some textual basis, but is nevertheless a reconstruction, and one I found, immodestly, an improvement. So it is because I have tried the concept, and explored its dimensions a bit—the variety of goods we may trust others not to take from us, the variety of security or insurance we have when we do, the sorts of defenses or potential defenses we lay down when we trust, the various conditions for reasonable trust of various types—that I am hopeful about its power as a theoretical and not just an exegetical tool.

I also found myself needing to use it, when I made a brief rash attempt at that women's topic, caring (invited in by a man philosopher [Baier 1982, a response to Frankfurt 1982], I should say). I am reasonably sure that it does generalize some central moral features both of the recognition of binding obligations and moral virtues, and of loving, as well as of other important relations between persons, such as teacher-pupil, confider-confidante, worker to coworker in the same cause, professional to client. Indeed it is fairly obvious that love, the main moral phenomenon women want attended to, involves trust. So I anticipate little quarrel when I claim that, if we had a moral theory spelling out the conditions for appropriate trust and distrust, that theory would include a morality of love in all its variants—parental love, love of children for their parents, love of family members, love of friends, of lovers in the strict sense, of coworkers, of one's country and its figureheads, of exemplary heroines and heros, of goddesses and gods.

Love and loyalty demand maximal trust of one sort, and maximal trust-worthiness, and in investigating the conditions for maximal trust and maximal risk we must think about the ethics of love. More controversial may be my claim that the ethics of obligation will also be covered. I see it as covered since to recognize a set of obligations is to trust some group of persons to instill them, to demand that they be met, possibly to levy sanctions if they are not, and this is to trust persons with very significant coercive power over others. Less coercive but still significant power is possessed by those shaping our conception of the virtues, and expecting us to display them, approving when we do, disapproving and perhaps shunning us when we do not. Such coercive and manipulative power over others requires justification, and is justified only if we have reason to trust those who have it to use it properly, and to use the discretion that is always given when trust is given in a way that serves the purpose of the whole system of moral control, and not merely for self-serving or morally improper purposes. Since the question of the justification of coercion becomes, at least in part, the question of the wisdom of trusting the coercers to do their job properly, the morality of obligation, insofar as it reduces to the morality of coercion, is covered by the morality of proper trust. Other forms of trust may also be involved, but trusting enforcers with the use of force is the most problematic form of trust involved.

The coercers and manipulators are, to some extent, all of us, so to ask what our obligations are and what virtues we should exhibit is to ask what it is reasonable to trust us to demand, expect, and contrive to get, from one another. It becomes, in part, a question of what powers we can in reason trust ourselves to exercise properly. But self-trust is a dubious or limit case of trust, so I prefer to postpone the examination of the concept of proper self-trust at least until proper trust of others is more clearly understood. Nor do we distort matters too much if we concentrate on those cases where moral sanctions and moral pressure and moral manipulation are not self-applied but applied to others, particularly by older persons to younger persons. Most moral pressuring that has any effects goes on in childhood and early youth. Moral sanctions may continue to be applied, formally and informally, to adults, but unless the criminal courts apply them it is easy enough for adults to ignore them, to brush them aside. It is not difficult to become a sensible knave, and to harden one's heart so that one is insensible to the moral condemnation of one's victims and those who sympathize with them. Only if the pressures applied in the morally formative stage have given one a heart that rebels against the thought of such ruthless independence of what others think will one see any reason *not* to ignore moral condemnation, not to treat it as mere powerless words and breath. Condemning sensible knaves is as much a waste of breath as arguing with them—all we can sensibly do is to try to protect children against their influence, and ourselves against their knavery. Adding to the criminal law will not be the way to do the latter, since such moves will merely challenge sensible knaves to find new knavish exceptions and loopholes, not protect us from sensible knavery. Sensible knaves are precisely those who exploit us without breaking the law. So the whole question of when moral pressure of various sorts, formative, reformative, and punitive, ought to be brought to bear (and by whom), is subsumed under the question of whom to trust when and with what, and for what good reasons.

In concentrating on obligations, rather than virtues, modern moral theorists have chosen to look at the cases where more trust is placed in enforcers of obligations than is placed in ordinary moral agents, the bearers of the obligations. In taking, as contractarians do contractual obligations as the model of obligations, they concentrate on a case where the very minimal trust is put in the obligated person, and considerable punitive power entrusted to the one to whom the obligation is owed (I assume here that Hume is right in saying that when we promise or contract, we formally subject ourselves to the penalty, in case of failure, of never being trusted as a promisor again). This is an interesting case of the allocation of trust of various sorts, but it surely distorts our moral vision to suppose that *all* obligations, let alone all morally pressured expectations we impose on others, conform to that abnormally coercive model. It takes very special conditions for it to be safe to trust persons to inflict penalties on other persons, conditions in which either we can trust the penalizers to have the virtues necessary to penalize wisely and fairly, or else we can rely on effective threats to keep unvirtuous penalizers from abusing their power—that is to say, rely on others to coerce the first coercers into proper behavior. But that reliance too will either be trust, or will have to rely on threats from coercers of the coercers of coercers, and so on. Morality on this model becomes a nasty, if intellectually intriguing, game of mutual mutually corrective threats. The central question of who should deprive whom of what freedom soon becomes the question of whose anger should be dreaded by whom (the theory of obligation), supplemented perhaps by an afterthought on whose favor should be courted by whom (the theory of the virtues).

Undoubtedly some important part of morality does depend in part on a system of threats and bribes, at least for its survival in difficult conditions when normal goodwill and normally virtuous dispositions may be insufficient to motivate the conduct required for the preservation and justice of the moral network of relationships. But equally undoubtedly life will be nasty, emotionally poor, and worse than brutish (even if longer), if that is all morality is, or even if that coercive structure of morality is regarded as the backbone, rather than as an available crutch, should the main support fail. For the main support has to come from those we entrust with the job of rearing and training persons so that they can be trusted in various ways, some trusted with extraordinary coercive powers, some with public decision-making powers, all trusted as parties to promise, most trusted by some who love them and by one or more willing to become coparents with them, most trusted by dependent children, dependent elderly relatives, sick friends, and so on. A very complex network of a great variety of sorts of trust structures our moral relationships with our fellows, and if there is a *main* support to this network it is the trust we place in those who respond to the trust of new members of the moral community, namely to children, and prepare them for new forms of trust.

A theory which took as its central question, "Who should trust whom with what, and why?" would not have to forgo the intellectual fun and games previous theorists have had with the various paradoxes of morality—curbing freedom to increase freedom, curbing self-interest the better to satisfy self-interest, not aiming at happiness in order to become happier. For it is easy enough to get a paradox of trust, to accompany or, if I am right, to generalize the paradoxes of freedom, self-interest, and hedonism. To trust is to make oneself or let oneself be more vulnerable than one might have been to harm from others—to give them an opportunity to harm one, in the confidence that they will not take it, because they have no good reason to (I defend this claim in Baier 1986b). Why would one take such a risk? For risk it always is, given the partial opaqueness to us of the reasoning and motivation of those we trust and with whom we cooperate. Our confidence may be, and quite often is, misplaced. That is what we risk when we trust. If the best reason to take such a risk is the expected gain in security which comes from a climate of trust, then in trusting we are always giving up security to get greater security, exposing our throats so that others become accustomed to not biting. A moral theory which made proper trust its central concern would have its own categorical imperative, could replace obedience to self-made laws and freely chosen restraint on freedom, with security-increasing sacrifice of security, distrust in the promoters of a climate of distrust, and so on.

Such reflexive use of one's central concept, negative or affirmative, is an intellectually satisfying activity which is bound to have appeal to those system-lovers who want to construct moral theories, and it may help them design their theory in an intellectually pleasing manner. But we should beware of becoming hypnotized by our slogans, or of sacrificing truth to intellectual elegance. Any theory of proper trust should not *prejudge* the question of when distrust is proper. We might find more objects of proper distrust than just the contributors to a climate of reasonable distrust, just as freedom should be restricted not just to increase human freedom but to protect human life from poisoners and other killers. I suspect, however, that all the objects of reasonable distrust are more reasonably seen as falling into the category of ones who contribute to a decrease in the scope of proper trust, than can all who are reasonably coerced be seen as themselves guilty of wrongful coercion. Still, even if all proper trust turns out to be for such persons and on such matters as will increase the scope or stability of a climate of reasonable trust, and all proper distrust for such persons and on such matters as increasing the scope of reasonable distrust, overreliance on such nice reflexive formulas can distract us from asking all the questions about trust which need to be asked, if an adequate moral theory is to be constructed around that concept. These questions should include when to *respond* to trust with *un*trustworthiness, when and when not to invite trust, as well as when to give and refuse trust. We should not assume that promiscuous trustworthiness is any more a virtue than is undiscriminating distrust. It is appropriate trustworthiness, appropriate trustingness, appropriate encouragement to trust, which will be virtues, as will be judicious untrustworthiness, selective refusal to trust, discriminating discouragement of trust.

Women are particularly well placed to appreciate these last virtues, since they have sometimes needed them to get into a position to even consider becoming moral theorizers. The long exploitation and domination of women by men depended on men's trust in women and women's trustworthiness to play their allotted roles, and so to perpetuate their own and their daughters' servitude. However keen women now are to end the lovelessness of modern moral philosophy, they are unlikely to lose sight of the cautious virtue of appropriate distrust, or of the tough virtue of principled betrayal of the exploiters' trust.

Gilligan's girls and women saw morality as matter of preserving valued ties to others, of preserving the conditions for that care and mutual care without which human life becomes bleak, lonely and, after a while, as the mature men in her study found, not self-affirming, however successful in achieving the egoistic goals which had been set. The boys and men saw morality as a matter of finding workable traffic rules for self-assertors, so that they not needlessly frustrate one another, and so that they could, should they so choose, cooperate in more positive ways to mutual advantage. Both for the women's sometimes unchosen and valued ties with others, and for the men's mutual respect as sovereigns and subjects of the same minimal moral traffic rules (and for their more voluntary and more selective associations of profiteers), trust is important. Both men and women are concerned with cooperation, and the dimensions of trust-distrust structure the different cooperative relations each emphasize. The various considerations which arise when we try to defend an answer to any question about the appropriateness of a particular form of cooperation, with its distinctive form of trust or distrust—that is, when we look into the terms of all sorts of cooperation, at the terms of trust in different cases of trust, at what are fair terms and what are trust-enhancing and trust-preserving terms—are suitably many and richly interconnected. A moral theory (or family of theories) that made trust its central problem could do better justice to men's and women's moral intuitions than do the going men's theories. Even if we don't easily agree on the answer to the question of who should trust whom with what, who should accept and who should meet various sorts of trust, and why, these questions might enable us better to morally reason together than we can when the central moral questions are reduced to those of whose favor one must court and whose anger one must dread. But such programmatic claims as I am making will be tested only when women standing on the shoulders of men, or men on the shoulders of women, or some theorizing Tiresias, actually work out such a theory. I am no Tiresias, and have not foresuffered all the labor pains of such a theory. I aim here only to fertilize.

3

Moral Judgment: Theory and Research on Differences between Males and Females

Mary Brabeck

A recent cartoon in a local newspaper depicted a man and a woman talking. The caption read, "Of course your mind is cleaner than mine, you change it more frequently." Most readers, deprived of the cartoon picture, would have no trouble guessing who was speaking and who was the object of the assertion. The cartoon speaks to a pervasive societal attitude—that one of the ways in which the sexes differ is in moral character. When a woman is portrayed as man's moral superior it is usually, as in the above cartoon, at the expense of her intellectual ability. Schopenhauer wrote, "The weakness of their reasoning faculty also explains why women show more sympathy for the unfortunate than men." More frequently, when differences between the sexes are claimed, women are portrayed as men's moral inferior. Freud characterized women this way:

> For women the level of what is ethically normal is different from what it is in men. Their superego is never so inexorable, so impersonal, so independent of its emotional origins. . . . they show less sense of justice, less ready to submit to the great exigencies of life, and they are more often influenced in their judgements by feelings of affection or hostility. (1961/1925, 257–258)

Women, it is frequently assumed, are more intuitive, empathic, selfless, kind- (and weak-) hearted (e.g., Florence Nightingale), while men are more deliberate, judicial, and rational in moral choices (e.g., Solomon).

Such stereotypes assume a dualistic categorization maintained on gender specific lines. Freud was the first to raise the idea to the level of theory. Since then, theories explaining sex differences in morality have abounded. Typically, a male standard is described using observations from a male sample. When females do not fit the scheme they are labeled deviant. Piaget, for example, found boys attentive to the rules of games and girls curiously lacking in that regard. Focusing on the standard set by boys he regarded the legal sense, necessary for morality, to be "far less developed in little girls than in boys" (1932/1965, 77). Kohlberg and Kramer (1969) reported the mean stage for men (stage 4, "Law and Order") differed from that of women (stage 3, "Interpersonal Concordance"), and on the basis of the one study speculated that this developmental lag may be due to different role-taking opportunities. Gilligan (1979, 1982a) notes that Erikson also maintained there were similar sex differences. Erikson's research showed that for men the identity-formation stage precedes intimacy; for women, the two are fused or identity is achieved through intimacy. Without changing the order of his psychosocial stages, Erikson retained the development of males as the norm against which females were found to deviate. These theories resound with a common theme: Men develop a rational moral attitude based on an understanding of alternative conceptions and a commitment to a universal abstraction. Women develop less of a concern for these abstractions, are more imbedded in particular concerns about individuals, more feeling than thinking, less committed, and, thus, more morally labile.

Recently, Gilligan (1977) has entered this discussion, bringing to it what she calls a "different [woman's] voice," which she claims helps to put the issues of sex differences in perspective. This paper will (1) summarize Gilligan's structural developmental theory and contrast her view with that of Kohlberg's justice morality; (2) examine the evidence for Gilligan's claims about sex differences and the related empirical results about sex differences from studies of moral cognition, altruism, and empathy; and (3) offer an evaluation of Gilligan's contribution to an integrated theory of morality.

Gilligan's Theory: An Ethic of Care and Responsibility

Freud, Erikson, Bettelheim, McClelland, and Levinson, have all, Gilligan notes (1977, 1982a), viewed women as intricately tied to the human relationships that form the basis for their identity. This view is not different from that articulated by Gilligan. The difference lies in the values placed on such development and the resulting psychology. For the others, the development of women was an aberration, a failure to develop according to the ideal plan. Gilligan accepts the assumption of differences between the nature of man and the nature of woman and sees a paradox in the observation that what marks women as unique also marks them as inferior:

The very traits that have traditionally defined the "goodness" of women, their care for and sensitivity to the needs of others, are those that mark them as deficient in moral development. The infusion of feeling into their judgments keeps them from developing a more independent and abstract ethical conception in which concern for others derives from principles of justice rather than from compassion and care. (Gilligan 1977, 484)

The focus in this society, Gilligan asserts, on individuation and individual achievement has led to a devaluing of the relational caretaking roles of women. The ability to achieve intimacy, maintain relationships, and act as caretakers, though valued, has typically been considered "'intuitive' or 'instinctive,' a function of anatomy coupled with destiny" (Gilligan 1979, 144). For Gilligan, these differences form the alternative, feminine, and essential side of moral considerations.

It is precisely the concern with particular moral situations, rather than abstract principles, with care for others and a desire to avoid inflicting hurt, rather than a care for the rights of others, with the maintenance of harmony and loving relationships, rather than the maintenance of moral rules, that Gilligan argues, constitutes a superior moral orientation. This, she claims, is characteristic of the morality of women.

Gilligan proposes that when the outline of morality is drawn with women in mind, the conception is different from that drawn as she claims Kohlberg has, with men in mind. For women, the moral problem arises from conflicting responsibilities rather than from competing rights and requires for its resolution contextual and inductive thinking rather than formal and abstract reasoning (Gilligan 1979). To describe development of this moral orientation, Gilligan proposes a model of structural progression of increasingly complex, differentiated, and integrated views of the morality of care, in which one is responsible for self and others. Thus, the infliction of hurt is viewed as the central moral concern superseding issues of fairness.

Gilligan (1977) describes three levels and two transition periods in development of the ethic of care.

The First Level: Orientation to Individual Survival. Here the self is the sole object of concern. Issues of survival of the self are of paramount importance and moral considerations emerge only when one's own needs are in conflict. Morality is a matter of imposed sanctions on the self.

The First Transition: From Selfishness to Responsibility. This transition reflects a definition of self within the attachments and connections made with others. One's own wishes and the responsibilities one has for another are now viewed as defining the conflict between what one "would" and what one "should" do.

The Second Level: Goodness as Self-Sacrifice. This is the level of the conventional view of women as caretakers and protectors. Moral judgments are derived from social norms and consensus. Concern for others, particularly the feelings of others and the possibility of inflicting hurt, is of major concern to people at this level. Goodness, equated here with self-sacrifice and the need for approval (typical of Kohlberg's stage 3), is joined with the desire to care for others.

The Second Transition: From Goodness to Truth. At this level women begin to see that a morality of care must include care of self as well as others. The situation, the intentions, and the consequences of an action are of primary import here, not the evaluation of others. A woman "strives to encompass the needs of both self and others, to be responsible to others and thus be 'good' but also to be responsible to herself and thus to be 'honest' and 'real' " (Gilligan 1977, 500). A heightened sense of responsibility for the decision accompanies the increased attention to one's responsibility to self as well as others.

The Third Level: The Morality of Nonviolence. The conflict between selfishness and responsibility to self is resolved at this level in a principle of nonviolence. A moral equality between self and other is achieved by equally applying an injunction against hurting: "Care then becomes a universal obligation, the self-chosen ethic of a postconventional judgment that reconstructs the dilemma in a way that allows the assumption of responsibility for choice" (Gilligan 1977, 504).

Gilligan has described a morality of responsibility based on a concept of harmony and nonviolence and a recognition of the need for compassion and care for self and others. This is in contrast to Kohlberg's morality of justice, which is based on a concept of reciprocity and fairness and a recognition that one must respect the rights of others as well as one's own. Gilligan's morality of responsibility is distinguished by an emphasis on attachments, issues of self-sacrifice and selfishness, and consideration of relationships as primary, while Kohlberg's morality of rights is distinguished by an emphasis on separateness, issues of rules and legalities, and consideration of the individual as primary. For Gilligan an ethic of care is achieved through perception of one's self as connected to others; for Kohlberg an ethic of rights is achieved through a process of separation and individuation of self from others. For Gilligan moral dilemmas are contextual and are resolved through inductive thinking; for Kohlberg moral principles are universal and are applied to moral dilemmas through formal and abstract thinking. For Kohlberg the development of principled moral reasoning proceeds through stages of invariantly sequential, hierarchically arranged stages, and is universal. For Gilligan the development of a principle of moral responsibility proceeds through stages of sequential, hierarchically arranged stages, and is found reflected in the voices of women. These differences are summarized in table 3.1.

Table 3.1

Comparison of Gilligan's Morality of Care and Responsibility and Kohlberg's Morality of Justice

	Morality of care and responsibility—Gilligan	Morality of justice—Kohlberg
Primary Moral Imperative	Nonviolence/care	Justice
Components of Morality	Relationships Responsibility for self and others Care Harmony Compassion Selfishness/self-sacrifice	Sanctity of Individual Rights of self and others Fairness Reciprocity Respect Rules/legalities
Nature of Moral Dilemmas	Threats to harmony and relationships	Conflicting rights
Determinants of Moral Obligation	Relationships	Principles
Cognitive Processes for Resolving Dilemmas	Inductive thinking	Formal/logical-deductive thinking
View of Self as Moral Agent	Connected, attached	Separate, individual
Role of Affect	Motivates care, compassion	Not a component
Philosophical Orientation	Phenomenological (contextual relativism)	Rational (universal principle of justice)
Stages	I. Individual Survival IA. From Selfishness to Responsibility II. Self Sacrifice and Social Conformity IIA. From Goodness to Truth III. Morality of Nonviolence	I. Punishment and Obedience II. Instrumental Exchange III. Interpersonal Conformity IV. Social System and Conscience Maintenance V. Prior Rights and Social Contract VI. Universal Ethical Principles

The Ethic of Care: Empirical Base

While Gilligan's theory of the morality of responsibility as separate from the morality of rights has been described in the literature (Gilligan 1977, 1979, 1982a), empirical evidence in support of her assertions is less available. Gilligan's notion of the morality of care is based on considerations of what is lacking in other developmental theories. Much of her writing addresses these deficiencies rather than summarizes the empirical observations based on tests of her theory. Research on her theory is also hampered by a lack of a published standardized interview.

Gilligan's original research involved interviewing twenty-nine women who were facing a decision about whether or not to have an abortion. This moral dilemma involves what Gilligan considers the central moral issue for women: the conflict between self and others when one must risk hurting. These subjects were interviewed about their choice, alternative options, the pros and cons of these options, the people and conflicts involved, and how the decision affected their sense of self and their responsibility to others. In addition, the women were given three of Kohlberg's hypothetical dilemmas.

Gilligan has examined her theory in two additional studies (1982a). In a longitudinal study she interviewed twenty-five students in their senior year of college and reinterviewed them five years later. Subjects were asked, as in the abortion study, to talk about their own experiences resolving moral dilemmas.

The third study, called "The Rights and Responsibility" study, further investigated the theory Gilligan developed on the basis of the two previous studies. Gilligan collected interviews from males and females between six and sixty years old, in nine age groups. No quantitative data are reported for any of these three studies. Evidence for Gilligan's theory currently rests on quoted excerpts from interviews and her interpretations of these selected excerpts.

Aside from the obvious problem of drawing conclusions about sex differences from the all-female sample of the abortion study, Gilligan's research also suffers the problems of any interview technique. While the interviews may be rich in exploratory data, generalizations from the small number are risky, probe questions may vary from subject to subject, and the representativeness of the excerpts cited by Gilligan is uncertain.

Nevertheless, these criticisms may be answered with future research. For now, confirmation of Gilligan's claim that women develop a morality of care and men a morality of rights must be sought in other lines of research. The first of these is the research of Kohlberg's theory of moral development, the theory that raised for Gilligan the issue of sex differences in morality. Subsequently, the related constructs of caring behaviors, altruism and empathy, will be reviewed.

Research on Sex Differences in Morality

While research on moral development suffers from a lack of consensus about a definition of morality, research on gender differences is further complicated, conflicting, and fraught with the problems frequently encountered in research comparing males and females (Jacklin 1981). Often the major aim of research is not directed at assessing sex differences, so that such analyses are done as an afterthought, and when sex differences are found, the results are not tied to any theoretical explanation. Frequently, studies which support the null hypotheses, that there are no sex differences, are not published, so that a slanted view of research findings is inevitable. Another confounding factor is that studies which support sex stereotypes are more readily accepted, even though males and females, at least during the early years, have been observed to be more similar than different (Maccoby & Jacklin 1974; O'Leary 1977; Tavris & Offir 1977).

Even studies that are designed to assess sex differences are difficult to compare. Sample characteristics and size differ, as do the instruments used to measure morality. Studies of Kohlberg's theory of moral reasoning using his interview format are even difficult to compare, as his scoring scheme has so many different versions.

A further cautionary note is necessary for a proper understanding of the relationship between Gilligan's theory and the literature review that follows. While studies of constructs related to Gilligan's notion of an ethic of care can shed light on her claim about sex differences, the studies summarized here do not directly investigate an ethic of care and cannot, therefore, be used as direct evidence to confirm or refute her theory. Principled reasoning, empathy, and altruism may or may not be components of the ethic she describes, and the analyses of sex differences in studies of those constructs may or may not be relevant to her claim of sex differences in a morality of care orientation. Additional research directly addressing this issue is needed to confirm or refute Gilligan's claims.

Meanwhile, a summary of the indirect evidence of her claim that there are differences in the morality of men and women will be offered here.

Research on Moral Reasoning

In part, Gilligan's argument with Kohlberg is methodological. She claims that his measure of moral judgment was derived from male research data (his original longitudinal study included only males) and that any deviation from this standard is viewed as a failure:

> The systematic exclusion from consideration of alternative criteria
> that might better encompass the development of women indicates

not only the limitations of a theory framed by men and validated by research samples disproportionately male and adolescent, but also the effects of the diffidence prevalent among women, their reluctance to speak in their own voice, given the constraints imposed on them by the politics of differential power between sexes. (Gilligan 1977, 490)

According to Gilligan's theory, sex differences in studies of moral reasoning as described by Kohlberg are to be expected. Given their presumed greater concern with relationships and issues of care, females ought to score predominantly at stage 3, "Interpersonal Concordance." Given their presumed greater independence and concern with the rights and issues of justice, males ought to score predominantly at stage 4, "Law and Order," or above.

Gilligan's argument that Kohlberg's scheme is sex biased is based in part on Holstein's (1976b) longitudinal study. In this study Holstein claimed, among other criticisms of Kohlberg's scheme, that the scoring standard used to measure moral reasoning is sex biased, that because of Kohlberg's original all-male sample, adult females are disproportionately found at stage 3, while males are predominantly at stage 4. Because Kohlberg's scheme is hierarchical this is tantamount to saying that women are less morally developed than men. Holstein supports her argument with the findings of Haan, Smith, and Block (1968), Hudgins and Prentice (1973), Kohlberg and Kramer (1969), and Turiel (1972). It is difficult to understand how Hudgins and Prentice support the claim, since they analyzed moral maturity scores of delinquent and nondelinquent mothers and sons and did not compare same-age subjects by sex. Turiel's 1972 study is unpublished, but a 1976 cross-sectional study was designed by Turiel as a test of sex differences in moral reasoning. Turiel's 1976 study reported that overall no statistically significant differences between the sexes were found in moral reasoning scores. At ages 10–11 and 12–14 girls outscored boys, while at ages 15–17 boys outscored girls. These mean differences, however, were only between .14 and .29 of a stage. While there was an age and sex interaction no main effect analyses were reported.

Haan et al. (1968) reported 41 percent of the females in her sample were at stage 3 and 39 percent at stage 4, while 22 percent of the males were at stage 3 and 43 percent at stage 4. Rest (1979) notes that this is "hardly evidence that stage 3 is a 'female' stage and stage 4 is a 'male' stage" (122).

Holstein's (1976b) own longitudinal data on sex differences are less than compelling. She measured boys and girls and their mothers and fathers over a three-year interval. At time 1 the mean moral maturity scores (MMS) were not significantly different for boys and girls, nor was there a significant difference at time 2 (though Holstein reports a "trend ($p < .20$) toward higher

scores" for boys (55). In the adult group fathers at time 1 showed a significantly higher MMS than mothers ($p < .001$) but this was not significant at
time 2.

Walker (1984) summarized seventy-two Kohlbergian studies that assessed sex differences in moral reasoning scores. Of twenty-nine samples of
children and early adolescents only four reported significant differences.
Walker dismisses one of these for incorrectly reporting a t value as significant. When differences were reported, they usually indicated more mature
development for females. From thirty-two samples of late adolescents and
youth only eight yielded significant differences. These differences indicated
more mature development for males. A relatively smaller number of studies
using adult samples (fourteen) reported a proportionally larger number of
significant differences (five) all favoring males. However, these differences
occur only when sex differences are confounded with education and/or occupation. Walker concludes that there is little evidence to support the claim
that stage 3 is model for women and stage 4 for men. He suggests methodological problems in scoring procedures, initial moral stage definitions, and
differential attainment of prerequisites for moral development (role-taking
opportunities, social experience) may account for the differences between
males and females that are reported.

When sex differences in moral judgment scores are found, chronological
age ought to be considered. It may be that females mature earlier and are
then matched by males during late adolescence. Using an objective measure
of Kohlberg's stages designed for their study, Freeman and Giebink (1979)
reported no significant sex differences among eleven- and seventeen-year-
olds, whereas girls at age fourteen outscored their male counterparts ($p >
.001$). When differences between the sexes in the moral judgment interview
scores are found, females seem to be advanced in the early years (Turiel
1976) and males in late adolescent and adult years (Haan, Langer, & Kohlberg 1976; White 1975). However, these results are not conclusive, because
some studies (Weisbrodt 1970) and college students (Arbuthnot 1975;
Fromming 1978) reveal no significant differences between the sexes, while
others (Blatt & Kohlberg, 1975) report female adolescents at the higher
stages more frequently than men.

Rest (1979) reviewed twenty-two studies that assessed gender differences
using the Defining Issues Test (DIT), an objective measure of Kohlberg's
stages, to measure moral reasoning. Of these only two studies reported a
significant correlation ($r = .25, p < .03; r = .25, p < .01$). In both studies
females scored higher than males. Rest concludes his review by saying that
"sex differences are rarely significant in junior high, senior high, college, and
graduate studies or adults. So it is not even true that at one age one sex has
an advantage and at another age the other sex does" (120). According to
Rest,[1] results of work completed since the 1979 summary are consistent

with this view. Additional published studies not cited in Rest's review also support that claim (Connolly & McCarrey, 1978; Prawat 1976). Garwood, Levine, and Ewing (1980) reported more males than females scored at stage 3 and more females than males obtained scores at principled stages. This is in contradiction to Haan et al. (1968), Holstein (1976b), and Gilligan's (1977) claims that stage 3 of Kohlberg is sex biased favoring women while later stages reflect a male orientation.

Research using the Piagetian (1932) model of moral stages is equally conflicting. These studies are difficult to compare because each uses a different instrument to assess morality of children. Some of these studies report males are more advanced (Guttman, Ziv, & Green, 1978; Lefurgy & Woloshin 1969), some studies report females more advanced (Roberts & Dunston, 1980; Sagi & Eisikovits, 1981). Others report no difference between the sexes (Simon & Ward, 1972; Lavoie 1974). In a related study, Hoffman (1977) reported that elementary school boys and girls showed an equal understanding of the rules in terms of moral obligations as opposed to punishment.

One possible source of support for sex bias, if it exists in moral reasoning tests, may be that the characters in the story dilemmas used by both Kohlberg and Rest are male. It may be that females, when they score lower than males, do so because they do not identify with the male protagonist. To test this possibility, Turiel (1976) used both male and female interviewers and used both male and female moral judgment interview forms. Neither the form of the interview nor the sex of the interviewer resulted in a significant interaction with a subject's age or sex.

Garwood et al. (1980) and Orchowsky and Jenkins (1979) independently investigated the impact of the sex of the protagonist on DIT scores. Freeman and Giebink (1979) measured the effect of the protagonists' sex on moral reasoning as defined by another objective test. None of these studies support Holstein's charge of sex bias in the instruments that measure moral reasoning. Of course, such bias in the original definition of morality may exist, but if it does it ought to be reflected in different scores obtained by males and females. Claims of sex differences in moral judgment appear to be overstated in light of the research results. Women may differ from men in moral orientation, but not as defined by either Kohlberg's interview or Rest's objective (1979) measure of moral judgment. Are there other ways in which the sexes express differences in morality? This question is addressed next.

Caring Behaviors

In the social psychology literature the ethic of care is often translated into empathy and altruism. Typically, these prosocial behaviors are studied in laboratory experiments by asking subjects to share rewards that have been earned or to make donations to a worthy cause, help a person who is apparently in distress, complete an affective questionnaire to measure empathy, or report their perceived similarity to a person.

A summary of the voluminous research on prosocial behavior is beyond the scope of this paper. This section is included to demonstrate that psychologists have attempted to empirically study the constructs of altruism and empathy which are logically related to Gilligan's morality of responsibility and ethic of care. It is, therefore, relevant for this investigation to examine the support in that literature for the claim to sex differences in these psychological constructs.

Mussen and Eisenberg-Berg (1977) note that sex serves as a moderating variable in very few studies of prosocial behavior. When sex differences are found to be statistically significant, girls are usually more helpful, generous, nurturant, and considerate than boys. Commenting on these differences, they wrote:

> Girls apparently receive more affection from their mothers than boys do and are more likely to be disciplined by induction and less by power-oriented techniques . . . or, as a result of training, girls may be more empathic with the needs and distress of others.
>
> Furthermore, in many cultures, helpfulness, and nurturance of others are considered more appropriate for girls than for boys; girls are therefore more frequently and more strongly rewarded for such behaviors by parents and others. (1977, 67)

Hampson (1981) suggests that helping behavior in children may be best understood as a person-situation interaction. He suggests that future research be directed toward examining individual differences that may account for different helping responses in similar situations. The next sections will examine the research on sex differences as possibly moderating person variables in altruistic and empathic responses.

ALTRUISM

The research on sex differences in altruism reveals little consistent differences between the sexes (Tavris & Offir, 1977). Krebs (1970) reported that out of seventeen studies of altruism in which sex differences among children were examined, nine showed a trend favoring girls, eight favoring boys. Only two of these studies reported a main effect that approached statistical significance ($p < .10$), both of these studies favored girls. Similarly, Krebs reported that most studies on adults failed to find sex differences in altruism.

Girls in this society, however, have a *reputation* for being more helpful and caring. Some researchers have tried to separate this reputation from the actual helping behavior. Shigetomi, Hartmann, and Gelfand (1981) replicated Hartshorne, May and Maller's (1928) classic study which noted that although girls were reputed to be far more altruistic than boys, the data showed girls were only slightly more altruistic in their behavior than boys. Shigetomi and colleagues tested 279 fifth and sixth grade children. They found that girls had significantly higher reputations for altruism (ratings of peers and teachers) than did boys, though girls scored significantly higher than boys on only two of the six behavioral measures of altruism.

Studies of altruism in adults are confounded by the fact that sex stereotypic behaviors are frequently used as the behavioral measure. For example, men are more apt to help a woman whose car has apparently broken down, assist a confederate who poses as a fallen down drunk, and pick up a hitchhiker (Deaux 1976). Gelfand and colleagues are currently investigating the possibility that sex bias in item content of altruism studies of children may account for the widespread notion that females are the more altruistic sex.[2] They are also conducting an extensive review of the literature on sex differences in altruism. Further claims about sex differences in altruism must await their investigation.

Helping behavior may be considered, however, separate from one's concern about inflicting harm on another, maintaining relationships, or judging moral issues from the perspective of an ethic of care. Empathy, the response to another's pain, may be a closer correlate to Gilligan's ethic of care and it is in the literature on empathy that sex differences are more consistently found.

EMPATHY

In their compendium of research on sex differences, Maccoby and Jacklin (1974) present evidence that suggests there are no consistent differences in empathy to be found between the sexes; both males and females were equally adept at understanding the emotional reactions and needs of others. However, calling Maccoby and Jacklin's conclusions premature, Hoffman (1977) reexamined and updated the literature on sex differences in empathy. Hoffman distinguished between cognitive empathy, or awareness of another person's feelings, and affective empathy. It is the latter, emotional response, that is frequently the stereotypic definition of empathy, and it is this type of empathy for which Hoffman's review supports the claim of sex differences: girls obtain higher vicarious affective arousal scores than boys. Studies of cognitive empathy, i.e., perspective taking and recognition of affect, do not yield such consistent results. These findings suggest that while males and females are equally likely to be aware of another's feelings and to recognize another's perspective, emotional reaction to another's feelings is more likely to come from females. Hoffman offers a number of explanations for why this difference occurs. There are differential socialization patterns: males act, females feel; there is a greater tendency of females to imagine themselves in another's distressing situation; or, he speculates, there is an innate empathic predisposition for females to experience relatively greater guilt over harming others.

Hoffman's conclusions about sex differences in empathy, however, are not unchallenged. Shantz (1983), in an extensive review of social cognition literature, notes the frequent stereotype that assumes girls are more "socially sensitive" than boys, but says that developmental literature does not currently support this assumption (72).

In summary, studies of sex differences in altruism and empathy frequently reveal more similarity than differences between males and females. When differences are found they slightly favor girls, though authors frequently suggest such differences are related to methodological problems and mediating variables (e.g., prior training, parental style of discipline). These studies suggest that the perception of sex differences in prosocial behavior is more prevalent than the research results for this perception support.

Thus far, empirical evidence has been presented that does not fully support Gilligan's claim about what is: namely, that males and females differ in moral orientations. Empirical studies are limited in that they can only describe what *is*, what can be observed about human behavior, and inferred about human thought. The next section will discuss the contribution Gilligan's theory makes to a description of what *ought* to be an adequate conception of moral judgment.

Toward an Integration of Justice and Care

Though she places a different value on the qualities, Gilligan is arguing as Freud, Erikson, Piaget, and Kohlberg have done before her: women are the more compassionate sex; affective concerns are more influential for them than for their male counterparts; they are more concerned about specific contextual moral choice, than universal principles. There is an intuitive appeal to these claims, which speaks to an essential truth in the assertions, a truth that persists even when the evidence contradicts it. Why does it persist? It may be that the truth about the different moral orientations of the sexes is a mythic truth rather than an empirical truth.

Myths, like religious beliefs, do not reveal empirical facts that support or refute scientific theories. They may, however, illuminate and direct attention toward critical questions for scientific inquiry. Bachofen (1967) has written: "Myth is nothing other than a picture of the national experience in the light of religious faith. . . . But to deny the historicity of a legend does not divest it of value. What cannot have happened was nonetheless thought. External truth is replaced by inner truth" (213–214).

Gilligan's often repeated argument with psychological theories (Gilligan 1977, 1979, 1982a, 1982c) is that these theories have ignored or devalued both fact and myth of women's development. She says, "Implicitly adopting the male life as the norm, they [psychologists] have tried to fashion women out of a masculine cloth" (1982a, 6). Gilligan's theory allows for examination of an "inner truth," a mythic belief about women, which may, through careful inquiry, expand our knowledge about what is true about morality.

Janeway (1971) has described our myths about women, what they are and why they persist. She argues that myths are responses to emotional needs and writes of one such need in today's society. Comparing the decade of the 1960s to that of the 1970s she says, "Where we once boasted that we were free, we are now more inclined to fear that we are alienated" (75). The truths that our myths perpetuate speak to satisfy felt needs. While the 1960s reflected a need to be independent and autonomous we are now expressing a need to be related and connected. Kohlberg's theory with its emphasis on the primacy of justice for each individual speaks to the first mythic need, Gilligan's theory with its emphasis on relationships, care, and nonviolence speaks to the second.

There is an essential tension between autonomy and interdependence, between the requirement of justice and the demands of mercy, between absolute moral principles and situation-specific moral action, between reason and affect. To resolve this tension by assigning half to males and half to females when evidence does not support that division is to reduce the complexity of morality, to cloud truth with myth, to do an injustice to the capacities of both sexes, and to lose an opportunity to revise and modify our theories of morality. It is this last possibility, Gilligan's contribution to a better understanding of the concept of morality, that is addressed in the remainder of this paper.

Gilligan and Kohlberg each assign a different place in their schemes to the development of relativism (Flanagan 1982; Kohlberg 1982). It is this difference that illuminates Gilligan's difference from Kohlberg and her unique contribution to an integrated theory of morality. For Kohlberg, relativism is a necessary step in judging a moral dilemma, the solution of which lies in absolute principles. In contrast, Gilligan's theory embraces relativism as the solution to moral choice. Quoting from the work of novelist George Eliot, Gilligan says, "Since 'the mysterious complexity of our life' cannot be 'laced up in formulas' moral judgment cannot be bound by 'general rules' but must instead be informed 'by a life livid and intense enough to have created a wide, fellow-feeling with all that is human'" (1982a, 130).

Noting Kohlberg and Kramer's (1969) finding that 20% of adolescents regressed in moral maturity scores, yet returned to principled stages by age twenty-five, Gilligan and Murphy (1979) argued that relativism is the result and reflection of the adolescent's struggle with the inevitable conflicts of human experience—the good do not always get rewarded, justice does not prevail, and seemingly good people engage in reprehensible action. These alarming insights lead to a rejection of universal, absolute rules (and principles) represented by authorities, and a retreat to a contextually relative position. This relativism is not, Gilligan argues, regression, but development and is the result, she claims (Gilligan & Murphy 1979), of confronting "the dilemma of the fact." That is, the problem of moral choice lies not only in an articulation of what one ought to do, but in applying that "ought" to concrete, practical, specific action. This is a distinction between the ideal and the real, the ethical principle and the ethical act. For Gilligan, morality involves love, caring, passion, not for an abstract universal principle but for a concrete, specific person: "The blind willingness to sacrifice people to truth . . . has always been the danger of an ethics abstracted from life" (Gilligan 1982a, 104). However, this is to embrace personal truths and affective moral sentiment and to renounce absolute and universal principles that may be rationally apprehended. As Blaise Pascal cautions, there are two extremes: to exclude reason, and to admit only reason. In fact, Gilligan's own ethic of care is a universal abstraction of a concrete imperative which she argues ought to govern moral choice: inflict no harm, leave no one abandoned.

Morality must be concerned with what one ought to do and that "ought" must be rationally defensible (Hare 1952; Rawls 1971). This demands attention to regulative principles as well as attention to the specific context. When the women in Gilligan's study (1977) faced the decision about whether or not to have an abortion they were engaged in making a personal choice about a particular situation which would affect identifiable people. In order to morally attend to the rights of, and potential harm to, all those affected, the context and particulars of each women's unique situation must be considered. However, a rational defense of the moral good reflected in each woman's individual judgment must attend to principles outside of one's experience or feelings about that experience.

Because decisions about moral action always exist within a specific context, moral choice is tied to the specific and relative situation. However, the relevant differences existing in any specific situation must temper one's application, but not definition of the moral good. Thus, contextual relativism may, as Gilligan argues, govern our *choices* of moral action and emotional response to moral dilemmas: absolutes, as Kohlberg argues, govern our definition and justification of what constitutes the moral good.

Rest (1983) has attempted to merge these disparate but related concerns that are relevant to a comprehensive moral theory. He has described four components of morality: (1) interpretation of a situation as moral and the appropriate affective response (outrage at a wrong committed, sorrow at a pain inflicted); (2) judgment about what constitutes the moral ideal or the just outcome; (3) decision about a course of action; and (4) an appropriate behavioral response. Rest places Kohlberg's theory in component 2, judgment of the ideal. It may be that Gilligan speaks to components 1 and 3. Her theory describes the ethic of care as constituting the thoughtful, motivating force of specific moral choice. Rest's multiple component model includes both absolute universal principles that guide moral deliberations about what *ought* to be, and contextually relative responses to the specific individuals affected by such choices. Kohlberg's universal principle of justice may govern the former while Gilligan's ethic of care and morality of responsibility may govern the latter. Future research that addresses these components of morality is needed to explore these issues.

Gilligan's theory enlarges the description of morality offered by Kohlberg. The ethic of care that Gilligan heard reflected in the voices of women and which exists in mythic beliefs about women, expands our notion of morality to include concern for interconnection, harmony, and nonviolence. Research results suggest that this enlarged conception of morality may be less sex specific than Gilligan had claimed. Her major contribution rests in a redefinition of what constitutes an adequate description of the moral ideal. When Gilligan's and Kohlberg's theories are taken together, the moral person is seen as one whose moral choices reflect reasoned and deliberate judgments that ensure justice be accorded each person while maintaining a passionate concern for the well-being and care of each individual. Justice and care are then joined; the demands of universal principles and specific moral choices are bridged, and the need for autonomy and for interconnection are united in an enlarged and more adequate conception of morality.

Notes

1. J. Rest, personal communication, 25 March 1982.
2. D. Gelfand, personal communication, 5 February 1982.

4

Gilligan and Kohlberg: Implications for Moral Theory

Lawrence A. Blum

Carol Gilligan's body of work in moral development psychology is of the first importance for moral philosophy.[1] At the same time certain philosophical commitments within contemporary ethics constitute obstacles to appreciating this importance. Some of these commitments are shared by Lawrence Kohlberg, whose work provided the context for Gilligan's early (though not current) work. I will discuss some of the implicit and explicit philosophical differences between Gilligan's and Kohlberg's outlooks and will then defend Gilligan's views against criticisms which, drawing on categories of contemporary ethical theory, a Kohlbergian can and does make of them.

Gilligan claims empirical support for the existence of a moral outlook or orientation distinct from one based on impartiality, impersonality, justice, formal rationality, and universal principle. This *impartialist* conception of morality, as I will call it,[2] in addition to characterizing Kohlberg's view of morality, has been the dominant conception of morality in contemporary Anglo-American moral philosophy, forming the core of both a Kantian conception of morality and important strands in utilitarian (and, more generally, consequentialist) thinking as well.

Recently impartialism has come under attack from several quarters. Bernard Williams' (1973, 1982, 1985) well-known critique takes it to task for leaving insufficient room for considerations of personal integrity and, more broadly, for the legitimacy of purely personal concerns. Thomas Nagel, though rejecting Williams' general skepticism regarding impartialist morality's claim on our practical deliberations, follows Williams' criticism of im-

Reprinted by permission from *Ethics* 98: 472–91. Copyright © 1988 by The University of Chicago Press.

partialism; Nagel (1986) argues that personal as well as impersonal (or impartial) concerns are legitimate as reason-generating considerations.

Gilligan's critique of Kohlberg and of an impartialist conception of morality is not at odds with these criticisms of impartialism, but it is importantly distinct from them. For personal concerns are seen by Nagel and Williams as legitimate not so much from the standpoint of *morality*, but from the broader standpoint of practical reason. By contrast Gilligan argues—drawing on the conceptions of morality held by many of her largely (but by no means exclusively) female respondents—that care and responsibility within personal relationships constitute an important element of morality itself, genuinely distinct from impartiality. For Gilligan each person is embedded within a web of ongoing relationships, and morality importantly if not exclusively consists in attention to, understanding of, and emotional responsiveness toward the individuals with whom one stands in these relationships. (Gilligan means this web to encompass all human beings and not only one's circle of acquaintances. But how this extension to all persons is to be accomplished is not made clear in her writings, and much of Gilligan's empirical work is centered on the domain of personal relations and acquaintances.) Nagel's and Williams' notions of the personal domain do not capture or encompass (though Nagel and Williams sometimes imply that they are meant to) the phenomena of care and responsibility within personal relationships, and do not explain why care and responsibility in relationships are distinctively moral phenomena.[3]

Thus Gilligan's critique of Kohlberg raises substantial questions for moral philosophy. If there *is* a "different voice"—a coherent set of moral concerns distinct both from the objective and the subjective, the impersonal and the purely personal—then moral theory will need to give some place to these concerns.

Gilligan does not suggest that care and responsibility are to be seen either as *replacing* impartiality as a basis of morality or as encompassing *all* of morality, as if all moral concerns could be translated into ones of care and responsibility. Rather, Gilligan holds that there is an appropriate place for impartiality, universal principle, and the like within morality, and that a final mature morality involves a complex interaction and dialogue between the concerns of impartiality and those of personal relationship and care.[4]

Kohlberg and Gilligan: The Major Differences

One can draw from Gilligan's work seven differences between her view of morality and Kohlberg's impartialist conception. The subsequent discussion will explore the nature and significance of these apparent differences.

1. For Gilligan the moral self is radically situated and particularized. It is "thick" rather than "thin," defined by its historical connections and rela-

tionships. The moral agent does not attempt to abstract from this particularized self, to achieve, as Kohlberg advocates, a totally impersonal standpoint defining *the* "moral point of view." For Gilligan, care morality is about the particular agent's caring for and about the particular friend or child with whom she has come to have this particular relationship. Morality is not (only) about how the impersonal "one" is meant to act toward the impersonal "other." In regard to its emphasis on the radically situated self, Gilligan's view is akin to those of Alasdair MacIntyre (1981, 1984) and Michael Sandel (1982).

2. For Gilligan, not only is the self radically particularized, but so is the other, the person toward whom one is acting and with whom one stands in some relationship. The moral agent must understand the other person as the specific individual that he or she is, not merely as someone instantiating general moral categories such as friend or person in need. Moral action which fails to take account of this particularity is faulty and defective. While Kohlberg does not and need not deny that there is an irreducible particularity in our affective relationships with others, he sees this particularity only as a matter of personal attitude and affection, not relevant to morality itself. For him, as, implicitly, for a good deal of current moral philosophy, the moral significance of persons as the objects of moral concern is solely as bearers of morally significant but entirely general and repeatable characteristics.

Putting contrasts 1 and 2 together, we can say that for Gilligan but not for Kohlberg moral action itself involves an irreducible particularity—a particularity of the agent, the other, and the situation.

3. Gilligan shares with Iris Murdoch (1970) the view that achieving knowledge of the particular other person toward whom one acts is an often complex and difficult moral task, and one which draws on specifically moral capacities. Understanding the needs, interests, and welfare of another person, and understanding the relationship between oneself and that other, requires a stance toward that person informed by care, love, empathy, compassion, and emotional sensitivity. It involves, for example, the ability to see the other as different in important ways from oneself, as a being existing in her own right, rather than viewing her through a simple projection of what one would feel if one were in her situation. Kohlberg's view follows a good deal of current moral philosophy in ignoring this dimension of moral understanding, thus implying that knowledge of individual others is a straightforwardly empirical matter requiring no particular moral stance toward the person.

4. Gilligan's view emphasizes the self as, in Michael Sandel's terms, "encumbered." She rejects the contrasting metaphor in Kohlberg, drawn from Kant, in which morality is ultimately a matter of the individual rational being legislating for himself and obeying laws or principles generated solely

from within himself (i.e., from within his own reason). Gilligan portrays the moral agent as approaching the world of action bound by ties and relationships (friend, colleague, parent, child) which confront her as, at least to some extent, givens. These relationships, while subject to change, are not wholly of the agent's own making and thus cannot be pictured on a totally voluntarist or contractual model. In contrast to Kohlberg's conception, the moral agent is not conceived of as radically autonomous (though this is not to deny that there exists a less individualistic, less foundational, and less morality-generating sense of autonomy which does accord with Gilligan's conception of moral agency).

A contrast between Gilligan's and Sandel's conception of encumbrance, however, is that for Sandel the self's encumbrances are forms of communal identity, such as being a member of this or that nation, religious or ethnic group, class, neighborhood, whereas for Gilligan the encumbrances are understood more in terms of the concrete persons to whom one stands in specific relationships—being the father of Sarah, the teacher of Maureen, the brother of Jeff, the friend of Alan and Charles. In that way Sandel's "encumbrances" are more abstract than Gilligan's.

5. For Kohlberg the mode of reasoning which generates principles governing right action involves formal rationality alone. Emotions play at most a remotely secondary role in both the derivation and motivation for moral action.[5]

For Gilligan, by contrast, morality necessarily involves an intertwining of emotion, cognition, and action, not readily separable. Knowing what to do involves knowing others and being connected in ways involving both emotion and cognition. Caring action expresses emotion and understanding.

6. For Kohlberg principles of right action are universalistic, applicable to all. Gilligan rejects the notion that an action appropriate to a given individual is necessarily (or needs to be regarded by the agent as) universal, or generalizable to others. And thus she at least implicitly rejects, in favor of a wider notion of "appropriate response," a conception of "right action" which carries this universalistic implication. At the same time Gilligan's view avoids the individual subjectivism and relativism which is often seen as the only alternative to a view such as Kohlberg's; for Gilligan sees the notions of care and responsibility as providing nonsubjective standards by which appropriateness of response can be appraised in the particular case. It is a standard which allows one to say that a certain thing was the appropriate action for a particular individual to take, but not necessarily that it was the "right" action for anyone in that situation.

7. For Gilligan morality is founded in a sense of concrete connection and direct response between persons, a direct sense of connection which exists prior to moral beliefs about what is right or wrong or which principles to accept. Moral action is meant to express and to sustain those connections to

particular other people. For Kohlberg the ultimate moral concern is with morality itself—with morally right action and principle; moral responsiveness to others is mediated by adherence to principle.

Impartialist Rejoinders to Gilligan

Faced with Gilligan's challenge to have found in her respondents a distinct moral orientation roughly defined by these seven contrasts, let us look at how Kohlberg, and defenders of impartialist morality more generally, do or might respond to this challenge. Eight alternative positions regarding the relation between impartial morality and a morality of care in personal relations suggest themselves.

1. Position 1 denies that the care orientation constitutes a genuinely distinct moral orientation from impartialism. Strictly speaking there is no such thing as a morality of care. Acting from care is actually acting on perhaps complex but nevertheless fully universalizable principles, generated ultimately from an impartial point of view.[6]

2. Position 2 says that, while care for others in the context of relationships may constitute a genuinely distinct set of concerns or mode of thought and motivation from that found in impartialist morality, and while these can be deeply important to individuals' lives, nevertheless such concerns are not moral but only personal ones. My caring for my friend David is important to me, but actions which flow directly from it are in that respect without moral significance.

Position 2 treats concerns with relationships as *personal* or *subjective* ones, in Nagel's and Williams's sense. Such a view is implied in Kohlberg's earlier and better-known work (e.g., 1981; part 1 of Kohlberg et al. 1984), where impartialism was held to define the whole of (at least the highest and most mature form of) morality and to exclude, at least by implication, relational or care considerations. In his most recent work, replying to Gilligan, Kohlberg claims to have abandoned this consignment of care in personal relations to an entirely nonmoral status; but this view nevertheless continues to surface in his writing.[7]

In contrast to positions 1 and 2, the remaining views all accord, or at least allow for, some distinct moral significance to care.

3. Position 3 claims that concerns of care and responsibility in relationships are truly moral (and not merely personal) concerns and acknowledges them as genuinely distinct from impartiality, but it claims that they are nevertheless secondary to, parasitic on, and/or less significant as part of morality than considerations of impartiality, right, universal principle, and the like. Kohlberg makes three distinct suggestions falling under this rubric. (a) Our personal attachments to others intensify our sense of the dignity of other persons, a sense of dignity which is ultimately grounded in an impar-

tialist outlook. Thus the husband's love for his wife intensifies and brings home to him more vividly her right to life, shared by all persons. (b) In a different vein, Kohlberg says that impartialism defines the central and most significant part of morality—what is obligatory and required—whereas the area of personal relationships is supererogatory, going beyond what is required. The demands of justice must be satisfied, but action on behalf of friends, family, and the like, while good and even perhaps admirable, is not required. Thus care is, so to speak, morally dependent on right and justice, whereas impartiality, right, and justice are not morally dependent on care. (c) The development of care is psychologically dependent on the sense of justice or right, but not vice versa.[8]

Position 3 differs from position 2 in granting some moral status to the concerns of relationship; care for friends is not only personally important but, given that one has satisfied all of one's impersonal demands, can be morally admirable as well.

4. Position 4 says that care is genuinely moral and constitutes a moral orientation distinct from impartiality, but it is an *inferior* form of morality precisely because it is not grounded in universal principle. On the previous view (3), the concerns of a care morality lie outside the scope of impartialist morality and are less significant for that very reason. In 4, by contrast, a care morality and an impartialist one cover, at least to some extent, the same territory; the same actions are prescribed by both. I may help out a friend in need out of direct concern for my friend; this action has some moral value, but the action is also prescribed by some principle, stemming ultimately from an impersonal perspective. And it is better to act from impartial principle than care because, for example, impartial morality ensures consistency and reliability more than care, or because impartialism is (thought to be) wider in scope than is care morality (covering impersonal as well as personal situations). So on view 4, acting out of direct care for a friend has some moral value but not as much as if the action stems from a firm and general principle, say, one of aid to friends.

This view might naturally regard the morality of care as a stage along the way to a more mature impartialist morality, and such a construal is suggested in some of Kohlberg's earlier writings, where care responses are treated and scored as "conventional" morality (in contrast to the more developed "postconventional" morality)—as conforming to social expectations of "being good."

Position 4 is importantly different from positions 1 and 2. For position 4, even though all the demands of a care morality can be met by impartialist morality, still a moral agent could in general or in some set of circumstances be animated by care morality entirely independent of impartialist morality. For positions 1 and 2 there is no such thing as a morality of care independent of impartialist morality.

5. Position 5 acknowledges a difference between care and impartiality but

sees this as a difference in the objects of moral assessment; care morality is concerned with evaluation of persons, motives, and character, while impartialist morality concerns the evaluation of acts.[9]

6. In position 6, considerations of an impartialist right set side constraints within which, but only within which, care considerations are allowed to guide our conduct. Considerations of impartiality trump considerations stemming from care; if the former conflict with the latter, it is care which must yield. If out of love for my daughter I want her to be admitted into a certain school, nevertheless, I may not violate just procedures in order to accomplish this. However, once I have satisfied impartialist moral requirements in the situation I am allowed to act from motives of care.

Such a view is found in recent defenses of a neo-Kantian position by Barbara Herman (1983), Onora O'Neill (1975, 1984), Stephen Darwall (1983), and Marcia Baron (1984). And these writers generally see this view as implying view 3, that care is a less important element of morality than is impartiality. However, this implication holds only on the further assumption that considerations of impartial "rightness" are present in all situations. But many situations which involve care for friends, family, and the like seem devoid of demands of justice and impartiality altogether. In such situations care is the more significant consideration. And if such situations constitute a substantial part of our lives, then even if impartialist morality were a side constraint on care—even if it were granted that when the two conflict the claims of impartiality always take precedence—it would not follow from this that impartially derived rightness is more significant, important, or fundamental a part of morality than care. For in such situations care will be operating on its own, no considerations of impartiality being present to constrain it.[10]

Thus by itself the side-constraint view of the relation between impartiality and care seems to leave open the possibility that a morality of care is a central element in a morally responsible life. In this way, view 6 is weaker as a critique of Gilligan than the previous five views (except perhaps 5), all of which relegate care to an inferior, subsidiary, or nonexistent (moral) role. It is only with the additional, implausible, assumption that impartialist moral considerations apply in all situations, that 6 implies 3.

But it might be thought that no defender of a Kantian-like view in ethics would accord such legitimacy and allow such importance to a nonrationalist, non-principle-based dimension of morality as I am construing in position 6. Let us examine this. As an interpretation of Kant, this neo-Kantian, side-constraint view (of O'Neill, Herman, and others) sees the categorical imperative essentially as a tester, rather than a generator, of maxims; the original source of maxims is allowed to lie in desires. This view rejects a traditional understanding of Kant in which moral principles of action are themselves derived from pure reason alone.

Nevertheless, such an interpretation leaves ambiguous the moral status accorded to the different desires which are to serve as the basis of maxims. The categorical imperative can, on this view, declare a desire only to be permissible or impermissible. But if we compare compassion for a friend or care for a child with a desire for an ice cream, or for food if one is hungry, then, even if both are permissible inclinations (in some particular situation), the compassion seems more morally significant in its own right than the desire for ice cream.

If the neo-Kantian admits this difference in the moral status of desires, she is then left with acknowledging a source of moral significance (the value of compassion compared with the desire for ice cream for oneself) which is not itself accounted for by the (neo-)Kantian perspective itself, but only bounded by it; and this is the position 6 discussed here—that care in personal relations does constitute a distinct dimension of morality, alongside, and subject to the constraints of, impartialist considerations of right.

To avoid this slide to position 6, the neo-Kantian can accept a moral distinction between types of permissible desires, but attempt to account for this distinction in some kind of Kantian way—for example, by seeing the greater moral value of some desires (e.g., compassion) as a reflection of respect for rational agency, or of treating others as ends in themselves, or something along that line.[11] A different move would be to bite the bullet of denying, as Kant himself seems to have done (in the notion that "all inclinations are on the same level"), any moral difference between a permissible compassion and a permissible desire to eat ice cream. Whether either of these incompatible positions is itself persuasive is a question that I cannot take up here.

The point of this excursus is to suggest that if one sees the thrust of impartialist morality as setting side constraints on the pursuit of other concerns, such as care in personal relationships, it will be difficult to avoid view 6, in which care in personal relationships is accorded some moral significance, and a moral significance which cannot be systematically relegated to a status inferior to that of impartiality.

7. Position 7 claims that, while care consideration are distinct from universal principle and impartiality, and while they are genuinely moral, nevertheless their ultimate acceptability or justifiability rests on their being able to be validated or affirmed from an impartial perspective.

This view distinguishes the level of practical deliberation from that of ultimate justification and sees the level of deliberation (in this case, care in personal relationships) as taking a different form from that provided by the standard of justification (that is, impartiality). On view 7, from an impartial and universal standpoint one can see how it is appropriate and good that people sometimes act directly from care rather than from impartialist considerations.

This view is distinct from view 1 in that there care considerations were held to be really nothing but considerations of universal principle, perhaps with some nonmoral accoutrements, such as emotions and feelings. Unlike views 1 and 2, view 7 acknowledges that care is (part of) a genuinely distinct form of moral consciousness, stemming from a different source than does impartialism and not reducible to it. Impartiality gives its stamp of approval to care but does not directly generate it; care thus does not reflect impartiality.

View 7 is weaker than view 6 as an assertion of the priority of impartiality over care. It does not, for example, claim that impartialist considerations always trump care ones but allows the possibility that care might in some circumstances legitimately outweigh considerations of impartiality. It allows the possibility that, on the level of deliberation and of the agent's moral consciousness, care would play as central a role as impartiality. The superiority of impartiality to care is claimed to lie merely in the fact that, even when the claims of care are stronger than those of impartiality, it is ultimately only an impartial perspective which tells us this.

Position 7 sees impartiality as more fundamental to morality than care because it is impartiality which ultimately justifies or legitimizes care. Yet this view seems an extremely weak version of impartialism; for unlike positions 1 through 4 (and perhaps 5 and 6), it is compatible with Gilligan's own claim that the care mode of morality legitimately plays as significant and central a role in the morally mature adult's life as does the impartialist mode. View 7 does not even require the moral agent herself to be an impartialist, as long as the mixture of care and impartialist considerations which animate her life can in fact be approved of from an impartial point of view.[12]

8. A final position bears mentioning because it is prominent in Kohlberg's writings. This is that the final, most mature stage of moral reasoning involves an "integration of justice and care that forms a single moral principle" (Kohlberg 1983, 343). This formulation taken in its own right—according care and justice equal status—does not really belong in our taxonomy, which is meant to cover only views which make impartiality in some way more fundamental to morality than care.[13] In fact, Kohlberg does not spell out this integration of care and justice, and the general tenor of his work makes it clear that he regards care as very much the junior partner in whatever interplay is meant to obtain between the two moral perspectives. So that, it seems fair to say, Kohlberg's understanding of the position mentioned here actually collapses it into one of the previous ones.[14]

In assessing both Gilligan's claim to have articulated a distinct voice within morality and the impartialist's response to this claim, it is important to know which counterclaim is being advanced. These eight views are by no means merely complementary to each other. The earlier views are much more dismissive of the moral claims of care in personal relationship than are the latter. It is an important confusion in Kohlberg's work that he attempts to occupy at least positions 2, 3, 4, 6, and 8, without seeming to be aware that these are by no means the same, or even compatible, philosophical positions. (On the other hand, there is a noteworthy tentativeness in some of Kohlberg's formulations in the volumes I have drawn on, which suggests that he was not certain that he had yet found an entirely satisfactory response to Gilligan.)

Before taking on some of these impartialist responses, the connections between such an inquiry and the controversy between virtue ethics and Kantian or utilitarian ethics bears some comment. Some of the seven contrasts drawn between Gilligan's and impartialist views characterize as well the contrast between a virtue-based ethic and its rivals; and some of the impartialist counterarguments against these contrasts are ones which are directed against virtue theory. Nevertheless, it should not be thought that all of the concerns of a moral outlook or sensibility grounded in care and relationship can be encompassed within what currently goes by the name of "virtue theory." And the converse of this is true also; as Flanagan and Jackson (1987, 627) point out, attention to some of the concerns of virtue theory, for example, an exploration of some of the different psychological capacities contributing to a lived morality of care in relationships, would enrich the care approach.

Moreover, while Gilligan herself points to the existence of two distinct moral voices, once having questioned and rejected the notion of a single unitary account of the moral point of view, one might well question further why there need be only two psychologically and philosophically distinct moral voices. Why not three, or five? I would myself suggest that, even taken together, care and impartiality do not encompass all there is to morality. Other moral phenomena—a random selection might include community, honesty, courage, prudence—while perhaps not constituting full and comprehensive moral orientations, are nevertheless not reducible to (though also not necessarily incompatible with) care and impartiality. A satisfactory picture of moral maturity or moral excellence or virtue will have to go beyond the, admittedly large, territory encompassed by care and impartiality.

The Moral Value of Care: Response to Impartialist Positions 1 and 2

The foregoing, largely taxonomic discussion is meant primarily to lay out the conceptual territory in which the various impartialist responses to the claims of personal care in morality can be evaluated. A full discussion of views 1 through 7 is impossible, and I would like to focus most fully on positions 1 and 2, which most forcefully and conclusively deny that there is anything morally and philosophically distinct in the morality of care. Building on these arguments, I will conclude with briefer discussions of views 3 through 7.

Position 1 denies the contrast, drawn in points 1 and 2 (see above, "Kohlberg and Gilligan: The Major Differences"), between the particularity involved in Gilligan's perspective and the universalism of Kohlberg's; position 2 asserts that, whatever there is to such a distinction, it is without moral significance. Position 1 claims that, when a moral agent acts from care for another, her action is governed by and generated from universal principle derived from an impartial point of view. This means more than that there merely exists some principle which prescribes the action in question as right; for that is the claim made in position 4 and will be discussed below. The mere existence of a governing principle would be compatible with the agent's action conforming to that principle by sheer accident; she could, for example, perform an action of aiding as prescribed by some duty of beneficence, but do so for a wholly self-centered reason. There would be no moral value in such an action. What position 1 requires is that the agent who is acting from (what she regards as) care be drawing on, or making at least implicit use of, such an impartialist principle.

Both views 1 and 2 imply that what it is to be a morally responsible person—say, within the domain of personal relations—is captured by the conception of an agent coming to hold, and acting according to, universal principles. Let us approach this claim by considering some principles which might be considered universal and impartial and which might be thought to be applicable in the domain of personal relations, such as "Be loyal to friends," "Nurture one's children," and "Protect children from harm." Each particular morally right or good act within an agent's role (as friend, as parent) would be (according to this claim) prescribed by some such principle, which applies to anyone occupying the role and which is in that sense universal.[15] Benefiting the particular friend or child will then be an application of universal principle to a specific situation governed by it.

Yet while it may be true that, say, a father will regard himself as accepting general principles of protecting and nurturing his children, it does not follow that applying those universal principles is all that is involved morally in protecting and nurturing his children. I want to argue that what it takes to bring such principles to bear on individual situations involves qualities of character and sensibilities which are themselves moral, and which go beyond the straightforward process of consulting a principle and then conforming one's will and action to it. Specifically I will argue that knowing that the particular situation which the agent is facing is one which calls for the particular principle in question and knowing how to apply the principle in question are capacities which, in the domain of personal relations (and perhaps elsewhere too), are intimately connected with care for individual persons. Such particularized, caring understanding is integral to an adequate meeting of the agent's moral responsibilities and cannot be generated from universal principle alone.

Consider the general principle "Protect one's children from harm." Quite often it is only a parent's concerned and caring understanding of a particular child which tells her that the child's harm is at stake in a given situation and, thus, which tells her that the current situation is one in which the principle "Protect children from harm" is applicable. One adult viewing a scene of children playing in a park may simply not see that one child is being too rough with another and is in danger of harming the other child; whereas another adult, more attentive to the situation, and more sensitive about children's interaction, may see the potential danger and thus the need for intervention and protection. Both adults might hold the principle "Protect children from harm"; yet the second adult but not the first rightly sees the situation at hand as calling for that principle. Gilligan suggests that the sensitivity, caring, and attentiveness which leads the second adult to do so are moral qualities. This is supported by the foregoing argument, that such capacities are essential to the agent's being a morally responsible person in the way which the principles in question are meant to articulate.[16]

In addition, care for particular persons often plays a role in knowing *how* to apply a principle to a situation, even once one knows that the situation calls for it. In order to know what it is to nurture, to care, to protect (his children) from harm, a father must take into account the particular children that his children are, the particular relationships that have evolved between himself and them, and the particular understandings and expectations implicit in those relationships. For example, suppose a father has to decide whether and how to deal with a situation in which his daughter has hit her younger brother. He must take into account what various actions, coming from himself in particular, would mean to each of them. Would his intervention serve to undermine (either of) his children's ability to work out problems between themselves? Would punishing his daughter contribute to a pattern of seeming favoritism toward the son which she has complained of recently? How might each of the children's self-esteem and moral development be affected by the various options of action open to him?

The father's knowing the answers to these questions requires caring about his children in a way which appreciates and manifests an understanding of each one as an individual child and human being, and of each of their relationships to each other and to himself. Such a particularized caring knowledge of his children is required in order to recognize how the various courses of action available to the father will bear on their harm in the situation. Merely holding or averring the principles "Protect one's children from harm" or "Nurture one's children" does not by itself tell one what constitutes harm (and thus protection and nurturance) in regard to individual children and in a given situation.

So it is no support to the impartialist view to assert that the role of particularity in moral action lies in the application of general role-principles to the particular case; for, I have argued, that process of application itself draws on moral capacities not accounted for by impartialism alone. Both knowledge of the situation and knowledge of what action the principle itself specifies in the situation are as much part of accomplishing the impartialist's own goal of acting according to the principle as is the intellectual task of generating or discovering the principle. Yet they are tasks which cannot be accounted for by an impartialist perspective alone.

I suggest then that both universality and particularistic care play a role in morally responsible action within personal relationships. Remember (see above) that it is no part of Gilligan's view to advocate *replacing* a concern for impartiality with care in personal relationships. If so, then acknowledging some role for universal principle even in the domain of personal relationships does not lead one to positions 1 or 2, which leave no distinct moral role for care in personal relations at all.[17]

Nevertheless, the foregoing argument should not be taken to imply that all morally good action within personal relationships does in fact involve application of universal principle; my argument has been only that even when it does it often requires some care for particular persons as well. But one can certainly imagine individually worthy actions of friendship or parenthood which are animated not by a sense of applying principle but by a direct care for the friend or child. This can even be (though it is not always) true of unreflective and spontaneous impulses of care. But in addition, care which is direct and unmediated by principle need not be unintelligent, impulsive, or unreflective; it can be guided by intelligent attention to the particular friend's or child's good, yet not be derived from universal principles regarding children or friends in general.[18]

If care in personal relations is granted to be of moral significance, both as an integral part of what it is for one's life to be informed by certain principles of responsible friendship, parenthood, and the like, as well as in its own right, then we must reject both position 1—that there is no difference between care and universal, impartial principle—and position 2—that while there may be a difference it is of no moral significance.[19]

Is Care a Universal Principle?

One can imagine the following response to my argument against positions 1 and 2: "All right. One can acknowledge that specific relationships are central to the moral life of the individual and that, therefore, care for specific persons in its various modes of kindness, friendship, compassion, and the like are important human qualities which have a claim on being considered moral. Furthermore, one can admit that a moral decision-procedure characterized by strict impartiality cannot be made to generate all the forms of moral response appropriate to this domain of morality.

"Nevertheless, in acting from love, care, compassion, is that moral agent not acting from some kind of 'principle'? Does not Gilligan want to say that everyone should be kind and caring, responsible to those to whom they are connected? Is she not saying we should all follow the principle, 'Be responsible within one's particular relationships,' or even 'Be sensitive to particulars'? If so, is she not therefore proposing a morality which is meant to be universal, indeed to be based on universal principle?"

This objection is useful in bringing out that in one important sense a morality of care is meant to be a morality for all. It is not a relativistic morality in the sense of applying to some but not others or of being confined to one particular group.[20] However, the objection presents itself as if it were a defense of the strongest impartialist view, namely, position 1 (or perhaps position 2). Yet the notion of "universal principle" in the objection has moved entirely away from the sense in which universal principle is meant to *contrast* with a morality of personal care. It has become a notion which encompasses emotional response and which acknowledges that moral action—acting according to that principle—requires a care for particular persons which cannot be exhaustively codified into universal principles. In that sense it is a notion of "universal principle" which has abandoned the pure rationalism, the pure impartiality, and the sense that adherence to universal principle alone (perhaps together with a strong will) is sufficient to characterize the moral psychology of Kohlberg's maturely moral agent. It acknowledges that other moral capacities, involving perception and sensitivity to particulars and care and concern for individual persons, are equally central to moral agency. Such a view no longer involves a critique of a particularistic morality of care in relationships.

Response to Impartialist Views 3 through 7

Positions 3 through 7 will be considered more briefly. But first, one more point about position 2. Suppose it were replied to the argument of the previous section that the capacities of care, sensitivity to particular persons, and the like, may be good, and perhaps even necessary for the application of moral principle, but—precisely because they are not themselves a reflection of universal principle, impartiality, rationality, and the like—they are not themselves moral.

Naturally if "moral" is defined in terms of impartiality, then anything outside of impartiality—even what is a necessary condition of it—is excluded. But then no independent argument will have been given as to why such a definition should be accepted.[21]

Let us consider position 3 in light of Kohlberg's suggestion that care in personal relations be seen as "supererogatory" and therefore secondary to or less significant than impartialist morality. "Supererogatory" can mean different things. If supererogatory is taken to imply "having greater merit," then those who exemplify care would have greater merit than those who merely fulfilled obligations. In that case it would be hard to see why that which is supererogatory would have less importance than that which is merely obligatory.

On the other hand, if "supererogation" implies strictly "going beyond (impartial) duty" (with no implication of superior merit), then it seems implausible to see care in personal relations as supererogatory. For there would be no duties of the personal sort which acting from care within personal relations involves doing more of, since duties would all be impartialist. Yet if duties (or obligations) of personal relationship are countenanced, then, leaving aside questions about whether these can in fact be encompassed within an impartialist framework (see n. 17, below), it becomes implausible to regard all forms of care as going beyond these; for one thing, many caring actions can themselves be acts which are in fact obligatory. Out of care I may do something for a friend which I am in fact obliged to do anyway. But also many acts of friendship, familial care, and the like seem outside the territory of obligation altogether rather than involving more of the fulfillment of obligation.[22]

Finally, if supererogation is taken more generally to refer to that which is (morally) good but not required, with no implication either of superior merit or of going beyond duty, then it seems contentious to relegate that which is supererogatory to a less significant domain of morality than that governed by impartial obligations. That (on this view) impartialist obligations are *requirements* while the supererogatory would not be, would mean only that one needed to satisfy the former first. This is the position taken in 6, and, as argued in the discussion of that view, nothing follows about which domain or orientation within morality is the more significant or valuable. For it can plausibly be argued that that which is (morally) good but not required casts a much wider net than the merely obligatory, and is, at least in that regard, a much more significant part of a typical human life.

View 4 says that, while care is distinct from impartiality and does have moral significance, it has less moral value than impartiality, which can also fully encompass all of its demands. The picture here is of a range of morally bidden acts, which are prescribed by both care and impartiality (though impartiality extends beyond this range as well).

First of all, it can be doubted whether all of the actions bidden by care morality can be seen as generated by principles of right or duty; as mentioned above, many caring actions seem outside the obligation structure altogether. But leaving this point aside, actions stemming from principles of right and acts stemming from care are not simply identical acts prompted by different motives. Leaving aside the problems of recognizing the situation as calling for the principle and knowing how to apply it (see above), it is also true, as suggested in the fifth contrast between Gilligan and Kohlberg, that within personal relations actions grounded in principle or duty alone will often not be seen by their recipients as expressing an attitude or emotion thought to be proper to that relationship. Thus while I can, out of adherence to a principle of aiding friends, do something to aid my friend, that action will not have entirely fulfilled what a fuller notion of friendship bids of me, which is to perform the action of aiding as an action expressing my care for my friend (see Stocker 1981). If emotionally expressive action is an integral part of appropriate behavior within personal relationships, then a philosophy grounded in rational principle alone will be importantly deficient in this domain and cannot be seen as superior to one of care.

View 5 regards a morality of care as concerning the evaluation of persons and impartialist morality as involving the evaluation of acts. This seems unsatisfactory in both directions. Most important, care morality is meant to encompass not only inner motives but outward acts, specifically, as argued immediately above, emotion-expressing acts. Care involves a way of responding to other persons and does not merely provide standards for the evaluation of agents. What is true of a morality of care, which view 5 may be pointing to, is that it rejects a sharp distinction between act and motive which would allow for a standard of act evaluation wholly separate from one of agent evaluation.[23]

Apart from what has been said in the presentation of those views, positions 6 and 7 raise philosophical issues beyond the scope of this paper.[24] Nevertheless, as we noted in those discussions, neither of these views, as they stand, put forth a strong challenge to Gilligan's views or to a morality of care.

Finally, it might be felt that the impartialist counterpositions discussed in this paper have served to push some of the seven contrasts, discussed earlier in the paper, into the background. This seems true. At the outset I claimed that Gilligan's work is of the first importance for moral philosophy, and that pursuing its implications for an adequate moral theory will take one into territory not readily encompassed within the categories of contemporary ethics. This paper is meant only as a preliminary to that enterprise, clearing out of the way some of the intellectual obstacles within contemporary ethics to pursuing some of these more radical directions.[25]

Notes

1. See esp. Gilligan 1982a, 1983, 1986b; Gilligan & Wiggins 1987; and Lyons 1983.

2. The notion of an "impartialist" outlook is drawn from Darwall 1983.

3. A detailed argument for this point is given in my essay (1986), esp. 357–59.

4. This is perhaps a slightly oversimplified picture of Gilligan's views, as there is also some suggestion in her writings that there is a deep flaw present in the impartialist/rationalist approach to morality which is not present in the care/responsibility approach. One possible construal of Gilligan's view in light of this seeming ambiguity is that she rejects any notion of justice as (morally and psychologically) *fundamental* or foundational to other virtues—especially to care, compassion, and the like. And that she rejects a conception of justice which is dependent on purely individualistic assumptions such as are sometimes seen as underlying more "foundational" views of justice. On this reading Gilligan would, e.g., reject any notion of justice generated from something like John Rawls' original position (though Rawls has recently argued that this individualistic characterization does not apply to his view; see Rawls 1985). Yet on this construal of Gilligan's views, she *would* accept a notion of justice which exists as one virtue among others, interacting with and no more fundamental than they. It is not clear how this acceptable, nonfoundational notion of justice is to be characterized in Gilligan's work. In her (Gilligan & Wiggins 1987) paper at the twentieth annual Chapel Hill colloquium she suggests that it is to be conceived as something like "protection against oppression." It is not clear whether, or how, this characterization is meant to connect with a nonfoundational notion of "fairness," e.g., (see Walzer 1983).

5. In Kohlberg (1984, 291), Kohlberg says that his view is distinguished from Kant's in including a role for "affect as an integral component of moral judgment or justice reasoning." Despite this remark, Kohlberg's more frequently rationalistic characterizations of his views do not bear out this contention. What is true of Kohlberg, as we will see below, is that he sometimes allows a legitimacy to care (as involving emotion) as a moral phenomenon, though, as we will also see, he is not consistent in this acknowledgment. But even when he thus acknowledges care, Kohlberg almost always relegates it to a secondary or derivative moral status. In this regard it is not clear that Kohlberg's view is significantly different from Kant's, who, at least in some of his writings (especially the *Doctrine of Virtue*), allowed a secondary place for emotions in morality.

6. Kohlberg (1982) has himself taken such a position; however, this view appears hardly at all in his most recent writings (1984), in which he attempts to answer Gilligan's and others' criticisms. There are several minor variations on the view that care *is* impartiality. One is to say that impartialist philosophies have all along been cognizant of the special moral ties and claims involved in particular personal relationships and have mustered their resources to deal with these. (Sher 1987, 187–88, is an example.) Another is to acknowledge that, while care is an important aspect of the moral life which has been largely neglected by impartialist theories, care considerations are nevertheless able to be fully encompassed by impartialism without disturbance to its theoretical commitments.

7. Kohlberg et al. (1983; 360), where Kohlberg says that many of the judgments in the care orientation are "personal rather than moral in the sense of a formal point of view."

8. The first two suggestions (a and b) are made in Kohlberg (1983; 229), and the second (care as supererogatory) again in Kohlberg (1983; 307). The last (c) is articulated by Flanagan and Jackson (1987).

9. I owe the delineation of this position to William Lycan (in personal correspondence).

10. It might be replied here that even if impartialist considerations do not arise in all situations, nevertheless, one must be concerned about them beyond those situations; for (on view 6) one must be committed beforehand to giving them priority over care considerations and so must be concerned with situations in which such considerations might arise, or in which one is not yet certain whether or not they are present. Yet even if this were so, it would not follow that one must be constantly on the lookout for the impartialist strictures. An analogy: that considerations of life and death tend to trump or outweigh most other moral considerations does not mean that, in order to avoid causing death, one must in all situations be on the lookout for the possibility that one might be doing so. I cannot here consider the further impartialist rejoinder that even when there are no impartialist strictures or considerations anywhere on the horizon, a commitment to heeding them still permeates all situations, and this grounds the claim that the impartialist dimension of morality is more fundamental and significant than care, even in the sphere of personal relations. The conclusion does not seem to me to follow from the premise; the inference seems to go from a hypothetical concern to an actual one. But more needs to be said on this (see Slote 1985, particularly "Morality and the Practical").

11. This view is taken by Barbara Herman (1985, 458).

12. I do not discuss position 7 in this paper, as I have attempted to do so in my essay (1986, esp. 351–53), where I argue that it is false. (For more on this, see n. 24 below.)

13. For this reason I have omitted views which defend some role for impartiality merely by claiming that it is not incompatible with care in personal relations. (Such a view is suggested, e.g., by Schneewind [1986, 73], though the argument there is about autonomy rather than impartiality.) For this view does not by itself grant impartiality any more significance than care; it simply says that the claims of impartiality do not get in the way of those of care. While such views are sometimes presented as if they constitute a defense of Kantian or some other impartialist ethical view, in fact by themselves (e.g., apart from views such as 1 through 7) they do not seem to me to do so.

14. Worthy of further exploration is the fact that, while Gilligan would agree with this formulation in its apparent granting of something like equal status to justice and care, Gilligan does not see the relation between the two voices as one of "integration" so much as the model of a full appreciation of the not readily integrated claims of both.

15. There is another, somewhat more colloquial, sense of "universal" which implies independence from particular roles. But for now I will adhere to the more formal, philosophical sense of "universal" as implying applicability to anyone meeting a certain description (here, occupying a certain role within a personal relationship).

16. I do not mean to imply that every situation presents a significant issue of moral sensitivity or perception involved in knowing that a principle applies. If a child

reaches to touch a hot stove, no one observing the situation could fail to see that here one needs to keep this from happening. But situations in life often do not come with their moral character so clearly declared to any and all beholders, a fact which is often masked in discussions of examples in philosophy, where the moral character of the situation is already given in the description.

17. Note that the argument so far has been couched in terms of "universality." But universality is not the same as impartiality. A morality of personal relationship roles (such as father, friend) is not fully impartialist unless the precepts governing such a morality are derivable from the position of pure impartiality postulated by the impartialist view. For a criticism of this supposition, see my essay (1988a), where it is argued that even if a role morality, such as that involved in parenthood, is applicable "universally" to all parents, the content of the moral precepts involved in it cannot be derived, even indirectly, from the impartialistic moral standpoint in which, from the point of view of the agent, each individual is to count for one and no more than one. If this is so, the acceptance given in the argument of the present paper to (some role for) universality is not tantamount to an acceptance of the same role for impartiality. But the argument advanced therein to show that universal principle itself cannot cover the whole territory of morality will apply ipso facto to the narrower notion of impartiality.

18. For a more elaborate argument that care and concern can be intelligent and reflective without involving moral principle, see my 1980 work, esp. chap. 2.

19. There seem to be a range of different types of moral personalities, a range in which both universal principle and care for particular persons have varying degrees and kinds of involvement and interaction with one another. To some persons, responsible friendship and parenthood comes more naturally than to others; they find it easier to keep attentive to, to remain in touch with the needs of, to consistently care for friends and children. By contrast, others, also responsible as friends and parents, might find it more often necessary self-consciously to remind themselves of the general principles governing friendship and parenthood—to use their principles to get them to do what the others do without an even implicit recourse to principles. Of course, the operation of principle in a person's motivation does not always show itself in explicit consulting of that principle. One might have so internalized a principle that one acts on it almost automatically, without having to call it up in one's mind. Yet, as positions 2, 3, 4, 6, and 7 acknowledge, there is still a difference between acting from an internalized but universal principle and acting purely from care and concern for a specific individual, even if this difference is hard to make out in many specific instances. It is only position 1 which denies such a distinction entirely. That there can be a range of differences among persons in the degree to which universal principles animate their actions does not mean that one can imagine a fully responsible moral agent for whom they play no role at all. It would be difficult to imagine a person fully confronting the complex responsibilities of modern parenthood and friendship without giving some thought to the general responsibilities, formulable as principles of some sort, attaching to the various roles which they inhabit. Yet at the same time it should not be forgotten that some people who are not especially reflective about their general responsibilities seem as if instinctively to know how to act well toward their

particular friends, or toward their or others' children, much better in fact than some other people who are nevertheless quite articulate about the appropriate principles of responsible friendship and parenthood. To insist that seemingly unreflective persons must be acting according to general principles of action even when they are not able to articulate any such principles nor to recognize as their own ones suggested to them by others—to insist on this is to be blinded by rationalist prejudices.

20. This does not mean that Gilligan's view of morality is incompatible with all forms of relativism. Gilligan does not, I think, aspire, as Kohlberg does, to a timeless morality valid for all people in all historical times and cultures. It seems to me that Gilligan's view is compatible with the qualified relativism suggested in Williams 1985, chap. 9—the view that, e.g., a care morality is appropriate for any culture which is a real historical option for us; but we cannot say that it either is or is not valid for ones which are not. Something like this view is suggested in Gilligan & Murphy 1979.

21. For a more detailed argument for not excluding considerations of care from the domain of the moral, see my essays (1986, esp. 361; 1988). See also the presentation above of position 6, in which the argument presented there has the force of shifting to the defender of Kant the burden of proof of denying moral worth to care and compassion and of restricting moral worth to that which is done from a sense of duty.

22. For an argument that many morally worthy acts of friendship, familial care, and the like, lie outside the structure of obligation or duty altogether, see my 1980 work, chap. 7.

23. For a sustained critique of the sharp separation between act and motive presupposed in view 5, see Hudson 1986, esp. chap. 3; and Blum 1981, chap. 7.

24. Some of the issues concerning view 7 are addressed in my 1986 essay, esp. 350–54. There it is argued that the reflective point of view outside of the specific individual's caring for his friend, from which it can be seen that the individual's caring action is a good one—or that compassion, concern for specific individuals' welfare, and similar traits and sentiments can be acknowledged as having moral value—cannot be identified with the specific standpoint of "impartiality" found in impartialist moral theories. Such impartiality is, it is argued, only one possible reflective viewpoint. If this is so, then it is no support for position 7 to argue that all rational beings would include principles of care, compassion, and the like, as part of an ultimately acceptable morality, for the standpoint from which these rational beings do so is not necessarily an impartialist one.

25. Some of this work can be found in writings of Baier (1985a, 1986a, 1986b, 1987a) and in Noddings (1984).

5

Justice, Care, and Gender:
The Kohlberg-Gilligan Debate Revisited

Owen Flanagan and Kathryn Jackson

I

In 1958, G. E. M. Anscombe wrote, "It is not profitable for us at present to do moral philosophy; that should be laid aside at any rate until we have an adequate philosophy of psychology, in which we are conspicuously lacking" (186). Anscombe hinted (and she and many others pursued the hint) that the Aristotelian tradition was the best place to look for a richer and less shadowy conception of moral agency than either utilitarianism or Kantianism had provided.

In the same year Anscombe published "Modern Moral Philosophy," Lawrence Kohlberg completed his dissertation at the University of Chicago, a dissertation that laid the foundations for what has been the dominant program in moral psychology for the last twenty-odd years. The contrast between the sort of Aristotelian philosophical psychology Anscombe envisaged and Kohlberg's program could not have been starker. Anscombe recommended that the concepts of "*moral* obligation and *moral* duty . . . and of what is *morally* right and wrong, and of the *moral* sense of 'ought,' ought to be jettisoned . . . because they are survivors . . . from an earlier conception of ethics which no longer survives, and are only harmful without it" (1958, 186). Kohlberg meanwhile claimed that people at the highest stage of moral development "answer [moral dilemmas] in moral words such as *duty* or *morally right* and use them in a way implying universality, ideals and impersonality" (1981, 22). And while Anscombe pointed to Aristotle as the possible proof that ethics could be done with a more robust and realistic conception of moral agency than the will-o'-the-wisp Enlightenment conception which Iris Murdoch describes as "thin as a needle" (1970, 53) and Alasdair MacIntyre depicts as "ghostlike" (1982), Kohlberg derided Aristotelianism, calling it the "bag of virtues" model; and he explicitly rejected the view that personality is divided up "into cognitive abilities, passions or motives, and traits of character." Instead, he proposed that virtue is one and "the name of this ideal form is justice" (1981, 30–31). For Kohlberg the morally good person is simply one who reasons with, and acts on the basis of, principles of justice as fairness.

Despite the fact that Kohlberg's theory has come to dominate the thinking of moral psychologists (but hardly the thinking of moral philosophers who think about moral psychology), critics abound. One of the more widely-known challenges to Kohlberg's theory comes from his colleague and former collaborator, Carol Gilligan. Over the past fifteen years, Gilligan has been listening to women and men talk about morality. Her book, *In a Different Voice* (1982a), is both a challenge to the comprehensiveness of Kohlberg's theory and a revealing look at the way liberal society distributes various psychological competencies between the sexes. Gilligan describes a moral universe in which men, more often than women, conceive of morality as substantively constituted by obligations and rights and as procedurally constituted by the demands of fairness and impartiality, while women, more often than men, see moral requirements as emerging from the particular needs of others in the context of particular relationships. Gilligan has dubbed this latter orientation the "ethic of care," and she insists that the exclusive focus on justice reasoning has obscured both its psychological reality and its normative significance.

Whereas justice as fairness involves seeing others thinly, as worthy of respect purely by virtue of common humanity, morally good caring requires seeing others thickly, as constituted by their particular human face, their particular psychological and social self. It also involves taking seriously, or at least being moved by, one's particular connection to the other (see Flanagan & Adler 1983). Gilligan's claim is that once the dispositions that underlie such caring are acknowledged, the dominant conception of moral maturity among moral psychologists and moral philosophers will need to be reconceived (Gilligan 1983; also see Blum 1980).

The purpose of this essay is to gain some perspective on the philosophical stakes in the moral psychology debate by surveying and critically evaluating Gilligan's writings subsequent to her book—writings in which she attempts to extend, clarify, and defend her views—as well as recent work of Kohlberg's, in which he responds to Gilligan's challenge. Some recent philosophical literature is also discussed.

II

One issue in need of clarification is the precise nature of the ethic of care and its relation within moral personality to the ethic of justice. In her most recent writings, Gilligan characterizes the two ethics as "different ways of viewing the world" that "organize both thinking and feeling" (1986a, 1986b, 1986c), and she returns continually to the imagery of a gestalt shift (e.g., the vase-face illusion) to make it clear that she thinks that the two ethics involve seeing things in different and competing ways. The justice orientation organizes moral perception by highlighting issues of fairness, right, and obligation. Indeed, a person entirely in the grip of the justice orientation may be able to see a problem as a moral problem only if such issues can be construed in it. The care orientation meanwhile focuses on other saliencies: on the interconnections among the parties involved, on their particular personalities, and on their weal and woe.

The claim is that typically one orientation dominates moral thinking and that the direction of dominance is gender linked. Recent research shows that while most people introduce both care and justice considerations when discussing moral problems, over two-thirds present three-quarters or more considerations in one mode or the other. Furthermore, men and women distribute themselves bimodally on the justice and care ends of the scale (Lyons 1983; Gilligan & Wiggins 1987).

It is significant that there are such differences in the way men and women conceive of the moral domain and in the way they choose to talk about the moral issues they confront in real life. But two things must be kept in mind. First, although one way of conceiving of moral problems dominates, most individuals use both orientations some of the time. Therefore the differences between two individuals with contrasting dominant orientations will be more like the differences between two people—one of whom tends to see physical objects in functional terms and only secondarily in aesthetic terms, and another person with reversed dominance—than like the difference between occupants of totally alien universes. Second, the data on how people in fact conceive of morality have no simple and direct implications on the issues of how the domain of morality is best conceived, what virtues and reasoning skills are required by morality, and how best a particular moral issue is construed.

One need not be committed to any implausible version of moral realism to maintain that the most defensible specification of the moral domain will include issues of both right and good, that moral life requires a multiplicity of virtues, and that the description under which a particular problem is best understood is at least partly constrained by the kind of problem it is. The first two points seem fairly obvious, so let's focus on the third.

In several places, Gilligan suggests that every problem that can be construed morally can be construed from either the justice or care orientation (Gilligan 1986b; Gilligan & Wiggins 1987). Suppose this is right. Imagine someone who sees the problem of repaying or forgiving foreign loans as an issue of *love* between nations; or a mother who construes all positive interactions with her children as something they are *owed*. There may still be good reasons for preferring one construal over another. Generally speaking, there are two sorts of grounds that might recommend one construal over another and thus that might recommend educating moral agents to be disposed to make one interpretation rather than another. First, there might be normative reasons. Although a particular type of issue, say, parent-child relations, can be construed theoretically from the perspective of either of Gilligan's two orientations, the different construals lead to different kinds of worlds, one of which is more desirable than the other, all things considered. Second, there might be reasons having to do with our basic psychological makeup for making use of different dispositions and reasoning strategies for dealing with different kinds of problems. For example, if one accepts Hume's insight about the difficulty of widening fellow feeling indefinitely, then it makes sense to inculcate beliefs and principles which produce moral sensitivities in situations where no positive feelings exist among the parties.

The data Gilligan and her coworkers have gathered point to the existence of something like such a psychological division of labor with different kinds of moral problems drawing out different kinds of moral response. Recall that most people use both orientations some of the time and that the choice of orientation depends at least in part on the type of problem posed. Indeed, standard Kohlbergian dilemmas, such as the Heinz dilemma (should Heinz steal the drug which could help his dying wife from the avaricious pharmacist who will not sell it at a fair price?), generate the highest number of justice responses in both sexes; and hypothetical stories that highlight inequality or attachment result in higher rates of justice and care responses, respectively, for both men and women (Gilligan & Wiggins 1987). This is true despite continuous findings of gender differences in responses to open-ended questions about the nature of morality and one's own real-life dilemmas, as well as in the ratio of justice versus care responses to hypothetical moral dilemmas.

Such findings regarding the domain specificity of moral response, especially in light of the point about better and worse construals, indicate that although Gilligan's gestalt-shift metaphor is illuminating in three ways, it is unhelpful and misleading in two others. First, it is helpful in drawing attention to the fact that just as some people have trouble ever seeing one or the other available images in a gestalt illusion, so too there are some people who have trouble understanding talk of rights or alternatively talk of love; they just can't see what you are talking about. Second, the metaphor highlights the findings that for most individuals one way of seeing moral problems dominates the other way of seeing to some degree, and that the direction of dominance is correlated with gender. Finally, the metaphor draws attention to the fact that there are some moral problems—abortion, for example—the proper construal of which is deemed by all parties to be a matter of the greatest importance, but for which the proper construal is an issue of deeply incompatible perception.

There are undoubtedly also problems of less monumental importance for which there are no clear grounds for preferring one construal over the other. In one study by a member of Gilligan's group, teenagers of both sexes were good at switching from their preferred orientation when asked if there was another way to think about a certain problem, but all subjects believed that their preferred mode gave rise to the most defensible solution. Barring radical discrepancies from a normative point of view as to what action is prescribed or how things turn out, there may well be nothing definitive to say about the preferability of one construal over the other in many specific cases (although there might well be objections to general dominance of one orientation), since personal style, even if socially constructed and gender linked, has certain saving graces on the side of cognitive economy once it is in place. Or to put the point more contentiously: in some cases the preferred mode of moral construal may be the most defensible simply because it is preferred.

Nevertheless, what is misleading about the gestalt metaphor is that, just as not all visual stimuli are ambiguous in the way gestalt illusions are, so too not all moral issues are so open to alternative construals. To be sure, the psychological apparatus involved in moral appraisal involves learning and underdetermination in a way visual perception does not, and thus moral construal is more tradition sensitive than visual perception. But again there may be both normative reasons and reasons of cognitive economy for teaching moral agents to be sensitive to certain saliencies (e.g., anonymity among parties, prior explicit contracts) in such a way that these saliencies are more or less sufficient to generate one construal (e.g., a justice construal) rather than some other. As we have seen, some of Gilligan's own data indicate that something like this happens for at least some problems for both men and women.

The second and more important way the gestalt metaphor is misleading has to do with the fact that there is a deep and important difference between visual perception and moral construal which the metaphor obscures. Whereas it is impossible to see both the duck and the rabbit at the same time in the duck-rabbit illusion, it is not impossible to see both the justice and care saliencies in a moral problem and to integrate them in moral deliberation. This is because moral consideration, unlike visual perception, takes place over time and can involve the assimilation and accommodation of as much, and as messy, information as we like. It is wrong, therefore, to suggest, as Gilligan does in one place, that the two perspectives are "fundamentally incompatible" (Gilligan 1986b; also see Lyons 1983).

The point is that there is no logical reason why both care and justice considerations cannot be introduced, where relevant, into one and the same reasoning episode. *Heinz*, after all, should steal the drug because it is *his* wife; and his wife should get the drug because *any* human life is more important than any avaricious pharmacist's desire to make some extra money.

This is not to deny that in some cases construing a particular problem from both perspectives will block moral clarity about what should be done (see Flanagan & Adler 1983), nor is it to deny that for the sake of normative elegance and psychological stability it will be important to have some, even imperfect, decision-procedure to resolve such conflicts. But, as we have suggested, one possibility is that the saliencies construable in a particular situation will make different sorts of considerations differentially relevant to that situation and, in that way, will keep intractability (but, possibly, not a sense of moral costs) to a minimum. The important point is that there is no impossibility in imagining persons who are both very fair and very caring and who, in addition, have finely honed sensitivities for perceiving moral saliencies and seeing particular problems as problems of certain multifarious kinds.

Thinking of moral psychology as variegated, as composed of a wide array of attitudes, dispositions, rules of thumb, and principles that are designed for multifarious sorts of situations, suggests a move in a more virtue-theoretical direction and, thus, a return to the sort of conceptual model that has been out of favor in the cognitive-developmental tradition since Piaget's *The Moral Judgment of the Child* (1932).[1] Indeed, the more plausibility one assigns to an Aristotelian conception of moral psychology, the more credible will be the suspicion that Gilligan's expansion of Kohlberg's model to include two general orientations is still insufficiently fine-grained to be adequate from either a psychological or normative point of view. There are three reasons for this. First, we still lack a clear (and remotely complete) taxonomy of the various dispositions—the cognitive and affective attitudes—that constitute the care orientation, and the same goes for the justice orientation. This failure to provide a more fine-grained analysis is more understandable for Kohlberg than for Gilligan. After all, Kohlberg believes that morality is decidedly not a matter of special-purpose virtues, dispositions, and reasoning strategies but, rather, consists of the application of a unified general-purpose style of thinking. But there is every reason to think that Gilligan's program would benefit from moving in a more virtue-theoretical direction, insofar as the conception of moral agency she describes is potentially so much thicker than Kohlberg's, embedded as it is in self-conception and social context.

In the second place, we lack a careful analysis of the differences between good and morally problematic or even corrupt kinds of care. Care can be corrupt either because of qualitative features of the caring relationship (e.g., it is based on insincerity or coercion) or because of the relationship's content (e.g., the parties have bad aspirations for each other or give sensitive attention to meeting each other's corrupt needs and desires). (See Baier 1986b; Gilligan does some of this in her own attempt to emulate stage theory: 1982a, 105.)

Third, even if we accept the plausible view that moral psychology is neither totally modular (as in vulgar Aristotlianism) nor totally unified and general purpose (as in vulgar Kantianism) but, rather, is tiered, containing both virtuous and vicious dispositions to think and react in certain ways as well as a general higher-level moral orientation (which may or may not have power over the lower levels), there is good reason to think that there are more than two such general orientations.[2] For example, Charles Taylor (1982) has described moral outlooks guided by the commitments to personal integrity, to perfection, and to liberation which cannot be assimilated under either of Gilligan's two rubrics, let alone under Kohlberg's one (see Miller 1985 for descriptions of some even more alien moral orientations); and it is hard to see how virtues like courage or moderation fall under either orientation.

The issues of the scope of morality and the range of realizable moral concepts are of the utmost importance. What moral psychologists conceive of as possible determines how they understand and classify moral personalities. But if the possibility range is too narrowly conceived or too culture bound or too gripped by a contentious normative conception, actual psychological realities may be missed.

In addition to these issues, there is still the important question of precisely what sort of adjustment Gilligan thinks work such as hers warrants in our conception of moral maturity. She was not clear on this matter in her book, and her recent work still shifts between the ideas that the two ethics are incompatible alternatives to each other but are both adequate from a normative point of view; that they are complements of one another involved in some sort of tense interplay; and that each is deficient without the other and thus ought to be integrated.

One might think that our claim that there is no logical incompatibility between the two ethics and thus no logical problem with bringing both kinds of considerations to any problem (which is not to imply that the two sets of concepts can be applied without conflict in every place) means that there is nothing to block the tactic of pursuing the integrationist strategy less hesitantly. But here Gilligan has some interesting things to say about the psychological origins of the two orientations. Although there may be no logical incompatibility between the concepts of justice and care, Gilligan suggests in many places that there is a deep-seated psychological tension between the two perspectives, a tension rooted in the fact that the two ethics are built out of etiologically distinct underlying competencies which make different and competing psychological demands on moral agents. It is the differences in origin and underlying cognitive and motivational structure which make integration of the two orientations in particular moral agents hard to realize and which, at the same time, explain the data on gender differences.

Gilligan accepts a roughly neo-Freudian account of early childhood. This account turns on two main variables: (1) the psychological situation of the child as both dependent and attached; and (2) the typical differences between maternal and paternal relations with the child. The basic story goes like this: The child has continuous experiences of both her relative powerlessness vis-à-vis her parents and her powerful attachment to them. The experiences of powerlessness and inequality give rise to the search for independence and equality and thereby provide fertile ground for the notions of fairness and autonomy (and their opposites) to take root. Meanwhile, the experiences of deep attachment and connection, of moving and being moved by others, provide the ground for the dispositions that will guide later attachments—for compassion, love, and altruism. Together "the different dynamics of early childhood inequality and attachment lay the groundwork for two moral visions—of justice and of care" (Gilligan & Wiggins 1987).

Even if one accepts that it is the alleged tension between the two kinds of early experiences that grounds the tension between the two ethics (one might be skeptical on grounds that there is a high degree of overlap between the two kinds of experiences), this tension does not explain the data on gender differences. Here Gilligan follows Nancy Chodorow's (1978) influential analysis of gender differentiation. Initially, for children of both sexes, the relationship with the primary caretaker, typically the mother, is one of powerful attachment and identification. However, as the child gets older and begins the project of carving out a self-concept, she starts to identify strongly with her same-sex parent, and parents reinforce this identification. In the typical family where the mother has a greater nurturing role than the father, boys will have to shift their initial identification with the mother to the father. Girls, meanwhile, do not need to reorient their initial identification but only to intensify the one that already exists. This means that the project of separation is more salient and more pressing for boys than for girls. Furthermore, because of the mutual feelings of identification between mother and daughter, girls will have richer experience than boys with attachment and connectedness. According to Chodorow,

> Boys . . . have to curtail their primary love and sense of empathic tie with their mother. A boy has been required to engage in more

emphatic individuation and a more defensive firming of experienced ego boundaries. . . . Girls emerge from this period with a basis for "empathy" built into their primary definition of self in a way that boys do not. (1978, 166–67)

Assuming this story is true, it should be obvious, first, that there is nothing necessary (although there may be biological and social pressures in certain directions) about the way we arrange nurturance, or about the particular ways parents treat their male and female children, and thus the story is not required to turn out exactly the way it now does. If there were greater sharing in nurturance by both parents, the process of acquiring a self-concept would not make such different demands and rest on such different experiences for boys and girls. Resultant attitudes about autonomy, attachment, and so on might not be as different as they now are. But, second, the latter analysis does indicate why, given current practices (with their long cultural histories), we cannot be sanguine about the possibilities for inculcating moral sensibilities which support both a rich sense of justice and care and a well-developed sense of autonomy and connection in one and the same agent.

Full-fledged integration aside, it is important to consider what role, if any, the experiences and dispositions which underlie each ethic have in contributing to morally good forms of the other. Again, it is important not to lose sight of the fact that the early experiences of powerlessness and attachment overlap.

Annette Baier has made some interesting suggestions in this regard. Her basic insight is similar to Hume's about the problem with Hobbes' state-of-nature hypothesis, namely, it ignores the fact that for any human interaction to take place, including even "a war of each against each," there must first be family and nurturance. Otherwise the helpless infant will not survive its first nights.

Baier argues first that theories of justice, including Rawls', need to assume that there will be loving parents in order to ensure the stability of a just society and the development of a sense of justice in new members:

Rawls' theory like so many other theories of obligation, in the end must take out a loan not only on the natural duty of parents to care for children . . . but on the natural virtue of parental love. . . . The virtue of being a *loving* parent must supplement the natural duties and obligations, if the just society is to last beyond the first generation. (Baier, 1985, essay 2 in this volume)

Second, Baier argues that the dispositions to be fair and to keep contracts presuppose (psychologically and normally, but not logically) that the agent has been cared for and has had experiences of trust.

Promises presuppose both experience of longer on-going trust relationships *not* necessarily initiated by any voluntary act (with parents or with friends) so that the advantages of such future-
involving mutual trust be already clear, and also an already established climate of trust enabling one to chose to get close enough to
a stranger to exchange words or goods or handshakes with him.
(Baier 1986b)

Baier's argument suggests the further insight that the moral disposition to
be just normally presupposes not only that the agent is attached to certain
abstract concepts and ideals, but also, more fundamentally, that he is attached to and cares for his community, and that he has a sense that his own
good and that of those he cares for most is associated with general adherence to these ideals. Without such cares and attachments, first to those one
loves and secondarily to some wider community to which one's projects and
prospects are intimately joined, the moral disposition to justice—as opposed to the purely prudential disposition to justice—has no place to take
root.

There is no objection in principle to using one set of virtues and dispositions to support or strengthen another set. The point is simply, as Baier puts
it, that "a decent morality will *not* depend for its stability on forces to which
it gives no moral recognition" (Baier, essay 2 in this volume)

III

The question arises as to what Kohlberg makes of the ethic of care and
the various dispositions and experiences that constitute it. What sort of recognition does he think this ethical perspective deserves? What is its relation
to the conception of morality as justice that he more than anyone else has
championed?

At first, Kohlberg (1982) flirted with the strategy of simply denying that
there is such an ethic and thereby denying that there is anything of *moral*
psychological importance to recognize. Kohlberg admits that initially he
found Gilligan's work unwelcome and preferred to read it as concerned with
ego psychology but not with moral psychology (1982, 514). This suggestion
in itself displays a very unrealistic view about the isolation of moral psychology from overall personality.

Lately Kohlberg seems to have come around to seeing that Gilligan's challenge was more apt than he first admitted. In two long coauthored essays
(both with Charles Levine and Alexandra Hewer) in the second volume of
his collected papers (1984), Kohlberg attempts to set forth a more complete
and satisfactory response to Gilligan's work. On an initial reading, Kohlberg
appears to concede many of the main points of contention. Reflecting on his

original theory, he writes, "I assumed that the core of morality and moral development was deontological; that is, it was a matter of rights and duties or prescriptions" (225). These "starting assumptions led to the design of a research instrument measuring reasoning about dilemmas of conflicting rights or the distribution of scarce resources, that is, justice concerns. We did not use dilemmas about prosocial concerns for others that were not frameable as rights conflicts" (304). "We admit, however, that the emphasis on the virtue of justice in my work does not fully reflect all that is recognized as being part of the moral domain" (227).

In speaking specifically of his standard measurement tool, Kohlberg says, "We do agree that our justice dilemmas do not pull for the care and response orientation, and we do agree that our scoring manual does not lead to a full assessment of this aspect of moral thinking" (1984, 343; see also 305–7, and 622–23). Kohlberg now recommends, therefore, understanding his theory as a "rational reconstruction of justice reasoning; emphasizing the nomenclature 'justice reasoning,' since the . . . stages have more typically been called stages of moral development [by him]" (1984, 224).

Despite such concessions, it is really quite difficult to put one's finger on how Kohlberg now intends his theory to be interpreted, and sometimes what is conceded with one hand seems to be withdrawn with the other. Indeed, on closer reading, it is hard to read Kohlberg as completely sincere in the latter concessions, for he also puts forward a variety of claims that are at odds with them.

For example, although Kohlberg now acknowledges that his theory is not comprehensive, he continues to promote a restricted conception of morality which belies this concession. In particular, he continues to make two common but questionable claims about the nature of morality. First, there is the claim that all moral judgments have certain formal features such as prescriptivity (i.e., they entail obligations) and universalizability (1984, 293–96). Second, there is the claim that "*moral* judgments or principles have the central function of resolving interpersonal or social conflicts, that is, conflicts of claims or rights" (216).

Both points are problematic. With regard to the first point, imagine a complex judgment about how one can best help a friend who is depressed. The judgment here will involve assessment of particular features of both parties. What one can do for a friend is, after all, determined in large part by the kinds of persons both are, the characteristic patterns of interaction between the two, and so on. It is implausible to think that there is anything interestingly universalizable about such a judgment or that there is necessarily any judgment of obligation involved. Indeed, where friendship or love truly exists, thinking about what one is obligated to do can, as Bernard Williams has put it in a related context, involve "one thought too many" (1982, 18).

With regard to the second point, the same example serves to show that it is simply not obvious that morality has the central function of resolving "conflicts of claims or rights." To be sure, this is an important function of moral theory, and the function most visible in public debates, but to conceive of this function as central and other functions of morality as peripheral is to beg the interesting question of how best to conceive of the domain of morality. There is too much moral energy expended on self-improvement and the refinement of character, on respectful interactions with loved ones, friends, and strangers, and on supererogation for such a claim to be acceptable without considerable defense. None is given.

At one point Kohlberg stresses that his conception of "morality as justice best renders our view of morality as universal. It restricts morality to a central minimal core, striving for universal agreement in the face of more relativist conceptions of the good" (1984, 306). And in many places he emphasizes that there are two senses of the word "moral"—one sense is that of "the moral point of view" with the alleged formal features, the other sense refers to "personal" issues—to things like friendship, family relations, supererogation, and so on (232). Kohlberg points out that how one treats the latter issues is widely acknowledged to be a relative matter (but, one must stress, not completely relative).

Still, two issues must be kept distinct. It is one thing to want to study a certain kind of moral thinking because it is more stable (the function of a theory of justice is, after all, to produce such stability in interpersonal relations among individuals who may have no personal connections) or because it is easier to talk about in terms of the theoretical framework of cognitive-developmental stage theory. Kohlberg (1984, 236–49) makes it clear that one reason he prefers to study justice reasoning is that he thinks that there are "hard" stages, that is, stages which satisfy standard Piagetian criteria of universality, irreversibility, and so on, of justice reasoning (see Flanagan 1984 for doubts about this), but not of reasoning about personal issues. But such theoretical attractions are irrelevant to the issues of psychological realism, normative adequacy, and the domain of the moral.

Once Kohlberg's proprietary attempt to restrict our conception of the domain of the moral is seen for what it is, his "total disagreement" (1984, 342) with Gilligan regarding gender differences is of little moment. Kohlberg clings to the fact that such differences are minimal or nonexistent in studies using his standard justice dilemmas as the test instrument (see Walker 1984 for a review; but see Baumrind 1986 for a criticism of Walker). The fact remains that there are, as Kohlberg acknowledges (350), gender differences in preferred orientation, in response ratios, and so on, even if there are none for one restricted type of moral problem. Such findings point to differences in moral psychology unless one implausibly restricts the domain of inquiry.

In several places Kohlberg tries a more interesting tactic than the one of restricting the conception of morality to what he studies. This tactic starts by accepting that "personal morality" is part of the domain of the moral (1984, 234–35) but then moves to claim that justice lies in some subsuming relation to this morality. In speaking specifically of Gilligan's work, he says, "The two senses of the word *moral* do not represent two different moral orientations existing at the same level of generality and validity" (232).

The overall strategy is to make an argument for the "primacy of justice," either by arguing that considerations of justice trump considerations of care when the two conflict, or by arguing that justice is in some sense necessary for care but not the other way around (see Kohlberg 1981, xiii; Kohlberg 1984, 305).

The first idea, that the demands of justice must be met before all others, is a familiar one within the context of liberal political theory. However, it is important to emphasize that, even within the liberal tradition, the claim that justice is trump applies in the first instance to the arrangement of basic social institutions. Many liberal philosophers are hesitant about any simple and straightforward extension of the deontological constraints governing political practices to individual behavior.

Furthermore, even if one holds that considerations of justice are overriding at the individual level, nothing follows about how often considerations of justice are germane. If, as seems the case for most of us, the larger part of moral life takes place in situations and contexts in which considerations of justice are not especially relevant, then the "primacy of justice" might be an important principle to have, and sensitivities to issues of justice will need to be well honed; but the virtue of justice will not be doing most of the work in the actual moral lives of most persons.

The second idea—that justice is necessary for care—comes in two forms. First, there is the claim that conditions of social justice must obtain for the personal virtues associated with both justice and care to thrive. "It seems to us . . . that morally valid forms of caring and community presuppose prior conditions and judgments of justice" (Kohlberg 1984, 305). Second, there is the claim that the personal virtue of justice is necessary for the personal virtue of care. "In our view special obligations of care presuppose, but go beyond, the general duties of justice, which are necessary, but not sufficient for them" (229). "More than justice is required for resolving many complex moral dilemmas, but justice is a necessary element of any morally adequate resolution of these conflicts" (370).

The first point is important. There is something obviously right about the view that morality is not a purely individual project and that personal virtue takes root best in a just society. But once we push things back to the basic social conditions necessary for morality, we come again upon the point that all societies, just or unjust, stable or unstable, egalitarian or nonegalitarian, presuppose prior relations of care between new members and those members involved in child rearing. There is in the end something misleading in the widely-held view that justice is the first virtue of society. Indeed, although it is wise to resist lexically ordering the basic virtues required for an ongoing morally good society or for a morally good personality, there is no incoherence in putting care first when it comes to creating the possible conditions for family, wider community, and individual character in the first place.

The second point—that personal justice has some essential connection to the other virtues—comes in several versions. The strongest and most implausible claim is that personal justice is sufficient for moral goodness overall. With the possible exception of Plato, no one has held this view. The reason is that it is easy to imagine someone who espouses and abides by some defensible conception of justice but who is morally deficient in other ways.

Kohlberg intends something weaker than the implausible sufficiency claim. His proposal, however, is ambiguous between two different claims: (1) that experiences of fairness and the development of the disposition to be just are necessary for the causal formation of whatever psychological competencies turn out to be associated with Gilligan's ethic of care, but not vice versa; and (2) that the display of any other virtue necessarily presupposes possession of the virtue of justice, but not vice versa. Showing either claim 1 or 2 would help support the claim that the two ethics do not "exist at the same level of generality and validity."

With regard to claim 1, we have already expressed the opinion that experiences of care and caring have an important role in laying the foundations for any ethical sense whatsoever (see Noddings 1984 for someone who makes too much of this point). Hence we already have grounds for doubting the claim that justice has some unique foundational status with regard to the formation of other virtues or to overall moral psychology.

When one focuses less on the basic experiences necessary for developing a moral sense and looks more closely at the sort of explicit moral instruction that takes place between parents and children (something neither Gilligan nor Kohlberg does), the claim that the acquisition of the personal virtue of justice has unique foundational status also seems implausible. To be sure, parents often say things like, "Kate, look how sad David is; he deserves a turn too." But it is most plausible to read such statements as presupposing that some of the competencies, dispositions, and beliefs required by justice and care are required by morally good forms of either. It is hard to see how we could teach children about kindness without teaching them certain things about fairness, but it is equally hard to see how we could teach them about fairness without teaching them certain things about kindness and sensitivity to the aims and interests of others. The situation is one of mutual support rather than a necessary condition in only one direction.

The fact that normally both justice and care are built out of some of the same underlying competencies does not imply, however, that a mature sense of justice is necessary for the display of the other virtues or for responding to every particular moral problem (claim 2 above). First, there are some persons whom we think of as virtuous in certain ways and in certain domains, but who we do not think are very fair or just; and the same holds true in the other direction. Second, it is possible to imagine individuals in whom beneficence is so sensitively and globally developed that the virtue of justice, as normally conceived, is not only unnecessary for the display of the other virtues, but is even unnecessary in situations in which ordinary persons with less saintly personalities would need to call upon it. Third, and setting such moral exotica aside, there are many moral problems which have nothing to do with justice. It is implausible, therefore, to think the personal virtue of justice is necessarily implicated in our dealings with such problems.

To question the truth of the necessary condition claim as a psychological thesis is not to deny what is normatively important about it. A morally good life overall requires fairness because the possession of the virtues associated with care might well, if not tempered by justice, result in immorality, for example, chauvinism, in certain circumstances. But the same holds true in the other direction.

In several places, Kohlberg tries to make the normative point but links it with the implausible psychological one. He says, "In our philosophic end point of moral reasoning, the hypothetical sixth stage, there occurs, we believe, an integration of justice and care that forms a single moral principle" (1984, 344). And elsewhere he claims that the two orientations converge at the highest stage because the "principle of persons as ends is common to both" (356).

This way of talking is misleading in two respects. First, Kohlberg now acknowledges (1982, 523; 1984, 215) that his highest stage of moral development is purely hypothetical; that in over twenty-five years of research, he and his colleagues have been unable to confirm the existence of stage 6. This means that the claim that justice and care converge at the highest stage to "form a single moral principle" is a claim for which there is no empirical evidence. Second, it is extremely doubtful, for reasons Gilligan and others (Blum 1980) have expressed, that a normatively adequate moral psychology is best thought of in terms of the possession of a single unified faculty and, even less plausibly, in terms of the possession of a "single moral principle."

Still, Gilligan's own view that morality consists of "two voices" needs further refinement, development, and defense before its full psychological and normative importance is clear. We need to know more about many things, including the precise nature and extent of the gender differences, the social causes of these differences, content effects, the fine-grained features of the ethic of care, the role of the competencies it makes use of in justice reasoning, and the plausibility of carving morality into only two voices.

IV

The view that there is one ideal type of moral personality—a unique way moral psychology is best ordered and moral reasoning conducted—is the psychological side of the coin whose other face contains the image of morality as a unitary domain with a determinate and timeless nature. Much recent work in moral philosophy has questioned this view of morality as a clearly carved domain for which a unified theory can be produced. Such work suggests that our attitudes and expectations about underlying moral psychology may also need to be revised. Rejection of the doctrine of the "unity of the moral" (Taylor 1982) may also require rejection of its close relative—the doctrine that there is one ideal type of moral personality.

A reasonable hypothesis is that moral personality occurs at a level too open to both social and self-determination for us to expect there to be any unique and determinate set of dispositions, capacities, attitudes, and types of reasoning which ideally underwrite all moral responsiveness. This means that we will have to learn to tolerate and perhaps applaud a rich diversity of good moral personalities. The fact that this will be hard for those still in the grip of the doctrine of the "unity of the moral" in no way belies the possibility that this is the right road to go.

Notes

1. The rest of cognitive psychology, of course, has gone increasingly homuncular.
2. Both Gilligan and Kohlberg take narrative data to be a fairly accurate index of the more general orientation. This is problematic. The relationship between first-person speech acts and underlying psychology is a widely discussed issue in contemporary philosophy of mind and cognitive psychology, and there is reason to think that our deficiencies in giving accurate self-assessments run very deep. Confabulation is an especially salient worry when the speech acts are being offered in response to issues which connect so obviously as do moral problems with issues of self-worth and with how one is perceived by others. Gilligan and Kohlberg are strangely silent on such matters.

Part II
EXPANDING THE QUESTION

6

Women, Morality, and History

Linda J. Nicholson

When Women's Studies first emerged in the early 1970s, many expected it to bring forth some very basic challenges to the existing academic disciplines. Since it was clear that gender has been a basic social organizing principle of all known societies, it was sensed that a perspective which made gender itself the issue would produce a potentially powerful new lens through which to view our past and present. That sense has been vindicated. Women's Studies has produced novel and indeed sometimes revolutionary means of viewing the subject matter of a variety of disciplines.

One such example is recent feminist scholarship in moral theory. Moral theory, as it has been traditionally taught in most British and American philosophy departments, has consisted of the writings of such men as Plato, Aristotle, Hume, Kant, Bentham, and Mill. Some feminist scholars have begun to make the increasingly convincing argument that the content of the theory produced by such men has not been uninfluenced by the almost universal masculinity of its creators. While some might counter with the argument that the predominant masculinity here signifies only that it has been men who have been given the resources for discovering that which is universal to the human condition, many feminists have responded that the masculinity of the authors has affected the very content of the theory itself. Thus, insofar as these theorists claimed to be articulating that which is universal to the human condition, they were mistaken.

I agree with the feminist argument. The point I wish to make in this essay is that it needs more careful formulation and elaboration than it has sometimes been given. In particular, there needs to be more stress on the point

Reprinted by permission from *Social Research* 50: 514–36. Copyright © 1983 by the journal.

that gender has been an important factor in influencing moral perspective and moral theory because gender has been an important factor in influencing the concrete circumstances of people's lives. Thus, in elaborating how gender has shaped moral perspective and moral theory we need to examine in depth the nature of such circumstances rather than relying too heavily on such shortcuts as "feminine" and "masculine."

There are specific reasons why such shortcuts, while often helpful, can sometimes be misleading. For one, they incline us to overlook the point that, while gender is and has been a fundamental social organizing principle, it is not the only such organizing principle. Other factors, such as race, class, and the sheer specificity of historical circumstances also profoundly affect social life and thus a moral perspective. Thus, insofar as we talk about a "feminine" or "masculine" moral point of view we run the risk of not seeing how what we are describing reflects the gender viewpoint of a certain race or class at a certain time. We thus tend to commit the same kind of error of false generalization that motivated the initial rebellion.

Kohlberg's Masculine Bias

To illustrate these points I would like to begin by examining some of the feminist scholarship which has emerged in moral theory. One of the major contributors to this discussion has been Carol Gilligan, responding to the moral-development theory of Lawrence Kohlberg. Kohlberg claimed to discover certain universal structures of moral development which underlie all human moral perspectives. These structures were viewed by Kohlberg as formal, that is, as compatible with a wide variety of specific moral positions. They also were described by him as possessing an invariant internal order such that movement among the stages follows a certain unilateral direction. Kohlberg and his associates steadily revised the exact specifications of the stages in light of empirical findings. In spite of such revision, there does appear one consistent general characteristic of the sequence as a whole, and that is that movement through the stages tends to be marked by greater abstraction. Thus, according to Kohlberg's model, as people's moral reasoning progresses toward the higher levels, it appears influenced less by reference to the consequences of actions on specific persons or communities and more by reference to abstract and universal principles. This was quite clear in a definition Kohlberg once gave of his highest stage, stage 6, "The Universal-Ethical Principle Orientation":

> Right is defined by the decision of conscience in accord with self-chosen *ethical principles* appealing to logical comprehensiveness, universality and consistency. These principles are abstract and ethical (the Golden Rule, the categorical imperative); they are not

concrete moral rules like the Ten Commandments. At heart, these are universal principles of justice, of the reciprocity and equality of human rights, and of respect for the dignity of human beings as individual persons. (Kohlberg 1980, 59)

Because of a lack of empirical confirmation, stage 6 has occupied a controversial place in the theory. However, even stage 5, which concerns the protection of individual rights, is more marked by appeals to nonparticularistic concerns than stages 3 and 4, characterized by reference to conventional norms. Similarly, reference to what is conventionally acceptable is itself more universalistic than the perspective found in Kohlberg's lowest two stages, which emphasize the personal consequences of individual actions.

An obvious question which can be raised about this position is whether it describes a sequence universal to human beings per se, or whether it represents a culturally biased perspective. Kohlberg, to deal with such an objection, empirically tested his model in a variety of divergent cultures. He found that even in cultures as diverse as the United States, Great Britain, Mexico, Turkey, Taiwan, and Malaysia, the predictive capacity of the stages and their sequence was confirmed (1980, 60). Kohlberg did note that not all societies or groups within a given society did as "well," that is, progressed through the stages at as fast a rate or reached in as great a number, if at all, the higher three stages (1980, 60). Kohlberg dealt with this type of divergence by arguing that not all social experiences are equally conducive to moral development (1982, 518)

If we ignore for the moment the ability of Kohlberg's model to predict movement along the stages successfully, the fact of divergence of rate and extent of moral development across cultures does speak in favor of the possibility of cultural bias. The point could be made that those who score low do not suffer from a lack of opportunity to reach the highest possible level of moral capacity but possess a type of moral reasoning poorly captured by Kohlberg's model. Thus, those who are classified by Kohlberg as "failures" might, from an alternative perspective, be viewed as "counterexamples." This is the type of objection which Gilligan raised against Kohlberg.

Specifically, Gilligan argued that Kohlberg's model of moral development evidences a masculine bias; its notion of development is skewed in favor of certain values more central to male than to female socialization. In part, Gilligan based her argument on the work of Nancy Chodorow. Chodorow, a sociologist heavily influenced by psychoanalytic and object relations theory, has drawn attention to a culturally universal difference between early female and male socialization: that the first and primary caretaker for girls but not for boys is a member of the same gender as they. One consequence of this difference is that young boys, to develop their own identity as masculine, must negate their early identification with their mothers. As a result, young boys tend to see social relationships as potentially threatening to their sense of self; protection against threats to their sense of autonomy takes on a high value in their lives. Young girls on the contrary incline toward defining themselves in terms of their connection to others. Thus, where men tend to fear engulfment by others, women fear abandonment. Chodorow also argues that because of the predominance of early parenting by women, young boys acquire knowledge of masculinity in a much more removed and abstract manner than young girls acquire knowledge of femininity; the role models of young boys are more frequently absent and distant figures. A consequence here is that abstract norms and rules play a greater role in the development of male gender identity than in the development of female gender identity.

Gilligan supplements these arguments with certain empirical studies. She draws on the work of Janet Lever, who notes one interesting difference in the games of young boys and girls—the games of boys are more marked by conflict resolved through the creation of rules. The games of young girls tend to involve smaller numbers of people and imitate patterns of interaction of adult life. This kind of play, Gilligan notes, leans less "toward learning to take the role of 'the generalized other,' less toward the abstraction of human relationships" than that of boys. On the other hand, "it fosters the development of the empathy and sensitivity necessary for taking the role of 'the particular other' and points more toward knowing the other as different from the self" (Gilligan 1982a, 9–10).

From such studies as those of Chodorow, Lever, and others, Gilligan notes certain general differences in masculine and feminine personality structures which incline toward general differences in types of moral reasoning. Boys and men tend to evidence strong concern with issues of rights and autonomy; noninterference is a highly valued good. They tend, more than females, to feel comfortable with rules that abstract from the particularities of situational concerns; they are more at ease than females with resolving hypothetical dilemmas. Girls and women, on the contrary, evidence a stronger orientation toward relationships and interdependence. Their moral judgments tend to be tied to feelings of empathy and compassion and to be situationally rooted. Their moral thinking in general tends to be contextual rather than categorical, to evidence in higher frequencies than males a response like "It depends" (Gilligan 1982a, 18).

Following from such arguments, Gilligan claims that Kohlberg's model, with its increasing emphasis toward abstraction from the particular, evidences a masculine bias. This bias, she argues, was made possible by his earliest empirical study from which he derived his model. That study used only boys as subjects. She claims that, given the bias within the theory, it is not surprising that girls tend to score significantly lower than boys on Kohlberg's scale.

Kohlberg responded to Gilligan's argument in a variety of ways. He noted studies which show no significant difference in the results of men and women (Kohlbeg 1982, 517–18). Kohlberg claimed to incorporate components of Gilligan's critique within the model; he also argued that, while Gilligan's points have relevance to certain components of moral reasoning, those which concern content and orientation, they become more irrelevant for the more formal issues of structure with which he is concerned (Kohlberg 1982, 514–16).

The "Masculine" in Western Moral Theory

At a later point in this essay I will deal with these responses. For now it is sufficient to note that even if there are components of Kohlberg's model which remain untouched by Gilligan's argument, that argument remains important in and of itself. Much of Western moral theory, independent of Kohlberg, has evidenced many characteristics which could be labeled "masculine" along the lines suggested by Gilligan.

This is a position argued by Lawrence Blum. Blum focuses particularly on a certain tradition within moral philosophy which he calls "moral rationalism," best exemplified in the thought of Kant and Hegel. He notes that, within this tradition, many of the features of that which has been seen as distinctively moral parallel those features traditionally thought of as masculine. Thus, for both Kant and Hegel the following qualities define that which is moral: rationality, self-control, strength of will, consistency, acting from universal principles, and adherence to duty and obligation. Moreover, these philosophers define the morally good "man" as specifically lacking the following qualities: sympathy, compassion, kindness, caring for others, and human concern—in short, those qualities associated with the emotional component of human nature which has also been linked with femininity (Blum 1982, 287–88).

Blum relates this association between qualities of gender and qualities of morality to the differences in the kinds of worlds in which men and women have been expected to operate. Thus whereas large-scale public institutions such as the state must abstract from the needs of particular persons and govern through the creation of universal laws, the family as bonded through intimacy and love is concerned with the particular and concrete. Thus, Blum argues:

> The male world of work in corporate and governmental bureaucracies requires a *certain* kind of "universalist" outlook (though this outlook is ultimately compatible with serving private or parochial interests), a suppression of personal emotion, an adherence to procedures which abstract from personal emotion, an ad-

herence to procedures which abstract from personal attachment, inclination, concern for particular others. Similarly love, personal attachment, emotional support and nurturance are appropriate to the distinctive tasks of the family. To the extent that men are allotted to the former realm and women to the latter, different sorts of attributes and characteristics will be required of the different sexes. And society will have to provide a form of sex-differentiated socialization which prepares men and women for these societal roles. (Blum 1982, 298–99)

This association between gender and forms of social organization is important to stress. It is also important to stress the historicity of this particular association between the family and the state to which Blum alludes. While certainly, some notion of a male/female distinction and of a gender division of labor may range over a wide variety of cultures, it is only with the growth of the more nuclearized family and the nation-state in the early modern period in the West, and particularly amongst the middle-class, that masculinity and femininity take on many of those specific qualities with which we are now familiar. Thus, it is only with the development of the family in the seventeenth and eighteenth centuries as an emotional unit bonded by feelings of affection among its members that there also begins to develop the ideal of the female as a being more emotional and affective than the male. Similarly, while a nondomestic public sphere requiring abstract rules extends far back into the past, it is only with the emergence of the modern nation-state that the importance of nonpersonal law as a means of order becomes emphasized and with it the association of certain traits with the "masculine."

The separation between a domestic sphere characterized by particularity and emotion and a public sphere characterized by abstract, impersonal rules may also be related to economic changes occurring in the West in the early modern period. Alfred Sohn-Rethel (1978) has argued that it is in those early societies where external trading first began that there emerges that kind of abstract thinking we call mathematical. His claim is that this kind of thinking arises only when it becomes necessary to develop formal modes of classifying objects for purposes of exchange. His point might be enlarged upon to claim that, while trade is carried out in many societies prior to the early modern period, it is only in the West at this time that internal trade begins to become the principle upon which economic activity as a whole is structured. Indeed, the emerging dominance of exchange as a motive for production is what we take as defining a "market economy." [1] Thus, insofar as the activity of exchange becomes a principal mode of activity in early modern Western society then, in light of Sohn-Rethel's argument, what would also follow is the centrality of that kind of abstract thinking we associate with mathematics.

We might elaborate the distinctiveness of that kind of cognitive abstraction. typified by mathematics with the help of a distinction made by Susan Buck-Morss. She distinguishes between the activity of abstraction per se, which she claims is basic to all human language competence, and what she calls abstract formalism. The latter, she states, is typified by a separation of form from content.[2] In other words, following her point, we might say that what distinguishes abstraction from abstract formalism is that in the latter what is abstracted is formal rather than concrete. This elaboration makes sense of a point she notes about Piaget and his tests: that while Western children perform well on such tests, others such as the Kpelle of Liberia do not, tending to grasp things by their "function" (Buck-Morss 1974, 42). In other words, the point here is not that the Kpelle do not abstract but that the criteria upon which they do are different from those of children in the West. This characterization of abstract formalism by its separation of form from content has direct relevance for one of Kohlberg's responses to Gilligan. Kohlberg argued that, whereas Gilligan's points might have relevance in assessing the differing contents of people's moral judgments, his model is concerned with the more formal structures of moral reasoning. This reply, however, still leaves unanswered the question of whether the separation of form from content is itself a function of a certain culturally rooted perspective rather than endemic to moral reasoning per se.

This idea that the separation of form from content might have something to do with a specifically modern Western mode of thinking allied to a separation of domestic and nondomestic spheres of activity can also be helpfully elaborated through the work of Roberto Unger. Unger situates the form/content distinction within a broader epistemological separation which he argues is basic to liberal thought. According to Unger, a liberal worldview structures our experience around the following dichotomy. On the one hand stands the order of reason, thought, form, rules, and means. On the other exists the order of desire, feeling, content, substance, and ends. Similarly, the order of ideas stands opposed to the order of events as objectivity is opposed to subjectivity. Unger expresses this basic polarization in the following:

> The estranged and the resigned share a common view of the relation of thought to life. They both believe that there is a public realm of factual and technical discourse and an intimate world of feeling. Within the logic of private emotion all religion, art, and personal love is arrested, and from it all rational thought is banished. The narrow conception of reason as a faculty addressed to the public rather than to the private life, to means rather than to ends, to facts rather than to values, to form rather than to substance, is necessarily accompanied by the cult of an inward reli-

giosity, aesthetic, and morality that thought cannot touch, nor language describe. (Unger 1975, 27)

This mapping of reason, form, means, etc., with a public sphere, and desire, content, ends, etc. with a private has the important manifestation that it is only the sphere of the former which is seen to unite us, while the sphere of the latter is believed to constitute our particularity. Thus, Unger notes that, following from this view, it is only when we are reasoning that we are seen to "belong to a public world because knowledge, to the extent it is true, does not vary among persons. When desiring, however, men are private beings because they can never offer others more than a partial justification for their goals in the public language of thought" (Unger 1975, 45). What is eliminated from such a perspective is the possibility of objective value and subjective reason.

Reason and Desire

Unger's framework provides us with a helpful means for explicating modern Western moral theory. The two major traditions in that theory are the deontological, exemplified in the theory of Kant, and the teleological or naturalistic, represented in utilitarianism. Unger describes these respectively as a "morality of reason" and a "morality of desire." He argues that both express the above polarization. Whereas a utilitarian position accepts the validity of concrete desires being "factored" into moral judgments, it attempts to overcome the privacy and therefore incomparability of such desires through the use of an arithmetical calculus. The problem, however, is in trying to make public and comparable that which has already been constituted as private and incomparable. Given such a premise, arithmetical tools must prove worthless, for, as has often been pointed out, how can one measure the intensity of a desire? The deontological tradition similarly breaks down on its acceptance of the separation of the private and the public. Unlike a morality of desire, which accepts the validity of incorporating concrete desires into moral judgment, a morality of reason denies the validity of making reference to desires. It is reason alone, apart from motivation by any particular desire, which legislates morality. The traditional problem here is that such a position must move between vacuity and inconsistency. To the extent that moral judgment can be created apart from reference to particular desires, it is too empty to provide concrete direction in moral decision-making. To the extent, however, that it incorporates any substance into that which it legislates, it becomes inconsistent as a theoretical position. Kohlberg's position, as in this latter tradition, evidences a weakness along similar lines. To the extent that each of his stages does constitute a recognizably distinct orientation, it is in danger of being the reflection of a particular worldview; to avoid giving content to the stages is also, however, to take away the means of empirically testing the concrete instantiation of the stages or to make such testing interpretive. This problem is also revealed in the following ambiguity: One means by which Kohlberg and his associates justify the progressive nature of the stages is by arguing that structural components of earlier stages become content components of later stages (Puka 1982, 475, n. 13). This justification, however, seems to raise certain problems for the form-content distinction itself.

Both the deontological and naturalistic positions cannot only be situated within the modern separation of private and public, they can also be explicated by reference to specific changes occurring in the relation of private and public over the past several centuries. In the eighteenth century, when Kant was writing, the relation of the state to the private sphere of family and desire was relatively remote; the state set only the formal preconditions within which the family could operate. By the latter part of the nineteenth century, the state had begun to take on a more active role in regulating both the family and the economy. Moreover, economic activities had themselves become more "public," moving out of the interior of the household and into interpersonal, "public" space. Many of the needs of the family were now fulfilled through the consumption of factory-produced objects rather than as a consequence of private, household activity. Thus, private desire became more the concern of impersonal regulation and production, making understandable the emergence of a moral theory such as utilitarianism, which attempted to organize and calculate private desire.

From the perspective of this type of analysis, Kohlberg's theory would therefore be viewed as in accord with much of modern Western moral theory, wherein movement away from particularity toward abstraction has come to represent a cognitive and attitudinal good. That evaluative principle, while making possible Kohlberg's measurement of people from all cultures, would, according to this position, itself represent a principle most in accord with the values of one.

This type of historical analysis, besides situating Kohlberg's theory, provides us with certain means for responding to arguments Kohlberg puts forth in its defense. One argument, earlier put aside, was Kohlberg's claim on the predictive capacity of his model. This capacity might be explained by the nature of the separation of private and public in modern Western society and its growing dominance. The family is the source of socialization in all contemporary societies. However, with the growth of such a separation, for some children the norms and values of the family become superseded by the norms and values of the public sphere. Modern schooling is an important agent in this transformation.[3] Because this is so, while one may find children moving from the moral particularity characteristic of intimate relations to the moral abstraction characteristic of impersonal, public relations, one will rarely (if at all) find movement in the opposite direction. Similarly, for various historical reasons, a form of social organization characterized by a separation of the private and the public has been and continues to be a dominant mode, replacing those forms of social organization not characterized by such a separation. Thus, here again one will find cultures developing a public sphere but not find cultures moving toward the elimination of such a sphere. For these kinds of historical reasons, it is not surprising that the direction exemplified by Kohlberg's model will be found in the movement of many people today.[4]

One of the problems involved in arbitrating between Kohlberg's theory and my historical critique is that to some extent Kohlberg allows history into his theory. Thus, as earlier noted, Kohlberg employs a semi-environmentalist position and argues that access to certain types of social environments is conducive to development along his stages. Thus if Western, middle-class, white children tend to progress faster through his stages and reach higher stages in greater numbers than children of other countries or other groups in Western countries, this would follow, in harmony with his theory, as a result of their exposure to those social environments which encourage such movement.

The problem, however, is that while Kohlberg does appear to allow for such an historical component in his theory, he also appears to want to deny the relevance of history for his theory. This later tendency is reflected in his characterization of his stages as universal, in apparent correlation with the universality of certain constant differentials in social life. This confusion is illustrated in the following passage:

> My general theory relates differential social experiences in terms of opportunities for social role taking to a differential rate of moral development. Of particular importance for development to later stages of moral reasoning (stages 4 and 5) are opportunities for power, responsibility and participation in the secondary institution of society (i.e. institutions of government, law and economy, in contrast to the primary institutions of society such as the family, the adolescent peer group, and other small face-to-face groups). Also of importance to rate of development is higher education, as the Colby et al. longitudinal study shows. (Kohlberg 1982, 518)

In the above quotation Kohlberg seems to imply a universal social distinction between what he describes as "primary" and "secondary" institutions. Noteworthy, however, is that the institutions he employs to illustrate this distinction, such as the family, the adolescent peer group, and institutions of government, law, and economy, are modern, at least as differentiated spheres of relationships. While all societies possess some type of family, not all societies differentiate family activities from economic or legal activities in the way implied in the above quotation. Kohlberg therefore cannot base a universality of his model on any such universality in social organization. The consequence, however, of this argument is that, if Kohlberg wishes to combine his model with an environmentalist position, he will also have to impute the same historical contingency to his model that attends to those forms of social organization he argues are conducive to development within it.

Another means of stating the above criticism would be to say that Kohlberg's description of moral change is, or may be, an accurate description of the direction moral change has tended to take in modern Western society. One reason, however, why Kohlberg would be against such a characterization of his model is that he would wish to view the principle of increased abstraction, which marks movement along the stages, not as *a* good, according to the value system of a particular society, but as *the* good. It is this wish which inclines his theory to commit the "naturalistic fallacy," that is, of arguing from the fact that people tend to move in a particular direction in moral reasoning to the conclusion that such movement is desirable. Kohlberg recognizes that he needs to ground the claim philosophically that the higher stages are "higher" or more adequate. However, he mitigates this admission by arguing that his model is compatible with a variety of moral theories. Noteworthy, however, is the fact that the diverse moral theories Kohlberg points to as compatible with his model, including those in both the utilitarian and deontological traditions, are all moral theories of modern, industrial society (Kohlberg 1982, 524).

As a final remark on problems with Kohlberg's model, it is important to note a methodological weakness which it shares with other cross-cultural models: the problem of equivocation. A means by which many theorists project the values of their own culture onto others is to use key words in an ambiguous manner. For example, Kohlberg's and Piaget's emphasis on "abstraction" ought to be precisely interpreted as a stress on "abstract formalism," for, as earlier noted, while it might be said that the process of abstraction is endemic to human existence, that which their studies test for need not be. A similar kind of equivocation can be found in Kohlberg's use of the term "justice" in the following passage:

> Justice, the primary regard for the value and equality of all human beings and for reciprocity in human relations, is a basic and universal standard. As social psychologists, the author and his colleagues have gathered considerable evidence to indicate that the

> concepts of justice inhere in human experience and are not the
> product of a particular cultural world view. (Kohlberg 1980, 57)

Certainly, if such phrases as "primary regard for the value and equality of
all human beings" and "reciprocity in human relations" are interpreted
broadly, we might find them applicable to all human societies. The danger,
however, is that such phrases also have a meaning which is more specific to
our society, where "justice" and "reciprocity in human relations" primarily
refer to certain types of interactions of strangers in an impersonal public
sphere. To trade on ambiguities between such specific and broad interpretations is to court projecting our own meanings onto societies where they do
not hold.

Women's Development

While from the type of historical perspective earlier described, Kohlberg's
theory suffers from a variety of weaknesses, the same, however, can be said
of Gilligan's critique. Gilligan, unlike Kohlberg, is much more cautious
about generating a cross-cultural position. Thus, she specifically states that
"No claims are made about the origins of the differences described or their
distribution in a wider population, across cultures, or through time" (Gilligan 1982a, 2). However, while making such disclaimers, Gilligan also
speaks of a "woman's voice" and "women's development." The use of such
expressions without supplementation by an historical account, which would
make clear of which women under what circumstances her descriptions
might be generally true, leads to a certain implicit false generalization. What
tends to get ignored are such factors as class, race, and again sheer changes
in history as variables in her analysis. This problem is accentuated by her
following Kohlberg in generating a stage theory which makes "higher" or
normative certain types of responses.

To show how these problems are evidenced, it is helpful to describe briefly
the model of female development she offers in response to Kohlberg's:

> In this sequence, an initial focus on caring for the self in order to
> ensure survival is followed by a transactional phase in which the
> judgment is criticized as selfish. The criticism signals a new under-
> standing of the connection between self and others which is artic-
> ulated by the concept of responsibility. The elaboration of this con-
> cept of responsibility and its fusion with a maternal morality that
> seeks to ensure care for the dependent and unequal characterizes
> the second perspective. At this point, the good is equated with car-
> ing for others. However, when only others are legitimized as the
> recipients of the woman's care, the exclusion of herself gives rise to

problems in relationships, creating a disequilibrium that initiates the second transition. . . . The third perspective focuses on the dynamics of relationships and dissipates the tension between selfishness and responsibility through a new understanding of the interconnection between other and self. (Gilligan 1982a, 74)

In short, women, according to Gilligan, move from initial selfishness to a position which gives undue consideration to the needs of others and finally to a position which integrates the needs of both self and other.

As with Kohlberg's model, one can offer an historical account to explain why the model Gilligan offers might describe the stages many contemporary women traverse in their moral development. An initial period of selfishness understandably attends the moral cognition of many children and adults in highly individualistic modern Western society. Within such a society, coextensive with the development of the type of private/public separation earlier described, female children have also been encouraged to abandon such selfishness in conjunction with their socialization in becoming "feminine." This has been particularly true for white, middle-class girls, for whom the ideal of femininity has always been more possible to attain and thus has been more directly influential in shaping behavior than it has been for many black, poor, and non-Western women. Even, however, for white middleclass females, the ideal of femininity has become increasingly problematic since the middle of the nineteenth century as many have moved into the public sphere, acting increasingly as political and economic beings. Particularly over the last thirty years, many such women have had to overcome the conflicts endemic to the conjunction of traditional "feminine" socialization with new expectations for functioning as autonomous individuals. Understandably, therefore, many have had to learn how to integrate a nurturant and an individualistic stance.

This is a very rough historical analysis. If this essay were to take a different direction it could be made more polished. It is sufficient, however, to illustrate how such an account could enable Gilligan to deal with certain questions otherwise left unanswered by her arguments. As earlier noted, Gilligan had claimed against Kohlberg that one evidence of his model's gender bias was the fact that females tended to score lower than males on his tests. One way Kohlberg responded to this objection was to point to studies which showed that at least in some cases, particularly those where such factors as education and opportunities for role-taking were controlled, women performed equivalently with men (Kohlberg 1982, 518). This finding would of course follow from the above historical analysis which argued that it was women's traditional exclusion from the public sphere, and not their gender per se, which made them "outsiders" to Kohlberg's model. However, given that such a model reflects a particular set of values reflective of certain social arrangements, Gilligan could still describe it as biased, independent of the fact that some women now perform equivalently with men.

There does appear, however, a tension between the above type of historical analysis and the stage model Gilligan suggests as an alternative to Kohlberg's. From the perspective of the historical analysis, the various types of responses she describes might be characterized as adaptations to different historical circumstances rather than as "stages" in moral development. Thus, what Gilligan describes as the lowest level of female moral response could be seen as an adequate response of those whose lives necessitate that considerations of self—or, as Gilligan describes it, considerations of "survival"—be given first priority. Women who respond at the second level could be seen as embodying what we think of as traditional sex-role socialization, again an adequate response in certain circumstances. Finally, women whose responses are at Gilligan's highest level could be viewed as leading the kinds of lives increasingly typical of Western professional women. The point, however, similar to points made against Kohlberg, is that to assume that these responses are progressively more moral is to make normative the circumstances and responses of a particular social group. Thus, it could be said that Gilligan's stage model of moral development is as biased against non-Western, nonwhite, and non-middle-class women as was Kohlberg's, only now minus the sexism.

Gilligan argues that we need to recognize two different modes of social experience in contrast to the unitary mode which has traditionally been attended to. Thus, she states:

> The failure to see the different reality of women's lives and to hear the differences in their voices stems in part from the assumption that there is a single mode of social experience and interpretation. By positing instead two different modes, we arrive at a more complex rendition of human experience. (Gilligan 1982a, 173–74)

It may be asked, however, why we need to limit our understanding to the recognition of only two modes. Are two possibilities that much more preferable to Kohlberg's one? One of the important insights that has emerged in feminist politics of the last twenty-year period is that there is no singular entity "woman." The recognition of this point does not entail an acceptance of the liberal/individualistic position that general claims are not permissible within public discourse. We can recognize that social theory requires a certain amount of abstraction, and thus a certain degree of forgetfulness of the complexity of all of our lives. However, at this point in the political/cultural history of North America, any abstractions which cut the human voice into two, while certainly representing a vast improvement over those abstractions which construed it as one, seem much too limited.

Notes

This essay is a slightly modified version of "Women, Morality, and History" which originally appeared in *Social Research* 50, no. 3 (Autumn 1983).

1. For an elaboration of the defining conditions of a market economy, see Polanyi 1957.
2. She also points to Marx as noting the connection between abstract formalism and industrial capitalism and Lukács as arguing the dominance of this form of cognition in contemporary capitalist society. While Buck-Morss' paper focuses primarily on Piaget and only secondarily on Kohlberg, many of her arguments parallel those I make in this paper; Buck-Morss 1975, 38.
3. For more on this point, see Nicholson 1980.
4. This argument that it would be impossible to find people today unaffected by the separation of private and public parallels an argument Eleanor Leacock (1977) makes. She argues for the impossibility of finding a contemporary society which does not evidence gender oppression because Western imperialism brought gender distinctions with it in its contact with nonindustrial cultures.

7

Some Cautionary Words for Historians

Linda K. Kerber

In a Different Voice is a study of psychological theory written by psychologist Carol Gilligan. It makes only a single, brief reference to women's history. Nevertheless, the book has been widely read and often acclaimed by historians, some of whom now seem to be attempting to integrate its findings and suggestions into their own scholarship. Since most of this work is at the prepublication stage, appearing at present in working papers and discussed in professional conversations, the following remarks are intended to encourage second thoughts and a more careful reading of Gilligan's work.

Like feminist historians, Gilligan criticizes the long-established pattern in academic research of establishing norms based on men's experience alone. Building on the theories of Nancy Chodorow and other ego psychologists, Gilligan stresses the necessarily different early experiences of girls, who understand at a very young age that they are like their mothers, and boys, whose first psychic task is to learn that they are not and can never grow up to be like their mothers. The socializing effects of this contrast create gender differences: for boys, "a self defined through separation": for girls "a self delineated through connection" (Gilligan 1982a, 35). The tasks of adolescents are therefore markedly different as well. Adolescent boys need to learn to manage relationships despite their basic and central sense of separation and individuality while girls must struggle to establish a separate identity while maintaining relationships. Ultimately, Gilligan argues, men and women claim different moral imperatives: women feel "a responsibility to discern and alleviate the 'real and recognizable trouble' of this world" while men's moral imperative "appears rather as an injunction to respect the rights of others" (100).

Reprinted by permission from *Signs: Journal of Women in Culture and Society* 11: 304–10. Copyright © 1986 by The University of Chicago Press.

Although Gilligan calls for studies of other ethical dilemmas (126) and reminds her readers that we should all seek an ethics both of justice and of care (62–63), the primary research on which the book rests is a study of women—and only women—confronting a decision about abortion. But it cannot be surprising that themes of responsibility and care emerge in women's articulation of their concerns about abortion. Gilligan alleges that the tendency to see "moral dilemmas in terms of conflicting responsibilities" (105) is a distinct characteristic of women's decision-making, but conflicting responsibilities—to oneself, to the fetus, to its father, to one's own parents and family—are necessarily embedded in a decision on abortion. The theme of care is equally present; if a pregnancy is chosen, the child's need for care will transform the mother's life. The conclusions that Gilligan reports are implicit in the central question of the project itself.

Meanwhile, we are given no accompanying study of men's responses to a similar challenge. Do not men also in some circumstances find themselves similarly stretched on the rack between selfishness and responsibility? Were we to listen to men during their process of decision on, say, draft resistance, might we not also hear similarly anguished contemplation of their responsibility to their families, to the needs of those who depend on them for care?

Despite Gilligan's occasional explicit warnings that her work is preliminary and the implicit warning that broad generalization is dangerous from experimental work done on such a small scale—one quite interesting study of self-concept includes only five women and nine men (158ff.)—the argument that women define themselves through relationships with others, through a web of relationships of intimacy and care rather than through a hierarchy based on separation and self-fulfillment, runs as a leitmotif through the book, giving it much of its structure and much of its attractiveness.

In a Different Voice is part of a major feminist redefinition of social vocabulary. What was once dismissed as gossip can now be appreciated as the maintenance of oral tradition; what was once devalued as mere housewifery can be understood as social reproduction and a major contribution to the gross national product. Gilligan is invigorating in her insistence that behavior once denigrated as waffling, indecisive, and demeaningly "effeminate" ought rather to be valued as complex, constructive, and humane. Yet this historian, at least, is haunted by the sense that we have heard this argument before, vested in different language. Some variants of it are as old as Western civilization itself; central to the traditions of our culture has been the ascription of reason to men and feeling to women. This bifurcated view of reality can easily be traced at least to classical Greece, where men were understood to realize themselves best in the public sector, the polis, and women in domesticity. Ancient tradition has long been reinforced by explicit socialization that arrogated public power to men and relegated women to domestic concerns, a socialization sometimes defended by argument from expediency, sometimes by argument from biology. Although now Gilligan appears to be adding argument from psychology, her study infers at times that gendered behavior is biologically determined and at others that it, too, is learned, albeit at an earlier stage of socialization than previous analysts had assumed.

A more recent version of this dualism, prevalent in the nineteenth and early twentieth centuries, is the doctrine of "separate spheres." Nearly twenty years ago, Barbara Welter (1966) pointed to a pervasive descriptive language by which women were measured, "the cult of true womanhood." This language located woman's "proper sphere" in the home and associated with it the cardinal virtues of domesticity, piety, purity and submissiveness. Women were understood to realize themselves through care for their families and through nurturance of relationships within them. Such rigid role definition may also have been a mode by which middle-class women maintained their upwardly mobile state. "It is no accident," Gerda Lerner wrote in 1969, "that the slogan 'woman's place is in the home' took on a certain aggressiveness and shrillness precisely at the time when increasing numbers of poorer women *left* their homes to become factory workers."

Ten years ago, Carroll Smith-Rosenberg (1975) gave a new understanding to this separation of spheres when she argued that it had made possible psychologically sustaining relationships among women and had been congruent with strong bonds of female friendship, affection, and love. As interpreted by Smith-Rosenberg, and many historians who wrote after her, the separation of spheres could offer advantages as well as the disadvantages emphasized by Welter. It could sustain a distinctive women's culture which embraced creativity in the domestic arts, distinctive forms of labor, and particular patterns of nurturing relationships. For the last decade a rich literature and a lively debate among historians have explored the nuances of this nineteenth-century ideology: Was it constraining to women? Should it be understood as a way in which a culture coped defensively with social change and the transformation of the Industrial Revolution? Ought the "separate female sphere" be understood as a source of strength for women, a psychic room of their own?

Although she makes no mention of it, Gilligan actually enters the dialogue about the separation of spheres. Her formulations suggest that what was once called a separate sphere of nurture and self-sacrifice was in fact a personality called into existence by women's distinctive psychological development rather than a result of explicit socialization. Her conclusion that women "define their identity through relationships of intimacy and care" (Gilligan, 1982, 164) is congruent with claims made in the nineteenth century in defense of a separate sphere of women.

In her single use of historical argument, Gilligan suggests that when Mary Wollstonecraft and Elizabeth Cady Stanton called for self-development and self-respect they were in effect saying that the search for identity through relationships of intimacy and care had gone far enough; that is, they were directly attacking the doctrine of separate spheres on the grounds of the psychological damage it had done. In effect, critics of Wollstonecraft and Stanton were right in complaining that both claimed for women a male psychological style. But Gilligan does not explore the psychological limitations of the female "voice" that she identifies, and the effect of her argument is to encourage the conclusion that women really are more nurturant than men, less likely to dominate, and more likely to negotiate than are men—just as Gilligan's women and girls do when considering the Heinz dilemma, the classic case in which a man named Heinz must decide whether or not to steal a drug needed by his dying wife. Perhaps there was—and is—something in the separation of spheres that is more than mere socialization. Perhaps when Victorians claimed that women were intrinsically more peaceable than men, they knew something that Gilligan has just rediscovered. Perhaps.

But the reification of separate spheres, now freshly buttressed by Gilligan's study of psychological development, poses major dangers of oversimplification. As Ellen DuBois (1980, 31) warned five years ago, single-minded focus on women's own culture brings with it the risk of ignoring "the larger social and historical developments of which it was a part" and does not "address the limitations of the values of women's culture," the ways that they restrained and confined women. A rigid dualism makes no room for analysis of the sort offered by Estelle Freedman in her important essay, "Separatism as Strategy," in which she contends that distinctive female institutions like schools, clubs, and settlement houses can be thought of as a public version of the female separate sphere that has "helped mobilize women and [been used by them to gain] political leverage in the larger society." Freedman argues that women have been most effective politically when they have reserved for themselves a territory free of contamination by male aggressiveness from which they might operate as critics of culture. When she calls for continued support of separate female institutions, Freedman explains, she does so "not because the values, culture, and politics of the two sexes are biologically, irreversibly, distinct, but rather because the historical and contemporary experiences that have created a unique female culture remain both salient for and compatible with the goal of sexual equality" (Freedman 1979, 513, 523, 525).

What, then, are the risks of relying on women's allegedly "different voice"? One danger, I think, is a familiar variety of feminist self-righteousness. Historically the rhetoric of feminism has spoken with two voices: one that claimed for women the natural rights of all human beings, and one that claimed that women were different from—and, usually better than—men. One major wing of suffragist feminism, for example, relied heavily on a rhetoric which grew out of the separation of spheres and maintained that women were more law-abiding, more peace-loving, and more charitable than men. Give women the vote, the argument went, and the streets would be clean, child labor would be eliminated, war would be at an end. One antisuffragist, Annie Nathan Meyer (1908; 1938) of New York, thinking of spread-eagle politics, called this wishful thinking "spreadhenism." Suffragists were right in expecting that support for peace movements and progressive legislation would come from newly enfranchised women, but they were wrong to predict that most women would support a political agenda drawn up from the concerns central to women's sphere. Newly enfranchised women voted as the interests of their race and class dictated, just as our own contemporaries have recently done. It is no surprise that the more extensive promises to usher in a new world made by suffragists could not be fulfilled.[1]

I agree with Gilligan that our culture has long undervalued nurturance and that when we measure ethical development by norms more attainable by boys than by girls our definition of norms is probably biased. But by emphasizing the biological basis of distinctive behavior (departing here from Chodorow, who emphasizes learning), Gilligan permits her readers to conclude that women's alleged affinity for "relationships of care" is both biologically natural and a good thing.

The other risk is one of romantic oversimplification. If women can be counted on to care for others, how are we to deal with self-interest, selfishness and meanness of spirit which women surely display as much as do men? If we let the cycle of historical revisionism come full circle, are we not back once again in the world of the angel in the house? And if we permit that, how are we to deal with the occasions when women's supposed ethic of relationship and care does not seem to have been an adequate moral imperative for all men or all women? Even Elizabeth Cady Stanton was not above making a racist appeal to white men that they choose white women for enfranchisement before black men. A recent book of essays on women in Weimar and Nazi Germany gives evidence of the attraction of housewives' organizations to fascism, the desertion of Jewish members by the German feminist movement, and the support for Nazi eugenics by the organization of German Women Doctors which quickly moved to expel its own Jewish members (Bridenthal et al. 1984).

It seems well established that little boys face a psychic task of separation that little girls do not. But let us not be in haste to conclude that most or all of what have been called the characteristics of separate spheres emerge naturally from women's own distinctive psychology, biologically rooted in patterns of maturation. Much, perhaps most, of it may well be rooted in the distinctive socialization of young girls in a culture which has always rested on the sexual division of labor, which has long ascribed some social tasks to men and others to women, and which has served as a mechanism by which a patriarchal society excludes one segment of the population from certain roles and therefore makes easier the task of producing hegemonic consensus. Gilligan describes how women make lemonade out of the lemons they have inherited. She does not tell how to transform the lemons into chocolate.

Note

1. See Kraditor, 1965, 49–50. For the ease with which suffragism's emphasis on women's special virtue could cooperate with white supremacy arguments, see Kraditor 1965, 140–70.

8

The Culture of Gender:
Women and Men of Color

Carol B. Stack

Gilligan's assertion that there is a female model for moral development, and that this model appeals to responsibilities rather than to rights, echoes similar developments in feminist anthropological thinking of the 1970s. Anthropological research published in that decade uncovered a set of oppositions between maleness and femaleness primarily derived from studies of non-class-based societies. For example, Sherry Ortner and Harriet Whitehead (1981), in their introduction to *Sexual Meanings,* emphasize that women in the societies described by the book's contributors tend to be more involved with private and particularistic concerns, with relationships, and with welfare of their own families than they are with the more general social good. Men, on the other hand, are more universalistic and have a concern for the welfare of the whole. Their suggestion—in full agreement with the earlier assumptions of Michelle Rosaldo and Louise Lamphere (1974) on the universal distinction between the public domain and the domestic domain—is that these notions are nearly universal. Until the last few years, these gender-based principles of opposition and dualism were recognized as the premises underlying feminist theory's heritage from anthropology.

Gilligan, in keeping with other feminist theorists studying the construction of gender, discovered enduring self-images that guide women through their lives—images set in contrast to the thoughts and actions of men. In Gilligan's model, women are more inclined to link morality to responsibility and relationships and to their ability to maintain ongoing social ties than are men. They achieve power and prestige through caring for others, and, Gilligan argues, their embeddedness in relationships should not be considered a developmental liability. Male development is linked to morality, fairness, rights, and rules, and to the social good; men forge their identities in relation to the external world and strive for personal autonomy.

Within the academic fields of psychology, sociology, anthropology, and history and in a variety of theoretical feminist models, several assumptions seemingly shared by Gilligan as well as influenced by her theory constitute the current dogma: (1) Men and women differ significantly in their construction of themselves in relationship to others. (2) Women and men experience issues of dependency differently. (3) Women and men experience class differently. (4) Women's work is perceived differently from men's work. (5) Boys and girls experience relationships differently. (6) There is a male and a female model for moral development. Feminist thinking across the disciplines links the construction of gender to these differences or oppositions.[1]

Preliminary analysis of data from my ongoing research with black return migrants to the rural South reveals inconsistencies between this accepted feminist theory and findings derived from interviews. Returnees' discussions of the dilemmas of adulthood, the meaning of social ties, and the shared visions of maturity, as well as the principles that they set forth as they consider these topics, confirm Gilligan's own observation that the cross-cultural construction of gender remains unexplored.

Data from my study of return migration confirm my deeply held conviction from earlier studies that the caste and economic system within rural southern communities creates a setting in which black women and men have a very similar experience of class, that is, a similar relationship to production, employment, and material and economic rewards (Stack 1974; Stack & Hall 1982). Intriguing hypotheses arise from this insight. The data suggest that under conditions of economic deprivation there is a convergence between women and men in their construction of themselves in relationship to others, and that these conditions produce a convergence also in women's and men's vocabulary of rights, morality, and the social good. I view black women's and men's contextualization of morality and the meaning of social ties as a cultural alternative to Gilligan's model of moral development, with a different configuration of gender differences and similarities.

Gender consciousness emerges from a negotiation between material conditions and cultural ideologies, from a negotiation between what is out there (historical conditions, class- and race-specific experiences, age and generations, the ecology of life course) and what we see with (the assumptions and interpretations that we have in our minds, our shared models of the world, our visions and dilemmas of adulthood). While it is extremely difficult to create a theory that makes it possible to negotiate between these two models, my aim is to demonstrate the importance of bringing race, class, consciousness, and generation to theory-building and the construction of gender (Dill 1983).

My previous study, *All Our Kin,* examined the cultural strategies of black women within the network of family relationships in urban communities, never making explicit questions concerning male and female adult development. My current research focuses on the return migration of black women, men, and children from the urban Northeast to the rural South, exploring the meaning of social ties and the dilemmas of adulthood within the context of their migration experience. Between 1975 and 1980, the black population in the South grew by two million, the largest decennial increase for blacks in any census region in history (Joint Center 1982). Changing migration patterns reflect a new social movement that forecasts a dramatic spatial reorganization of population, and the restructuring of the social, cultural, and material conditions of migrants' lives, including the set of arrangements for organizing the gender system within family networks.

In the detailed life histories of return migrants, both women and men describe with force and conviction the strength of their kinship ties to their rural southern families and the nature of these ties that bind. For many of the black men and women I interviewed, the relation to a home place has been and is the lodestar that provides place and context, meaning, continuity, and identity. As urban migrants, they with their families were satellites to home places, magnetized to the core. Their rural kin ties somberly represent spirit and purpose, fate, circumstance, and obligation. A collective social conscience among these migrants manifests itself in several cultural strategies: concern for reciprocity, commitment to kin and community, and belief in the morality of responsibility.

The data I have analyzed from this return migration study reveal an African-American model of moral development. Men and women alike redefine and recontextualize moral dilemmas and the principles they use to think about them. These women's and men's voices, in unison with one another, appear to be very different from those on which Gilligan and Kohlberg based their models of relatedness and moral reasoning. However, the data used to generate this preliminary critique of gender-related theories of moral development were collected for a different purpose and were based on a different methodology from that used by moral-development theorists. The life histories and the discussions of people's thoughts about migration choices, however, provide a starting point for placing Gilligan's theory in the context of culture and class. In future interviews with male and female return migrants, I will be using some of Gilligan's methods, slightly modified, in order to generate more precisely comparable data.

Gilligan's theory of women's moral development has taken root in native soil. It is a powerful and persuasive theory that derives a female model of moral development from the moral reasoning of primarily white, middle-class women in the United States. The model fits the data, and it fits the conceptualizations of many feminist researchers. However, as black and third-world feminist researchers have emphasized, gender is a construct shaped by the experience of race, class, culture, caste, and consciousness.[2] Future research must contribute another dimension to the construction of feminist theory: it should provide a critical framework for analyzing gender consciousness and a cautionary reminder to those theorists who think that gender construction is the same in all societies.

Notes

1. Relevant sources for these assumptions, in addition to Gilligan, include Petchesky 1983; di Leonardo 1984; Quinn 1982; and J. B. Miller 1976.
2. See Dill 1983; Hooks 1981; Hull, Scott & Smith 1982.

9

Women's Rationality and Men's Virtues: A Critique of Gender Dualism in Gilligan's Theory of Moral Development

John M. Broughton

I have a great mother complex. I want to help people and be kind to them. I was told to work on that stuff—be more aggressive and more full. And it all depends on how you look at it. I am sort of happy with the way that I am. I am fairly good looking. And I am intelligent. And I think I am a pretty nice person. . . . I really enjoy being with other people and getting close to people. That is possibly the most meaningful thing for myself right now, just being close to people. I guess I really like to communicate with people and get feedback from people on a deep level. . . . (What makes you feel committed?) The fact that I know them really well and are getting close to them and know what some of their needs are, and some of their wishes and some of their fears, as they do for me. I feel committed when I get close to somebody. (What obligations do you feel towards these people?) To be honest with them, not to do anything which would hurt them.

—Gilligan's Subject #15

Moral versus Cognitive Sex Differences

It may not be purely accidental that discussions of psychological differences between men and women customarily have the same point of departure in the domain of the specifically *moral* aspects of the psyche. In these discussions, it is often Freud's (1925/1961, 1931/1961) notorious observations concerning the relative degrees of morality in men and women that are used to motivate closer examination of the issues.

It may be reasonable to argue that it is the peculiarly contentious nature of Freud's observations that makes his distinction between the sexes so salient. However, it seems possible that it is his particular use of *moral* attributes as features distinctive of sex, and his assumption, following Weininger (Millett 1970), that they could be transmitted only by *fathers*, that gives his

---

Reprinted by permission from *Social Research* 50, no. 3: 597–642. Copyright © 1983 by the journal.

remarks their edge. Generally speaking, where the psychological differences between men and women have been explained in terms of contrasting cognitive attributes (e.g., Strong 1943; MacKinnon 1962; Witkin et al. 1962; Maccoby 1966), there has been less outcry and fewer accusations of sexism. To some extent, any explicit statement of sex differences is controversial and, especially in recent years, is likely to have come under intense critical scrutiny. However, the suggestion that men and women are cognitively different typically seems to be experienced as less disturbing or threatening than the intimation that they are morally different.

This situation may have something to do with the fact that within our positivistic culture, claims about cognitive differences are more, easily seen as free from value-judgments. This would appear to be so for three reasons. First, cognition itself is usually seen as being oriented to fact rather than value. Second, assessments of individuals' different moralities are more easily perceived as attempts to establish differences in these individuals' moral *worth*. Third, the assessment of cognitive differences seems to be more amenable to established scientific procedures of objective measurement. Thus, the fact that Freud's observations about sex differences were not based on traditional scientific methods and were nonmetric in character is often used to discredit them.

However, this common-sense contrast between "scientific," cognitive, value-free assessments and "speculative," moral, value-laden interpretations has been obscured by Lawrence Kohlberg. Kohlberg has used rigorous scientific methods of measurement (see Colby et al. 1983) to establish a theory of moral development parallel to Piaget's cognitive stage theory. Furthermore, he has claimed that research reveals a pattern of sex differences in moral judgments, with the majority of adult women reasoning at "conformist" stage 3 while adult men typically reason at "legalistic" stage 4 (Kohlberg & Kramer 1969).

Kohlberg's position could not be dismissed as biologistic, as Freud's had been, since Kohlberg had explicitly contrasted his "interactionist" assumptions about development with Freud's "maturationist" ones. The sex differences were not innate or learned but "developed." Genetics was supplanted by genesis, but without abandoning the concept of human nature (Blasi 1976), thus advancing the progressivist trend away from biological versions of medieval substances and essences. This combination of qualities in Kohlberg's theory has elevated moral psychology to the level of a postreligious system which appears to prove once and for all on scientific and humanistic grounds Eve's lesser moral worth than Adam's. The hierarchical ordering of stages implicit in the developmental nature of the theory seems to make it quite clear that men are morally superior to women, not just different from them. There is a certain irony to this since, in an earlier work, Kohlberg replaced Freud's asymmetrical treatment of boys' and girls' awareness of their sex with a more egalitarian developmental concept of symmetrical gender identities (Kohlberg 1966). This cognitive alternative to Freud became one of the mainstays of Chodorow's more recent and influential rejection of the traditional psychoanalytic theory of gender (Chodorow 1978).

"Fish Gotta Swim, Bird Gotta Fly": Gilligan's Sex-specific Psychology

The finding of male superiority on Piagetian measures of "formal operations" (Neimark 1975; Modgil & Modgil 1976) has received hardly any attention at all. But the findings on Kohlberg's measure of "moral maturity" have stirred up considerable debate. Perhaps the most dramatic outcome of this controversy is the work of Carol Gilligan (1977, 1979, 1982a; Dulit 1983). Much as various psychoanalytic theorists, most of them women, had criticized the Freudian "sexual phallic monism" that made girls' development a function of a felt penis-lack (Chasseguet-Smirgel 1976), Gilligan has aimed to undermine Kohlberg's "sexual moral monism" that made women's moral development into a stage 4 lack. She does so by arguing—along the lines first suggested by Virginia Woolf's concept of "gynocentrism" and later developed more fully in a psychological direction by feminist writers such as Jean Baker Miller (1976), Evelyn Keller (1978), and Susan Griffin (1978)—that there is a double rather than a single human nature: there is a qualitatively different set of stages in women's moral development. These stages represent the progressive emergence of an orientation to affective qualities of sympathy, caring, and tolerance of ambiguity which ground an ethical focus on responsibility and nonviolence, "the ideals of human relationships—that everyone will be treated with equal respect and that no one will be left alone or hurt" (Gilligan 1981, 66). Following Gutmann (1965), Bakan (1966), and Chodorow (1978), she claims that underlying this moral vision is a concept of self as "connected" rather than "separate," subject #15's comments at the start of this paper being a classic example.

Gilligan aspires to an "ethics of ambiguity" in which abstract features of moral decision-making are contextualized in terms of immediate situational factors, especially those originating in the specificity of interpersonal relationships. Gilligan's dimorphism resembles the common opposition drawn between Gestalt psychology and early structural psychology. Like gestaltists, women have a synthetic sensibility, focusing on wholes and the texture of relations and configurations, rather than analyzing things in terms of parts, elements, or boundaries. They are sensitive to and dependent upon context, and this is the reason for their ability to see ambiguities. Their understanding is more "perceptual," more immediately "experiential," and less ordered in terms of cognitive or logical abstractions from—or representations of—experience. They cross boundaries and see unexpected similarities. Their intelligence exhibits what Guilford described as "divergent" rather than "convergent" qualities (Guilford 1957).

This divergent, synthetic, contextual mental configuration, Gilligan argues, is and should be normative for women. It would appear that only a woman who fully embraces such a moral orientation, to the exclusion of other ethical positions, reasonably can be called a fully developed woman.

Kohlberg's claim that development is essentially a step-by-step movement toward formal principles of justice concerning rights and duties Gilligan sees as holding only for men. She argues that women appeared to be reasoning at a lower moral level than men because they were being evaluated with respect to a male criterion that was inappropriately applied to women. For example, if subject #15's style of discourse excerpted at the beginning of this article were to be applied to the relational feelings and commitments of the characters in the "Heinz dilemma," #15 would be scored "stage 3" or "interpersonal conformist." In addition, she stresses that the use of hypothetical dilemmas as the basis of Kohlberg's measurement instrument leads to a systematic and discriminatory underestimation of women's moral potential. That potential, she argues, can be realized only in relation to the context of personal life problems that are located in relation to a concrete self and other, that require action, and that occur in areas where women have the power to choose, such as in the situation of having to decide whether or not to have an abortion (Gilligan & Belenky 1980). Paradoxically, in this latter study, administration of the Kohlberg instrument was a central part of the procedure, and the findings from it were a central part of the reported results. The selective retention of the Kohlberg instrument, despite its supposed nonvalidity for women, remains to be explained.

Gilligan's alternative moral vision carries with it the clear implication that men harbor an illusory reality. She sees men as guilty of what Hampshire (1959, 1978) has called "false individuation," the illegitimate reduction of the complex ongoing flow of everyday moral situations and behavior to a definite grid of discrete actions and fixed elements which fail to reflect the true difficulties and nuances of the ethical life. The feminist sociologist Jessica Benjamin (1987) has referred to men's illusory autonomy as "false differentiation," and has linked it to an instrumental rationality. Gilligan too sees men's morality as instrumental and, like Parsons (Parsons & Bales 1955), opposes to it female "expressiveness."

The Empirical Validity of Gilligan's Theory

To what degree does Gilligan's account really fit the empirical facts? How much of an interview can be interpreted adequately in terms of the descriptions she presents? In order to assess this most fairly, an analysis was made of one of Gilligan's own interviews, in fact, one of her favorites—subject

#63. Gilligan has been wont to use this rich and satisfying thirty-five-page transcript to typify the phenomena that her theory appeals to. This is an interview with a young, educated, unmarried, white, middle-class woman who had had an abortion and whose interests had since turned to medicine.

It must be acknowledged that almost all of the values and beliefs central to Gilligan's theory of women are to be found in this interview. Nevertheless, almost all of the "rational" concepts that she attributes to men are to be found there too! There are repeated affirmations of "independence," "self-control," "conserving your energy," "not splitting [your]self" (i.e., self-consistency), and other notions that would appear to be more compatible with the idea of a "separated" male self rather than a "connected" female self. This orientation is well captured in #63's recommendation of "arguments that protect individual freedom. . . . What's important is individual freedom and decision . . . individual determination." She stresses as a central guide the capacity for individual decisiveness: "Your life force or some life force given to you by God . . . does sustain. That is enough to make you very hard." Furthermore, many of her statements reflect a concern for the "overall good," to be understood as morally specifiable in terms of a person's "not impinging on somebody else." This rather liberal conception of morality, defined individualistically and privatistically, seems much closer to that view which Gilligan attributes to the typical male (e.g., Gilligan 1982a, 19).

In addition, #63 appears to be rather fluent in the supposedly "male" language of rights. "What right has the state to lock up anybody?" she inquires. In connection with the American Medical Association's opposition to Medicaid, she becomes an explicit proponent of the "rights" orientation: "You have a right to say something about somebody's actions and you don't have a right to mess with their psychological and moral beliefs. . . . I think of a lot of things you should be crying 'Rights!' " Gilligan correctly predicts that, as a woman, #63 will be concerned with people's suffering. However, even that concern is voiced by #63 in terms of rights: "Where do you have the right to cause human suffering?" she asks rhetorically. Gilligan stresses the primacy of the "responsibility orientation" over the "rights orientation" in women. However, #63 argues explicitly that responsibilities are grounded in rights: "People suffer, and that gives them certain rights, and that gives you a certain responsibility."

On the issue of moral obligation, Gilligan again turns out to be correct. In conformity with the womanly voice, #63 does reject the notion of obligation. But on closer inspection we find that this is only because she assumes that duty is to be equated with external coercion: "I don't like the idea of duty. [It's like someone] told you to do it." Thus, she can hardly be said to have rejected any concept of moral obligation in terms of conscience, or an internal sense of necessity.

From Gilligan's point of view, #63 reflects the "female" concern with human relationships. However, a careful examination of the text reveals that the subject thinks of relationships in an impersonal way rather than a personal one. In the famous "Heinz dilemma" of Kohlberg, she says that Heinz should respect his relationship to his wife because "he owes her something" for what she has done for him previously. Elsewhere, she describes the ideal relationship as one where there is a "giving of realistic information." For #63, therefore, human relatedness is cognitive, not affective, and is based upon a relatively mechanistic principle of concrete exchange. #63 also passes beyond the boundaries of Gilligan's description of women's personalized understanding of social relations to emphasize in a rather "masculine" manner the extrapersonal aspects of morality. Defining morality, she asserts that "there is a personal and sociological aspect to it, and beneath that are both these in making moral decisions." Under "sociological," she includes "economics" and "class structure."

All but one of the excerpts cited so far are from the unstructured, autobiographical part of Gilligan's interview. However, when Gilligan comes to the part where she employs the dilemmas from Kohlberg's instrument, #63 becomes even more "masculine" in her responses. First, she appeals to a notion of "justice": "You can break laws because the laws are not too just." Her opinion is, "I think he should do it" (i.e., steal the drug to save his dying wife). Since she does not believe in moral obligation, on account of its coerciveness, she retreats to the position that "You do the best you can." However, she elevates that homily to the level of what she calls a "principle." She says, "It would be living out his principles, in a sense, to do it." In contrast to Gilligan's claim that women's morality is affective and personal in orientation, #63 insists that "politically, it doesn't make a damn bit of a difference how you feel about the other people involved. It is the *principle* involved." That this is not merely a casual use of words, concealing an otherwise situationally relativistic ethics, is suggested by the way in which she goes on to explain her underlying reasoning:

> The principle is you have the duty to go about doing positive action to prevent death. . . . I think it is a universal value. . . . It was a natural thing. "Do it this way." I generally feel there are universal considerations. That is part of the natural system and order of things. . . . It is kind of the values that come from life situations. But then again, those are universal. . . . Since they [values] are not relative, I assume they are natural. . . . Considerations about what is just and what isn't I think have to develop after you're born. . . . Morality is sort of a philosophical consideration.

Contrary to Gilligan's wish, and much to the horror of the interviewer, this favored female subject insists upon restating, more or less, the basic tenets of the Kohlbergian theory of moral development! This is all the more impressive, since at the beginning of the interview #63 had firmly rejected Kohlberg's theory, about which she claimed to know a good deal.

Due to his sex role, the present author decided that it would be only fair to look at one of the interviews that Gilligan uses to illustrate the "male" form of moral reasoning, a subject referred to affectionately, yet noncontextually, as "#32." Again, to some extent, Gilligan's predictions are borne out. This young man (also white and middle class, unmarried, yet living with a woman) says that Heinz is "morally obligated" to steal the drug and that "it is objectively right to do so, because of the priority of the woman's life over his [the druggist's] right to get money." He defines morality as "an appeal to reason."

Nevertheless, with a slight shift of questioning from "should one" to "would one"—a common elision in a Gilliganian interview—he explains where the sense of obligation originates:

> In the immediate situation, that is where it came from. When you say "wife," I sort of get a feeling of love and tenderness, that in his situation that is probably where—. It wouldn't strike me in that situation, if I were doing it for my wife. I wouldn't feel as though it were my obligation to steal it. It is something that I would obviously want to do, and as though a part of me would be dying if I didn't do it.

He emphasizes the importance of being "put in a situation where I can help," and admits that "I don't feel sort of called on to help people on the other side of the world." When he is asked "What is morality or ethics?" he replies:

> Generally, it means to me acting in a way not to hurt . . . being decent to other people. And by "decent" what do I mean? Something like, well, not taking advantage of other people, not hurting them. . . . And, I mean, I think that morality does include the feeling that I should help people when I am in a position to help somebody.

Here, #32 appears to espouse an ethic of responsibility. In so doing, he conforms to Helen Weinreich Haste's (1981) finding, in a reanalysis of Kohlberg's data, that moral orientations to responsibilities are commonly found in male subjects (e.g., Kohlberg's case 42, described by Haste [1983]).

#32 goes on to elaborate his view of the moral.

> (What does it mean to you to say that something is morally right or morally wrong?) It means that relates to what a person does or

has done in that situation, involving people, interaction. . . . It somehow arises from the situation. . . . Somehow, morality is more what happens between people. . . . Morality has to do with the way one acts towards other people. . . . You would want to be able to make other people feel comfortable. . . . I am having trouble thinking in completely abstract terms, and I can't quite think off-hand of situations to put myself in. . . . I don't always feel that something can be objectively right or wrong. . . . In the case of abortion, I would say that is more a personal value.

The fact that such examples are not isolated instances is confirmed in an ironic way by Gilligan herself. In her article with Murphy (Murphy & Gilligan 1980) she presents material from two subjects to document the existence of thinking that is clearly and consistently "contextual relativism." On inspection of this paper, it turns out that both these subjects are male! What is more impressive is Murphy and Gilligan's observation that these men moved *out of* the formalistic "male" mode of thinking *into* the contextual "female" mode, which the authors construe as an irreversible developmental transformation! Of course, Gilligan could defend herself by pointing out that the psychological dimorphism which she has described, rather than being an absolute one, reflects only differential *tendencies* in men's and women's thinking. Although the complete crossover in the case of these two men would still be very hard to account for, it must be admitted that she has offered us in her book some strong examples of her typical "male" and "female" tendencies appearing respectively in men and women. What more graphic illustration of her point could there be than #15's comments which head the present essay? Isn't this a convincing illustration of the Chodorowian "connected self" central to Gilligan's theory? The example becomes even more compelling in the following additional excerpt from the interview with #15, which reveals the thrill and risk of transcending boundaries and barriers:

It is hard to describe, but you know when the level of communication is taking place just by how it makes you feel. It is just the self . . . being touched by somebody else without all the crust around it to protect it from being touched, with that stuff all stripped away. The deeper self. . . . When I get more in contact with this deeper universal stuff, somehow some of these distinctions and divisions fall away and there is more of a union. . . . I have been told that one of my problems is I get almost smotheringly close to people and show my real self. People tell me they get smothered and feel like they lose their identity and they become merged in some inseparable hold, which is scary. And I guess I am looking for some love affair which takes the mystical "two are now one" sort of thing. But that frightens a lot of people I have run into. Just getting too close in the effort to show real selves. But you start losing selves sometimes, and you lose separate identities.

Only one problem: #15 was a man!

The Vanishing Sex Difference between Gilligan's and Kohlberg's Theories

The upshot of the previous section is that Gilligan does not demonstrate convincingly that women's reasoning fits her three-stage description. In the Kohlbergian style, she presents only short excerpts from her interviews, leaving us unclear as to whether or not the moral discourse that remains in the rest of the interviews can be accounted for adequately under one or another of her three levels. There is no assurance of the representativeness of the excerpts she gives us. Since she does not report the kind of heterogeneity that I have been able to identify in her own interviews, a special kind of selectivity seems to have occurred in her interview analysis. Even in the case of the excerpts that she does present, her interpretations and paraphrases appear not to do total justice to what her subjects were saying. For example, the interviewees often appeal to notions of equality in a way that fits her scheme no more than it does Kohlberg's (Parsons 1979). Conversely, it appears that the interview material that she presents underdetermines the interpretation that it is supposed to establish. For example, why should we take the statement of Gilligan's nineteen-year-old who is facing her second abortion and does not know whose role to take as the dilemma of "the feminine identification of goodness with self-sacrifice" (Gilligan 1982a, 496) rather than as a classic instance of the intractable contradictions of the simple "empathic" role-taker described by Kohlberg's stage 3?

Gilligan tries to distinguish her sequence as one of increasingly sympathetic and harmonious relations between "self and other," but this is hardly much of a contrast to Kohlberg's notion of increasingly equilibrated relations of "role-taking." "Sympathy" and "role-taking" would appear to be related in some way, and how "harmony" and "equilibrium" could be distinguished conceptually is not at all self-evident. Similarly, she tends to treat equality, caring, responsibility, nonviolence, etc., as though they were principles of general validity, not just values possessing local usefulness. In this respect, her view approximates that of Frankena (1973), according to whom principles of justice are rationally compatible with principles of beneficence.

Moreover, Gilligan's "stages" are not very different from Kohlberg's. Her first level of "selfishness and survival" appears to be more or less identical with Kohlberg's "preconventional" morality. Her second level, at which the need for approval and the desire to help others converge in a "self-sacrificial goodness," is easily confused with Kohlberg's third stage, as we have just seen. Kohlberg's stage 3 "interpersonal concordance" morality includes concerns for love and caring as well as a concern for the fulfillment of role expectations.

Even Gilligan's third level, which we might expect to reveal the contrast best, is similar in many ways to Kohlberg's postconventional level. True, the idea of self-other interdependence is more general and less specifically moral than Kohlberg's notion of decentered role-taking. However, the two constructs seem quite compatible. Gilligan tends to make them appear opposites by contrasting women's "responsibility orientation" with men's emphasis on abstract and absolute rules, rights, duties, and principles. There are at least six features of this supposed antinomy indicating that she may have exaggerated the opposition.

First, Kohlberg is careful to distinguish rights from rules; the latter are central only in conventional morality. Second, rights (and their correlative duties) are not abstract or decontextualized (Kohlberg 1982). Even in law, the very business of judgment is a complex decision concerning the contextual appropriateness of applying general notions of rights to particular, concrete situations (Levi 1948).

Third, Gilligan asserts that "the morality of rights differs from the morality of responsibility in its emphasis on separation rather than attachment, in its consideration of the individual rather than the relationship as primary" (Gilligan 1979). However, rights and duties are concerned precisely with social relatedness, and the very reciprocity of a right and a duty captures that concern. This is not to deny that individualism and privatism are central to Western legal and moral systems. They certainly are, and so pervasive are they that Gilligan herself does not escape them. For example, she studies her subjects as separate, thinking minds abstracted from their sensuous, ongoing life context and relationships; she encourages women's quest for independence, autonomy and self-sufficiency; and, especially noteworthy, she talks about an abortion as entirely the concern of the pregnant woman. Nor does emphasizing the interpersonal make one less of an individualist; the very idea of interindividual relationships has always been at the heart of individualism (Waterman 1981).

Fourth, rights and duties are not absolute (Dworkin 1977). Only at the conventional level could they be so construed. Even within the utilitarian or social-contract orientation of Kohlberg's stage 5, what is morally right and what moral rights are to be upheld are always relative to particular systems of utilities or consensual social ideas. Once it is granted that rights and duties are not absolute, then the "flexible," "relative" virtues that Gilligan espouses appear less unlike rights and duties. For example, Gilligan and her subjects seem to presuppose something like "the right of all to respect as a person," "the right to be treated sympathetically and as an equal," and "the duty to respect and not to hurt others." It is certainly not the presence or absence of prescriptivity that distinguishes Gilligan and Kohlberg. For example, as can be seen in the quotation from Gilligan (1981) in the second section of this article, she speaks of the "ideals of human relationships." Given that she is so uncompromising about what these ideals are, it is difficult to see in what way she is not here recommending more or less binding rights and duties or perhaps even "principles" of personal welfare and benevolent concern. We may conclude that, by Gilligan's own standards, insofar as women treat sympathy, equality, and nonviolence as optional choices dependent on situational factors they depart from being moral *and* from being women.

Although, at best, Gilligan's third level resembles Kohlberg's postconventional level, at worse it resembles the upper half of his conventional level, stage 4. By confounding rights with fixed and absolute rules, she confuses postconventional with conventional moral judgment. This may account for her tendency to select as female "virtues" qualities conventionally or traditionally attributed to women, and her tendency to see development as progressive adaptation to these stereotypical norms. At other times, she succeeds in distinguishing postconventional from conventional but truncates Kohlberg's theory at the fifth stage, making him appear to be either a legal positivist or a social-contract utilitarian. If this were the case, then her criticisms of him for subordinating welfare to justice would be inappropriate, since that distinction can be made clearly only beyond stage 5. It is precisely Kohlberg's notion of universalizable principles of justice based on ideal role-taking that is designed to protect morality from a narrow legalistic or absolutistic interpretation, to criticize utilitarian welfare concerns compatible with social Darwinism, and to prescribe the right thing to do even in areas of life experience where there are no relevant specified rights. Thus, a fifth caveat to Gilligan is: "Principles are not the same as rights." In fact, it is via moral principles that any given system of rights and duties is evaluated; principles serve to legitimize ethically adequate moral and legal systems and to delegitimize inadequate systems (Kohlberg 1973; Habermas 1975; Dworkin 1977). Gilligan appears not to realize that Kohlberg's metaethical position is strictly deontological and cannot be reduced to the teleological metaethics grounding stage 5.

Finally, Kohlberg's sixth stage of morality incorporates self, responsibility, nonviolence, and even a kind of caring in a way what makes the Kohlberg/Gilligan contrast seem less extreme. The final stage reintroduces the self as equal in a manner quite similar to Gilligan's transition from "self-sacrificial" to "interdependent" morality. It also includes notions of responsibility along with its conception of universal moral obligation. Responsibility, like affectional relation, is one of the content areas for all the Kohlberg stages, and, thanks to Blasi (1981) as much as to Gilligan, it has been elevated recently to a more formal role in the theory (Kohlberg 1982). While Kohlberg has not incorporated communitarian ethics explicitly in his final stage, principles of nonviolent resistance would appear to be part of the universalizable content of that stage. He refers to the example of Gandhi as much as Gilligan does, although in doing so he pays more attention to acts of resistance and civil disobedience in the face of an unjust state. Gilligan does not seem very concerned with societal transformation, given her desire to imbed women even more deeply in the domestic and personal aspects of welfare in civil society.

It is this confinement that leads Gilligan to split caring from justice, failing to see that, while justice requires abstraction, it is intended as the abstract form that caring takes when respect is maintained and responsibility assumed for people whom one does not know personally and may never come to know. Therefore, Gilligan does not seem to acknowledge the importance of respect or responsibility in the relationship of a government to its nation's citizens, or nation-states to each other, or of states, governments, and citizens to past or future generations. "Caring" is limited as the basis of an ethical orientation unless it can overcome the parochiality that its association with friends and family tends to convey (cf. Rustin 1982). It may be true that Kohlberg's claim that "love is a local form of justice" is an inadequate attempt to generalize concepts from the public and judicial sphere of morality to the intimate domain and, at best, works only in atypical cases of interpersonal life, like Kohlberg's dilemma of "Joe and his father." Nevertheless, Gilligan appears equally unrealistic in wishing that all social phenomena be based on concrete affectional ties. To limit and privatize the moral domain by inflating the Judeo-Christian concept of goodness and love leads to the problems described by Sidgwick (1893, 105–15, 238–48) and Frankena (1973, 56–57, 79–94). As the latter says, "The life of pure love . . . is not the moral life. . . . Love by itself gives us no way of choosing between different ways of distributing good and evil" (Frankena 1973, 56–57). A principle of help or care does not work in situations where helping one agent harms another. Even in the Heinz dilemma this is a problem; shouldn't Heinz "care" for the druggist too? More dramatically, this undifferentiated humanistic ethic of care can lead to tragedies like Vietnam: the rationale given for the intervention in Southeast Asia was one of altruistic concern to help a suffering ally. Similarly, unqualified nonviolence is insupportable, as we can infer from the contradictions that Gandhi embodied, especially in his attitude toward the Nazi slaughter of the Jews (Erikson 1969).

The egalitarian ethic that Gilligan recommends to us is part of liberalism, yet a part forgetful that, within the liberal tradition, equality must be balanced with *liberty*. Nowhere in Gilligan's ethic is the need for freedom voiced. In particular, it would appear that women do not need to be free in order to reach the maximum of their developmental potential. The liberation of women is not necessary to reach Gilligan's level 3, much as it is dispensable in reaching Kohlberg's stage 6. For cognitive-developmental theorists, issues surrounding oppressive asymmetrical relations of illegitimate authority and the abuse of power do not have to be engaged because the mind, in the full course of its development, rises above mere concrete relations of oppression by envisaging the perfect mutuality and reciprocity of symmetrical human relationships from which unwarranted power differentials and the corruption of authority have been eliminated. Gilligan's women are doubly free, since they subvert men's rational mastery by constructing a different worldview, a view of a world in which mastery has no place.

The Dubious Empirical Status of Sex Differences in Moral Development

A decade ago, Maccoby and Jacklin's (1974) review of research on childhood exposed the myth of pervasive psychological sex differences. They showed that, contrary to stereotypical norms, there is no clear evidence that girls are more passive, dependent, compliant, anxious, timid, withdrawn, self-effacing, suggestible, impulsive, nurturant, or social than boys; nor are they less analytic (including field independent), decontextualized, active, competitive, achievement oriented, organized, or planful.

Although Gilligan announces that "the differences between the sexes are being rediscovered in the social sciences" (Gilligan 1979, 432) and others seem to be in agreement (e.g., Golding & Laidlaw 1979–80; Flanagan 1982; Kegan 1982), it is still far from clear that the existence of such differences with respect to moral development has been established. The debate over the existence or nonexistence of sex differences in moral judgment scores was triggered by an early study that found sex differences in favor of men (Haan et al. 1968). At that time, Kohlberg and Kramer (1969) explained the findings as follows: "Stage 3 interpersonal concordance morality is a functional morality for housewives and mothers; it is not for businessmen and professionals." This interpretation is peculiar, given that most of the subjects in the Haan study were students, among whom one might expect to find relatively few housewives and mothers or businessmen and professionals.

Since then, Keasey (1972); Blatt and Kohlberg (1975); Turiel (1976); Holstein (1976); Levine (1976); Haan, Langer, and Kohlberg (Haan et al. 1976); Erickson et al. (1978); and Gibbs, Widaman, and Colby (1982) found no sex difference in childhood or adolescence; and Weisbroth (1970); Berkowitz et al. (1980); and Gibbs, Widaman, and Colby (1982) found no sex difference in early adulthood. However, Fishkin, Keniston and MacKinnon (1973) found one for adults, Erickson et al. (1978) and Bussey and

Maughan (1982) found a sex difference for young adults, Haan, Langer and Kohlberg (Haan et al. 1976) found one in early and middle adulthood, Kuhn et al. (1977) found one in middle adulthood, and Holstein (1976) found a transitory difference in middle adulthood. Like Kohlberg and Kramer, Erickson et al. (1978, 3) concluded that the differences could be attributed to social role-taking opportunities: "Late adolescent and adult males in our society are afforded greater opportunities to take on roles of responsibility having societal import, and . . . females' sex role socialization has discouraged such activity for women."

Undaunted by her own finding of no sex differences in a study of students that was controlled for educational privilege (Murphy & Gilligan 1980), Gilligan reanalyzed these and other data, and in the process brought to light some sex differences in means and distributions of scores. In opposition to Kohlberg and Kramer, and Erickson et al., Gilligan, Langdale, and Lyons (1982, 83–93) argued that, given the educational parity of their male and female subjects, such differences could not be attributed to social role-taking opportunities but must instead be attributed to a sex bias in the Kohlberg theory and scoring system.

In a review of cross-cultural tests of Kohlberg's theory, Blasi and Broughton (in press) found several instances of sex differences. Admittedly, there was a tendency for the sex differences to be a little larger in cases where the difference was in favor of men. In addition, there was a tendency for men to exhibit a wider range of stages of reasoning. However, where sex differences were found, they were equally often in favor of women (e.g., in the Bahamas) as they were in favor of men (e.g., in Israel). Furthermore, in the U.S. and cross-cultural longitudinal studies, the rates of development over time were commensurate for male and female subjects, with a tendency for females to advance more rapidly.

Overall, the findings indicate that the existence of a sex difference in moral development, at least of the Kohlbergian variety, is still open to question, especially for the age groups prior to adulthood.

The findings that perhaps contradict Gilligan's claims most directly are those reported by Norma Haan (1978). Haan identified what she calls an "interpersonal morality" that contrasts with the "formal morality" described by Kohlberg. Much as Gilligan has suggested, despite its greater internal inconsistency, subjects were found to prefer this interpersonal morality in action situations, while there was a trend toward greater use of formal morality in dealing with hypothetical dilemmas. Formal reasoning, in fact, was found to be a liability in action situations, subserving mental processes of defensive isolation and intellectualization and tending to paralyze action. In this and another (1975) study Haan found that reasoning level was higher regarding a real-action situation than it was regarding a hypothetical one. Furthermore, she found that interpersonal moral reasoning diverges increasingly from the formal type with development. Again in concordance with Gilligan, Haan found that ego processes play an important role in interpersonal morality but not in formal morality. However, *no sex difference was found in the use of these two moralities*; both female and male subjects tended to prefer to use interpersonal moral reasoning in the action situations. Moreover, the experience of the action situations was found to advance both kinds of morality equally, suggesting a common developmental mechanism.

Other empirical findings cast doubt upon the dichotomy of moralities that Gilligan describes. For example, men's capacity for moral commitment based on sympathetic caring, a desire for social harmony, and a dedication to nonviolence, despite their simultaneous penchant for rationality, is testified to by several studies. Keniston's *Young Radicals* comes first to mind (1968). Keniston's in-depth examination of the moral character, development, and politics of the male activists revealed that their status was postconventional on Kohlberg's scale, while exhibiting all the virtues of responsibility, sympathy, caring, etc., that are supposed by Gilligan to be incompatible with that status. Furthermore, departing from Chodorow's characterization, Keniston revealed through an extensive clinical procedure that these young men's beliefs and activities were grounded in a warm, personal relationship to their mothers, one that had not been rejected but had continued into adulthood as a source of identity. A parallel finding appears in Zahaykevich's (1982) research on Russian dissidents (all male). All the subjects were found to be postconventional according to Kohlberg's scheme. She identified three types of dissenter, only one of which, the "abstract rationalist" type, was characterized by an emphasis on reason as a moral guide. The other types—"heroic romantic" and "carnivalesque historicist"—eschewed abstract rationality and emphasized community, relationship, and personal solidarity as the bases of morality and political action. They saw cultural, spiritual, and aesthetic values as central to ethics. All the dissidents studied were committed to nonviolent resistance, and none evinced the kinds of fantasies of violence that Pollak and Gilligan (1982) find in their male subjects.

Concerning Gilligan's claims about the "separate" and "connected" self, there is one study in particular that supports the dualistic view (Carlson 1971), although Gilligan herself does not cite it. However, several phenomenological studies of the structure of self find the same kind of dividedness into public and private in both sexes (Laing 1960; Winnicott 1965; Broughton 1981). Gilligan claims that there is a sex difference in Eriksonian ego-identity development, but a recent review by Weiss shows that the findings are quite mixed, with many showing similar trajectories for men and women (Weiss 1983). Several other studies of the development of the ego reveal very similar patterns for male and female subjects. Perry's (1968) scheme for intellectual-ethical development applies to both men and women (cf. Parker 1978). Fowler (1981) found that his stage of religious identity applied equally to men and women. Basseches' (1980) levels in the development of "dialectical thinking" applied equally to his male and female subjects. In a study of ten samples of men totaling five hundred subjects between the ages of eleven and fifty-one, Loevinger and colleagues found the same stages of ego development as in women (Redmore et al. 1970). In Broughton's (1978) study of developmental levels in child, adolescent, and young-adult world-views, male subjects exhibited no differences from female subjects. Of particular note is the fact that rationalist and irrationalist philosophies appeared as a function of age and developmental status, not as a function of gender. Following Freire's and Gilligan's interview method of allowing subjects to define their own problems and issues, Golden (1983) identified in high-school students four sequential developmental cycles in which norms of achievement and affiliation were first established and then relativized, contextualized, and criticized. In longitudinal and cross-sectional studies, both male and female students were found to pass through these phases of value change; there were no sex differences in development.

All six of these investigations are particularly relevant to Gilligan's claims, since all six developmental schemes involve a hierarchy of increasing "contextuality" and decreasing "absoluteness." Indeed, it was from Perry's scheme (developed on male subjects) that some of Gilligan's understanding of women's contextual relativism was derived. This comes as no surprise to the psychologists of cognitive style who have known for a long time that boys exhibited both "convergent" and "divergent" forms of mental activity (Getzels & Jackson 1962; Hudson 1968), and that supposed sex differences in analytic reasoning (e.g., field independence) were hard to substantiate (Maccoby & Jacklin 1974). In addition, in the study conducted by Kuhn et al. (1977) both tolerance of ambiguity and empathy were found to be a function of moral level and not of gender.

Womanhood as a Moral Concept

Gilligan's alternative to Kohlberg "doubles up" on it, preserving a parallel with it rather than replacing it. Without her always realizing it, this doubling up or paralleling strategy has the consequence of challenging many of the assumptions upon which Kohlberg's approach originally was founded. For example, Gilligan implicitly has shifted the metaethical ground of the psychology of normative ethics, supplanting Kohlberg's "deontological" approach to morality with an "aretaic" one that is oriented to *virtues* (Frankena 1973; cf. MacIntyre 1982) and that describes qualities of the ideal person and the good life rather than prescribing the rights and obligations that comprise a just society. Gilligan's view is similar in many respects to

Aristotle's account of the different virtues appropriate for men and women in the first book of his *Politics*.

An important aspect of this metaethical shift, not less significant on account of its obviousness, is that the step from Kohlberg to Gilligan entails a rearrangement of human psychology such that moral development is now seen as fused with the development of gender itself. As Kohlberg (1966) had suggested a decade earlier, sex-role is not what the social-learning theorists tried to convince us it was. Rather, it can be conceived in terms of "gender identity," a rational cognitive construction which is not learned but undergoes successive developmental transformations via a process of self-socialization. In this sense, sex is no longer to be seen as a matter of "roles" imposed from without. Gilligan's theory aspires to synthesize these two parts of cognitive-developmental theory that Kohlberg had kept separate, at the same time undermining his claims, first, that the process of gender formation was essentially the same for both sexes, and, second, that it was purely a matter of identity. Instead, much the same way Freud appeared to do, Gilligan makes gender a specifically moral issue. Despite a certain kinship with Erikson, she does not attach herself primarily to his theory of identity formation. Neither does she draw her ideas from the gender identity paradigm of Kohlberg's earlier paper. Furthermore, she does not entertain the possibility of sex differences in cognitive development. Psychological sex dimorphism is confined to moral development. Thus, womanhood is defined as a specifically moral status. Given the developmental dimension, gender is not a given; one can only gradually *become* a woman. In de Beauvoir's words, "Woman is a becoming" (1953, 30). However, in Gilligan's book, one cannot become a woman without developing specific, circumscribed values and commitments in the moral domain, including stipulated metaethical commitments to an aretaic or virtues orientation rather than a deontological or justice orientation. Thus, some female people never really become properly gendered. Those whose development ceases at the second level of self-sacrificial morality are to be conceived not only as not fully moral but also as not fully women. To be a "moral" person, in the strict sense of the term, one must attain the fullness of one's potential as a gendered individual.

Women Do Not Develop

There are other ways in which Gilligan's claims undermine the Kohlbergian paradigm. For example, she challenges the primacy of structural form. The morality that she recommends (for women, at least) is relatively *content*-oriented, in the sense that it is the particulars of concrete selves and their actual ongoing personal relationships to concrete others that ground moral decision-making and action. Sometimes it appears as though it is not the *actual* relational contents that are crucial but rather the *way* in which such concreteness is taken into account. To the extent that this is what Gilligan intends, we might say that it is not content itself that grounds moral decision-making but rather the general form of content, the manner of its being cognized and employed in ways of social behaving. Thus, content is almost raised to the level of form in this interpretation.

This is perhaps why Gilligan looks more like a theorist of "personality traits" than a moral developmentalist. The differentiae used to distinguish women and men look very much like the stock bipolar traits of individual-differences psychologists: field-dependence/independence, tolerance/intolerance of ambiguity, open/closed-mindedness, impulsiveness/reflectiveness, flexibility/rigidity, etc. (Cattell 1965). In a sense, she borrows what she would call a "male" style here, preferring congeries of abstract psychic elements over the relational concept of "structure." Gilligan thus embodies the unfortunate tendency of all psychologists of sex differences to gravitate toward a psychology of traits (Sherif 1979).

Comprehending exactly what Gilligan intends is complicated by the fact that, at times, she does not seem to be elevating content above structure so much as raising *action* above thought. In the latter case, then, we would say that women's morality inheres in a way of behaving rather than a way of dealing with the concrete particulars of personal relationships and commitments. Perhaps another way of saying the same thing is that she wishes to elevate *function* above structure, in which case it is not so much a dispensing with thought but emphasizing its functional value in practice, in its capacity to inform commitments and guide activity in the complex nexus of interpersonal relatedness. Such a functional approach tries to compensate for the excessive intellectualism of the structural approach by giving a salient role to *experience,* not in the abstract sense of assimilation and accommodation of conceptual schemes but in the sense of what it feels like to grapple with specific relational events such as those involved in an abortion decision. It is argued that women's moral experience is qualitatively different from men's (Gilligan, Langdale & Lyons 1982).

Paradoxically, however, Gilligan fails to question the original oppositions between form and content, thought and action, structure and function, concept and experience, abstract and concrete. She leaves women in almost the same position that Aristotle left them, representing matter while men represent form, the form that is given to matter (Whitbeck 1976).

While the attempt to resuscitate the concepts of concreteness, content, action, practicality, function, and experience, which structural approaches have tended to suffocate, is well intentioned, running them all together into an undifferentiated mass tends to lead to a crude romanticism that rejects rationality uncritically, often using as the basis of the argument precisely those principles of rationality (e.g., noncontradiction) that are being rejected. This kind of romanticism is typical of attempts to "feminize" logocentric psychological theories and is not specifically feminist in any way (Broughton 1984). Since such attempts conform to the very dichotomies presupposed by the logocentric theories in the first place rather than calling them into question, they tend to perpetuate the status quo, to affirm the established division of labor, and to foreclose the possibility of radical transformation. Intractable duality offers only the appearance of liberation from a "male" monism. In fact, it leaves us with little more than its mirror image. In this, Gilligan's rebellion exemplifies what Barrington Moore (1968) calls "conservative solidarity" and Richard Sennett (1981) terms "disobedient dependence." Gilligan repeats the pragmatists' attempt to secede from positivism, and in so doing joins the pragmatist illusion that the problems of formalism can be solved by returning to functional concepts of action-based inquiry and context-sensitive problem-solving.

A disturbing consequence of the revolt against structure is that it implies that women do not develop. As I have tried to demonstrate elsewhere (Broughton 1982), the concept of "development" in modern Western thought is tied to a model of hierarchically ordered structural systems. Insofar as Gilligan rejects the formal, abstract quality of such systems, and (at least for women) abandons the distinction of competence and performance that they require, she perforce gives up the possibility that women's consciousness undergoes systematic transformation through an equilibration process. This is tantamount to being unable to explain the movement from one stage to another. Indeed, it is tantamount to dispensing with the whole notion of "stage." This radical step is foreshadowed in the way that Murphy and Gilligan rejected both differentiation-integration and sequential transformation as criteria of more morally-developed positions (Murphy & Gilligan 1980, 97–100).

Strictly speaking, then, Gilligan's reinterpretation implies that only men develop, while women pass through "phases," "types," or "positions." This may account for the fact that, as she reports, her female subjects can proceed through her levels relatively rapidly (Gilligan & Belenky 1980). Indeed, the process of making an abortion decision sometimes appears more like a Wernerian "microgenesis" than a set of structural transformations. Thus passage through the levels is a kind of functional adaptation, akin to moving through the phases of problem-solving, task-performance, or "coping" as described in the literature of popular psychology. This kind of movement looks much more like something "produced" than something developing, as Lasch (1976, 7–8) has pointed out. Gilligan's account of femininity therefore approximates traditional feminist social-learning views within which it is construed as an artificial sex-role manufactured to fit particular social needs and requirements. Masculinity, on the other hand, would seem to be less a product of society than an autonomously evolving, transcultural developmental outcome.

Dimorphism is more infectious than Gilligan realizes. Despite her attempts to confine it to the content of male and female development, it tends to spread to the level of the form of life itself, making the transformational experiences of men and women different in kind. Men develop; women are produced.

Trait Psychology and Ethical Relativism: Are There More Than Two Genders?

What Piaget and Kohlberg achieved for psychology was the replacement of intellectual "factors" and personality "traits," defined arbitrarily in terms of age norms, by developmental differences ordered and evaluated in terms of their relation to a final telos or end-point which was explicitly and rationally justified on philosophical grounds (Elkind 1969; Kohlberg & de Vries 1971). Gilligan's attempt to retain the evaluative order and telos, without the philosophical justification of why movement through the order is to be construed as a rational progress, leaves her in a precariously inconsistent position. It is not unlike the position in which Jane Loevinger finds herself (Broughton & Zahaykevich 1977, 1980), indeterminate between a logically ordered developmental stage hierarchy and a relativistically defined set of types or trait clusters. This kind of inconsistency can be accommodated only by giving up one of the two conflicting metatheoretical assumptions—developmental or type/trait—or by transcending both in a new synthesis, a theoretical innovation. Coincidentally, Noam, Kohlberg, and Snarey have recently attempted such a maneuver themselves, although without a great deal of success (Noam et al. 1983; cf. Broughton 1983a).

Insofar as Gilligan dismisses Kohlberg's competence measure (the hypothetical dilemmas and the corresponding structural scoring system) and looks only at everyday moral-affective functioning, she gives up on the possibility of distinguishing potentiality from actuality, moral capability from moral performance. While this distinction is itself problematic in a variety of ways, she fails to acknowledge its complexities and so lapses into a kind of situational or contextual relativism (Frankena 1973). This is in addition to her "gender relativism." In general, her conceptual apparatus is much more conducive to a thoroughgoing relativism, including cultural and ethical relativism, than to any kind of universalist account (see, especially, Murphy & Gilligan 1980).

Relativism leads to all kinds of paradoxes, not the least of which is that to be consistent a relativist must be a nonrelativist about relativism, since its opposite (nonrelativism) is not considered even relatively valid. A parallel problem arises with "tolerance of ambiguity." Is one to be tolerant even of intolerance of ambiguity? If Gilligan were to embody genuinely the contextual relativism and tolerance of ambiguity that she holds as the highest virtues of womanhood, then she would have to be accepting, not rejecting, of structure, principles, and formal reasoning and would have to give up the specific qualities that she has so unambiguously attributed to women! Even were we to grant that women have the qualities that she attributes to them, those qualities would be bound to conflict and interfere with each other, since they have no rational consistency with one another. For example, women are required to be tolerant of ambiguity and simultaneously to be unambiguously caring and responsible. A similar problem arises for women who aspire to subjective "field dependence" without acknowledging that the latter logically requires the existence of a field that is objectively distinct from that which is dependent on it. The ambiguity between field dependence and field independence is presumably one which is not to be tolerated by the field-dependent woman. Such conceptual paradoxes are not confined to Gilligan's theory. For example, they appear earlier in Loevinger's theory of ego development in women (Broughton & Zahaykevich 1980).

In supplanting rational ethical rights and obligations with concrete commitments based on contextual and interpersonal sensitivity, Gilligan conflates the moral with the social and both with the practical. Here she is in agreement with her above mentioned subject #63, who summarizes her response to the Heinz dilemma by saying, "It is kind of more practical considerations than moral." Gilligan refers to her ethics as one of "best fit," where the "actual consequences of choice" become central in evaluating the morality of that choice. The possibility of moral objectivity is given up as a rationalist's pipe dream (Murphy & Gilligan 1980, 83). Thus Gilligan conforms to the greater pragmatism of the female voice that she documents empirically in her 1979 paper (435, 444). Her relativism extends and exaggerates this dispersion of the ethical; it has as its ultimate consequence the admission that it is no longer possible to say what morality is or to give any clear rational ground for it—what she calls the "ineluctable uncertainty of moral choice" (Murphy & Gilligan 1980, 83). The positivists rub their hands in glee as "philosophical speculation" is banished, so that ethics can then be absorbed easily into the world of facts. Moral problems are nothing but "dilemmas of fact," in Murphy and Gilligan's felicitous phrasing. "Ought" is thus reduced to "is" and prescriptive to descriptive, just as philosophical moralists from Dewey (Dewey & Tufts 1932) to Kohlberg (1971) had warned. Under Gilligan's interpretation, morality becomes simply the diversity of forms that it is found to take, or the diversity of things which are taken to be morality. Women's morality, and therefore also their very gender itself, becomes reducible to the "is," the order of more or less contingent "personality" factors, which in turn can be rendered empirically as psychological and social traits or processes observed at particular points in time and space. Generalizations from such observations become entirely dubitable, in tune with Gilligan's exhortations to women that they eschew the general in favor of the particular. (Presumably men would tend to make such generalizations, but women would not understand or believe them!)

Arguably, to the same degree, it follows from Gilligan's account that there ceases to be any particular thing called "gender." If the sexes are mutually exclusive, then "gender" denotes nothing in particular, serving only as a nominal rubric under which fall two specific forms of transformational psychological system. If men and women are nonoverlapping forms of mental life, "gender" is reducible without loss to "male plus female" and degenerates to the point of serving only a purely descriptive function. Since there is nothing to assure us that these two transformational systems cumulatively exhaust all psychological possibilities, there is no a priori reason why one might not discover a third gender, or a fourth, perhaps corresponding to nondeontological and nonaretaic metaethical systems.

The Denial of Self-Deception, Desire, and Being

In psychology, the notion that males and females exhibit different kinds of "self" can be traced to David Gutmann's (1965) paper on women and ego-strength and David Bakan's (1966) book on "agency" and "communion," both authors having been influenced primarily by psychoanalytic theory. Thus, Gilligan's dualism could be said to have its roots in the psychoanalytic tradition. Although she does not acknowledge the work of either Gutmann or Bakan, she does link her dualism to Chodorow's sociological "object relations" approach. However, there is something peculiar about this liaison, given that the assumptions of the cognitive-developmental approach are fundamentally incompatible with psychoanalytic theory. In fact, in both Piaget and Kohlberg, the developmental-stage idea was formulated in explicit opposition to Freudian theory, rejecting the concepts of primary process, repression, and the conflict-ridden dynamic unconscious, and discounting the centrality of sexuality and aggression, the significance of concrete attachments or objects-choices, and the formation of self and morality through processes of introjection and identification. By positing each "stage" as a complete replacement of the prior stage, the developmental approach eliminates the role of memory. Moreover, by extending the process of gender formation and moral development from childhood into adolescence and early adulthood, the formative role of early experience is further erased.

Despite her sensed affinity for Chodorow, Gilligan actively subscribes to all these departures from the psychoanalytic tradition. In particular, by limiting women's morality to the conscious, conflict-free sphere of the developing ego, she denies the possibility of self-deception. She ignores the Freudian revelation that we have an interest in not knowing ourselves and so hides from sight women's collusion in their own oppression (the later being "projected" into the male morality of mastery). As long as Gilligan asks her subjects only what they think of themselves, and accepts what they say at face value, she cannot distinguish insightfulness from defensiveness, knowledge from wishful thinking, or fact from fantasy. In trying to restore the subject to cognitive structuralism, she has collapsed subjectivity and objectivity into a flat, one-dimensional psychology. It is an idealist psychology in which self and self-concept are assumed to be identical. Small wonder then that Gilligan's women offer little resistance to traditional views of what women are and what their place is. Much as her interview offers them no way to penetrate their own self-mystifications, it offers them no way to penetrate the cultural mystifications of femininity. They are left without reason or desire for emancipation.

In Gilligan's Cartesian framework, knowledge is split from interest as mind is from body and reason from emotion. When gender is equated with cognitive style, it is severed from sexuality. The central iconography of abortion potentiates the fantasy of the total mastery of women's bodies by women's minds. Perhaps an even more contentious segregation of pure consciousness from the psychosomatic is attempted when Pollak and Gilligan (1982) interpret projective-test data cognitively rather than clinically in order to show that women are naturally nonaggressive. Gilligan's answer to Freud's question "What do women want?" seems to be "They don't want anything!" When a cognitive self and a moral worldview rule the psyche, desire, either sexual or aggressive, is largely irrelevant. What is there left, then, for women to do but to accept their nature, adjust to their social location, and retreat into the comfort of their "difference"? There is no sense in desiring another or in "aggressively" resisting oppression when life's travails are all in the mind.

The net result of this inexorable mentalism is that thinking is elevated to the point of its divorce from being. In actuality, Gilligan is not looking for evidence that her subjects are sympathetic, caring, responsible, or nonviolent. She is satisfied as soon as these qualities are manifested as espoused values in speech. It is enough that the "voice" or narrative style are different. Development is thus close to learning to talk in a certain way.

This, in turn, predisposes Gilligan's view to class and ideological biases. There is, in fact, a strong resemblance between her level 3 and what Bernstein (1975) has described as "new middle-class" discourse, or Reisman has termed the "other-directed" style of the modernized white-collar world. Carlson's 1971 paper, otherwise quite sympathetic with Gilligan's position, contains a literature review showing that the different cognitive styles which Gilligan describes are not to be found in nonwhite or nonmodernized groups and, furthermore, are subject to major historical alterations.

Conclusion

It is not the purpose of this critique to deny the contribution that Carol Gilligan has made to our understanding of the psychology of either gender or moral development. In drawing attention to the multiplicity of metaethical assumptive frameworks, she has offset any Kohlbergian tendencies to theoretical imperialism. In suggesting that women's experience is different from men's, she has reminded us that even the charismatic authority of the monolithic term "development" cannot distract us from the reality of human differences. In arguing for the salience of love, care, and commitment, she has restored to the focus of our vision the complex opposition between private and public morality.

Neither is it the purpose of this essay, in questioning the sharp distinction that Gilligan has drawn between herself and Kohlberg, to defend the latter's theory, which is surely subject to a number of serious criticisms (Broughton 1978b, 1983a). In fact, Kohlberg *accepts* much of Gilligan's theory (e.g., Kohlberg & Power 1981) and, insofar as he does so, the current critique takes issue with both theorists and their *folie à deux*.

Neither is it the purpose of this review to deny the existence of differences in general between the sexes or the reality of psychological gender differences in particular. Rather, in an attempt at a dialectical treatise on difference, I have sought to reveal some of the various contradictions that arise when a vision of gender is constructed in terms of a dualistic psychology. For example, Gilligan's separation and sharp contrast of "male" and "female" normative ethics and metaethics seems, in her own terms, extremely "masculine" in its emphasis on difference and boundary, its abstraction of the mind from life, and its tendency to essentialize gender, removing it from the context of relationships, discourse, culture, societal structure, and processes of historical formation. She subscribes to the very decontextualized binary logic that elsewhere she eschews as the false consciousness of a mystifying male moiety (Chodorow 1979).

How, then, can Gilligan account for the crossovers documented above even in her own interviews? At times, following other gender dualists like Daly (1978) and Ruddick (1980, 1984b), she covers herself by saying that the two forms of consciousness are not always mutually exclusive. Thus, sometimes, she backs off from the dual typology to a trait theory (e.g., Gilligan 1982a, 2), admitting that there are moments when men speak in the female voice and women speak in the male voice. However, as in Ruddick and Daly, such concessions are made infrequently and rarely with conviction. The reason for this is that to dwell on the overlap of genders undermines the whole explanatory framework. Is a man speaking in the feminine voice at that moment a woman? Or is he merely a female impersonator? At least at the intuitive level of "Who is female and who is male?" gender is a relatively clear distinction, and when slippage is permitted between gender and "voice" the latter loses its power to serve as either an explanation or an illumination of the former. Like "hysterical versus obsessive," "extroverted versus introverted," or "flexible versus rigid," the notion of "connected versus separated" voice then assumes the stature of a mere personality dimension. Such is the cost of backing down from a "type psychology" to a "trait psychology" (Cattell 1965, 54–55).

It is one of Gilligan's assumptions, following Virginia Woolf, that women's voice may be suppressed in a male-dominated culture, with the consequence that women's only alternative to silence may be to imitate male reasoning. As Lanser and Beck (1979) have put it, "Such a masculinization of women's minds is a patriarchal commonplace." They describe how this process tends to produce a "double voiced" discourse. This certainly could account for the appearance of the language of individualism, separation, rights, and justice in women's discourse. In addition, one of the things that Gilligan is pointing out about women is their contextual relativism, which allows them to appreciate different "voices."

However, the reverse case, the appearance of the female voice in men's discourse, cannot be explained along either of these lines. Since men are not oppressed by women, men are not the victims of "matriarchal feminization." Also, if the natural male tendency is to accentuate separation and boundary, and to be intolerant of ambiguity or plurality, then it should be most unnatural for men to appreciate or borrow the female voice. Thus, either an additional explanatory principle must be invoked or the thesis of "patriarchal masculinization" needs to be repealed and some substitute interpretation located to account for the symmetrical crossing over of voices exposed by empirical observation.

There is a sense in which gender is not indispensable to Gilligan's account. That is, she appears to be engaged in a broad metaphysical and epistemological task, a revival of liberal romantic idealism and mentalism requiring the collapse of some standard distinctions (e.g., subjectivity/objectivity and ideology/reality) and the erection or resurrection of others (e.g., cognition/affect, knowledge/interest, and mind/body). Such a philosophical task tends to take on a life of its own, apart from the additional considerations of whether or how such oppositions might be aligned with "male/female." One might also regret the strategic error of tying such oppositions to gender, since any synthesis of opposed terms then appears to undermine the distinctness of the sexes. As we have seen, her philosophical polarizations do not work. In fact, their revival of a thoroughgoing Cartesianism flies in the face of two centuries of philosophical critique (Cocks; McMillan 1982). Worse, as Flax (1980) has so interestingly shown, Descartes' dualisms themselves reflect a traditionally macho rejection of anything symbolizing the feminine. Thus, the empirically observable crossing over of voices is matched by the failure of Gilligan's conceptual polarizations.

However, the failure of these oppositions need not imply a retreat to androgyny, with its strange language of "masculine femininity" and "feminine masculinity." Admittedly, as writers from Hegel to the structuralists and critical theorists have pointed out, there are general social conditions of work, class, ideology, discourse, and mass culture that tend to homogenize men and women, making them in the same general image. Yet within that sameness, polarization may be introduced at any point where it might stabilize structures or modulate conflict. Gilligan's dualism appears to be one such surface polarization, constructed within the interests of a liberal individualism that can only benefit from more deeply inscribing the pseudoantinomies of rationality and irrationality that constitute its ideological foundation. In generating more talk about gender—indeed, in rendering gender itself as a form of speech or "voice"—developmental psychology augments the circulation of individualistic discourse and intensifies the flow of power that permeates its various surfaces, including the psychosomatic interiors of its various interlocutors.

The critical possibilities that emerge from Gilligan's undertaking arise at the point of opposition to Kohlberg's rationalism. However, in the absence of a grounded understanding of rationality or a dialectical vision of relation, the critical moment slips away. First, Gilligan mistakenly assumes that to reject Kohlberg's theory is to dispense with rationality as a basis for moral judgment, at least for women. In other words, she assumes that Kohlberg's account of "rationality" is an adequate one. A more parsimonious approach would be to work at the necessary task of examining Kohlberg's theory critically, while reserving the right for women to be rational under some description of reason less narrow than Kohlberg's.

Second, in confounding rationality with dogmatism, obsessive formality, and intellectualization, Gilligan's critique approximates a romantic position of direct opposition to judgment, limitation, and separation. On the rebound, she moves to an emphasis on the Dionysiac crossing and dissolution of boundaries. Such a counterposition entails two problems. On the one hand, it suggests an eternal return to a point psychologically prior to gender, which would preempt the desired distinction of women's consciousness from men's. On the other hand, it tends to support a psychodynamically regressive tendency toward infantile fusion with the mother. Such a romanticism has difficulty sustaining a distinction between a critique of false individuation and an argument for infantilization. As Benjamin's Hegelian analysis has pointed out, psychological development requires not a return to infantile connectedness but a dialectical reconstruction of dependence, in which individuation is reconciled with the need to have one's subjectivity recognized (Benjamin 1987). Gilligan misinterprets Chodorow's view of women. Chodorow (1978) characterized women's psychological structure not in terms of a simple tendency to connect but in terms of a complex and fragile preservation of the tension between merger and individuation.

There are echoes here of the classic Freud-Jung debate (see, e.g., Freud 1914/1963). Freud warned against a mystical developmentalism that undermined the basic psychoanalytic concept of unconscious wish. He saw in Jung an attempt to view gender as a duplication (Elektra as double of Oedipus), to render as complementary polarities achieving balance through development what were, in reality, the components of critical contradictions that only analytic insight and sublimation could modulate. In Gilligan's polarized developmental construction of gender on the basis of mirror-image traits, there is a return to the notion of symmetrical male-female complementarity. Early on, under the pressure of theoretical as well as clinical considerations, Freud gave up on the idea of gender symmetry. Although he proposed the notion of negative or "shadow" Oedipal complexes underlying the bisexuality of men and women, he was opposed to Jung's "animus/ anima" conception (later adapted by Winnicott) on account of its implications of symmetry.

Augmenting Freud's insight, Lacan has pointed to the social origins in humanistic ideology of the idea that genders are symmetrical complementaries (Mitchell & Rose 1982). He interprets the persistence of this antidialectical distortion as psychodynamically rooted in the infantile illusion that desire is reducible to satisfiable need, and that male and female be mutually the exclusive objects of that satisfaction. This symmetrical pseudomutuality is reproduced in Gilligan's rational-affective dualism, and also at her highest stage where asymmetry of desire, power, or communication is precluded a priori by the assumption of a natural tendency to harmonious self-other equality.

What's lacking in Lacan? Admittedly, his structuralist presuppositions leave him with crippling difficulties in understanding object relations, internalization, and fantasy, in explaining the way in which boys and girls assume the garb of their respective genders, in accounting for the personal rather than societal dimension of sexism, and in permitting any constructive departure from gender norms. Nevertheless, his clinical and conceptual struggles with gender leave us with some helpful directions for thinking the issue through from a point of view that is both psychodynamic and hermeneutic. First, his Hegelian unfolding of "being" provides a developmental perspective that is neither liberal individualist nor cognitivist. It therefore allows us to see the political struggle involved in gender identity, to distinguish gender from sex-role or self-interpretation, and to recuperate the existential significance that sex and gender have to us. Second, only the introduction of some asymmetry into both gender and cross-gender relations can preserve sexual distinction from a precipitous collapse into the blended voices of androgyny. At the same time, the basis of this asymmetry in the paradoxical nature of desire provides a way of understanding the important, tense, and yet variable link that gender has to sexuality. It is this connection to mutual sexual desire that works as a guarantee against androgynous uni-sexuality.

Third, *pace* Gilligan, gender is fundamentally a symbolic issue. The power of the masculine and feminine inheres to a significant degree in what they symbolize to men and women. This helps us to grasp the importance of discursive interaction, and the power relations that it mediates, in the never-ending negotiation of gender relations. It helps us to understand the sensuous, aesthetic quality of the relations between gendered individuals. It further helps in highlighting the liability of male and female, the degree to which they are subject to gradual or sudden changes of meaning, even to the point that they may turn dialectically into each other in the mutual permeation of interlocutors' being. Not least of the advantages of an appreciation of variability is that the tension between heterosexuality and homosexuality is not excluded.

Fourth, dwelling upon symbolism and significance implies both continuity and discontinuity. On the one hand, there is a symbolic tradition of masculinity and femininity borne by culture that is a constant reminder of the origins of present sex and sexuality in the activities and experiences of previous generations. On the other hand, the requirement that the symbolism of gender and sexuality be interpreted anew in each generation, even in each relationship, introduces a space for subjective will and objective novelty. This encourages a sensitivity to the ways in which gender and sexuality are both culturally diverse and historically formed and projected, while still presenting an insolubly rich field of discourse and struggle for each new pairing and each new social group.

These ontological, asymmetrical, sexual, symbolic, historical, cultural, hermeneutic, and intersubjective qualities of gender cry out for a vision more complex and with greater descriptive scope than a dualistic psychology of development has yet been able to offer. Gender and sexuality are phenomena that are in a relation of friction with superimposed cultural or ideological stereotypes and individual self-interpretations. It is the recognition and continuation of that friction which helps to make being gendered simultaneously entertaining and poignant. If we fail to recognize that friction, for whatever reason, we anesthetize ourselves to the sensuous texture and creative possibilities of being female or male.

Part III
CHECKING THE DATA

10

Two Moralities? A Critical Discussion of an Ethic of Care and Responsibility versus an Ethic of Rights and Justice

Gertrud Nunner-Winkler

Gilligan has recently claimed that there are two contrasting approaches to morality: an ethic of care and responsibility and an ethic of justice and rights (1977, 1983; see also Murphy & Gilligan 1980; Gilligan, Langdale & Lyons 1982). The first approach, more typical for females, corresponds to the experience of the self as part of relationships, as "connected self"; moral judgments consider specific details of concrete situations and are guided by an interest in minimizing the overall harm done. The justice orientation, more characteristic of males, on the other hand, is an expression of an autonomous, independent, "individuated" self; moral judgments follow principles defining rights and duties without "due" consideration of specific circumstances and costs implied. Gilligan accuses Lawrence Kohlberg of stating the justice orientation as the only valid moral orientation, thus neglecting the contribution of the other approach to morality.

In this essay I shall try to reinterpret Gilligan's position. First, differences noted between the "male" and the "female" approach, as far as they are moral, I take to be differences not in ethical position but in emphasis of one against the other of two types of moral duties. Second, the consideration of situational particularities does not discriminate between the two moral orientations. Third, a considerable part of the sex-specific differences are not moral differences: Gilligan's description of an ethic of care and responsibility includes questions concerning the conception of the good life that do not belong to morality proper. In the last part of the essay I shall attempt to derive several hypotheses about sex-specific moral preferences formulated in

Reprinted by permission from W. Kurtines and J. Gewirtz, eds., *Morality, Moral Behavior and Moral Development*: 348–61. Copyright © 1984 by John Wiley & Sons, Inc.

terms of theoretical distinctions introduced in the first part and shall test them against empirical data collected in a study on adolescent development.

The Distinction between Perfect and Imperfect Duties

For theoretical clarification I consider a distinction that was introduced by Kant in his *Metaphysik der Sitten* (1797/1977) and later elaborated especially by B. Gert in his *The Moral Rules* (1973), namely, the distinction between perfect and imperfect duties. Perfect duties are *negative* duties, that is, duties of omission (e.g., do not kill, do not cheat, etc.); imperfect duties are *positive* duties, duties of commission, which, however, do not prescribe specific acts but only formulate a maxim to guide action (e.g., practice charity). This maxim thus delineates a broad set of recommendable courses of action some of which the actor realizes by, at the same time, applying pragmatic rules and taking into account concrete conditions, such as individual preferences, contingencies of location in space and time, and so on.

Perfect duties, because they require only *not* to act, can, at least in nonconflictual cases, be followed strictly by everybody at any time and location and with regard to everybody (Gert 1973). Imperfect duties, on the other hand, can never be observed completely: it is impossible to practice charity all the time and with regard to everybody. Positive maxims do not define limits of their application, do not specify which and how many good deeds have to be performed and whom they are to benefit so that the maxim can be said to have been followed. Due to this latitude, the following of maxims requires what Kant calls power of judgment (*Urteilskraft*). The asymmetry between perfect and imperfect duties is also reflected in the differential reactions to transgression. The failure to meet perfect duties is considered a vice (*Laster*), the failure to meet imperfect duties is lack of virtue (*Untugend*).

The Ethic of Care and Responsibility as an Ethic of Imperfect Duties; The Ethic of Rights and Justice as an Ethic of Perfect Duties

The characteristics Gilligan (1977) enumerates show the ethic of care and responsibility to be primarily an orientation to imperfect duties, the ethic of rights and justice to be primarily an orientation to perfect duties. Thus, the most eminent goals of the ethic of care are the wish to care for and help others, to meet obligations and responsibilities, a concern for others and feelings of compassion, a responsibility to discern and alleviate trouble in this world (511). This orientation to imperfect duties finds its most concise expression in one woman's statement in an interview: "Is it right to spend money on a pair of shoes, when I have a pair of shoes and other people are shoeless?" (510). The very form this reflection takes, the interrogative, is proof of its being derived from an imperfect duty, namely, the principle of charity, which does not define its own form of application, its own limits, and the degree to which it is binding.

The ethic of rights and justice, on the other hand, is depicted as being mainly concerned with rights of individuals and their protection, that is, ways of ensuring that rights of individuals will not be interfered with by others. Such rights, it seems, are conceived to be invulnerable, absolute rights valid at all times and places and for all persons; they are conceived as rights corresponding to perfect duties. No one would deny that both kinds of duties are considered part of one morality, the unity of which is constituted through adherence to some universalizing procedure. How, then, is Gilligan's claim that it is still a question of contrasting moral approaches to be understood. I think it can be interpreted to mean that females (1) feel more obliged to fulfill imperfect duties than males; and (2) in cases of conflict will more likely opt for the fulfillment of imperfect duties, whereas males will insist more rigidly on having the perfect duties respected. The first part of the statement, I think, is more adequately construed as a difference in moral action and moral character and not as a difference in ethical position, for the latitude of imperfect duties per definition requires that individuals make use of their moral understanding to derive concrete action decisions. This kind of difference in interpersonal orientation parallels the distinction between diffuse and specific role relationships that Talcott Parsons (1964, 65ff., 153ff.) notes: in diffuse relationships, that is, relations between relatives, friends, neighbors, it is assumed that one may ask for any kind of support, and the burden of proof rests with the role partner who withholds help. In specific relationships, on the contrary, the kind of help that may legitimately be asked for is clearly specified and limited, and the burden of proof rests with the partner demanding support. The hypothesized sex-difference in orientation might thus be a consequence of the fact that traditionally females are much more exclusively involved in diffuse relationships than are men and therefore feel bound to meet any need arising, whereas men are much more used to specific relationships and tend first to question the other person's "right to demand help." This hypothesis I shall take up in the last part of the essay.

The interpretation that in cases of conflict females opt for fulfilling imperfect duties, and males perfect duties, implies a difference in ethical positions insofar as females might be assumed to reverse the male order of priority of perfect over imperfect duties. Yet this interpretation is implausible, for Gilligan ascribes to the ethic of care an orientation to contextual particularities—"It is the reconstruction of a moral dilemma in its contextual particularity which allows an understanding . . . and thus engages the compassion and tolerance considered previously to qualify the feminine sense of justice" (1977, 511)—which is incompatible with an a priori strict ordering of one set of rules over the other. In fact, it is precisely this consideration of contextual particularities that Gilligan sees as lacking in the ethic of rights and justice—"Kohlberg retains his conception that principles of justice are context free" (1983, 83). This differential awareness of situational specifics marks one of the main differences between the two ethics.

The plausibility of this implied equation between an orientation to imperfect duties and to contextual particularity, respectively, to perfect duties and their contextual independence will be discussed in the following passages. I want to show that this equation holds true only for a very specific aspect of Kant's moral position that is shared by scarcely anyone, namely, that perfect duties allow no exceptions. It does not hold true for Kohlberg, even though he presents his construction of rights in such a misleading way that it does provoke the kind of criticism Gilligan voices.

The Role of Situation-specific Knowledge in Moral Judgment

In the nonconflictual case, the following of perfect duties presupposes scarcely any knowledge of situational specifics. As all that is required is not to act in a specified way at any time or location and with regard to everybody, all one needs to know are some general empirical facts valid for all situations (e.g., what substances are poisonous, giving strong enough poisons to a human being will kill him or her, etc.) or at best some narrowly limited specific facts (e.g., if that person does not receive a specific medicine now, he or she will die) or truth-values for specific statements (e.g., it is true that x happened). Yet the range of concrete facts one might need to know is clearly confinable and can deductively be determined: only those facts are relevant that pertain immediately to the rule in question; that is, for the rule "do not kill," relevant facts are all potential risks to life; for the rule "do not lie," only the empirical truth of statements asked is relevant.

Imperfect duties, on the other hand, require situation-specific knowledge, for they demand contextually situated decisions in regard to when and where to act and in regard to whom. Thus, Gilligan's proposition that the ethic of care takes situational details into account, whereas the ethic of rights does not, seems plausible: imperfect duties require by their logical characteristics a concrete specification that perfect duties do not. Yet the picture gets more complicated as soon as one considers cases where duties collide. Only if one assumes that there are rules without exceptions can there be any moral judgments that can be made without taking note of situational specifics. This actually is Kant's position. Kant (1959) maintains that perfect duties enjoy absolute priority over imperfect duties, that is, allow for no exceptions. Thus, he explicitly states that even if lying to a murderer might save a friend's life, it cannot be justified, for "truthfulness ... is a *perfect duty valid under all circumstances*" (205).[1]

This position is extreme, however, and is shared by scarcely anyone. In modern discussion the justifiability of exceptions to rules is widely accepted. It finds a clear expression in the differentiation between actual duties and prima facie duties that W. D. Ross (1930, 8–31, 61f.) introduced: rules are valid only prima facie, that is, under normal circumstances, when there are no other moral considerations that bear on the decision. In Gert's (1973) exposition, the "except" clause plays the same role. Thus, Gilligan's claim that the ethic of care is oriented to situational particularities that the ethic of rights will neglect is valid only at first sight. For even to observe perfect duties requires—if exceptions are deemed justifiable—that the question of consequences of different courses of action in a specific situation has to be examined: for it might well be that the imperfect duty to prevent harm may in a concrete case legitimately override obligations following from a perfect duty. Therefore I think one cannot very well hold context orientation to be a feature that constitutes contrasting approaches to morality. Context orientation is a prerequisite for *all actual moral judgments*.

One problem still remains open: how moral decision is to be reached in such cases of conflicting duties. Moral choice in dilemmas is based on a process of reflection on the potential universalizability of the specific solution, found by taking all particulars of the concrete situation into account. It is this compatibility of universalism with an orientation to situational particularities that has often been overlooked. Hare makes this point very lucidly in his distinction between universality and generality: "The thesis of universalizability does not require moral judgments to be made on the basis of highly general moral principles. . . . Moral development . . . consists in the main in making our moral principles more and more specific by writing into them exceptions and qualifications to cover kinds of cases of which we have had experience" (1963, 40).

It may very well be true that people will come up with different solutions: People will differ in the weight they will give to various considerations. As Gert puts it: "One man might publicly advocate killing one man in order to save ten others. . . . Another man might not publicly advocate violation in this situation. He might feel that a significant decrease in the protection from violations of the rule plus general anxiety due to added uncertainty more than offsets the possible benefit" (1973, 99). This is true because "evils are ranked in too many diverse ways" (ibid., 126). It might also be true that sex-specific differences in the ranking of evils might show up; thus, for instance, I would assume, in accordance with the hypothesis put forward earlier, that females might weigh consequences on the level of the social system as less grave than consequences on the level of interpersonal relations. Yet this could be taken to be a sex-specific filling in of a latitude that is conceded within the limits of morality, whereby morality is understood as constituted through an obligation to some universalizing procedure, that is, to impartiality.

One minor point may still be noted pertaining to the question of methodology. Gilligan tends to see Kohlberg's use of hypothetical dilemma as another indication of the abstraction of moral problems from the "contingencies of human social existence" she criticizes in him:

> While the analytic logic of justice is consonant with rational social and ethical theories and can be traced through the resolution of hypothetical dilemmas, the ethic of care depends on the contextual understanding of relationships. . . . While the analytic logic of justice can be traced through the deductive resolution of *hypothetical* dilemmas and the understanding of systems of rules, the ethic of care is manifested through the understanding of *actual* situations of moral conflict and choice. (1983, 9–10)

I think this is a misunderstanding. If exceptions are allowed, concrete circumstances have to be taken into account in solving a moral conflict—be it a hypothetical or an actual conflict. There is a difference, namely, that in actual dilemmas one can never be sure whether facts are correctly perceived. Yet this difference lies on the level of empirical truth of descriptive statements, not on the level of normative judgment.

Kohlberg's Position

The main criticism Gilligan directs against Kohlberg is that he neglects situational particularities in making moral judgments: "Kohlberg built a theory of moral development on a unitary moral conception of fairness and justice. . . . Thus the social concept of moral decision was replaced by the structures of formal thought which provided a rational system for decision that was autonomous and *independent of time and place*" (1983, 7). Kohlberg's "principles of justice [are] *context-free* and [can] generate *objectively right* solutions to moral problems" (Murphy & Gilligan 1980, 83). Yet by the logic of his own moral convictions Kohlberg by necessity must orient his moral judgments to concrete situational circumstances. This is because in a conflict between perfect and imperfect duties he not only maintains—unlike Kant—that the perfect duty *may* be violated, but almost requires that it *must* be violated; that is, Kohlberg adopts a radical female position, however ironic this may sound. Thus, for instance, in the Heinz dilemma the issue is whether Heinz may break into the druggist's store to steal a drug to save his wife's life. In terms of the distinctions introduced earlier, the Heinz dilemma depicts a conflict between a perfect duty (not to steal) and an imperfect duty (to prevent evil, namely, the death of the sick woman). Kant would have denied that Heinz may break into the store: if one may not lie in order to save a life, one may not steal either. Kant (1959) gives another example that proves the same point: a man has been entrusted with a large sum of money. The owner dies without the heirs knowing anything of the deposit. The man, a charitable and philanthropic person, lost all his fortune without any fault of his own; his wife and children are starving. The heirs, however, are unkind, rich, and wasteful, and "it were just as well that the additional wealth were to be thrown into the ocean" (1959, 82). Even in this extreme situation the man may not keep the money to feed his wife and children, for "it is wrong, it contradicts duty" (82)—that is, it is wrong under all circumstances, context free.

Kohlberg, quite on the contrary, demands that Heinz steal the drug "because the right to life supersedes or transcends the right to property" (Colby, Gibbs, Kohlberg, et al. 1979, 80). This justification rests on the assumption of a clear hierarchy of differentially binding duties and obligations. Yet whereas in Kant the hierarchical ordering of duties is based on their formal characteristics (perfect duties, as they are negative duties, which can be followed and are to be followed under all circumstances and with regard to everybody, are superordinate to imperfect duties, which only formulate maxims that can never be completely followed), Kohlberg seems to posit the hierarchy of rights by content: "There is a hierarchy of rights and values. Stealing is justified as serving a universal right to or value of life which is prior to laws" (ibid.). Because of its utmost priority, this universal right to life is henceforth treated as if it were a perfect right corresponding to a perfect duty in Kant's sense: it is a right that must be granted universally; that is, it implies seemingly perfect duties regardless of concrete circumstances or of personal ties. Thus, for Kohlberg it is as much a duty to steal for a stranger as it is to steal for one's own wife: "It would be right to steal for a stranger because the right to life should be accorded universally to all men whose lives can be saved regardless of personal ties" (ibid., 82). The problem with this position is that "saving life" by its structural characteristics is an imperfect duty, which does not specify its own limits: a universally accorded right to life implies the universal duty to save "all men whose lives can be saved regardless of personal ties," even if that would require violation of property rights. Thus we all are not only required to give away all the money we own but also justified—in fact, maybe even obliged—to rob all banks as well as all members of our society who own more than they need to feed themselves, so as to be able to save the starving children in the third world, whose sad fate is well known to all of us.[2]

I assume Kohlberg would not support such a revolutionary Robin Hood strategy. If this were correct, it follows that, for Kohlberg as well, decisions in moral dilemmas hinge on concrete circumstances: thus, it may be justifiable to rob for one's own wife or even a stranger one has met, but it may be less justifiable to rob with the intent to send the money to India. Yet in Kohlberg's own justifications, the factual dependency of moral judgments on a consideration of concrete circumstances is veiled; thus, Gilligan rightly denounces the neglect of situational contingencies on Kohlberg's part. This neglect, though, I take—in contrast to Gilligan—not to be characteristic of a certain type of morality, the morality of rights and justice; rather, it is because Kohlberg has not clearly recognized the logical structure of imperfect duties. This can be seen from the misleading formulation he uses. He speaks of a universal right to life, which seems to imply a universal, hence perfect, duty to save life. Perfect duties, however, can be formulated only in the negative: All one can say is that every human being has a right not to be killed, disabled, deprived of freedom by others.

Morality versus Questions of the Good Life

Thus far only part of Gilligan's position has been discussed: the assumption that an orientation to care can be juxtaposed to an orientation to rights, whereby only the former takes situational particularities into account, whereas the latter denies their relevance. The second half of this assumption has been refuted: consideration of concrete situational details is indispensable for *all* moral judgments (if exceptions are allowed). The first part has been reformulated: females feel more obliged to fulfill imperfect duties of charity, whereas males adhere more strictly to the perfect duties of noninterference, although both types of duty belong to morality.

Yet Gilligan's conceptualization of the two approaches to morality is more encompassing than has hitherto been stated. Gilligan sees them as emanating from different experiences of the self in the world: "The principle of nonviolence and an ethic of care . . . informs the world of the connected self, the principle of fairness and an ethic of justice . . . informs the world of the separate self" (Gilligan, Langdale & Lyons 1982, 42–43). The experience of the self in the world is itself a process of development, described for the ethic of care as the unfolding of the concept of responsibility. I think that in this conceptualization of the "connected self" and of stages of responsibility, moral orientation and development is mixed with aspects of ego development and with questions of the good life. To substantiate this claim I will analyze two examples. In the first, concerning ways of conflict resolution in child's play, "social connectedness" is interpreted by Gilligan, Langdale and Lyons as the basis of a specific moral orientation, although it might well be simply an expression of specific ego interests. The second example concerns reflections about life plans at pregnancy; in the decision of this issue questions of the good life are confounded with moral problems.

In the first example, two six-year-olds respond to the dilemma "created when, in playing with a friend, they discover that they and their friend want to play a different game." Characteristic of the little girl are the following statements: "*We don't have a real fight*" and "we agree what we should do" and "we should play one . . . , then the other"; while the little boy starts out by stating: "I wanted to stay outside—he wanted to go in" and ends with the statement "*I would do what I want—he would do what he wants.*" The italicized statements are pointed out by the authors as especially good exemplifications of the contrasting principles of care versus fairness. As long as it is so described, however, this dilemma is not a moral dilemma, but the inner conflict of an individual choosing among his or her own conflicting needs. Each child has two desires: the desire to play a specific game and the desire to play with a specific friend. The little girl forgoes the chance to play the preferred game (at least for some time) yet in return maintains the chance to play with the friend. The little boy, on the other hand, proves to be more interested in playing the preferred game, though be it alone, than in playing with his friend. Thus far each child may have chosen among different needs that proved not to be simultaneously satisfiable. There is nothing moral about this choice: it is well known that females are more interested in relationships and males more in things (objects).[3] Neither one nor the other of these preferences is morally more recommendable. Gilligan might consider this very construction of the dilemma to be a male version, while she sees it as a moral dilemma, that is, not as an intraindividual choice among one's own conflicting needs but as an interindividual choice between satisfying one's own needs or the needs of others. Yet I do not think that it really is a moral question. Adequately satisfying each other's needs is what a good relationship means. If a relationship is not good, that is, if both partners cannot find satisfaction and enrichment in sharing alter's interests, separating and searching for a more congenial partner might—so long as no other considerations must be considered, such as marriage and children—be better than a permanent pseudomoral adoption to alien interests.

Once the friendship dilemma comes to be seen as a moral dilemma of conflicting needs of ego and alter, however, the central issue of imperfect duties arises immediately: how far to go in fulfilling the needs of alter. It is this issue around which Gilligan presents the female moral development as revolving. Different levels of the conceptualization of responsibility formulate different answers: on the first level, responsibility centers on the self and on relationships that are self-serving; on the second level, responsibility orients to the needs of others such that the satisfaction of one's own needs is considered selfish, and self-sacrifice is deemed as "good"; on the last level, the focus of responsibility is shifted to the relationship itself, the stability of which is comprehended as depending on the fulfillment of the needs of self *and* other. This developmental sequence, although it answers a central problem of imperfect duties, is too narrowly conceived as moral development: it is a more encompassing learning process; it is a process of the development of self as an autonomous person, as a competent actor. Thus, on the third level the insight is developed that the second-level understanding of good-ness as self-sacrifice is a welcome device to avoid taking upon oneself the responsibility for one's own actions. And it is only on the third level that the individual can clearly recognize his or her own needs and interests and sepa-rate them from externally obtruded ones, and becomes willing to assume the responsibility for the consequences that the following of one's own needs may entail. This competence is a prerequisite for all life choices (career, part-ner, worldview, political conviction, etc.), of which moral decisions make up only one part.

Gilligan, I think, unduly treats this general process of ego development as moral development and treats as moral choices what in reality are decisions about ways of life. This can be seen very clearly in the way Gilligan (1977) presents her interviews on abortion. The women questioned answer not the issue of whether an abortion is morally justifiable but rather questions of the "good life": namely, "What kind of person do I want to be?" "What kind of life do I want to lead?" This claim may seem unjustified, for most of the women do start off the discussion with formulating moral considerations, such as, "I don't believe in abortion. Who can say when life begins" (1977, 497), or even "It is taking a life" (499). Yet in fact these considerations do not enter the decision process; the question of abortion is dealt with as a choice between different ways of life. This can be seen if one examines the kind of reasons that are put forward by the same woman who considers abortion as taking life. Among the reasons she lists for having an abortion are the fear of losing a good job, losing independence, difficulties in handling the relationship with the father of the child; among the reasons against hav-ing an abortion she mentions enjoying more home life, being admired by others for bringing up a child alone; having less feelings of guilt. Another woman is quoted as comprehending through pregnancy her own "inner conflict between the wish to be a college president and to be making pottery and flowers, having kids and staying home" (1977, 508).

I do not want to deny that morally relevant considerations do sometimes enter into the question of life choice. Thus, for instance, the woman quoted earlier hesitates about a professional career for fear of losing her compas-sion on the way up. Yet most considerations mentioned concern morally neutral ego goals, such as a desire for a fulfilling occupation or the desire to avoid internal conflicts of priority between family and job, and the decision seems mainly to involve a morally neutral balancing out of different ego interests.

To summarize, I tend to think that not all the differences Gilligan sees as constitutive for two contrasting approaches to morality are really differ-ences in moral orientation. Social connectedness is largely a result of greater social- than task-oriented interests; stages of responsibility describe a process of disentangling self from conformity expectations, which is a general process of ego development inasmuch as conformity expectations extend to many nonmoral issues. It may still be true that females feel more obliged than males to fulfill imperfect duties, to answer to concrete needs of others, even at their own costs. It also seems plausible that this characteristic is, as Gilligan suggests, a consequence of women's greater social involvement. It might also be, however, merely a consequence of an inability to recognize and stand up to one's own needs, that is, a consequence of lack of ego strength, of an inability to say no. If this is true, the status of a "female" approach to morality would be very ambiguous, indeed.

Some Data Concerning Sex Differences in Moral Judgment

In this last section I employ the data Rainer Doebert and I have collected. We interviewed 112 male and female adolescents in the age range of sixteen to twenty-two years and of different socioeconomic backgrounds. The interview covered intensity of adolescent crisis, moral judgment, coping and defense styles, parental patterns of conflict resolution and child rearing, political socialization, and so on. It was not designed specifically to test sex-specific morality, yet some of the results may serve to test the following hypotheses derived from the assumptions of an ethic of care and responsibility:

1. Females feel more bound by imperfect duties than do males; that is, in a conflict between a perfect and an imperfect duty females will more likely opt for transgression of the perfect duty.
2. In moral decisions females will take more situational details into account.

To test these hypotheses, a subsample of ninety-eight subjects was drawn from the original study, that matched male and female subjects on educational background and, as far as possible, on age as well. The subjects are distributed as shown in table 10.1.

To test the first hypothesis, three different morally relevant decisions will

Table 10.1
Distribution of the Sample over the Variable Age, Education, and Sex

Variable	Male			Female		
Education	High	Medium	Low	High	Medium	Low
Number of subjects	15	16	17	15	17	17
Average age	18.5	17.1	16.2	19	16.8	16.5

be used. The first concerns the decision in Kohlberg's mercy-killing dilemma: A woman who is incurably ill and suffers unbearable pain asks the doctor for an extra dose of morphine to make her die. Should the doctor give it to her or refuse it? This story depicts a conflict between a perfect duty, do not kill, and an imperfect duty, relieve pain. The action decision was classified into four categories:

1. The doctor should give the drug, notwithstanding the law, because the woman suffers so much and should be allowed to decide for herself (active mercy-killing).
2. The doctor should not give the drug, because the law is legitimate; at most he may stop excessive medical support (passive mercy-killing).
3. The doctor should not give the drug so as not to risk punishment.
4. Undecided: the doctor should, because of pain, yet should not, because of punishment.

The subjects' responses are distributed over these four categories as is shown in table 10.2.

The data show that in this dilemma females do not feel more bound by the imperfect duty to relieve pain. If anything at all, females more eagerly seek to avoid punishment. This finding might be taken as proof of the female tendency to consider consequences in making moral decisions, yet the moral ambiguity of this tendency is that it is not specified how consequences for the different persons involved are to be balanced. Any procedure balancing costs to ego versus benefits to alter would, I assume, have to make use of some universalizing procedure.

In the second morally relevant decision, subjects were asked to pass a moral judgment on the following action: A person talks an old-age pensioner into ordering a useless journal. The judgment could take the following form: I find this action very bad (for a score of 3), pretty bad (2), not particularly bad (1). From the "female" point of view, this action might be interpreted as exploitation of a weak or poor elderly person by a skillful

Table 10.2
Distribution of Answers to the Mercy-Killing Dilemma

Response	Male	Female
Doctor should—pain	30	24
Doctor should not—law	7	8
Doctor should not—punishment	11	14
Undecided	1	3

salesperson who simply tries to maximize his or her own profits at all costs. From the "male" point of view, one might defend this action as a legitimate pursuit of business interests, based on the assumption that all market partners can take care of themselves and look out for their own interests. Thus, one might expect females to condemn this action more than males. This is not the case, however: The average evaluation of this action by males and females is identical; both find it pretty bad (for the average score of 2.0).

For the third morally relevant decision, the same format (with a scale of 1–3) was used for an evaluation of the following action: A person does not want to lend some money to a friend and therefore pretends not to have any money. Again, females might be expected to deny help less readily when asked for it, and therefore to condemn this action more strongly. Again, the data do not bear out this expectation: males and females alike judge this action as not particularly bad (for the average scores—males 1.4, females 1.3).

To test the hypothesis that in moral decisions females will take more situational details into account, responses to the following dilemma (taken from Gleser & Ihilevich 1969) depicting an interpersonal conflict were analyzed. "You live with your aunt and uncle, who have taken care of you since your parents were killed in an accident when you were only five years old. One stormy night you have a date with a friend, but your aunt and uncle will not let you go out because it is late and the weather is bad. You are about to leave anyhow when your uncle issues the order: 'You stay at home because I said so.'" No situational details were considered to have been taken into account in responses such as these: "I'd go anyhow"; "That's none of his business"; "I'd be furious and leave." Situational details were considered to have been taken into account in these: "I would go, if the date was very important to me, if not, I'd stay"; "If I'd accepted them as parents, I would stay, because I respect them"; "It depends how they handle conflicts in other situations—if they forbid everything, I'd go"; "If we were meeting in a group and it was only 8 o'clock, I'd go; if we were meeting alone and it was 10 o'clock I'd stay at home."

Of the subjects, fourteen of the males and twelve of the females considered concrete situational particularities when making their decisions on how to act in this interpersonal conflict. Those taking situational details into account are slightly older (.35 years) and of higher socioeconomic background (of the lowest educational level, only 16 percent, of the two higher levels, 42 percent consider concrete circumstances).

Certainly one could not hold the analysis of these few data to be an adequate test of sex differences in moral judgment. Still, it should be noted that the data presented do not lend support to the assumption that females (at least in the age range tested) observe imperfect duties more closely than do males or give more consideration to contextual particularities.

Notes

1. Cf. "It cannot be that opposing rules are simultaneously obliging: if it is [strict] duty to act according to one rule, then it is not only not duty to act according to a contrary one, but it is even undutiful. Thus a collision of duties and obligations is unthinkable. It can be, though, that two reasons of obligations collide. . . . [In that case] it is not the stronger obligation but the stronger reason of obligation that dominates" (Kant 1797/1977, 330).
2. Gilligan, Langdale & Lyons 1982 also points out this difficulty in Kohlberg (pp. 52–53, interim report).
3. This difference in interests also is reflected in career choices. In our study, for example, 27 percent of girls but only 5 percent of boys mentioned "contact with other people" as one of the most important criteria in selecting among different careers. On the other hand, 25 percent of the boys and only 12 percent of the girls report specific factual interests that they want to follow up in a career, such as interest in cars and in natural sciences.

11

Sex Differences in the Development of Moral Reasoning: A Critical Review

Lawrence J. Walker

Kohlberg's (1969, 1976, 1981) theory of moral reasoning development has been criticized as being biased against women (e.g., Gilligan 1977, 1982a; Haan 1977; Holstein 1976b). The allegation of sex bias is a serious charge against any psychological theory and is even more controversial when leveled against a theory of moral development. The minimal foundation for such a interpretive claim against a theory would be evidence indicating greater moral maturity for males than for females. For this reason it seems appropriate to review the existing research literature to determine whether consistent sex differences in reasoning about moral dilemmas have been found and, if so, what explanations might account for these differences. Such a review is necessary since the assertions regarding sex bias and sex differences in moral reasoning are becoming bolder and more frequent and are found not only in scholarly writing but also in textbooks and the popular press (e.g., Gilligan 1982c; Saxton 1981). Although the current controversy revolves around a contemporary theory of moral development, the issue is not new; historically, women have often been regarded as morally inferior to men (e.g., Freud 1925/1961).

The charge of sex bias might be warranted for two reasons. First, a theorist could explicitly advocate or popularize a poorly founded claim that the sexes are fundamentally different in rate and end-point of moral development. For example, Freud (1925/1961) asserted that women lack moral maturity because of deficiencies in same-sex parental identification. Second, a theorist might offer no such opinion, but define and/or measure moral maturity in ways that inadvertently favor one sex or the other and thus create

Reprinted by permission from *Child Development* 55: 677–91. Copyright © 1984 by the Association for Research in Child Development.

a false impression of real differences in moral maturity. The allegations of sex bias against Kohlberg's theory have been based primarily on the latter reason.

Gilligan (1977, 1979, 1982a, 1982b) has been the most articulate critic alleging sex bias in Kohlberg's theory. She contends that Kohlberg's theory and scoring system are insensitive to characteristically feminine concerns for welfare, caring, and responsibility, and that Kohlberg, in failing to recognize the principled nature of these concerns, has denigrated such thought to lower stages. She argues that Kohlberg's conception of morality is androcentric in that there is an emphasis (particularly at the higher stages) on traditionally masculine values such as rationality, individuality, abstraction, detachment, and impersonality—an emphasis that is reflected by the assertion that justice is the universal principle of morality.

Kohlberg's Theory

A brief description of Kohlberg's theory (1969, 1976,1981) may be helpful at this point. He has postulated six stages in the development of moral reasoning. The initial two stages form the preconventional level. People at this level (primarily children) conceive of rules and social expectations as being external to the self. In stage 1—punishment and obedience—right is defined by literal obedience to authority and the avoidance of punishment and physical damage. In stage 2—individualism, instrumental purpose, and exchange—right is defined as serving one's own interests and desires and as letting others do likewise; cooperative interaction is based on terms of simple exchange. The conventional level subsumes stages 3 and 4. People at this level (primarily late adolescents and adults) identify with, or have internalized, the rules and social expectations of others, including authorities. In stage 3—mutual interpersonal expectations, relationships, and conformity—right is defined as concern for shared feelings, expectations, and agreements that take primacy over individual interests. In stage 4—social system and conscience maintenance—focus is on the maintenance of the social order and the welfare of society or the group by obeying the law and doing one's duty. Stages 5 and 6 form the postconventional and principled level. At this level, people (a small minority of adults) differentiate themselves from the rules and expectations of others and think in terms of self-chosen principles. Stage 5—prior rights and social contract or utility—has utilitarian overtones in that right is defined by mutual standards that have been agreed upon by the whole society and by basic rights and values. In Stage 6—universal ethical principles—right is defined as accordance with self-chosen, logically consistent principles that are abstract and ethical and that all humanity should follow. It should be noted that Stage 6 has been dropped except as a theoretical construct because of its absence in Kohlberg's longitudinal data (Colby, Kohlberg, Gibbs & Lieberman 1983).

In Kohlberg's approach, moral development is assessed by responses to a number of hypothetical moral dilemmas that currently entail the following issues: life, law, morality and conscience, punishment, contract, and authority. Scoring of these responses according to Kohlberg's manual (Colby, Kohlberg, Gibbs, et al. 1984) can yield two measures: a global stage score and a moral maturity score. The global stage score is determined by the modal stage of reasoning, with a minor stage being included if the second most frequent stage has 25 percent or more of the scored responses. The moral maturity score (MMS), a more quantitative measure, is given by the sum of the products of the percentage of usage at each stage multiplied by the number of that stage: it can range from one hundred to five hundred.

Kohlberg (1976) claimed that the order of the stages is invariant, but he predicted variability in rate and eventual end-point of development. There are two main determinants of rate of moral development: (1) attainment of appropriate levels of cognitive development, and (2) exposure to appropriate sociomoral experiences. Kohlberg (1973b, 1976) has hypothesized that cognitive development is a necessary but not sufficient condition (i.e., a prerequisite) for the development of moral reasoning. This claim has been supported by studies (e.g., Kuhn, Langer, Kohlberg & Haan 1977; Walker 1980) that indicate that attainment of a moral stage requires the prior or concomitant attainment of the parallel cognitive stage.

Level of moral development is influenced not only by cognitive prerequisites but also by exposure to sociomoral experiences (Kohlberg 1969, 1973b). The essential feature of these social experiences for moral development is the provision of role-taking opportunities in conflict situations. These experiences arise both through interpersonal relationships with family and friends and through real participation in the economic, political, and legal institutions of society. The effect of these experiences is thought to be a function not only of their quantity but of their quality in terms of the degree to which they afford opportunities for leadership, communication, decision-making, and responsibility. Both of these determinants of rate of moral development (cognitive prerequisites and sociomoral experiences) may be useful in explaining variability in moral reasoning between groups (e.g., socioeconomic classes, cultural groups, the sexes).

The Issues of Sex Bias

Kohlberg's philosophical defense of his model of moral reasoning development (e.g., Kohlberg 1981) may seem to reinforce the view expressed by Gilligan and others that he considers thinking at the higher stages to be detached, disinterested, and unmindful of the concrete realities of interpersonal relationships. However, there are two problems with that conclusion. First, it fails to recognize the self-limiting scope of Kohlberg's approach to moral development. His theory is a *cognitive* theory that deals with the adequacy of justifications for solutions to moral conflicts. It does not speak directly to the issues of moral emotions and behaviors, although Kohlberg (1978) has admitted the necessity and desirability of going beyond "cognition." Second, this criticism fails to recognize the contextual basis of principled moral judgment in action (versus abstract descriptions). Kohlberg (1982) argues that there is no conflict between using moral principles and being contextually relative in moral judgment. Principled moral reasoning is contextually relative since it can be sensitive to aspects of a given situation in ways that rule-bound moral reasoning cannot. Boyd's (1979) interpretation of principled moral reasoning in terms of its accompanying "psychological postures" demonstrates the concrete aspects underlying such reasoning. For example, central to Kohlberg's conception of mature moral reasoning is the attitude of mutual "respect for persons" as ends, not means (Boyd 1983). It should be remembered in this context that principled moral thinking is not the exclusive domain of moral philosophers but has also been used by activists such as Martin Luther King and Mother Teresa of Calcutta (Kohlberg 1981).

Gilligan's (1977) response to the bias she saw inherent in Kohlberg's theory was to postulate an alternative stage sequence for the development of women's moral reasoning. These stages were derived from interviews with twenty-nine women who were considering having an abortion. In the first level that Gilligan described, the orientation is to individual survival in that the self is the sole object of concern. The following transitional level represents a movement from this self-centered orientation toward responsibility that entails an attachment to others. In the second level, goodness is seen as self-sacrificial caring for others in order to gain their acceptance. The second transitional level represents an attempt to be responsible to self as well as to others and is based on notions of honesty and fairness. In the third level, the orientation is to a morality of nonviolence, and caring is seen as a universal obligation. Unfortunately, the only data that have been presented as yet to support this proposed stage sequence have been anecdotal (Gilligan 1982a). None of the usual types of evidence for a stage sequence (i.e., longitudinal, cross-sectional, or experimental) has been reported. Nor has she provided an explanation as to why males and females may develop different orientations to moral judgment. Despite this lack of empirical support, her claim that the sexes follow different developmental pathways is, nevertheless, intended as a major challenge to the cognitive-developmental assumption of the universality of stage sequences (Gilligan 1982b).

If there is sex bias in Kohlberg's approach, how could it have arisen? A trite response is that, because Kohlberg is a man, he has taken a masculine point of view in theorizing about moral development. An equally trite rejoinder would be to point out that Kohlberg has had a number of female colleagues, including the senior author of the recent editions of the scoring manual (Colby et al. 1984). A second and much more serious possible source of bias is that the stage sequence has been constructed from the longitudinal data provided by an exclusively male sample (Colby et al. 1983). This lack of representativeness is a real threat to the generalizability of the model and could easily be a source of sex bias, but to date, no data have been presented to show that females do not follow Kohlberg's sequence of stages. Nonetheless, it is impossible to determine whether the same stages and sequence would have been derived if females had been studied originally. A third potential source of bias is the predominance of male protagonists in the moral dilemmas used as stimulus materials in eliciting reasoning. Females may have difficulty relating to these male protagonists and thus exhibit artifactually lower levels of moral reasoning. The effect of protagonists' sex on moral reasoning has been examined in a number of studies. Bussey and Maughan (1982) found more advanced reasoning with same-sex protagonists (for male subjects only). Freeman and Giebink (1979) also found more advanced reasoning with same-sex protagonists (for female subjects only). On the other hand, Orchowsky and Jenkins (1979) found more advanced reasoning with opposite-sex protagonists, and Garwood, Levine, and Ewing (1980) found no evidence of differential responding when protagonist sex was varied. Thus, the data are equivocal regarding this potential source of bias.

To summarize, it is possible that sex bias exists in Kohlberg's theory, in particular because of his reliance on a male sample, but this remains to be determined. This review was undertaken to examine the consistency of sex differences in moral reasoning.

Sex Differences in Moral Reasoning

This review of the literature covered all studies using Kohlberg's measure in which sex differences in development of moral reasoning were examined. A study was excluded (a) if only one sex was assessed; (b) if there was no report or analysis of sex differences; (c) if age and sex were confounded (e.g., comparing mothers and their sons); (d) if subjects were selected according to stage; (e) if the date had been reported previously in another study (e.g., Kuhn et al. 1977; Haan, Weiss & Johnson 1982 both reported data that had been previously reported by Haan, Langer & Kohlberg 1976); or (f) if some objective measure of moral reasoning (such as the Defining Issues Test [DIT]) was used instead of Kohlberg's interview measure. There were several reasons for excluding studies using the DIT and similar measures: it is not appropriate for children and early adolescents; it does not stage-type (instead it yields continuous indexes, the "P" or "D" scores); it relies on stage definitions that differ somewhat from Kohlberg's (cf. Kohlberg 1981; Rest 1979); and Rest (1979) has already provided a brief review of DIT research on sex differences. He found that DIT studies were fairly consistent in failing to reveal significance sex differences.

It is important to note that the exclusion from this review of studies that did not examine sex differences implies that the review probably overestimates the incidence of sex differences in research on moral development. It is reasonable to assume that most of the researchers who did not report a sex difference found the sexes to be similar. The fact that differences are more likely to be published exacerbates the problem and makes Type I error more likely (what Rosenthal 1979 labeled the "file-drawer problem").

Since the concerns regarding sex bias in Kohlberg's theory have focused primarily on the conventional and principled stages (e.g., Gilligan 1977), it is possible that sex differences would only become apparent in adulthood, when such moral reasoning is predominant. To clarify this issue, a developmental analysis of sex differences in moral reasoning seems appropriate. Therefore, the studies to be reviewed are presented in three tables that divide the life span into the somewhat arbitrary periods: (a) childhood and early adolescence, (b) late adolescence and youth, and (c) adulthood. A finding for each sample within a study is provided if there were separate analyses or a nonsignificant interaction between sample and sex. Unless otherwise noted, a nonsignificant finding indicates that both the main effect of sex and any interactions with sex were not significant; that includes studies involving repeated measures, which are designated "experimental design" or "longitudinal design," as appropriate. A number of researchers who did not analyze sex differences did present enough data (e.g., the number of males and females at each moral stage) to allow me to do such an analysis (typically conducting a Kolmogorov-Smirnov test for ordinal data; Siegel 1956), and that is noted.

Childhood and Early Adolescence. The results of research in which sex differences in moral reasoning in childhood and early adolescence were examined are summarized in table 11.1. There were thirty-one such studies, involving a total of 2,879 subjects who ranged in age from about five years to seventeen years. The pattern revealed is that sex differences in moral reasoning in childhood and early adolescence are infrequent; for the forty-one samples, only six significant differences were reported.

One of these differences (White 1975) cannot be taken at face value since the reported statistical analysis is actually not significant, contrary to the author's conclusion. This leaves five significant findings. Biaggio (1976) found that girls in her Brazilian sample of ten-, thirteen-, and sixteen-year-olds were more advanced in moral reasoning that the boys (MMS = 275 vs. 235). Blatt and Kohlberg (1975, Study 2) found pretest differences among

Table 11.1

Studies Examining Sex Differences in Moral Reasoning in Childhood and Early Adolescence

Study	Sample	Findings	Comment
Baumrind[a]	9 years ($N = 164$)	N.S.	finding based on data obtained from author and calculated by me via the Kolmogorov-Smirnov test; for a description of this study see Baumrind 1982
Bear & Richards 1981	11–13 years ($N = 60$)	N.S.	
Biaggio 1976	10 years ($N = 30$); 13 years ($N = 30$); 16 years ($N = 30$)	girls > boys	Brazilian sample
Bielby & Papalia 1975	10–14 years ($N = 12$)	N.S.	
Blatt & Kohlberg 1975 (Study 2)	11–12 years ($N = 66$) 15–16 years ($N = 66$)	apparently N.S. for younger group; girls > boys for the older group	experimental design; an age x sex interaction was found, but no analysis of the simple main effects was reported
Davidson 1976	7–13 years ($N = 176$)	N.S.	
Gibbs, Widaman & Colby 1982	4th grade ≃ 10 years ($N = 26$)	N.S.	
	5th grade ≃ 10 years ($N = 30$)	N.S.	
	7th grade ≃ 12 years ($N = 23$)	N.S.	
	7th grade ≃ 12 years ($N = 35$)	N.S.	
	9th grade ≃ 14 years ($N = 18$)	N.S.	
Gilligan, Langdale, Lyons & Murphy 1982	8 years ($N = 16$) 12 years ($N = 16$) 15 years ($N = 16$)	N.S. N.S. N.S.	
Haan 1978	13–17 years ($N = 56$)	N.S.	

Table 11.1
Continued

Study	Sample	Findings	Comment
Haan, Langer, & Kohlberg 1976	10–15 years ($N=42$)	N.S.	
Holstein 1976b	initially 13 years ($N=53$)	N.S.	3-year longitudinal design
Kavanagh 1977	14–15 years ($N=48$)	N.S.	experimental design
Keasey 1972	6th grade $\simeq$ 12 years	N.S.	
Krebs 1967	6th grade $\simeq$ 12 years ($N=123$)	N.S.	no analysis by author; finding based on data from his Table 3 and calculated by me via the Kolmogorov-Smirnov test
Krebs & Gillmore 1982	5–14 years ($N=51$)	girls > boys	
Kuhn 1972	K–2d grade $\simeq$ 5–7 years ($N=68$)	N.S.	
Leming 1978	7th grade $\simeq$ 13 years ($N=30$)	N.S.	
Parikh 1980	12–13 years ($N=20$); 15–16 years ($N=19$)	N.S.	Indian sample; age x sex interaction not examined
Saltzstein et al. 1972	7th grade $\simeq$ 13 years ($N=63$)	girls tended to be at stage 3, while boys tended to cluster at lower stages	
Selman 1971 (Study 1)	8–10 years ($N=10$)	N.S.	
Simon & Ward 1973	11–12 years ($N=60$)	N.S.	British sample
Sullivan et al. 1970	12 years ($N=40$) 14 years ($N=40$)	N.S. N.S.	

Table 11.1
Continued

Study	Sample	Findings	Comment
Taylor & Achenbach 1975	K–2d grade ≃ 5–7 years ($N=30$); retardates matched for MA ($N=30$)	N.S.	
Timm 1980	5th grade ≃ 11 years ($N=80$)	N.S.	
Turiel 1976	10–11 years ($N=63$) 12–14 years ($N=62$) 15–17 years ($N=85$)	girls > boys for the two younger groups; girls ≃ boys for the older group	an age x sex interaction was found, but no analysis of the simple main effects was reported
Walker 1980	9–13 years ($N=101$)	N.S.	experimental design; no relevant analysis by author; finding based on data of initial sample and calculated by me via the t test
Walker 1982	10–13 years ($N=50$)	N.S.	experimental design
Walker 1983a	10–12 years ($N=60$)	N.S.	experimental design
Walker, de Vries & Bichard 1984	13–14 years ($N=16$)	N.S.	
White 1975	7–8 years ($N=15$) 9–10 years ($N=42$) 11–12 years ($N=54$) 13–14 years ($N=23$)	N.S. N.S. N.S. claims boys > girls	Bahamian samples the validity of the analysis is suspect since the t value reported is actually n.s.
White, Bushnell, & Regnemer 1978	8–17 years ($N=426$)	N.S. (except for data previously reported by White 1975)	Bahamian samples; cross-sectional, longitudinal, and sequential designs

[a]D. Baumrind, personal communication, March 3, 1982.

their 15–16-year-olds that favored girls (316 vs. 275). Krebs and Gillmore (1982) found that the girls in their sample of 5–14-year-olds evidenced slightly more advanced moral reasoning than the boys. Turiel (1976) found differences favoring girls for 10–11-year-olds (268 vs. 254) and 12–14-year-olds (308 vs. 279). Finally, Saltzstein, Diamond, and Belenky (1972) found that girls tended to be classified at stage 3, whereas boys tended to be classified primarily at stages 1–2, but also at stages 4–5 (these stages were collapsed for analyses). It should be noted that one-third of this sample was classified at stages 4–5. Such high scoring for young subjects seems anomalous, especially according to current scoring procedures. (Revisions in scoring and stage definitions will be discussed in a later section).

To summarize, sex differences in moral reasoning apparently are rare early in the life span and, when they occur, indicate more mature development for females, although even these infrequent differences are relatively small.

Late Adolescence and Youth. The results of research in which sex differences in moral reasoning in late adolescence and youth were examined are summarized in table 11.2. There were thirty-five such studies, involving a total of 3,901 subjects who were mostly high-school and university students. As was found earlier in the life span, sex differences in moral reasoning in late adolescence and youth are infrequent: only ten of the forty-six samples yielded significant sex differences.

Three of these sex differences are of dubious relevance, as the researchers either failed to provide appropriate statistics to substantiate their claims (Alker & Poppen 1973; Fishkin, Keniston & MacKinnon 1973) or conducted highly questionable analyses. (Lockwood 1975 used incorrect error terms in his analysis of variance).

Two other researchers found that, although there were no overall sex differences, sex did interact with other variables. Arbuthnot (1975) found an interaction between sex and sex role identity that indicated that both women and men with nontraditional sex role identities had higher moral reasoning. Levine (1976) found that women used more Stage 3 reasoning than men did on the standard dilemmas involving fictitious characters, whereas there were no sex differences on modified dilemmas involving primary others (i.e., one's own mother or best friend).

Five additional findings indicating significant sex differences in late adolescence and youth remain to be discussed. Arbuthnot (1983) found that women in his university sample evidenced more advanced moral reasoning than men (by about one-third of a stage). Bar-Yam, Kohlberg, and Naame (1980) reported two significant differences in a study of Israeli high-school students. In both the Moslem-Arab and Youth-Aliyah samples, boys had higher levels of moral reasoning than girls (296 vs. 249, and 376 vs. 350, respectively). Both samples were drawn from ethnic groups where the status

Table 11.2
Studies Examining Sex Differences in Moral Reasoning in Late Adolescence and Youth

Study	Sample	Findings	Comments
Alker & Poppen 1973	undergraduates ($N=192$)	men were more likely to be at the preconventional or principled levels	no descriptive statistics and no statistical analyses provided
Arbuthnot 1975	undergraduates ($N=78$)	N.S. main effect of sex, but interaction with sex role identity	nontraditional sex role identities were associated with higher moral reasoning for both sexes
Arbuthnot 1983	undergraduates ($N=207$)	women > men	
Bar-Yam, Kohlberg & Naame 1980	kibbutz-born 15–17 years ($N=19$)	N.S.	Israeli samples
	Christian-Arab 15–17 years ($N=37$)	N.S.	
	Moslem-Arab 15–17 years ($N=25$)	boys > girls	
	Youth-Aliyah 15–17 years ($N=12$?)	boys > girls	Youth-Aliyah were disadvantaged immigrants who were sent to kibbutzim
Berkowitz, Gibbs & Broughton 1980	undergraduates ($N=82$)	N.S.	experimental design
Bielby & Papalia 1975	15–19 years ($N=12$) 20–34 years ($N=12$)	N.S. N.S.	
Bush & Balik 1977	undergraduates ($N=40$)	N.S.	experimental design
Bussey & Maughan 1982	undergraduates ($N=40$)	men > women, also interaction	Australian sample

Table 11.2
Continued

Study	Sample	Findings	Comments
		with sex of protagonists in dilemmas	
D'Augelli & Cross 1975	undergraduates ($N = 133$)	N.S.	no analysis by authors; finding based on data from their Table 4 and calculated by me via the Kolmogorov-Smirnov test
Edwards 1978	16–21 years ($N = 40$) undergraduates ($N = 52$)	N.S. N.S.	
Evans 1982	high-school students ($N = 81$)	N.S.	experimental design
Fishkin, Keniston & MacKinnon 1973	undergraduates ($N = 75$)	women tended to be stage 3; men tended to be stage 4	no descriptive statistics and no statistical analyses provided
Froming 1978	undergraduates ($N = 200$)	N.S.	
Gibbs, Arnold, Ahlborn & Cheesman 1984	14–18 years ($N = 60$)	N.S.	experimental design; sample composed of delinquents
Gibbs, Arnold & Buckhart 1984	11–21 years ($N = 177$)	N.S.	
Gibbs, Widaman & Colby 1982	14–17 years ($N = 165$) 10th grade $\simeq$ 16 years ($N = 34$) 10th and 11th grades $\simeq$ 15 years ($N = 23$) undergraduates $\simeq$ 19 years ($N = 51$) undergraduates $\simeq$ 19 years ($N = 38$)	N.S. N.S. N.S. N.S. N.S.	experimental design

Table 11.2
Continued

Study	Sample	Findings	Comments
Gilligan, Kohlberg, Lerner & Belenky 1971	high school 15–17 years ($N=50$)	N.S.?	boys and girls differed by only 11 MMS points, but no analysis was reported
Gilligan, Langdale, Lyons & Murphy 1982	19 years ($N=16$)	N.S.	
Haan 1975	undergraduates ($N=310$)	N.S.	
Haan, Langer & Kohlberg 1976	16–20 years ($N=78$)	N.S.	
Haan, Smith & Block 1968	university students and Peace Corps volunteers ($N=510$)	more women than men were at stage 3 (41% vs. 23%); no apparent differences at other stages	no analysis by authors; finding based on data from their Table 2 and calculated by me via the Kolmogorov-Smirnov test
Haan, Stroud & Holstein 1973	16–35 years ($N=58$)	N.S.	sample composed of "hippies"
Haier 1977	undergraduates ($N=112$)	N.S.?	men and women differed by only 7 MMS points, but no analysis was reported
Kahn 1982	12–19 years ($N=30$)	N.S.	Irish sample; finding based on analysis provided by Kahn[a]
Kavanagh 1977	17–18 years ($N=48$)	N.S.	experimental design
Leming 1978	11th grade ≃ 17 years ($N=30$)	N.S.	
Levine 1978	undergraduates ($N=300$)	N.S. main effect of sex, but	

Table 11.2
Continued

Study	Sample	Findings	Comments
		interaction with content of dilemma	
Lockwood 1975	8th grade ≃ 14 years (N = 30); 11th grade ≃ 17 years (N = 28)	claims boys > girls	the validity of analysis is suspect since incorrect error terms were used (see his Table 3)
Maqsud 1980a	16–19 years (N = 57) 17–19 years (N = 56)	N.S. N.S.	Nigerian samples
Maqsud 1980b	14–17 years (N = 97)	N.S.	Nigerian samples
Murphy & Gilligan 1980	initially undergraduates (N = 26)	N.S.	longitudinal design
Simon & Ward 1973	14–16 years (N = 60)	N.S.	British sample
Small 1974	undergraduates (N = 48)	N.S.	experimental design
Sullivan et al. 1970	17 years (N = 40)	N.S.	
Walker, de Vries & Bichard 1984	15–17 years (N = 16)	N.S.	
	undergraduates 17–24 years (N = 16)	N.S.	

[a]J. Kahn, personal communication, November 22, 1982.

of women had traditionally been low, with few opportunities for decision-making within the family and society and with typically low levels of education. It is interesting to note that no differences were found in the kibbutz and Christian samples, in which attitudes could be expected to be more egalitarian.

Bussey and Maughan (1982) found that men in their university sample evidenced more advanced moral reasoning than women. My analysis of data presented by Haan, Smith, and Block (1968) for their study of university students indicated that women were overrepresented at stage 3. This study may involve some mis-scoring of stage of moral development (a possibility that Haan 1971 has noted). There are two bases for this suggestion. First, subjects responded to the dilemmas in questionnaire format rather than the recommended interview format (Colby et al. 1984), which would result in more ambiguous responses and hence less reliable scoring. Second, moral stage definitions have been significantly altered since that study was conducted, in part because of the anomalous scoring of many subjects in their university sample as being preconventional.

To summarize, sex differences in moral reasoning in late adolescence and youth are rare, as was the case earlier in development. In contrast to the data from childhood and early adolescence, however, most studies in which sex differences were obtained indicate more mature development for males, although the differences, once again, were small (i.e., less than half a stage).

Adulthood. The results of research in which sex differences in moral reasoning in adulthood were examined are summarized in table 11.3. There were thirteen such studies, involving a total of 1,223 subjects who ranged in age from twenty-one years to over sixty-five years. Sex differences in moral reasoning in adulthood are slightly more frequent than earlier in the life span; or, alternatively, sex differences are more frequent in this generation than in later generations. (It is impossible to separate developmental and cohort differences with these data.) For the twenty-one samples considered, four significant differences were reported, all favoring men.

Unlike previously discussed studies that involved rather homogeneous samples of school and university students, in the studies of adults that revealed differences in moral reasoning, sex was often confounded with educational and/or occupational differences. Haan et al. (1976) found that men scored higher than women in both their 21–30-year-old sample and their 47–50-year-old sample (parents of the younger group). According to Haan (1977), the older women in this study were mostly housewives. The occupational status of the younger women was not described.

In the two remaining studies that revealed differences, sex was similarly confounded with occupational differences. Holstein (1976b) found differences favoring men (409 vs. 366) on her first test but not on the retest. Nearly all the men in her sample had careers in business, management, or the professions, whereas only 6 percent of the women were employed. Similarly, Parikh (1980) found that men in her Indian sample scored higher than women (326 vs. 280). The men were all self-employed professionals, whereas most of the women were housewives. All of the remaining studies summarized in table 11.3 seem to have entailed more homogeneous samples and have not yielded significant sex differences. The Weisbroth (1970) study, for example, involved doctoral students and professional or semiprofessional employees in universities or teaching hospitals and revealed no differences. The men and women in the Buck, Walsh, and Rothman (1981) study, Gilligan, Langdale, Lyons, and Murphy (1982) study, and Walker (1983b)

Table 11.3
Studies Examining Sex Differences in Moral Reasoning in Adulthood

Study	Sample	Findings	Comments
Baumrind[a]	parents of 9-year-olds, ages not provided ($N = 284$)	N.S.	finding based on data obtained from author and calculated by me via the Kolmogorov-Smirnov test; for a description of this study, see Baumrind 1982; sample composed of married couples
Bielby & Papalia 1975	35–49 years ($N = 12$)	N.S.	
	50–64 years ($N = 12$)	N.S.	
	65 + years ($N = 12$)	N.S.	
Buck et al. 1981	parents of pre-adolescents, ages not provided ($N = 60$)	N.S.	sample composed of married couples; no analysis by authors; finding based on data from their Table 1 and calculated by me via the Kolomgorov-Smirnov test
Gibbs, Widaman & Colby 1982	mostly parents of undergraduates, mean age was 38 years ($N = 30$)	N.S.	
Gilligan, Langdale, Lyons & Murphy 1982[b]	22 years ($N = 16$)	N.S.	
	27 years ($N = 16$)	N.S.	
	36 years ($N = 16$)	N.S.	
	46 years ($N = 16$)	N.S.	
Haan 1974	Peace Corps volunteers, initially mean age was 23 ($N = 70$)	N.S. for both 1st and 2d test	longitudinal design; no analysis by author; finding based on data from their Table 4 and calculated by me via the Kilmogorov-Smirnov test

Table 11.3
Continued

Study	Sample	Findings	Comments
Haan, Langer & Kohlberg 1976	21–30 years ($N=83$) 47–50 years ($N=179$)	men > women men > women	Sample composed of married couples
Holstein 1976b	initially mean age was early 40s ($N=106$)	men > women on 1st test; N.S. on 2d test	3-year longitudinal design; sample composed of married couples
Nassi 1981	former Free Speech Movement arrestees ($N=26$) former student government leaders ($N=28$) random sample of former students ($N=23$)	N.S. N.S. N.S.	no direct analysis by author; finding based on data from her Table 2 and calculated by me via Fisher's test for each sample of subjects; average age of all three samples is 34 years
Parikh 1980	parents of teenagers, ages not provided ($N = 78$)	men > women	Indian sample; sample composed of married couples
Walker 1983a	23–84 years ($N=62$)	N.S.	sample composed of university employees
Walker, de Vries, Bichard 1984	graduate students 21–52 years ($N=16$)	N.S.	
Weisbroth 1970	21–39 years ($N=76$)	N.S.	

[a]It should be noted that, although my analysis revealed no significant difference between men and women, Baumrind (1982) did report a difference favoring men. Her finding was not included in this table because it was based on a subsample of the data provided by Baumrind (personal communication, March 3, 1982).

[b]Although Gilligan, Langdale, Lyons & Murphy (1982) found no differences in their analysis of MMSs, they did report a subsidiary analysis that indicated that more men than women displayed at least one instance of conventional reasoning. However, the relevant data as presented in their figure 2 indicates the opposite pattern. Thus, the appropriate interpretation of this analysis remains unclear.

study were comparable in education and occupational levels, and no differences in moral reasoning were found. Several other studies (Bielby & Papalia 1975; Buck et al. 1981; Haan et al. 1968; Holstein 1972; Keasey 1971; Parikh 1980) have provided direct evidence regarding the relation between moral development and a variety of social experiences (e.g., family discussions, education, occupation, political and social activity).

A widely-shared assumption (initially stated by Kohlberg & Kramer 1969) is that women fixate at stage 3, whereas men progress to stage 4, or, as alleged by Gilligan (1982a, 70), "the thinking of women is often classified with that of children." Even among the studies that yielded some evidence of sex differences, there is no evidence, in adulthood, for such a claim. The modal stage for both men and women in the Holstein (1976b) study and Haan et al. (1976) study (as reported by Haan et al. 1982 for a large subsample of their 47–50-year-old subjects) was stage 4, and the modal stage for both sexes in the Parikh (1980) study was stage 3. Thus, although sex differences may be reported in some studies, they tend not to be of the magnitude that has been suggested.

To summarize, it is apparent that sex differences in moral reasoning in adulthood are revealed only in a minority of studies, and even in those studies the differences tend to be small.

Meta-Analysis

The conclusion indicated by this review is that the moral reasoning of males and females is more similar than different. However, this traditional method of literature review has been criticized as being susceptible to biases and ignoring valuable information available in research reports. Meta-analytic procedures that enable reviewers to combine statistically the results of a series of studies are viewed as a more powerful and objective method than summary impression (Cooper & Rosenthal 1980), and therefore were used as an adjunct to the traditional review described above.

Rosenthal (1978) has provided a comprehensive discussion of meta-analytic procedures, which need not be duplicated here. One of the more powerful, yet simple and routinely applicable, methods is the Stouffer method. Briefly, the steps in this method are (a) compute the exact one-tailed p of the test statistic reported; (b) compute the Z score (the standard normal deviate) associated with each p value; (c) sum these Z scores and divide by the square root of the number of findings being combined; and (d) compute the appropriate p value for this overall Z score, which indicates the probability level for the observed pattern of findings. Step (a) requires that a test statistic with degrees of freedom be provided. However, since sex differences were often of secondary interest to researchers, many failed to report the statistics on which they made inferences of no differences or reported statistics without indicating direction. The solution adopted for this review, but one that may increase distortion, was to assume an exact finding of no difference and use $p = .50$.

This meta-analysis of the studies reported earlier in this paper tested the hypothesis that males are more advanced than females in moral reasoning development, and, although the trend was in the predicted direction, this pattern was not significant, $Z = +.73$, $p = .23$, one-tailed. Even this finding probably overestimates the incidence of sex differences, given the reporting and publishing biases discussed earlier. Thus, the conclusion yielded by the meta-analysis is consistent with that of the traditional review.

It is also important to note that Kohlberg has introduced both conceptual and procedural revisions to his theory in an attempt to account more adequately for his longitudinal data (Colby et al. 1983). The preconventional stages have undergone little revision, but the more advanced conventional and principled stages—the level of moral reasoning common to adulthood—have been significantly redefined. The extent of these changes is reflected in the low correlation (.39) between the scores yielded by the original and current scoring manuals (Carroll & Rest 1982). Revisions in scoring procedures (Colby 1978; Kohlberg 1976) have been twofold: (1) in the definition of the unit of analysis, and (2) in better differentiation of content from structure. Colby (1978) claimed that these revisions should eliminate the tendency to underestimate the reasoning of females because of particular content (e.g., focus on relationships, love, and caring).

Earlier studies, in particular, may have involved considerable mis-scoring (as previously argued for the Haan et al. 1968, and Saltzstein et al. 1972 studies) that may account for some of the reported sex diferences. Thus, it is interesting to note that all but two (Arbuthnot 1983; Bussey & Maughan 1982) of the research teams that found significant sex differences used early versions of Kohlberg's scoring manual: the 1958 version (Turiel 1976), the 1963 version (Saltzstein et al. 1972), the 1968 version (Haan et al. 1976),the 1971 version (Bar-Yam et al. 1980; Biaggio 1976), and the 1972 version (Blatt & Kohlberg 1975; Holstein 1976b; Parikh 1980). The version used by Haan et al. (1968) was not reported. It is unlikely that this pattern is coincidental, but fortunately there is more direct evidence regarding the effects of changes in scoring. Holstein (1976b) rescored data previously presented in a preliminary report (Holstein 1972). The modal stage for men according to both scoring methods was stage 4, but the modal stage for women changed from stage 3 with the older scoring method to stage 4 with the new scoring method. Thus, some of the reported sex differences in early studies may, in fact, represent measurement artifacts.

Conclusions

The allegation that Kohlberg's theory is biased against the moral reasoning of women has become more vehement and more frequently expressed. The primary basis for this claim is that Kohlberg relied solely on the data from his longitudinal sample of males to derive and validate his description of moral development. This review and meta-analysis of the research literature indicates that, contrary to the prevailing stereotype, very few sex differences in moral development have been found. Of the 108 samples summarized in tables 11.1–11.3, only eight clearly indicated significant differences favoring males. Furthermore, several of these studies yielding sex differences favoring men were methodologically flawed, primarily because sex and occupational/educational differences were confounded. In addition, most studies reporting sex differences relied on early stage definitions and scoring procedures.

Support for the null hypothesis (i.e., that there are no sex differences in stage of moral reasoning), such as has been amassed here, is usually not of any particular significance; but given the persistent belief that there are sex differences, this review may provide a heuristic perspective on a different issue. At the same time it is important to realize, as Kohlberg (1982) has noted, that the lack of stage disparity in moral reasoning between males and females does not preclude the possibility of sex differences in content within a stage (e.g., reliance on particular norms) or in the preferential use of various orientations in the making of moral judgments.

Rather than arguing over the extent to which sex bias is inherent in Kohlberg's theory of moral development, it might be more appropriate to ask why the myth that males are more advanced in moral reasoning than females persists in light of so little evidence. This review of the literature should make it clear that the moral reasoning of men and women is remarkably similar, especially given publication and reporting biases that make differences more likely to be reported. Perhaps it is time to focus our attention on other concerns, such as the questions of the role of cognitive prerequisites and sociomoral experiences in facilitating moral development and of the relationship of moral reasoning to moral emotions and behaviors.

12

Sex Differences in Moral Reasoning: Response to Walker's (1984) Conclusion that There Are None

Diana Baumrind

In a recent review of some fifty studies, Walker (1984, reprinted as pre-ceeding essay in this volume) concluded that there are no consistent sex dif-ferences or biases in Kohlberg's theory or measure of moral development. However, I will attempt to show that certain of the decisions Walker made were not well suited to the theory he was testing and resulted in a bias favor-ing findings of no sex differences. Therefore, research findings included in his review do not warrant the conclusion that there are no sex differences but suggest instead that the source and specific nature of these differences have yet to be established.

Understanding these differences is important because sex bias may be but one manifestation of a more pervasive cultural bias resulting from Kohl-berg's restriction of the meaning of morality to universal cognitive judg-ments about justice as fairness. The presence of sexual or cultural bias in his definition of morality would limit the scope of Kohlberg's theory and rec-ommend against universal adoption of his restrictive definition of morality, especially when applied to females, or citizens of second- and third-world countries.

This article includes three parts. In the first I demonstrate some of the shortcomings with Walker's (1984) analyses. In the second, I present addi-tional analyses of data from the Family Socialization Project (FSP). In the third, I relate Walker's analyses and the FSP data to more general issues concerning moral development.

Shortcomings of Walker's Analyses

In his review and meta-analysis, Walker includes data on three age periods: childhood, youth, and adulthood. Only the data on adulthood, however, are relevant to the controversy on sex differences, since the allegation of bias arises from the presences of sex differences in the attainment of the highest level of moral reasoning and not in differential rate of development. The differences favoring girls throughout childhood and early adolescence are easily explained by their accelerated general development. However, the finding of sex differences favoring adult men in so highly valued a personal attribute as moral maturity would be of great social concern. Fortunately for Kohlberg's theory, Walker concluded that only four of the twenty-one adult samples he considered showed significant sex differences (all favoring men). Unfortunately, Walker's analysis was flawed.

Walker included in the studies that did *not* show sex differences data on nine-year-old children and their parents from the FSP (Baumrind 1982). However, I reported a sex difference favoring fathers over mothers with the same data from the FSP. The purpose of the FSP study in which sex differences were reported was to determine whether the Bem Sex Role Inventory gender classification had predictive power over and above knowledge of biological sex on twenty child-rearing and personal measures. Among the significant effects of biological sex was that on Kohlberg stage scores. Hierarchical analyses of variance were used to test the effect on all dependent measures. However, Kohlberg stage scores, unlike the other nineteen dependent measures in that study, are discrete values intended to assess discontinuous theoretical entities. Therefore, the use of analysis of variance, while expedient in order to treat all twenty dependent measures similarly, was not appropriate.

Moral Development Is a Discontinuous Variable

Kohlberg, following Piaget, regards stages not as a measurement device but rather as the true nature of moral development. Therefore, it is not theoretically meaningful to treat stage scores as continuous in testing the hypothesis of sex differences. The Kolmogorov-Smirnov test used by Walker to test sex differences in moral reasoning on some of the largest samples in his review (including the FSP sample) assumes a continuous distribution and is inappropriate for the same reason as the use of analysis of variance in the Baumrind study. Because stages are discrete, and different stages or levels have different meanings, it is more appropriate to examine differences in frequency of men and women within a stage or stages than to compare the differences between mean stage scores of men and women. That is, the assumption of a continuous distribution leads to the question, "Is there a sex difference in level of moral reasoning?" rather than to the more specific and theoretically cogent question, "Is there a sex difference at a given stage in moral reasoning?" Thus one might argue that, as a consequence of women's focus on issues of caring, they would be overrepresented at stage 3 and underrepresented at the postconventional formal level of reasoning in the Kohlberg system. Practically, a general search for sex differences across stages may lead to the conclusion of no sex differences or only minimal sex differences, when in fact the possibility remains that a significant sex difference does exist at a particular stage or level but not across all stages or levels.

Proneness to Type II Errors

Walker has attempted to amass support for the null hypothesis, to argue that there are no sex differences in Kohlberg's stage system scoring. Apart from the logical impossibility of proving the null hypothesis, the method of analysis selected by Walker biased his results in favor of the null hypothesis he favored in three ways.

First, in reanalyzing other investigators' data (including data from the FSP), Walker chose to use the Kolmogorov-Smirnov test. That test, used under the conditions that Walker used it, is excessively prone to Type II errors, that is, it will fail to detect a (sex) difference when such a difference exists. The Kolmogorov-Smirnov test assumes a continuous distribution, which cannot contain ties (identical scores). But a stage theory contains six prototypic scores, of which only five are typically used, and requires by theory the presence of ties. The Kolmogorov-Smirnov test becomes increasingly conservative as the number of ties increases, and Walker introduced no correction for ties (personal communication to Steven Pulos, 27 November 1984).

Second, sex differences favoring males are found more frequently in the adult studies. However, Walker combined all studies cited in his first three tables into a single meta-analysis, even though only the adult data in his table 11.3 are crucial to the issue of whether sex differences in level of moral development exist, and the adult data comprise only 16 percent of the studies cited in his meta-analysis. In so doing, he increased the probability of failing to find sex differences favoring males.

Third, Walker did not take into account differences in sample size among the studies cited. With increasing sample size the power of the Kolmogorov-Smirnov test increases less rapidly relative to that of the t test or the Mann-Whitney test (Siegel 1956), making it more subject to Type II errors with sample sizes greater than thirty. All studies with a sample size of thirty or less failed to find significant sex differences, whereas four of the eleven studies with a sample size greater than thirty found significant differences. Another four of the eleven large sample studies were examined with the

Kolmogorov-Smirnov test, which is inappropriately conservative for the reasons just cited. One of these (FSP), as we will show, does reveal sex differences favoring males at the highest educational level.

Discounting Studies in Which the 1983 Manual Was Not Used

Walker argued that studies that do show sex differences can be discounted if they did not use the new conventions established by the 1983 scoring manual. FSP protocols were scored by the conventions established by the 1971 manual. However, FSP findings cannot be discounted on that account unless all studies using earlier manuals are discounted on the basis that the new manual represents Kohlberg's theory, and prior manuals do not. But the new scoring manual has already been criticized for questionable construct validity and ambiguously defined scoring standards (Cortese 1984).

Of particular concern is the absence of an empirical terminal stage. According to Walker (1984, 678), Kohlberg dropped stage 6 because it was absent from his longitudinal sample. Although stage 6 reasoning has been dropped from the scoring manual, it is evident from the numerous references to stage 6 in Kohlberg's newest collection of essays on moral development that it has not been dropped as *the* pivotal metaphysical ideal in the Kohlberg system (e.g., Kohlberg & Elfenbein 1981). In a structural theory of moral development such as Kohlberg's, the entire stage sequence, and each stage within the sequence, is teleologically determined by the ideal terminal stage. Kohlberg's stage 6 embodies Rawls' (1971) model of justice. According to Kohlberg, it was selected to assure a "hard" structural theory of stages that could "characterize the domain of justice in interpersonal interactions, just as notions of equilibration and reversibility characterize the domain of logico-mathematical and physical reasoning" (Kohlberg, Levine & Hewer 1983, 62). This terminal or ideal stage anchors Kohlberg's claim to having achieved rational consensus on the content of the right in conflicts about justice, "analogous to norms of scientific rationality in the philosophy of science" (Kohlberg et al. 1983, 62). The absence of an *empirically* defined ideal stage compromises the construct validity of the five preceding stages. By eliminating stage 6 as an empirical entity, Kohlberg has decapitated the corpus of his theory rather than merely doffed its empirical hat from its metaethical head.

It is indeed a matter of some concern that the correlation is only ".39 between the scores yielded by the original and current scoring manuals" (Walker 1984, 687–88). This correlation between two operational definitions of the "same" theory is strikingly low, resulting in less than 16 percent of shared variance between the scores obtained using the original and the current manuals. However, impartiality requires that if, on the basis of this low relation, one rejects any, one rejects *all* findings using the pre-1983 scoring manual, including, of course, the findings that there is no sex differences in level of moral judgment.

At this point in time, it is difficult to know what to make of the conceptual and procedural revisions that have recently been offered by Kohlberg and his colleagues (Colby, Kohlberg, Gibbs & Lieberman 1983; Kohlberg 1981, 1984; Kohlberg et al. 1983) to the stage theory of moral development. The 1983 scoring manual is different from the previous ones; it is not yet clear that it is better.

Discounting Studies Because the Significance of Sex Differences Is Nullified by Controlling for Education

Walker's second major challenge to the studies that showed sex differences favoring adult males is that these differences were confounded with social status. But if (a) stage score level and educational level are systematically interdependent in the real world, and (b) both are determined by social status, then eliminating sex differences by statistically controlling for educational level obscures rather than clarifies the challenge to Kohlberg's theory presented by the dependence in the real world of Kohlberg's stage score level on sex and social status.

Neither Walker nor Kohlberg have acknowledged that the highly significant relationship between Kohlberg's sociomoral level and social status variables (including education) in the general population represents a serious challenge to a theory of moral development. According to Walker, Kohlberg explains the relationship by saying that postconventional reasoning requires, in addition to a certain level of cognitive development, exposure to appropriate sociomoral experiences. Walker indicates that "These experiences arise both through interpersonal relationships with family and friends and through real participation in the economic, political and legal institutions of society" (1984, 678). However, neither Kohlberg nor Walker state the nature or the magnitude of the expected relationship between these two quite different kinds of qualifying experiences and Kohlberg stage score level, or whether one kind can substitute entirely for the other kind. Does the theory suggest a linear relationship between variables such as years of education or social status and stage score level, or is there instead a necessary threshold for each stage? If (as seems more consonant with the theory) the latter, what threshold is posited for each stage?

Of particular interest is the relationship between amount and quality of education and postconventional and, specifically, stage 6 reasoning. Kohlberg constructed his "theoretical definition of a sixth stage from the writings of a small elite sample; elite in the sense of its formal philosophic training and in the sense of its ability for and commitment to moral leadership" (Kohlberg et al. 1983, 60). It was also a male sample. Kohlberg observes that postconventional reasoning almost never occurs in preindustrial societies "because of their relatively simple degree of social-structural complexity and because their populations have little or no formal education" (Kohlberg et al. 1983, 133). However, Kohlberg does not specify what level of complexity and amount of formal education suffice to permit truly moral (i.e., stage 5 or stage 6) reasoning to germinate. Similarly, although the relationship between education and stage score level is known to be highly significant for men, less is known about the relationship for women. Further, it is not known whether the sex difference in stage score level favoring men exists uniformly at all educational levels. Although the data from the Family Socialization Project cannot address these questions for the population at large, they can do so for a socially and educationally advantaged group of mature, married couples. This sample is ideal for examining the interrelationships among sex, professional status, and postconventional reasoning, because it is skewed in the direction of higher educational and therefore higher Kohlberg stage score levels. Stage 6 reasoning typifies 21 of the 303 adults in the FSP sample.

Reanalysis of Data from the FSP

The reanalysis of the FSP data presented in this article takes the stage theory seriously by employing statistical techniques that treat the stages as discrete. These data will be used to probe Walker's conclusion that there are no sex differences in adult moral judgment level using Kohlberg's scale.

Method

Subjects. Subjects in the Family Socialization Project are middle-class, well-educated Caucasian individuals residing in the San Francisco Bay area, and consist of 164 nine-year-old children (78 girls, 86 boys) and most of their parents (158 mothers, 145 fathers), whose median ages were thirty-eight (mothers) and forty-one (fathers).

Data. As part of the second wave of data collection in a longitudinal study of the impact of family socialization practices on the social competence of children and adolescents, four Kohlberg dilemmas were administered to parents in interview form. The interviews consisted of four Kohlberg stories (Joe and his father, Son tells a lie, Heinz and the druggist, Wife wants euthanasia).

The interviews were scored by one rater using Kohlberg's 1971 scoring manual. Prior to scoring the rest of the protocols, the rater achieved 90 percent agreement in major score or major/minor reversal score with Constance Holstein (Holstein was trained by Kohlberg, e.g., Holstein 1976a) on twenty cases, ten training material cases and ten actual protocols. Following the conventions established by the 1971 manual, the transcribed interview is unitized and the central issue in each unit is identified. A single stage score is assigned to each unitized issue. "Global issue scores" representing modal characteristics of the subject's reasoning on a given issue across a range of questions or stories are then determined for each story and across all stories. A single "major" stage score is assigned if 50 percent or more of the global issue scores reflect this stage. A "minor" stage score is assigned if less than 25 percent but greater than 50 percent of the global issue weighted scores reflect a stage. The *Typical* moral stage score is the major stage score for the entire protocol. The *Maximum* moral stage score is the highest major or minor stage score obtained at least twice by the respondent for any of the four individual stories. A *Typical/Maximum* score was constructed to include information from both the Typical and Maximum scores in order to have a finer-grained classification of subjects and to avoid problems inherent in data with the restricted range of the Typical and Maximum scores. The Typical/Maximum score is the Typical moral stage score with sublevels corresponding to the Maximum score. For example, persons with a Typical score of 4 and a Maximum of 6 were assigned a score of 4,6; and persons with a Typical score of 4 and a Maximum score of 5 were assigned a score of 4,5. This scale is, of course, only ordinal.

The Typical and Maximum scores are used only when the frequency distribution of subjects is examined. When the relationship between moral reasoning and another variable, for example, education, is examined, then the Typical/Maximum score is used. If the analysis reported for the Typical/Maximum is conducted with the Typical score, the same results are found, but to a lesser degree, due to the greater sensitivity of the Typical/Maximum score. In all but one case the results are significant ($p < .05$) for both the Typical/Maximum score and the Typical score. The one exception is the Mann-Whitney comparison within educational levels 1 + 2 (table 12.3), where the z for the Typical score is 1.89, $p = .059$.

A variation of the Hollingshead and Redlich (1958) education scale, described in table 12.3, was used because it differentiates at the higher educational levels which are overrepresented in the FSP sample.

Results

Results to be presented demonstrate: (a) the presence of sex differences across stage score levels only when education is not controlled, (b) the presence of sex differences favoring men only at the postconventional level, and finally (c) the presence of sex-differentiated effects of educational level and employment status on stage score level.

Sex differences across stage score levels. If, in order to probe Walker's conclusions, equal interval levels and a continuous distribution for the scale are assumed, an analysis of variance for adults reveals significant effects favoring men, $F(1,302) = 5.42$, $p < .02$. With analysis of covariance, in which the amount of education is the covariate, the effect of sex is no longer significant. However, such an analysis is based on the assumption that the relation between education and moral development scores is the same for men and women. Later in this section I show that this assumption is unwarranted for the FSP data.

I have argued that statistics such as analysis of variance or t test are inappropriate because the construct of moral reasoning is theoretically discontinuous and the intervals between stages cannot be assumed to be equal. Therefore, for all the analyses that follow, ordinal and nominal level nonparametric statistics were selected.

Using the Mann-Whitney test, there was a significant difference favoring males ($z = 2.80$, $p < .01$). Thus, when education is not controlled, significant sex differences are found using ANOVA or the Mann-Whitney test, whereas none were found by Walker (1984) using the Kolmogorov-Smirnov test.

Sex differences within stage score levels. I have argued further that the most theoretically cogent analyses are conducted within rather than across stage score levels. Gilligan (1982a) has suggested that, characteristically, women are concerned with welfare, caring, and responsibility more than they are with abstract, universalistic justice. Accordingly, within the Kohlberg system, more adult women than men should be represented at the conventional level (stages 3 and 4, but particularly at stage 3) and fewer should be represented at the higher, postconventional levels (stages 5 and 6, but particularly at stage 6).

This hypothesis was examined using prediction analysis (Froman & Hubert 1980; Hildebrand, Laing & Rosenthal 1977) in which the adequacy of a model is assessed by determining the error cells in a contingency table— those cells that represent types of subjects that should not occur according to the theory—and then computing values of K (the proportion of subjects *observed* in all of the error cells) and U (the proportion of subjects *expected* in the error cells, given the marginal frequencies). An overall measure of a model's prediction success is given by $V = 1-K/U$. V can be directly interpreted as the proportionate reduction of errors that is achieved by the theoretical predications over the hypothesis of statistical independence. A test of statistical significance on V can be performed to investigate whether the error reduction is significantly greater than zero or greater than the reduction occurring in another model. The results (table 12.1) do not support the hypothesis (Kohlberg & Kramer 1969) that women "fixate" at stage 3. However, more women were found at stage 4, the other conventional stage, as measured by both the Typical and the Maximum scores. The prediction of

Table 12.1
Result of the Prediction Analysis with Number of Males and Females at Each Kohlberg Stage Score Level

Stage	Females	Males	V
Typical moral reasoning:			
2	11	4	———[a]
3	14	14	0
4	52	33	.19*
5	72	82	.10*
6	9	12	.18
N	158	145	———
Maximum moral reasoning:			
3	4	3	0
4	36	19	.28*
5	92	83	0
6	26	40	.25*
N	158	145	———

[a]No prediction concerning sex difference was made for preconventional stages, hence no analysis was conducted.
*$p < .05$.

fewer women at postconventional stages was supported at stage 5 for the Typical score and at stage 6 for the Maximum score.

Sex differences in the effect on stage score level of educational level and employment status. Based on data obtained primarily from men, Kohlberg and his colleagues have assumed that education and employment status are equally important determinants of stage score level for women. For example, Walker offers the nonemployed status of women as an explanation for their lower level of reasoning in Haan et al.'s sample (Hann, Langer & Kohlberg 1976). If he were correct, the moral level of employed women should be higher than that of nonemployed women. In fact, the fifty-nine FSP women who were not employed did not differ significantly in stage score level from their employed peers (Mann-Whitney, $z = .58, p = .56$). Further, the correlation between stage score level and educational level was significant for men (tau $= .19, p < .01$) but not for women (tau $= .05$). Thus, for women, in contrast to men (in this highly educated sample), neither educational level nor employment per se are important determinants of level of moral judgment.

Similarly, the impact of postgraduate education on stage 6 reasoning differs by sex. For males, but not for females, postgraduate education appears to be a necessary (although not sufficient) condition for stage 6 reasoning; of the twelve males at stage 6, eleven had at least a Master's degree, whereas this was true of only one of the nine stage 6 women, $x^2(1,N = 21) = 10.54$, $p < .001$.

Sex differences in stage score level within educational level. The educational level in men is much higher than that of women in the well-educated FSP sample (Mann-Whitney, $z = 8.33$, p $< .001$) as well as in the general population. As can be seen in table 12.2, the sex difference favoring men in educational level is significant for every stage represented, except for stage 2.

The final analysis was designed to ascertain if the higher stage score level of men exists at all educational levels, or instead exists only at the higher educational levels where men predominate. Mann-Whitney tests for sex differences in stage score within levels of education were calculated. For this analysis, educational levels 1 and 2 were combined, as were educational levels 6 and 7, to increase the number of women at the highest (MA and above) and men at the lowest (two years or less of college) levels of education: at the high end, only three women were assigned to level 1, whereas fifty-four men were; all ten parents at level 7 were women. It can be seen in table 12.3 that the direction of significant sex differences in moral reasoning is reversed at the lowest and highest educational levels: at the highest educational level (1 and 2), men obtain a higher moral level than women, as expected; but at

Table 12.2

Sex Differences in Education Level by Kohlberg Stage Score Levels[a]

Kohlberg Stage	Females			Males			Mann-Whitney Z
	Mdn	Q	N	Mdn	Q	N	
2	4	3–4	11	2	1–3	5	1.53
3	3	2–4	14	2	1–3	14	1.98*
4	4	3–5	52	3	2–3	33	3.11**
5	3	2–5	72	2	1–3	81	6.20***
6	3	3–4	9	2	1–2	12	2.87**

[a]Medians (Mdn) and Interquartile Ranges (Q) are based on the interval that contains the 50th, 25th, and 75th percentiles, respectively. Owing to the assumed ordinal nature of the construct, the interpolation method was not employed. One father at stage 5 had a missing response on the education variable and is therefore not included in this analysis.

*$p < .05$.

**$p < .01$.

***$p < .001$.

Table 12.3
Sex Differences in Typical/Maximum Stage by Level of Education[a]

Education Level[b]	Females			Males			Mann-Whitney
	Mdn	Q	N	Mdn	Q	N	Z
1 + 2	5,5	4,5–5,5	41	5,5	4,6–5,6	92	2.10*
3	5,5	4,4–5,5	38	5,5	4,5–5,5	27	.35
4	4,4	3,4–5,5	36	5,5	4,4–5,5	15	1.85
5	5,5	4,4–5,5	15	5,5	5,5–5,5	4	.85
6 + 7	5,5	4,4–5,5	28	4,4	4,4–4,4	6	2.88**

[a]Medians (Mdn) and Interquartile Ranges (Q) are based on the interval that contains the 50th, 25th, and 75th percentiles, respectively. Due to the assumed ordinal nature of the construct, the interpolation method was not employed.
[b]Education Levels: 1 = Ph.D., M.D., or J.D.; 2 = M.A.; 3 = B.A.+; 4 = B.A.; 5 = 3 years college; 6 = A.A. or 2 years college; 7 = 1 or fewer years of college.
*$p < .05$.
**$p < .01$.

the lowest educational level (6 and 7), women obtain a higher moral level than men.

Discussion

In this sample of well-educated husbands and wives, sex differences in Kohlberg stage score levels are found when either analysis of variance or more appropriate ordinal or nominal level nonparametric statistics are used. When educational level is not controlled, more women are found at stage 4 and more men at the postconventional level. Educational level and employment status are significantly related to men's but not to women's stage score level. As indicated above, for men, but not for women, postgraduate education appears to be a necessary (although not sufficient) condition for stage 6 reasoning to occur. In this sample, the difference favoring males is found only at the higher educational levels, where men predominate. When men and women with two years or less of college are compared, the stage score level of women is higher. These data demonstrate that the presence and direction of the sex difference in stage score level depend on the educational level of the population studied.

In the remainder of this article, I discuss two issues: (1) the presence or absence of sex differences as a function of educational level of the sample studied, and (2) the cultural bias in Kohlberg's theory and constructs (in contradistinction to his measure).

188 / Diana Baumrind

The Relationship of Educational Level to Sex and Stage Score Level

The presence of sex differences in stage score level depends on the educational level of the population studied. The inconsistency of sex differences across the studies reviewed by Walker may be explained by variations in educational level among the samples studied. If men and women are equated for education level and the educational range is midlevel, no sex difference in Kohlberg stage score is likely to be found. At the educational extremes, sex differences emerge, but in opposite directions.

The finding that, among individuals with a high school education but with two years of college or less, women score at a higher level than men, and indeed higher than other women with more education, has not (to my knowledge) been noted before. The reason for the finding may simply be that the high level of intelligence associated with postconventional reasoning guarantees more men than women that they will obtain a higher education. Alternatively, more women than men may take advantage of opportunities to resolve social conflicts at a high cognitive level in their interpersonal encounters, whereas more men than women may require the formal cognitive training provided by university education in order to apply principled reasoning to social-cognitive dilemmas. The finding that at the highest level of education more men than women use postconventional reasoning is consistent with results from almost all studies that do report a sex difference in adult stage score levels.

Kohlberg and Walker assume that when a control for education nullifies the sex difference in stage score level, it follows that the sex difference is spurious. However, educational level does not assess merely academic skills or knowledge of subject matter. It is in fact the best single index of social niche, indicating at its higher levels acculturation into the dominant values of the intelligentsia in Western society. Therefore, controlling for education begs the question in a dispute about the presence of sexual/cultural bias in Kohlberg's system. To the extent that sexual/cultural niche is controlled (by controlling for educational level), we must fail to find evidence of a sexual/cultural bias across stages.

It would be useful for Kohlberg or Walker to: (a) specify an educational threshold for each stage; (b) explain the sex difference in the "suitable" conditions necessary for postconventional reasoning to occur; (c) explain why postgraduate education is necessary for stage 6 reasoning to occur in men but not in women; and (d) explain why full moral development requires a college degree in any society.

Sexual/Cultural Difference versus Deficit

The presence of a strong educational effect (above a theoretically justifiable threshold) raises the troubling issue of cultural elitism, which may be manifested as an apparent sex bias, in the event that more women than men are excluded from the "right kind" of educational experiences either by discrimination or by their own choice. Kohlberg defends his system against the long-standing allegation of cultural elitism and ideological bias (e.g., Baumrind 1978; Reid 1984; Sampson 1981; Schweder 1982; Simpson 1974; Sullivan 1977) by attempting to distinguish between the intrinsic worth of persons and the value placed on their actions or judgments. As a stage 6 thinker, Kohlberg claims that he and his system hold that all persons are of equal worth. However, the logic of Kohlberg's position leads to the contrary, and common-sense, position that a person's moral worth *is* judged by his or her actions, and these actions in turn are dependent upon the quality of the moral judgments that guide them. Kohlberg implicitly agrees, because he regards moral development, defined as a change toward greater differentiation, integration, and adaptation as measured by "higher" stages on the Kohlberg scale, as *the* primary objective of a "truly democratic educational process" (Kohlberg 1981, 96). He also holds that there is a necessary, although complex, relation between moral judgment level and moral action, and that the relation is highest at the postconventional level, particularly at stage 6. Clearly, then, individuals differ in their moral worth, and, in the Kohlberg system, their moral worth is measured by stage score level.

The charge of sexual or cultural *bias* in Kohlberg's theory arises from his claim in "From *Is* to *Ought*" (Kohlberg 1981) that a developmentally advanced mode of reasoning about social issues, in particular, postconventional reasoning, is *morally* more mature than a developmentally prior mode, in particular, conventional reasoning. Were he to have claimed merely that conventional reasoning about such issues was more mature morally than preconventional reasoning he would have aroused little opposition, since in all societies children are socialized to internalize the mores of their society, and adults who reason about social issues at a preconventional level are regarded as socially immature. It is Kohlberg's claim that postconventional and, in particular, stage 6 reasoning is *morally* superior to conventional reasoning because it meets the criterion of universality that opens him to the charge of sexual/cultural bias. Postconventional reasoning occurs less frequently in Eastern cultures and second- and third-world countries and in women's thinking than in the reasoning of males with postgraduate educations. Yet Kohlberg claims "that there is a universalistically valid form of rational moral thought process which all persons could articulate assuming social and cultural conditions suitable to cognitive-moral stage development" (Kohlberg et al. 1983, 75). With equal access to such conditions, Kohlberg claims that no sex differences or cultural differences in moral level would be found. But in assuming that, with equal access, all cultures would choose such conditions, Kohlberg equates differences in the value placed on the universality criterion with deficits in orientation about morality.

Kohlberg chose to equate morality with justice because a justice orientation

> best renders our view of morality as universal. It restricts morality to a central minimal core, striving for universal agreement in the face of more relativist conceptions of the good.
>
> Another reason for focusing upon justice is our concern for a cognitive or "rational" approach to morality. . . . Possibly the most important reason for focusing on justice is that it is the most structural feature of moral judgment. . . . Justice "operations" of reciprocity and equality in interaction parallel logical operations or relations of equality and reciprocity in the non-moral cognitive domain. (Kohlberg et al. 1983, 93)

But Kohlberg's preference for reasoning about the logical priority of a principle such as life over an alternative principle such as property rights represents the peculiar bias of Western industrialized society (Reid 1984; Sampson 1981), particularly, of its male members. Moral leaders in non-Western societies do not appear to share Kohlberg's moral orientation. For example, in their study of African community leaders, Harkness, Edwards, and Super (1981) failed to find any instances of stage 5 or 6 reasoning. Similarly, some "postconventional" reasoners (such as kibbutz members) who share Western values but emphasize communal and collective moral principles rather than individualistic ones are partially missed or misunderstood by Kohlberg's model (Snarey, Reimer & Kohlberg 1985). Indeed, as Emler (1983) suggests, Kohlberg's higher stages may constitute secular humanist values couched in the abstract language of individual rights, reciprocity, distributive justice, and equity (Simpson 1974). Gilligan (1982a) claims that Kohlberg's notion presents an incomplete picture, and that there is a fundamentally dialectical tension between justice conceived as impartiality and justice conceived as compassionate concern. The latter expresses a *preference* for concrete, particularistic thinking shown by more of the highly educated women than men in the FSP study.

Morality has signified much more to philosophers throughout the ages than the "central minimal core" Kohlberg chooses to study. The kinds of phenomena Kohlberg's "minimal core" fails to encompass include: (a) judgments about what constitutes a good and meaningful life; (b) acts of social responsibility that go beyond right and duties to a commitment to transform society in accord with one's social ideal; and (c) special obligations to friends and family that arise from in-group identity. These omissions are central to alternative perspectives on what phenomena belong in the moral domain.

For example, Buddhists and Marxists, so different in most ways, share an understanding of individuals as socially embedded from conception, so that as individuals mature they become able to conceive of nature as their own real body; physical nature constitutes human beings' inorganic flesh and the social environment their organic flesh. Alienation is a consequence of separating oneself from the physical and social environment in which one is naturally embedded. This view of the individual as socially embedded rather than as autonomous and self-centered, and this emphasis on the importance of practical wisdom, are commonly thought to characterize more women than men and more individuals in second- and third-world countries than our own. It should generate a perspective on morality as practical, transformational, and concerned with concrete, particular persons and contexts.

By contrast, Kohlberg, in common with Kant, restricts the term "moral" to the formulation of universal, rational principles of objective and impartial treatment with the emphasis entirely on speculative wisdom (or *sophia*). Practical wisdom or praxis is relegated to the preconventional or conventional levels. Praxis is a term rooted in Judeo-Christian tradition that refers to the individual's and the community's commitment to realize the Good in ritual, custom, and ethical action. It was adopted by Marx to refer to the transformational, by contrast with the interpretive, function of human thought and action. Sexual/cultural differences emerge in studies that restrict morality to Kohlberg's minimal core because of its partiality toward a form of formal, abstract reasoning that is functionally ill-suited to the circumstances of individuals who occupy nonprofessional niches in any society, or who embrace collectivist objectives.

I agree with Kohlberg that a conception of ideal moral judgment should rest on an adequate conception of what it is. I affirm further than an adequate conception of ideal moral judgment should not rest on what it is not and cannot be. Were stages 5 and 6 equally distributed among both sexes, and all peoples, there could be no charge of sexual/cultural bias against the Kohlberg system (although the system could still be viewed as insufficient). But stages 5 and 6 are not equally distributed, and so the charge of bias cannot be dismissed as a myth. Further, some persons capable of universalistic moral reasoning reject it as an orientation because it is an idealized notion of morality that substitutes conformity of judgment to an ideal for conformity of action to judgment, and thus justifies not conforming one's morally relevant actions to one's moral judgments.

Ethical universalism neither is nor ought to be. Cultural pluralism, including ethical diversity, is beneficial to the survival of the human species, provided that all parties to a dispute are able to decentrate from their contradictory moral orientations and agree upon procedures for resolving practical disputes that arise from their differences about how life should be lived.

Those of us who want to investigate "moral" phenomena now speak in many different voices, precluding the use of the term "moral" for any one voice. Kohlberg and his colleagues have chosen to study the development of universal principles concerning justice as fairness. Other researchers have elected to study quite different phenomena within the moral domain. I recommend, therefore, that each of us select an operationally well-defined term with minimal surplus meaning to describe the theoretical construct we claim to have measured, and that we all agree to reserve the term "moral" for the domain that includes all such phenomena.

13

How Different Is the "Different Voice"?

Catherine G. Greeno and Eleanor E. Maccoby

Gilligan's book *In a Different Voice* was intended to right a wrong. In 1965 Jean Piaget wrote, "The most superficial observation is sufficient to show that in the main the legal sense is far less developed in little girls than in boys" (1965, 77). Several studies using Lawrence Kohlberg's moral development scale also reported sex differences (and male superiority) in the level of moral reasoning employed in response to hypothetical moral dilemmas (Alker & Poppen 1973). Gilligan argues that these supposed deficiencies of female development result from an injustice inherent in the research. She notes that the research paradigm, and the analyses of moral "levels," have been based primarily on the study of male subjects. As a result, psychologists have fallen into an observational bias; by "implicitly adopting the male life as the norm, they have tried to fashion women out of masculine cloth" (Gilligan 1982a, 6), and women's particular moral development "falls through the sieve" (31) of an androcentric research tradition. Gilligan's view is that with a less biased approach to moral thinking, one would find that women's thinking was somewhat different from men's, but not less mature. Psychologists have erred, not in believing that women are different from men, but that they are inferior to men; because women develop along a moral path that is distinct from that followed by men, existing research paradigms have failed them.

Because Gilligan addresses Kohlberg's paradigm primarily, it is well to be aware of certain features in his work, as well as some of the recent advances in theory, method, and findings (Kohlberg 1981; Colby et al. 1983). The major goal of Kohlberg and his colleagues has been to trace developmental change in moral reasoning. While Kohlberg originally thought he could distinguish six such levels, more recent work indicates that there are four that can be applied to the large majority of children and adults. These four levels form a clear developmental progression. That is, individuals move from one to the next as they grow older, and there is evidence for the claim that the four levels have validity for individuals from a variety of cultural backgrounds. The transition from level 3 to level 4 is of the greatest interest for our purposes. Level 3 is considered to be the first stage of adult reasoning. Some studies using Kohlberg's rating system found that women tended to remain scored there, while men more consistently matured to level 4 (Fishkin et al. 1973; Haan et al. 1968). Level 3 reasoning involves a concern with maintaining bonds of trust with others. The individual strives to be—and to be seen by others as—a "good" or "nice" person. The "good" or "right" action is that which will not hurt those with whom one has valued relationships. Shared feelings and agreements take priority over individual interests. The move to level 4 involves what might be called a move to a societal level of thought, where moral issues are considered in terms of a system of law or justice that must be maintained for the good of society. The higher level does not supersede or supplant the lower—persons who can think in societal terms about moral issues also can continue to think about the effects of their actions on other persons with whom they have relationships—but a new progression in thought has occurred. There can be no doubt that level 4 considerations do appear in an individual's thinking later than level 3 considerations. In this sense, the societal level is more mature.

Here Gilligan makes her primary departure from the work that precedes her. She argues that although the androcentric coding system used for Kohlberg's dilemmas shows women remaining at level 3 more often than do men, women are not in fact fixed at this relatively immature level but progress along a path different from that followed by men. Specifically, she believes that women move from an exclusive orientation toward serving others' interests to a greater emphasis on self-actualization. Thus, the "different construction of the moral problem by women may be seen as the reason for their failure to develop within the constraints of Kohlberg's system" (19).

Current work reveals, however, that Gilligan has been attacking a straw man. In a comprehensive review paper, Lawrence Walker considers sixty-one studies in which the Kohlberg paradigm is used to score moral reasoning for subjects of both sexes. These show that in childhood and adolescence, there is no trend whatever for males to score at higher levels than females on Kohlberg's scales. In adulthood, the large majority of comparisons reveal no sex differences. In the studies that do show sex differences, the women were less well educated than the men, and it appears that education, not gender, accounts for women's seeming lesser maturity. Throughout this large body of research, there is no indication whatever that the two sexes take different developmental paths with respect to moral thought about abstract, hypothetical issues (Walker 1984, reprinted as chapter 11 in this volume).

Because Gilligan's own writings do not include data on how girls and women change their moral thinking as they grow older, we do not know whether a different scoring system, based on Gilligan's formulations, would show differences in the sequence of developmental steps. For two reasons we think it highly doubtful that such differences will emerge if and when the necessary comparisons are made: (1) the number of men and the number of women who reach the different Kohlberg levels at successive ages are highly similar, which suggests that the sexes follow the same developmental path; and (2) thinking about moral issues is closely linked to, though not identical with, general cognitive development, and we know that the sexes do not differ in the average rate at which they climb the ladder of cognitive growth.

Of course, thinking about hypothetical moral issues is not all there is to morality. In retrospect, it is unfortunate that Gilligan focuses her attack primarily on the Kohlberg paradigm. Gilligan has other points to make about morality, and in the long run, her greatest contribution may be her work on these other aspects of moral decision-making. Women, Gilligan believes, are bound into a network of intimate interpersonal ties. Compared with men, they are more empathic and compassionate, more concerned lest they fail to respond to others' needs, and made more anxious by the threat of separation from their loved ones. All these things could be true even if the sexes did not differ in their thinking about abstract moral issues.

Gilligan is not the only writer to point to sex differences in the capacity for intimate interpersonal relationships. The claim that women are more oriented toward interpersonal relations has a well-established history in many forums of discussion. Women's predominance in the nurturance and care of young children is an accepted and cross-culturally universal fact. Theorists have used women's presumably greater interpersonal orientation to "explain" a wide variety of sex-linked phenomena, ranging from differences in mathematical or spatial ability to differences in the nature of the roles assigned to women in most societies. Talcott Parsons and R. F. Bales' (1955) distinction between the instrumental (masculine) and the expressive (feminine) functions in family organization provides an early example. The more recent work of Sandra Bem (1974) and of Janet Spence, Robert Helmreich, and Joy Stapp (1975) makes similar distinctions.

Research has indicated that there are indeed some robust sex differences that relate to Gilligan's concerns. For example, empathy and altruism have been frequently examined for sex differences (see Eisenberg & Lennon 1983). Self-report scores on these qualities are particularly striking: in each of the sixteen self-report studies reported by Nancy Eisenberg and Roger Lennon, women rate themselves as more empathic than do men. These sex differences are sometimes very large statistically. Also, it has been found that when observers, such as teachers or peers, are asked to rate qualities of people they know, females are rated as more empathic and altruistic than males (Swain et al. 1979). The stereotype of women's greater empathy and altruism is very strong, and, as Martin Hoffman (1977) points out in his review of empathy, "The relevant theorizing in the literature is in essential agreement with this stereotype. . . . There appear to have been no theorists who contradict [it]."

It is clear that women have a greater *reputation* for altruism and empathy than do men, and that women accept its validity. Whether the reputation is deserved is a more complicated question. There are many studies in which people are unobtrusively observed while confronting an opportunity to help others. In general, these studies do not show that women are any more likely than men to offer help. However, most of these studies involve situations in which the person to be helped is a stranger. It has become clear that an individual's helpfulness to strangers depends on a complex set of factors that may or may not be related to gender. Thus, a person's readiness to offer help depends on the sex of the person in need, on perceived risks entailed in helping, and on the helper's beliefs about whether he or she has the skills needed to be an effective resource (e.g., a man is more likely to offer to change a tire, a woman, to soothe a child). It should be noted that in real life most altruistic acts are performed for the benefit of persons close to us. We suspect that if a real sex difference in altruism emerges, it will be found with respect to helpful acts directed toward friends and intimates, not toward strangers. But this work remains to be done; so far a sex difference can be neither confirmed nor refuted.

Recent work on children's play groups indicates that even at a very early age males and females show decidedly different styles in social interactions (see Maccoby 1985). The research provides some evidence supporting a "agentive/expressive" distinction, similar to the one proposed by Parsons and Bales, but at a preadult phase of development. Girls' groups are smaller, most often a dyad or triad of "best friends" whose interactions are based on shared confidences. Boys' groups are larger and more task-oriented; that is, play tends to center on some goal-directed game or activity. These differences appear fairly early in childhood and are persistent. It is possible that some of the gender differences postulated in areas such as empathy and altruism stem from these early tendencies and preferences. An interesting parallel is, in fact, found in the literature on intimacy among adults. Women's relationships tend to focus on self-disclosure, and "liking" among women is highly correlated to the amount of self-disclosure that goes on in a relationship. For men the correlation between liking and self-disclosure is very low (Rubin & Schenker 1978). Self-disclosure tends to be a feature of intimacy and may be connected to the kind of network of interpersonal ties that Gilligan perceives. A great deal of work is left to be done on the exact nature of intimate relationships and possible gender differences therein.

When we read Gilligan, it is easy to be impressed by the elegance of her style and by the historical, philosophical depth of what she has to say. In these respects, her writing is very refreshing compared to the dry fact-citing of much of social science. It seems almost philistine to challenge the nature of her evidence. Many women readers find that the comments by women quoted in Gilligan's book resonate so thoroughly with their own experience that they do not need any further demonstrations of the truth of what is being said. The fact remains, however, that Gilligan claims that the views expressed by women in her book represent a *different* voice—different, that is, from men. This assertion demands quantitative, as well as qualitative, research. There is no sphere of human thought, action, or feeling in which the two sexes are entirely distinct. Reproductive activity is the area in which behaviors come closest to being truly dimorphic, but apart from this, the male and female distributions overlap greatly, and in most respects, men and women are more alike than they are different. A claim that the two sexes speak in different voices amounts to a claim that there are more women than men who think, feel, or behave in a given way. Simply quoting how some women feel is not enough proof. We need to know whether what is being said is distinctively *female*, or simply human. We believe that no researcher who makes assertions such as Gilligan's can escape the obligation to demonstrate a quantitative difference in the proportion of the two sexes who show the characteristics in question. Here, Gilligan's research, as cited in the book, is unsatisfying. One study on abortion decisions was understandably confined to women subjects, and we consequently cannot compare how women and men think about this issue. Another study by Susan Pollak and Gilligan, after comparing the responses of men and women to a set of pictured scenes, maintained that women are made more anxious than men by the isolation that is involved in achievement, while men are made anxious by intimacy. However, a recent attempt to replicate that study raises serious questions about the way the pictures were classified to elicit the sex differences. Other classification systems reveal no tendency for the sexes to differ in their anxiety about intimacy or separation (Pollak & Gilligan 1982; Bussey & Maugham 1982; Benton et al. 1983). Finally, Gilligan has not yet provided any evidence that boys and girls follow different developmental courses in their thinking about morality. The book's only evidence concerning children's responses to moral issues consists of quotations from two eight-year-olds and two eleven-year-olds. These quotations fit our stereotypes about boys and girls, and intuitively we may feel that Gilligan must be right. But can we remain satisfied with this level of evidence?

We can only sound a warning: women have been trapped for generations by people's willingness to accept their own intuitions about the truth of gender stereotypes. To us, there seems no alternative to the slow, painful, and sometimes dull accumulation of quantitative data to show whether the almost infinite variations in the way human beings think, feel, and act are actually linked to gender. Let us hasten to say that we are not arguing that the sexes do not differ in important respects. We only urge that claims about what these differences are should be subjected to the empirical tests that are the basis of social science.

14

A Methodological Critique

Zella Luria

In a Different Voice has had a predictably wide audience among women. Indeed, the six story-filled essays have an intuitive fit with how many women see themselves, especially in relation to men. Given the potential influence of this work in characterizing women's thinking, it becomes imperative to scrutinize the bases of its arguments and to ask whether the evidence is yet sufficient to warrant Gilligan's conclusions. If the evidence is found insufficient, what further research might be needed for a more rigorous test of the book's intriguing assertions?

Gilligan's work demonstrates her immersion in the field of adolescent development and the influence on her of psychoanalytic theory. In research (as well as in popular thought) on the psychology of adolescence, Sigmund Freud and Erik Erikson are critical figures; the theories and methodologies of both turn up repeatedly in all of Gilligan's writing here and elsewhere. The weaving of literary examples (presumably as metaphors), theoretical proposals, and loosely defined empirical research can be a winning but seductive design; occasionally Gilligan does not draw a clear line between theoretical speculation and discussion of data and slips from hunch, example, or metaphor to "proven fact." The structure of her work, to use a metaphor myself, is built of solid bricks intermixed with some of cardboard.

In Gilligan's interview work, for instance, the nature of the evidence is sometimes unclear. Although psychological work on adolescents has been criticized for relying too heavily on the single method of the semistructured interview that is favored by Gilligan, that method *can* be a useful technique

---

Reprinted by permission from *Signs: Journal of Women in Culture and Society* 11: 321–24. Copyright © 1986 by the University of Chicago Press.

if certain requirements of rigorous research are fulfilled. First, good samples must be carefully characterized by age, social class, education, and method of recruitment, so that readers can securely apply the findings to similar groups. In general, Gilligan's sample specification is inadequate to justify her group characterizations. For example, eight males and eight females at different ages do not make up a number sufficient to characterize all males and females. Then, too, samples, drawn from classes on moral development at Harvard University are dubious exemplars of students generally. Questionable, moreover, is the match within this sample itself between male and female students. Such matching does not occur in the central study of attitudes toward abortion. Twenty-nine women considering abortions in Boston may provide an important example of decision-making, but they cannot provide data on how men and women differ in such thinking.[1] None of this rules out the possibility that adequate, well-specified samples for interview could be studied. Gilligan, however, has not yet done it.

Second, interviews that yield discursive data such as explanations, personal histories, and discussion of abstract questions require objective rules that categorize the respondents' texts. The rules for categorizing—X is a caring answer, Y is a rationalization and is also an abstract answer, Z is an abstract answer with caring, and so on—must be specified to ensure that all investigators make the same decisions about what particular responses mean, regardless of the theory under study. If the measuring system is reliable, investigators who may not share biases or views should, by careful rule application, agree nonetheless on the categorization of interview answers. Since the group working with Kohlberg on the studies of moral development central to Gilligan's critique has had three coding schemes and since Gilligan tells little of her own, no reader can know if this second requirement—the reliable objective scoring system—has been met. Thus the reader cannot make a personal judgment on the author's understanding of a particular answer or on the way in which answers are classified.

Third, Gilligan's juxtapositions of disparate samples pose problems about combination rules. Even if all subjects were asked about Kohlberg's dilemma on Heinz and the pharmacist, what was the rationale for considering abortion candidates and Harvard students as combined sources for data on two gender voices? The interviews of twenty-nine pregnant women in the abortion study covered many questions necessarily absent from the Harvard students' interviews. After all, the family planning agency from which Gilligan recruited subjects expected her to talk about more than Heinz and the Kohlberg moral dilemmas. One is left with the sense that the combination of the data does not conform to the usual rules of psychological procedure—shared samples, shared procedure, shared scoring—but is the result of a somewhat impressionistic grouping of the stories Gilligan's subjects told. Obviously no psychologist would object to such a technique for deriving hypotheses, but Gilligan seems, at least, to be proffering it as a basis for proof.

It is highly likely that Gilligan is concerned with these issues of methodology. However, the book lacks any careful statement on them. One is left with the knowledge that there were some studies involving women and sometimes men, and that women were somehow samples and somehow interviewed on some issues as well as on the Kohlberg stories. Somehow the data were sifted and somehow yielded a clear impression that women could be powerfully characterized as caring and interrelated. This is an exceedingly intriguing proposal, but it is not yet substantiated as a research conclusion. The interesting answers to queries liberally sprinkled along with the case studies through the volume cannot substitute for objectively derived data.

Gilligan's hypothesis, moreover, gives rise to another question. Does she truly believe that we need one psychology for women and another for men? At the 1983 meeting of the Society for Research in Child Development, her response was no, but her book suggests that her answer is yes. She gives no evidence of the extent of overlap between male and female responses to Kohlberg moral dilemmas, as if the data consist of two virtually nonoverlapping curves. If there is one statement to be clearly and loudly stated to the public by students of sex differences, it is that overlap of scores by males and females is always far greater than the differences in those scores, particularly on psychological measures. We are not two species; we are two sexes.

It appears, then, that to yield so strong a theory as that which structures *In a Different Voice*, Gilligan has to some degree oversimplified the case and overinterpreted the data. Yet we might still ask whether her conclusions seem plausible when placed in the context of overall evidence. The lead review by Lawrence Walker in the June 1984 issue of *Child Development* [reprinted as chapter 11 in this volume] details the evidence on sex differences found in studies using the Kohlberg moral reasoning measure. No sex differences that can be measured in replicable, developmentally orderly, and statistically significant ways are cited in the review. Of the nineteen adult studies reported there, fourteen yield no significant sex differences and five find men ahead in measures of moral reasoning. When usual summary techniques are applied to add all the studies together, the data do not support any finding of a statistically significant sex difference. In the review's last table, however, there is a footnote citing results by Gilligan, Langdale, Lyons, and Murphy in an unpublished 1982 manuscript. Four samples of sixteen subjects—made up, one gathers, of eight men and eight women in each of four different age groups—were tested and showed no difference in average scores of men and women. A footnote suggests that "more men than women displayed at least one instance of postconventional (a higher stage) reasoning" [Gilligan, Langdale, Lyons & Murphy 1982, cited in Walker

1984, 686 (reprinted as chapter 11 in this volume)]. Are thirty-two men and thirty-two women the data base for Gilligan's different voices?

A recent doctoral thesis by Betsy Speicher-Dubin helps us to understand why some interpretations of sex differences may have been derived from older data. When social class is truly controlled, that is, by determining a married woman's class by her own education and work history rather than by her spouse's, sex differences do not appear. Results from the University of California Institute of Human Development at Berkeley based on archival data from the Oakland study—whose design was described by Harold Jones in 1939 and whose results relevant to this discussion were described by Speicher-Dubin in 1982—showed women coming out slightly ahead on the Kohlberg measure. As the match between male and female class and education becomes more equitable, it might be reasonable to expect that male and female scores may not be very different. The relevant literature is replete with instances of presumed sex differences (we call some of them stereotypes) that disappear when better controls are used. On the other hand, if one wants to find sex differences, as Gilligan apparently does, one can get them simply by not controlling for class and education. One further related point: a 1979 review of work on a Kohlberg-like test—the Defining Issues Test developed by J. R. Rest—concluded that sex differences are rarely significant among students at the junior high, senior high, college, or graduate level or among adults. It is not even true, therefore, that at one stage in life one sex has an advantage which the other assumes at a later stage (Brabeck 1983). This evidence has not since been disputed.

Curiously, all of this discussion began just as Kohlberg and his colleagues took a new scoring manual to press. A previous publication by that group includes an example in an appendix of how responses demonstrating care of others can be coded at all stages (Colby et al. 1983, 1984). Still, we cannot know whether Gilligan used such a method because her book contains no statement describing her interview and scoring criteria. Another recent review concludes that Gilligan's theory has been given wide scholarly attention, but "empirical evidence in support of her assertions is less available" (Brabeck 1983, 275, 277, reprinted as chapter 3 in this volume). I welcome the research that will test those assertions.

What is it that we want today as women and as feminists? That is not a question about evidence but about goals. Do we truly gain by returning to a modern cult of true womanhood? Do we gain by the assertion that women think or reason in one voice and men in another? Gilligan's view focuses on characteristics of the person; the situation is only a vehicle for the expression of the reasoning personality, whether that be caring or abstract. The same rationale has often been used to shunt people into the "appropriate" job. Social psychologists during the last decade have been struggling to free psychology of these views of personality produced in the 1950s for the good reason that people are not, in fact, all that predictable in different circumstances. People differ in how they size up situations and then in their behavioral responses (Bem & Funder 1978; Block & Block 1980; Magnusson & Endler 1977). Actually, Gilligan's tie to the Kohlberg method does not give her—or Kohlberg—a sound basis for talking about people's behavior, only for analyzing what they say, alas.

A reasonable goal seems to me to make women—and men—able to choose when to be caring and related and when to be concerned with abstract issues. (While I do not view abstraction and ability to care as opposites, for the sake of argument let us assume that they are nonoverlapping ways of thinking or behaving.) Modern women will need *not* to be always caring and interrelated, if indeed they ever were constantly so. And they are also in situations where being abstract and rights oriented is a necessity. My purpose as a feminist is to train women to choose their actions sensibly and flexibly, depending on the situations they confront.

Some of my students are frightened. All around them are striving women. Many of my students are feminists but are also somewhat timid, traditionally feminine, and unsure of their ability to manage the real overload of work and family. They are horrified by real-life competition for graduate school, for jobs, for men. How can we help such women deal with society today while trying to change it in productive ways? This seems to me to be the task. The world will not stop to let off those caring women whose fears and repugnance keep them from learning new choices. Surely Gilligan and I want one voice that allows both men and women a variety of differentiated responses. Anything else is a step backward.

Note

1. This sample is also unlike one of women who refuse to consider abortion, as can be seen in Kristin Luker 1984.

Part IV

FEMINIST ETHICS AND THE FUTURE OF CARE

15

Reply to Critics

Carol Gilligan

Among his many astute observations, William James (1907, 131) noted that when a new idea is introduced, the first response is to say that it is so obviously false, it is hard to see how anyone could believe it; the second is to say that it is not original, and everyone has always known it to be true. My critics are making both statements, but in doing so they introduce a central confusion. I am saying that the study of women calls attention to the different way of constituting the self and morality; they are focusing on the issue of sex difference as measured by standards derived from one sex only. In other words, my critics take the ideas of self and morality for granted as these ideas have been defined in the patriarchal or male-dominated tradition. I call these concepts in question by giving examples of women who constitute these ideas differently and hence tell a different story about human experience. My critics say that this story seems "intuitively" right to many women but is at odds with the findings of psychological research. This is precisely the point I am making and exactly the difference I was exploring: the dissonance between psychological theory and women's experience.

The sex difference issue was raised in a curiously unacknowledged way by those psychologists who chose all-male research samples, since the choice of a single-sex sample reflects an implicit premise of gender difference. But a sex-difference hypothesis cannot be tested adequately unless the standards of assessment are derived from studies of women as well as from studies of men. Otherwise, the questions being asked are: How much are women like men? Or, how much do women deviate from the male-defined standard?

It was in an effort to ask a different question that I wrote the book under

---

Reprinted by permission from *Signs: Journal of Women in Culture and Society* 11: 324–33. Copyright © 1986 by The University of Chicago Press.

discussion, seeking to discover whether something had been missed by the practice of leaving out girls and women at the theory-building stage of research in developmental psychology—that is, whether Piaget's (1965) and Kohlberg's (1969) descriptions of moral development, Erikson's description of identity development (1958),[1] Offer's description of adolescent development (1969), Levinson's (1978) and Vaillant's (1977) descriptions of adult development, as well as more general accounts of human personality and motivation, contained a consistent conceptual and observational bias, reflected in and extended by their choice of all-male research samples.[2]

The "different voice" hypothesis was an answer to this question. What had been missed by leaving out women was a different way of constituting the idea of the self and the idea of what is moral. Rather than seeing to what extent women exemplify what generally is taken to be self and morality, I saw in women's thinking the lines of a different conception, grounded in different images of relationship and implying a different interpretive framework. Attention to women's thinking thus raised a new set of questions about both male and female development and explained a series of observations that previously had not made sense. Discrepant data on girls and women, commonly interpreted as evidence of female deficiency, pointed instead to a problem in psychological theory.

That this problem affected women differently from the way it affected men seemed clear. Since women's voices were heard through a filter that rendered them confused and incoherent, it was difficult for men to understand women and for women to listen to themselves. In my book, I sought to clarify two related sets of problems, put forth in my subtitle: problems in psychological theory and problems in women's development. The argument was not statistical—that is, not based on the representativeness of the women studied or on the generality of the data presented to a larger population of women or men. Rather, the argument was interpretive and hinged on the demonstration that the examples presented illustrated a different way of seeing.

In defining a shift in perspective that changes the meaning of the key terms of moral discourse—such as the concept of self, the idea of relationship, and the notion of responsibility—I described an ethic of care and response that I contrasted with an ethic of justice and rights. I also cited as an empirical observation the prominence of the care perspective in women's moral thinking and used literary examples to amplify and extend the voices in my interview texts. My critics cannot make up their minds whether it is naive or self-serving to think of women as caring or whether this is a fact so obvious that it does not need repeating. But as they elaborate these contentions, it becomes increasingly apparent that the book they are discussing is different from the book which I have written (Gilligan 1982a).

They speak of the nineteenth-century ideal of pure womanhood and the romanticizing of female care: I portray twentieth-century women choosing to have abortions, as well as women college students, lawyers, and physicians reconsidering what is meant by care in light of their recognition that acts inspired by conventions of selfless feminine care have led to hurt, betrayal, and isolation. My critics equate care with feelings, which they oppose to thought, and imagine caring as passive or confined to some separate sphere. I describe care and justice as two moral perspectives that organize both thinking and feelings and empower the self to take different kinds of action in public as well as private life. Thus, in contrast to the paralyzing image of the "angel in the house," I describe a critical ethical perspective that calls into question the traditional equation of care with self-sacrifice.

The title of my book was deliberate; it reads, "in a *different* voice," not "in a *woman's* voice." In my introduction, I explain that this voice is identified not by gender but by theme. Noting as an empirical observation the association of this voice with women, I caution the reader that "this association is not absolute, and the contrasts between male and female voices are presented here to highlight a distinction between two modes of thought and to focus a problem of interpretation rather than to represent a generalization about either sex." In tracing development, I "point to the interplay of these voices within each sex and suggest that their convergence marks times of crisis and change." No claims, I state, are made about the origins of these voices or their distribution in a wider population, across cultures or time (Gilligan 1982a, 2). Thus, the care perspective in my rendition is neither biologically determined nor unique to women. It is, however, a moral perspective different from that currently embedded in psychological theories and measures, and it is a perspective that was defined by listening to both women and men describe their own experience.

The most puzzling aspect of my critics' position is their dissociation of women's experience from women's thinking—as if experiences common to women leave no psychological trace. Thus, Greeno and Maccoby cite examples of sex differences in their references to "women's predominance in the nurturance and care of young children [as] an accepted and cross-culturally universal fact" (1986, 313); to recent research indicating "that even at a very early age males and females show decidedly different styles in social interactions" (314); and to findings of sex differences "in the literature on intimacy among adults" (314). Kerber observes that "it seems well established that little boys face a psychic task of separation that little girls do not" (1986, 309). Yet in endorsing the position of no sex differences, they appear to believe that nothing of significance for moral or self-development is learned from these activities and experiences. The burden of proof would seem to rest with my critics to give a psychologically coherent explanation of why the sex differences they mention make no difference to moral development or self-concept. To say that social class and education contribute to moral development while experiences typically associated with gender are essentially irrelevant may say more about the way development is being measured than it does about the morality or gender.

In replying to my critics, I wish to address three issues they raise: the issue of method, the issue of theory or interpretation, and the issue of goals or education. The first question is what constitutes data and what data are sufficient to support the claims I have made. To claim that there is a voice different from those which psychologists have represented, I need only one example—one voice whose coherence is not recognized within existing interpretive schemes. To claim that common themes recur in women's conceptions of self and morality, I need a series of illustrations. In counterposing women's conceptions of self and morality to the conceptions embedded in psychological theories, I assume that a psychology literature filled with men's voices exemplifies men's experience. Therefore, in listening to women, I sought to separate their descriptions of their experience from standard forms of psychological interpretation and to rely on a close textual analysis of language and logic to define the terms of women's thinking.

Like all psychological research, my work is limited by the nature and context of my observations and reflects my own interpretive frame. There are no data independent of theory, no observations not made from a perspective. Data alone do not tell us anything; they do not speak, but are interpreted by people. I chose to listen to women's descriptions of experiences of moral conflict and choice, to attend to the ways that women describe themselves in relation to others, and to observe changes in thinking over time. On the basis of these observations and my reading of psychology, I made a series of inferences about the nature of sex differences, about women's development, about the concept of self, and about the nature of moral experience.

Seizing on the Lawrence Walker article recently published in *Child Development* (1984, reprinted as essay 11 in this volume), my critics claim that there are no sex differences in moral development because there are no sex differences on the Kohlberg scale. Thus they completely miss my point. My work focuses on the difference between two moral orientations—a justice and a care perspective rather than on the question of whether women and men differ on Kohlberg's stages of justice reasoning. On two occasions, I have reported no sex differences on Kohlberg's measure (Gilligan & Murphy 1979; Gilligan & Belenky 1980). But the fact that educated women are capable of high levels of justice reasoning has no bearing on the question of whether they would spontaneously choose to frame moral problems in this way. My interest in the way of people *define* moral problems is reflected in my research methods, which have centered on first-person accounts of moral conflict.

My critics are unaware that Walker's conclusions and use of statistics have been seriously challenged by two of the researchers on whose findings he most heavily relies. In replies submitted to *Child Development,* Norma Haan (1984) reports significant sex differences on the Kohlberg test, even when controlling for social class and education and using the new scoring method; Diana Baumrind (1986, reprinted as essay 12 in this volume) notes that the most highly educated women in her sample were less likely than other women or men to score at Kohlberg's postconventional stages because they were less likely to frame moral problems in terms of abstract principles of justice.[3] Thus, lower scores on the Kohlberg measure do not necessarily reflect lower levels of moral development but may signify a shift in moral perspective or orientation.

The example in my book of eleven-year-old Amy illustrates how a care perspective is rendered incomprehensible by the Kohlberg frame. This point is extended by interviews conducted with Amy and Jake when they were fifteen. At fifteen, both children introduce both moral perspectives in thinking about the Heinz dilemma, although the order of introduction is not the same. Amy's ability to solve the problem within the justice framework leads her to advance a full stage on Kohlberg's scale, but Jake's introduction of the care perspective signifies no advance in moral development, according to Kohlberg's measure. The Kohlberg test, in its equation of moral development with justice reasoning, does not adequately represent either Amy's or Jake's moral thinking. Amy's own terms remain at fifteen the terms of the care perspective, and from this standpoint she sees moral problems in the justice construction. To equate her moral development with her ability to reason within this framework is to ignore her perceptions; but it is also to encourage her, in the name of development, to accept a construction of reality and morality that she identifies as problematic. For Jake, the equation of moral judgment with the logic of justice reasoning encourages him to take the position that anyone disagreeing with his judgment has "the wrong set of priorities." He takes this stand at first when asked about the druggist's refusal to relinquish his profit, but then abandons it in the recognition that there is another way to think about this problem. At eleven, Jake saw the Heinz dilemma as "sort of like a math problem with humans"; at fifteen he recasts it as a story about two people whose actions can be interpreted differently, depending on the constraints of their situation, and whose feelings, when elaborated, evoke understanding and compassion. What had seemed a simple exercise in moral logic thus becomes a more complex moral problem.

If my critics had pursued their questions about method and evidence, they would have discovered that in 1983 Nona Lyons reported a systematic procedure for identifying justice and care considerations in people's descriptions of real-life dilemmas (1983; 1982), and Sharry Langdale, in a doctoral dissertation (1983), demonstrated that Lyons' method could be adapted for coding responses to hypothetical dilemmas. With a cross-sectional, life-cycle sample of 144 males and females who were matched for social class and education, Langdale found significant sex differences in the use of justice and care considerations. My critics also could have learned that Kay Johnston, in a recently completed dissertation (1985), created a standard method (using Aesop's fables) for assessing moral orientation use and preference. Johnston demonstrated that sixty eleven- and fifteen-year-old girls and boys from a middle-class suburban community were able to understand the logic of both the justice and care orientations, to use both strategies of reasoning in solving the problems posed by the fables, and to explain why one or the other orientation provided a better solution. She also found consistent sex differences in orientation use and preference, as well as variation across fables.

These studies and others confirm and refine the "different voice" hypothesis by demonstrating that: (1) the justice and care perspectives are distinct orientations that organize people's thinking about moral problems in different ways; (2) boys and men who resemble those most studied by developmental psychologists tend to define and resolve moral problems within the justice framework, although they introduce considerations of care; and (3) the focus on care in moral reasoning, although not characteristic of all women, is characteristically a female phenomenon in the advantaged populations that have been studied. These findings provide an empirical explanation for the equation of moral judgment with justice reasoning in the theories derived from studies of males; but they also explain why the study of women's moral thinking changes the definition of the moral domain.

My critics' readiness to dismiss findings of sex differences is evident as well in the fact that they cite the Benton et al. (1983) critique of Susan Pollak's and my (1982) study of images of violence, but overlook the three articles that followed in its wake: our reply (1983), "Differing about Differences," their response (Weiner et al. 1983), "Compounding the Error," and our rejoinder (1985), "Killing the Messenger." Pollak and I agree with Benton et al. that a priori classification of Thematic Apperception Test (TAT) pictures poses a serious problem in the classification they propose. Our study, however, relied on a content analysis of the violent stories written by women and men, an analysis that our critics ignore. This analysis revealed that, within the texts of the stories written (considered independently of the pictures), violence was associated with intimacy in stories written by men and with isolation in stories written by women. The report by Benton and her associates of sex differences in the incidence and location of violence are not inconsistent with our conclusions; however, their failure to conduct a content analysis suggests that their study was not a serious attempt at replication.

If the Walker article (1984, reprinted as chapter 11 in this volume) implies that questions about sex differences in moral development can be reduced to an issue of Kohlberg test scores, the Benton et al. critique (1983) suggests that questions about sex differences in violent fantasies can be reduced to an issue of picture classification. Given that researchers repeatedly find significant sex differences in the incidence of both violent fantasies and violent behavior, the rush to dismiss the exploration of these differences on the basis of picture classification seems like an attempt to paper over a huge social problem with a methodological quibble. My critics are concerned about stereotypes that portray women as lacking in anger and aggression; but they do not consider the lower incidence of violence in women's fantasies and behavior to be a sex difference worth exploring. Thus my critics essentially accept the psychology I call into question—the psychology that has equated male with human in defining human nature and thus has construed evidence of sex differences as a sign of female deficiency, a psychology that, for all the talk about research design and methods, has failed to see all-male research samples as a methodological problem.

My work offers a different perspective, on psychology and on women. It calls into question the values placed on detachment and separation in developmental theories and measures, values that create a false sense of objectivity and render female development problematic. My studies of women locate the problem in female development not in the values of care and connection or in the relationship definition of self, but in the tendency for women, in the name of virtue, to give care only to others and to consider it "selfish" to care for themselves. The inclusion of women's experience dispels the view of care as selfless and passive and reveals the activities that constitute care and lead to responsiveness in human relationships. In studies conducted by myself and my students, women who defined themselves in their own terms—as indicated by the use of active, first-person constructions—generally articulated the value of care and affirmed their own relational concerns. In thinking about choices in their lives, these women were able to adopt a critical perspective on societal values of separation and independence and to reject confusing images of women, such as "supermother" or "superwoman," that are at odds with women's knowledge about relationships and about themselves. Women's ability to act on this knowledge was associated in several doctoral dissertations with invulnerability to eating disorders, recovery from depressions, and the absence of depressive symptoms in mothers of young children.[4] But if my characterization is accurate, there is no question that this knowledge brings women into conflict with current societal arrangements and often confronts them with painful and difficult choices.

My critics and I share a common concern about the education of our women students, as well as, I assume, a more general concern about the future of life on this planet. In light of these considerations, how best might we approach the education of both women and men students? To label women's concerns about conflicts between achievement and care as a sign of weakness to render women frightened and fearful. This approach only reinforces the impression that women's fears are groundless. Women need to engage the problems created by the overload of work and family because these conflicts fall most heavily on women. But it is a disservice to both women and men to imply that these are women's problems.

That developmental psychology has been built largely from the study of men's lives is not my invention. While we may disagree about the particular nature of the problems in this representation, as women we do ourselves an immense disservice to say that there is no problem. Since morality is closely tied to the problem of aggression—an area where sex differences are uncontested—it may be of particular interest at this time for both sexes to explore whether women's experience illuminates the psychology of nonviolent strategies for resolving conflicts. I am well aware that reports of sex differences can be used to rationalize oppression, and I deplore any use of my work for this purpose. But I do not see it as empowering to encourage women to put aside their own concerns and perceptions and to rely on a psychology largely defined by men's perceptions in thinking about what is of value and what constitutes human development.

Notes

1. Erikson began his work on identity with returning war veterans in the 1950s and advanced it further in *Young Man Luther* (1958).
2. For a discussion of psychological norms based on studies of males, see McClelland 1975; Adelson & Doehrman 1980, and other essays in the same volume.
3. For a more extensive discussion of Amy's and Jake's moral reasoning at age fifteen, see Gilligan 1986a.
4. Steiner-Adair 1984; Jack 1984; Willard 1985. See also Attanucci 1984.

16

The Liberation of Caring: A Different Voice for Gilligan's "Different Voice"

Bill Puka

A compelling vision of "caring" and its role in women's development has evolved in psychology and gender studies (e.g., Miller 1976; Chodorow 1978; Gilligan 1982a; Noddings 1984). Gilligan's "different voice" conception of "care" as an ethical orientation and its contrast to the patriarchal preference for individual rights and justice has had a powerful impact on many fields, including philosophy. It has garnered an enthusiastic international following.

Many of Gilligan's supporters, however, are careful to note the formative nature of her account and its potential dangers. As some put it, "Gilligan has helped show that there is some gender difference here, centered around the relational and nurturent orientations of women. Now we must clarify what it is." Gilligan sometimes qualifies her own views similarly (Gilligan 1982a, 3, 126). Feminist analysis warns that attempting to distinguish woman's caretaking strengths from her socialized, servile weaknesses flirts with sexism itself. It runs the risk of transforming victimization into virtue by merely saying it is so, of legitimizing subjugation to gender in a misguided attempt at self-affirmation. This seems a typical pitfall for oppressed groups, especially in "personal consciousness-raising" approaches to liberation.

In this essay, I will pose a different voice for Gilligan's "different voice," an alternative hypothesis of what the caring difference might be. On this hypothesis care is not a general course of moral development, primarily, but a set of coping strategies for dealing with sexist oppression in particular. In the spirit of care, this hypothesis is designed to "satisfy everyone," including proponents and critics on each side. Foremost, it seeks to preserve care's strengths and the strengths of women's development. Yet in doing so, it

Reprinted by permission from *Hypatia* 5: 58–82. Copyright © by the author.

pares back some of care's presumed critical relevance to "justice theories" of development, making room for their virtues while deflecting much unnecessary controversy detrimental to care.[1] The alternative hypothesis also seeks to affirm feminist worries regarding care without threatening Gilligan's main insights or care's research potential.

I. The Two Alternatives

1. Care As Moral Development: Gilligan's Voice

Gilligan portrays care as both a general orientation toward moral problems (interpersonal problems) and a track of moral development. As an orientation or focus, care expresses an empathetic sense of connectedness to others, of being in relation with them, actually or potentially. As a track of development, care evolves from an egocentric form of self-care, through a more conventional sort of do-gooder care. It moves on, finally, to a self-chosen, self-reflective, and self-affirming form of mature caring (Gilligan 1982a, chaps. 3, 4).

At level 1 of this development, care is self-concerned and self-protective out of a sense of vulnerability. The caring individual seeks above all to avoid hurt and insure psychological survival. With increasing self-confidence and a sense of competence to relate effectively, she sees this protective orientation as selfish and irresponsible. Care then evolves into a more conventional form of caring for others that is socially effective in its adherence to accepted norms. At this second level, the caring person seeks the support and approval of others by living up to their expectations and serving their needs altruistically. On the one hand, this leads to psychological denial and the rationalization of care's slavishness, according to Gilligan. On the other, it breeds a conflicting sense of being put upon and of allowing it to happen, of using the guise of altruism and martyrdom to mask indirect self-interest. With the confidence to face this conflict, and oneself, however, the caring individual moves to level 3. Here she recognizes that self-concern is self-responsible, that an adult must balance care for others with care for self as the contexts of her various relationships require.

At both transition points in the care sequence, crises of vulnerability can lead to nihilism and despair, confusion and retreat from care, rather than development. That is, women progress and regress in care, rather than following an invariant, progressive sequence.

Care is defined by theme rather than gender, according to Gilligan (1982a, 2). Yet care also is the dominant, spontaneous expression of a "relational social perspective." Since a relational perspective arises spontaneously from the formation of female gender identity and role, care will be the female ethic of choice. (Males characteristically evolve a "separational" or individualistic social perspective, by contrast, and prefer a rights and justice ethic.) In addition, since the most prominent theories of moral development favor the theme of justice, since they "listen to male voices" primarily, these theories tend to discriminate against female development. They underrepresent, distort and undervalue its "different voice" of caring (Gilligan, 1982a, chaps. 3, 4).

2. Care as Subjugation and Liberation

The alternative "care as liberation" hypothesis portrays care primarily as a sexist service orientation, prominent in the patriarchal socialization, social conventions, and roles of many cultures. This care theme is seen best at Gilligan's level 2, which is dominated by "stereotypical feminine virtues" such as "gentleness and tact," and an overriding desire "not to hurt" or disappoint anyone, as Gilligan puts it (1982a, 76, 65). Here women "seek survival by trying to satisfy male expectations and find male approval in hopes of male support (1982a, 66–67, 72, 78).

On the liberation hypothesis, the focus of such a care theme can be adjusted by adult women to handle crises of hurt, domination, and rejection usually brought on by males in women's daily lives and relationships as clearly reflected in Gilligan's key studies (1982a, 2, 3). Such crises engender various responses, each of which has pros and cons. Care "development" or care *levels*, then, actually represent circumscribed coping strategies, of special use to women for facing crises of sexism. While these strategies may be ordered by coping effectiveness, they do not evolve from each other developmentally for the most part. They do not represent general systems of moral competence of the sort that cognitive stages do in classic theories of moral development.

Let us reconsider Gilligan's three levels of care through the lens of this alternative hypothesis. Care at "level 1" now becomes primarily a coping strategy for facing hurtful rejection and domination, not for orienting to moral issues generally. It copes with its context, sensibly, by "seeking survival" through self-protection (1982a, 75–76, 110–11). Yet the effectiveness of this strategy, its "sense of isolation, aloneness, powerlessness," as Gilligan puts it, can often lead to resuming the conventional, slavish approach of level 2 care. In Gilligan's research, such coping requires psychological denial and rationalization when used as a strategy adopted by adult women (1982a, 80–85). Level 2's slavishness is especially difficult to live with if one has reflected at all on one's role and treatment in sexist relationships as Gilligan's respondents have. We would not expect this reflective conflict to arise in the well-socialized girl.

To deal with these inner conflicts of level 2 coping, while facing additional domination and rejection by men, various strategies recommend themselves.

Level 3, where the balance between care for others and care for self is struck, is not the obvious alternative. One might revert to level 1 self-protectiveness again. Gilligan describes an assertive mode of this strategy which involves "deliberate isolation." Here one sees oneself as "a loner" who is self-sufficient and unfettered to a degree (1982a, 75, 89). This form of self-protection would be especially effective in dealing with level 2 aversion to slavish care and internal level 1 problems of powerlessness and isolation. Yet in addressing these problems in this way, one identifies with one's victimized retreat from care, mistaking it as one's self-affirming strength.

A like strategy of "care" would involve what Gilligan terms "moral nihilism" (1982a, 123–26). In its less despairing form, it is a more affirmative approach to self-interest than self-protection is—if nothing is really right or wrong, then "why care?", "Why not be selfish?"

Of course, one may not have the self-confidence for such self-affirmation, nor the luck of finding those modes of self-affirmation that "work for you." In this context, one may fall into moral confusion and hopelessness. Gilligan describes this "development" as well—"I'm still in love with him, no matter what he has done, and that really confuses me. . . . I can't get him out of my mind" (1982a, 124). Such regression in caring can also result from the servile strategy of trying level 2 "service orientation" over and over again, despite its failure. Gilligan terms these sorts of phenomena "cycles of repetition" and the "psychology of passivity," though she does not apply these descriptions to level 2.

When considering the basis of this reinterpretation thus far, three features of Gilligan's account are key. First, care is depicted as progressing and regressing, alternately, not necessarily as evolving in order of levels. Second, Gilligan does not claim, nor offer evidence, that lower levels of care generally occur earlier in development. And finally, Gilligan's studies do not observe any one respondent traversing all three levels of care in order, or otherwise. Therefore, the seemingly undevelopmental disorder or variability of care fits here.

There are, however, more effective coping strategies which care might try. Through the self-confidence gained by surviving abandonments and hurt, and reflectively learning their lessons, women may emerge to level 3 care. In this explicit "consciousness-raising" strategy, a woman seeks the "middle path" between self-protection and slavishness. She balances self-care with care for others more evenly. Level 3 care is clearly a more subtle and effective path for the sexist realities a woman faces than level 2 coping. It shows significant insight into the validity of benevolent virtues and compassionate response, along with acknowledgement of their dangers. Here a woman learns where she can exercise her strengths, interests, and commitments within the male power structure and where she would do better to comply with that structure. A delicate contextual balance must be struck to be effective here.

Since this approach carries forward some of the aversive "service orientation" of level 2, its internal effectiveness is enhanced by rationalization, as it was at level 2. Likewise, since the slavishness of this orientation is now more reflectively recognized than at level 2, effective rationalization must take a far more reflective and legitimating form. Thus, in this level 3 coping strategy, a woman takes personal responsibility for compliance. She portrays it as adult and self-chosen *in its selectivity,* and even virtuous in this selectivity. Furthermore, she abstracts and generalizes the strategy as a legitimate and even preferred ethic—a carefully balanced, caring-for-others-in-general ethic—from which males could learn much. She distinguishes such a service orientation from slavish level 2 conventionalism by recasting the *limits* of her social and moral power as the very *power* to be limited, to be tentative, contextual, and morally balanced in her exercise of power. Gilligan emphasizes the peculiar virtues of such contextualism and tentativeness in level 3 care (1982a, 54–55, 95, 100–102, 165–167).

Partial Developments

As should be apparent, support for this alternative "different voice" will derive from Gilligan's own text. The "care as liberation" hypothesis proposes that Gilligan's observations and *interpretations* of care *may* not best support her overall position that care constitutes moral development. At the least, they lend comparable support to the view that care is primarily a form of coping with sexism. Before we detail this support, a few reflections on the significance of this hypothesis are in order. We will begin with its relation to Gilligan's conception of moral maturity, to possible (sexist) biases in her interpretive theorizing, and to the nondevelopmental strengths of care she uncovers.

While the highest level for care shows a degree of cognitive liberation from sexist oppression, its "consciousness-raising" may not see through many sexist aspects of its own ethic. In this regard it is morally defective and incomplete rather than mature or adequate. Level 3 care does not accurately identify the causes of its "sense of service" in the sexist nature of social institutions and sexual politics primarily. Rather it "progressively" personalizes and legitimizes responsibility for this orientation as a desirable form of "taking control of one's life" and "taking responsibility for oneself," of learning to feel "adult" and "good about oneself" (Gilligan 1982a, 75–78, 82–85, 91–94).

Unfortunately, Gilligan's descriptions of care maturity at level 3 appear to reflect and legitimate this process. They portray only the effectiveness of care, not the inadequacies of self-alienation involved. These descriptions actually may compound the problem by portraying care's consciousness-raising approach to liberation as a *spontaneous* or *natural* development reflective of female gender. By making this approach dependent on *personal* confidence, psychological *self*-awareness, and on moral *self*-control and *self*-responsibility, Gilligan seemingly weakens the key connection her account draws between relational orientation and female gender identity.

In an account of care's progressive struggle with sexism, level 3 care might be faulted for its lack of political sense or institutional focus out of which a sense of solidarity with other women and a need for cooperative social action might derive. Care's almost total lack of social-institutional focus at level 3 certainly raises questions about its general moral adequacy. The attempt to balance serving others with self-care at level 3 does not solve the problem of slavishness. It merely tempers and accommodates to it in a morally questionable way. This accommodation is then intellectualized, especially in Gilligan's descriptions of level 3, by portraying it as a necessary complement to "male-oriented" justice (1982a, 100). (Marx described a similar tendency of crude communism to *universalize* private [alienated] property, including women as male property, in a misguided hope of moralizing it.) By contrast, a truly liberated ethic for women (and other oppressed groups) might speak in a truly new voice, expressing themes of unfolding, liberated experience. In so doing it might not promote either responsive responsibility or demand for individual rights in themselves or in combination. Hopefully this view of care addresses feminist concerns and those of critical theorists. Obviously it is framed primarily from the perspective of socialist feminism, though it hopes to accommodate radical and liberal feminist perspectives as well in the particular context it addresses.

At the same time, there can be no doubt that it is psychologically and morally better for women to cope with oppression in these caring ways than not at all. To be able to handle a circumscribed range of moral problems through a particular set of orientational strategies surely shows moral skill. Coming to certain valid moral beliefs and insights, working out one's caring stance on key interpersonal situations clearly, represents a moral advance in some cognitive-psychological domain. And of course, it is morally better that people see through oppression part way than not at all. This is true even when they deceive themselves when doing so; after all, self-deception is a skill of sorts in certain contexts. When such moral progress is accompanied by increased self-awareness and confidence, learning to take control of one's life and responsibility for oneself, additional moral progress is likely to result. These are all moral developments in women's conceptual orientations which Gilligan has uncovered perceptively and ordered artfully. Gilligan has detailed women's moral *socialization* well also, it appears.

Still, the evolution from somewhat duped and debilitated in some domain to somewhat disabused and functional in that domain differs from steadily progressive development in general competence. In this latter process we primarily move from fairly competent to progressively more so. Circumscribed moral coping skills tailored to gender-specific and oppressive contexts differ from broad systems of cognitive moral competence. Such systems organize and process the fundamentals of social experience for all, at the most basic level, while recognizing that much of our most salient experience is not of this sort.

Theories of human development in moral cognition, such as those of Piaget and Kohlberg, seek to chart the progression of such basic meaning and reasoning systems. As a result, care coping and its struggle for liberation need not be covered by the classic theories of moral development Gilligan criticizes. Nor do these theories discriminate against care when leaving such phenomena out. Likewise, such theories need not, and should not, cover the so-called "justice focus" that Gilligan associates with male gender preferences, nor any other "macho" ethic there may be. This is so even when such orientations primarily speak to male experience and reflect patriarchal competencies in sexist society.

The theories of Piaget, Kohlberg, and especially Freud should be criticized for *bias,* patriarchal and otherwise. However, where justice bias in basic cognitive *structure* is found, it will not likely discriminate against care orientation, as Gilligan describes this phenomenon. And, when such biases are removed, such caring is not likely to be better represented in these sorts of human developmental theories.

"Slave Morality" and Other Ideologies

The "care as liberation" hypothesis utilizes the speculative conceptual models and political jargon of critical theory for two reasons. First, it seeks to emphasize the uncanny relationship between care maturity, as Gilligan portrays it, and the "slave morality" phenomenon long recognized in this tradition. Second, it seeks to show how Gilligan's own critical approach to exposing patriarchy in classic moral development theory might apply to her own view. It does this, in part, by applying the sort of analysis Gilligan offers of level 2 caring to her level 3 caring.

Gilligan's critique, after all, tries to show how males "rationalize" their gender-identity needs through moral (justice) orientations. They claim such needs as their just due. Patriarchal theories then further "rationalize" this rationalization by abstracting and legitimizing it at its "highest" level as a generally applicable form of moral competence. The "care as liberation" hypothesis builds on Gilligan's own observations of how women rationalize their moral victimization at level 2. It suggests how care theory may further "rationalize" this circumscribed sort of rationalization by abstracting and legitimizing it (at its "highest" level) as a generally applicable form of moral competence. In offering this analysis I do not assume that women or victims of oppression generally suffer more "ideological distortion" *overall* than those who oppress them, far from it. Rather this analysis posits partial distortions of one sort, in relation to one sort of coping, and only to a degree.

The "slave morality" phenomenon, as we know, was identified most vividly in the spread of Christianity among poor and oppressed peoples. As Nietzscheans observed, for example, the Christian message of "love as service" appeals by transforming vices of subservience into virtues of redemption. "Bear your cross, be humble, meek, patient, and long-suffering for His sake. Love and give even to those who abuse you, asking nothing for yourself, and all will be given to you." Such a message appeals even more when it prescribes such virtues and distributes such burdens to all, as is especially notable in Christianity. Marx identified this ideological "opiate" in secular ideals as well, including ideals of communism. As noted, he predicted that proletarians, victimized by private property, would misconceive their liberation in the ideology of equal property, equal distribution of wealth. In this way they would at least share their victimization "after the revolution." For Marx, Nietzsche, and others, truly liberating moral revolution (or development) is not found in such selective validation of servitude as one climbs out of it. It does not consist in balancing or equalizing servitude. Rather, moral adequacy is found in a radical transformation of our understanding of human welfare and mutuality. Of course, this transformation need not overturn enduring virtues of the feminine, noted by radical feminists and Gilligan as well.

While the "care as liberation" hypothesis is not dependent on such speculative positions, nor the often slanted or overgeneralized observations that accompany them, it benefits from what common-sense plausibility they have.[2] (See Nicholson 1983 for a very interesting analysis in a related tradition.)

It is important to recognize, however, that challenges to the moral and psychological adequacy of care and coping, from a critical theory perspective, are somewhat secondary to the intent of this hypothesis. The "slave morality" analysis applies only to one aspect of the "consciousness-raising" component of level 3 care. The heart of "care as liberation" distinguishes care as socialization and skillful coping from care as general moral development. In this way, as noted, it preserves many of care's psychological strengths while fending off damaging countercriticisms from classic theories of moral development. There is no dispute, I take it, that Gilligan's contrast between care and justice, female relationality and male individuation, captures gender *socialization* by and large. Nor is there likely to be dispute that effective coping, for either gender, *might* vary these themes in ways that Gilligan's care levels depict. Rather the current Kohlberg-Gilligan dispute, for example, is over whether these levels are "cognitive-developmental." It is over whether they spontaneously evolve in a way that expresses holistic cognitive systems and their inherent processes of constructional self-transformation. Care need not enter this cognitive-developmental domain, nor theoretical controversy, to make its contribution.

It is also important to recognize that the explicitly feminist analysis of care coping I offer, while important in its own right, may be one aspect of a broader view concerning "response to authoritarianism." Care levels bear a strong resemblance to patterns of attitudinal assimilation and accommodation commonly observed among poor and oppressed groups, or in oppressive situational contexts. Taking the levels in order, their "oppression focus" may be rendered in common-sense terms: Level 1—protect yourself against harm from those in power. Ensure your psychological survival in the face of ongoing domination through strategies of self-protection and self-concern. Level 2—to overcome ongoing powerlessness, play the roles those in power set for you. Serve and sacrifice to gain their approval and support, thereby participating in their power and avoiding harm. Be circumspect in pursuing your true interests, or even in recognizing them. And maintain a sense of fulfillment and self-esteem in expressing the competencies of pragmatic service. Level 3—with the partial success of strategy level 2, and where otherwise possible, acknowledge your (nonthreatening) true interests. Ferret out spheres of power for pursuing these interests within the gaps of the established power structure. Embrace the competencies of those oppressed roles one cannot avoid. Identify with them and use them with one's "true" competencies as a source of evolving strength and pride.

Social scientists have observed this sort of pattern in the orientation of inmates in prison camps as associated with a related phenomenon, "identification with the aggressor" (Bettleheim 1943; A. Freud 1946; Sanford 1955). Kohlberg has also observed it in the prison communities he has studies (Kohlberg, et al. 1975; Jennings et al. 1983a, 1983b). There also are anecdotal accounts (novels, films, documentaries) of this pattern in blue-collar orientations toward authoritarian management and in "third-world" orientations toward the "economic imperialism" of industrialized nations.

In this context, it is notable that Gilligan portrayed care levels only in the responses of women facing the oppressive machinations of sexist institutions and relationships (1982a, 71–72, 107–8). In particular, Gilligan's respondents faced threats of male rejection and abandonment in love relationships due to unexpected pregnancies. They consciously saw their abortion decisions as severe crises for these relationships and themselves.

Again, the "care as liberation" hypothesis is not dependent on the sorts of global and anecdotal observations cited above, though it benefits from their strongest and most shared insights. This hypothesis can and will be supported from Gilligan's own account of care and its relation to the field of moral development.

II. Working Hypothesis

Since "care as liberation" is a working hypothesis designed for comparison with Gilligan's "different voice," its supporting case must be framed relative to Gilligan's as well. It must "argue" that Gilligan studies (a) socialization, reflective consciousness-raising, and coping more than moral development; (b) gender-based coping more than a care theme of coping which women happen to prefer; and (c) coping with oppression and especially sexism rather than more general coping with moral issues. The fact that this hypothesis derives its case from Gilligan's own text reflects Gilligan's own acknowledgement that care is influenced by socialization and coping with sexism. As noted, however, her account opts for the dominance of moral developmental processes in care's evolution, viewing other factors as secondary. This may be a function of the Kohlbergian framework from which her work stems. The "care as liberation" hypothesis questions this interpretation based on the nature of Gilligan's reported observations and research methods. Thus, while it poses different themes for care, it does so in Gilligan's own voice. (It is best thought of as part of an internal debate which Gilligan might have with herself, or which supporters might have among themselves, regarding how to voice the caring they hear.) We begin with points (b) and (c) above.

Women and Sexism

It is easy to misunderstand Gilligan's claim that the "different voice" is characterized by theme, not gender (1982a, 2). Care is not a theme that all women must prefer, or that all women have been observed preferring. Neither is it a theme males cannot adopt. However, it is the theme that Gilligan considers characteristic of women, not men. This is so, in the first instance, because Gilligan claims to have found an "empirical association" of this sort. But more important, it is so because Gilligan claims to have identified the apparent cause of this association, the relational orientation built into female gender-identity. Gilligan's research is aimed at uncovering this distinctively gender-based causal relation. Likewise, her research with colleagues and students is focused on the gender difference issue (Lyons 1982; Langdale 1983; Johnston 1984).

> The different voice I describe is characterized not by gender but theme. Its association with women is an empirical observation; and it is primarily through women's voices that I trace its development. But this association is not absolute, and the contrasts between male and female voices are presented here to highlight a distinction between two modes of thought and to focus on a problem

of interpretation rather than to represent a generalization about either sex. (1982a, 2)

In presenting excerpts from this work, I report research in progress whose aim is to provide, in the field of human development, a clearer representation of women's development which will enable psychologists and others to follow its course and understand some of the apparent puzzles it presents, especially those that pertain to women's identity formation and their moral development in adolescence and adulthood. (1982a, 3)

Notice the apparent inconsistency of aims in these two self-reflections, given that Gilligan's interpretations are illustrated with her research findings.

These findings were gathered at a particular moment in history, the sample was small, and the women were not selected to represent a larger population. These constraints preclude the possibility of generalization and leave to further research the task of sorting out the different variables of culture, time, occasion, and gender. Additional longitudinal studies of women's moral judgments are needed in order to refine and validate the sequence described. (1982a, 126)

Gilligan's research and account of care development, to which the last citations refer, is characterized by gender rather than theme. Chapters 3 and 4 of Gilligan's book, which encompass care levels, refer only to Gilligan's abortion study. This study sampled women only, in order to discover how women in particular think about moral issues, construct moral categories, and define moral language. Quite understandably, then, Gilligan faults Kohlberg's all-male sampling because he was not researching *male* development, but, supposedly, human development.

To derive developmental criteria from the language of women's moral discourse, it is necessary first to see whether women's construction of the moral domain relies on a language different from men and one that deserves equal credence in the definition of development. This in turn requires finding places where women have the power to choose and thus are willing to speak in their own voice. (1982a, 70)

Moreover, Gilligan's interpretive analysis of findings from this study focuses on gender difference by organizing the various caring themes of self-survival, feminine virtue and conformity, moral nihilism, and shared (caring) responsibility together under gender.

Yet, in addition, Gilligan characterizes her chosen moral issue, as in the abortion study, as focusing on problems of passivity and dependence that have been "most problematic for women," and as requiring a resolution of the conflict between sexist conventions of femininity and women's conception of adulthood (1982a, 69, 71). The subject of the study was designed to focus on "how women deal with such choices," "bring[ing] to the core of feminine apprehension . . . that sense of living one's deepest life underwater" (1982a, 71).

There is not only a clear emphasis here on gender, then, but a head-on confrontation with sexism. Moreover, this confrontation occurs in an especially sexist context, a sexist crisis. While Gilligan makes the crisis nature of the abortions study clear (1982a, 72, 107), she does not make clear how much the crisis is one of sexism itself. However, Gilligan emphasizes from the start the role of sexism in women's spontaneous and distinctive moral judgment more generally. Care orientation is introduced with illustrations from female respondents which show "a sense of vulnerability that impedes these women from taking a (moral) stand, what George Eliot regards as the girl's 'susceptibility' to adverse judgments by others, which stems from her lack of power and consequent inability 'to do something in the world'" (1982a, 66). As Gilligan puts this point further: "When women feel excluded from direct participation in society, they see themselves as subject to a consensus or judgment made and enforced by men on whose protection and support they depend and by whose name they are known" (1982a, 67). Gilligan illustrates her point vividly, through a respondent.

> As a woman, I feel I never understood that I was a person, that I could make decisions and I had a right to make decisions. I always felt that that belonged to my father or my husband in some way, or my church, which was always represented by a male clergyman. They were the three men in my life: father, husband, and clergyman, and they had much more to say about what I should or shouldn't do. They were really authority figures which I accepted. It only lately has occurred to me that I never even rebelled against it, and my girls are much more conscious of this, not in the militant sense, but just in the recognizing sense. . . . I still let things happen to me rather than make them happen. (1982a, 67)

Again, characterizing women's moral judgment *as a whole,* Gilligan notes that

> The essence of moral decision is the exercise of choice and the willingness to accept responsibility for that choice. To the extent that

women perceive themselves as having no choice, they correspond-
ingly excuse themselves from the responsibility that decision entails. Childlike in the vulnerability of their dependence and consequent fear of abandonment, they claim to wish only to please, but
in return for their goodness they expect to be loved and cared for.
This, then, is an "altruism" always at risk, for it presupposes an
innocence constantly in danger of being compromised by an
awareness of the trade-off that has been made. (1982a, 67)

More significant, then, is a continuing emphasis on the sexism problem
throughout Gilligan's discussion and her excerpts from respondents. This
continuing emphasis is found even when Gilligan's deliberate emphasis is
elsewhere. When Gilligan and her respondents speak of relationships, over
two chapters, there is scarce mention of the relational network of siblings
and friends that supposedly defines care's relational orientation. One would
expect some emphasis on a close female friend or two in an open-ended
interview about one's abortion decision. While there are some abstract generalizations about caring for "others," or for a "future child," in this text,
the only actual ongoing relationships emphasized are with "the boyfriend"
or "lover." Moreover, the egregiously sexist nature of these relationships
and of women's situations in them (especially regarding abortion) are emphasized in each case.

In discussing level 1 of care, for example, Gilligan notes that as a general
phenomenon, "Relationships are for the most part disappointing" (1982a,
75). As a respondent illustrates this point, "the only thing you are ever going
to get out of going with a guy is to get hurt" (75). Gilligan then notes that
"as a result, women sometimes choose isolation to protect themselves
against hurt" (75). Yet whether women choose isolation or not, the overall
orientation of self-care at level 1 is self-protective, not merely self-concerned
(75–77). And what women are protecting themselves against primarily, in
the responses that Gilligan cites, are the threats posed by characteristically
sexist rejection in love relationships, and in social responses to the abortion
crisis.

Gilligan's respondent Betty, for example, had her first abortion after being
raped. Afterwards she felt "helpless and powerless to obtain contraception
for herself because she did not have any money and she believed she needed
her parents' permission; she also felt powerless to deal with her boyfriend's
continuing harassment. In the end, she gave in to his assurance that he knew
what he was doing and would not get her pregnant, influenced by her belief
that if she refused, he would break up with her" (1982a, 109). She became
pregnant again because "no one was willing to help." "After I went to bed
with him he just wanted me to do everything he wanted to do . . . (disregard-
ing) the fact that I wanted my freedom." Thus Betty becomes preoccupied

with her own needs, as Gilligan puts it, "to ensure her own survival in a world perceived as exploitative."

At care level 1, a woman's thinking "focuses on taking care of herself because she feels all alone. The issue is survival." Gilligan continues, "In this mode of understanding, the self . . . is constrained by lack of power that stems from feeling disconnected" (1982a, 75). It is notable that Kohlberg's stages also trace an egoistic "concern for self" at his level 1 (stages 1 and 2). However, this egoism simply expresses self-interest, not protection against hurt and threat, especially not hurt or threat that puts one's very survival at stake. Presumably this is because Kohlberg and other moral developmentalists are trying to tap general competence in responding to the broad spectrum of moral problems, not to especially oppressive or threatening ones. However, adolescents and adults are observed to retreat to this egoistic level functionally, when faced with oppressive crises and threats (as in a prison environment). In this regard it is important to note in the above citations (and those following) how often the self-protective response of self-concern at level 1 seems to follow, not precede, the level 2 concern with "maintaining one's love relationship." It is important to note how often this concern sets care up for its fall. (This ordering of concerns, by levels, is not what we would expect in a developmental sequence.)

We see this regressive "retreat from care," from hurt in love relationships, in the reaction of moral nihilism and confusion which is the corollary to self-protection in Gilligan's account.

> Lisa, a fifteen year old, believing in her boyfriend's love, acceded to his wish "not to murder his child." But after she decided not to abort the child, he left her and "thus ruined my life. . . . I don't know what to do with my boyfriend gone. I'm still in love with him, no matter what he has done, and that really confuses me, because I don't know why I still do. . . . I can't get him out of my mind." (1982a, 123–24)

We see a similar reaction in a woman already working out of such reactions near the highest level of care.

> Sarah (a third respondent) had discovered the first pregnancy after her lover left her, and she terminated it by an abortion which she experienced as a purging expression of her anger at having been rejected. Remembering the abortion only as a relief she nevertheless describes that time in her life as one in which she "hit rock bottom." Having hoped to "take control of my life," she instead resumed the relationship when the man reappeared. Two years later, having again "left my diaphragm in the drawer," she became

pregnant. Although initially ecstatic at the news, her elation dissipated when her lover told her that he would leave her if she chose to have the child. (1982a, 90–91)

Level 2 care is said to show a general concern for serving others' needs sacrificially and thereby winning their approval. It tries to go along with shared norms and values which define the expectations others have of you. In this respect, it seems akin to Kohlberg's conventional stage 3 in which respondents play their "good boy"/"good girl" roles that others expect of them. Gilligan faults Kohlberg's system for classifying women's judgment at such a childlike level of care (1982a, 70).

However, in the excerpts in which Gilligan cites from respondents, the orientation of level 2 is tailored much more to serving "the boyfriend's" needs and sexist expectations in particular. A secondary focus is on living up to peculiarly sexist conventions of love relations, marriage, and family. There is an emphasis here, as we saw above, on "trying to please" out of the "vulnerability of dependence" and "fear of abandonment," and in the "expectation of being loved or cared for." The prescribed manner of pleasing invokes peculiar "feminine stereotypes" such as "deference to male judgment and strength," and "gentleness and tact" (1982a, 69, 79, 80). None of these key features of Gilligan's "altruism at risk" are key to Kohlberg's "good girl" orientation at conventional stage 3.

Consider the type of conventionality care espouses. Gilligan notes that respondents in her abortion study get pregnant in hopes of "making the baby an ally in the search for male support and protection or, that failing, a companion in male rejection" (1982a, 72). Pregnancy is also seen as "the perfect chance to get married and leave home," to overcome a sense of "powerlessness and disconnection" (1982a, 75), or as a way "to concretize our relationship" (1982a, 88) or "put the relationship to the ultimate test of commitment" (1982a, 72, 119). Yet abortion also is seen as a way to overcome this sense of powerlessness, to "continue the relationship [with the lover] and not 'drive us apart.'" "Since I met him he has been my life. I do everything for him, my life sort of revolves around him" (1982a, 81).

Gilligan observes that her respondent Ellen "considered herself 'fairly strong-willed, fairly in control' . . . until she became involved in an intense love affair . . . entertain[ing] vague ideas that 'some day I would like a child to concretize our relationship.' Abjuring, with her lover, the use of contraceptives . . . she saw herself as relinquishing control, becoming instead 'just simply vague and allowing events to just carry me along'" (1982a, 87–88). Even in evolving out of level 2, as Gilligan sees it, a woman "struggles to free herself from the powerlessness of her own dependence" when "pregnant by the same man" who made her have the abortion that kept them together (1982a, 81).

Aside from relationality, which defines the caring perspective overall, "not hurting" is its dominant orientation. Yet when Gilligan introduces this "common thread" in her initial excerpts from women's judgment, the thread that particularizes these concerns is "not hurting *boyfriends*." As one respondent puts it, "Not hurting others is important in my private morals. Years ago I would have jumped out of a window not to hurt my boyfriend. That was pathological. Even today, though, I want approval and love. . . ." As another respondent put it, "My main principle is not hurting people. . . . I'm afraid I'm heading for some big crisis with my boyfriend someday, and someone will get hurt, and he'll get more hurt than I will" (1982a, 65).

III. Socialization and Reflection

The above citations and the way they are cast, I believe, are representative of Gilligan's first two levels of care. Yet Gilligan's depiction of level 2 care also includes a more general "caring for others" emphasis alongside the focus on "serving males." In recent writings (Gilligan 1987; Gilligan & Wiggins 1988) an emphasis has been placed on caring in mother/daughter relations. These emphases in care could challenge the hypothesis that care coping is tailored to sexism. However, I believe that the discussions of care and mothering are highly speculative rather than merely interpretive in a social scientific sense. They concern a global "care orientation" that is very difficult to tie to care *levels* and the actual interview data from which they derive. This is why I have relied so heavily on Gilligan's original, book-length account of care in these discussions. And, of course, the "care as liberation" hypothesis does not claim that care *only* involves coping with sexism.

Moreover, the emphasis on care in general, at level 2, is precisely what we should expect if care truly is conventional at this level, as Gilligan claims. The key is that care fits traditional sexist socialization here, socialization in "service orientation" or service ideology, or a coping strategy based on this theme. Obviously the effectiveness of such a socialized conventional ideology depends on its somehow rationalizing the subservient role of women relative to men in society. And there is little dispute, I take it, that this socialized ideology does so in part by generalizing women's service orientation to others as a whole. Gilligan acknowledges this tendency by citing the Broverman stereotypes of gentleness, tact and other caretaking traits as "female stereotypes" (1982a, 79). These socially approved and fostered traits are to characterize woman's character, her moral self-concept and orientation to others generally, in sexist society. As Gilligan also notes, this very same rationalization, viewing oneself and one's activities as *generally* altruistic, is used explicitly by women at level 2. Here it handles inner conflict with the slavishness of conventional care. These are signs of care's strategic and partially reflective quality at level 2, as well as its more dominant socialization influence.

Therefore, if sufficient reason can be offered for preferring a socialization and reflection explanation for care over a cognitive-developmental account, the "care as liberation" hypothesis is supported. This will be our final task regarding the first two levels of care and, eventually, the third level. Since level 3 is more complex, it will have to be addressed at more levels. And, since it is a primarily "self-chosen" orientation, rather than a conventional one, we will emphasize the contrast between its reflective, "consciousness-raising" character, and the nature of cognitive-developmental processes. This approach will be clarified briefly at the outset.

While level 3 care copes with sexism in particular, it also retains the generalized focus on "caring for others" begun at level 2. The "care as liberation" hypothesis holds three factors responsible for this trend. First, there is the lingering influence of conventional care at this level. This is shown by the continuation of a basic service theme from level 2, now applied to oneself as well as others, combined with the failure to notice key deficiencies of this theme during reflection. Second, there is the "slave morality" phenomenon, providing a more elaborate version of level 2 rationalizing. It "legitimizes" caring service by generalizing its apparent virtues ideologically.[3] Third, there is the influence of truly liberated "consciousness-raising" or insightful reflection. In this process, some women uncover many of the morally valid and virtuous components of benevolence, as Gilligan recounts. These components properly express benevolence toward others in general. However, on the "care as liberation" hypothesis, Gilligan's account of level 3 overrates the fullness and adequacy of these discoveries. It also overrates their cognitive-developmental form.

To support the role of these three factors at level 3, our analysis should identify six features of care here: (1) the significant role of sexist socialization influences; (2) the superior role of reflection; (3) the peculiarly personal, insightful, or otherwise nongeneralizable form of that reflection; (4) its social-ideological character; (5) its moral defects, and the defective way that it is personalized and legitimized; and (6) the relative lack of evidence for cognitive-developmental processes there, or their significant influence. Since Gilligan cites very few level 3 respondents, it is difficult to draw extensive support for these features from the text. However, they all receive some support in the citations that follow, especially when considered in the context of Gilligan's research approach. The moral defects of mature care, suggested earlier, are elaborated in detail elsewhere (Puka 1988). The contrast I will outline between Gilligan's research and the approach of cognitive-developmentalists she criticizes is elaborated elsewhere as well (Puka 1990).

The task of our analysis is made easier by the fact that socialization, reflection, and cognitive-developmental processes exert very different degrees of influence on us. As shown in the research literature, and by common observation, socialization plays the dominant role in shaping our motivations, values, and ideologies. On this same basis we can assume that the power of female socialization in sexist "service orientation" is great. Gender studies, as a field, has greatly bolstered that assumption. Reflective learning and insight are a powerful factor in forming moral ideologies among adults, where the effects of earlier socialization are weakened or overcome. (The work of Perry [1964] provides excellent evidence for this, which Gilligan countenances greatly in defining level 3. This evidence is supported, despite appearance to the contrary, by Belenky et al. in *Woman's Ways of Knowing*.) The power of reflection here is greatly increased, we commonly observe, when compounded with the social reinforcements of one's reflective peers. In these contexts, the burden of proof is on the moral developmentalist (*any* moral developmentalist) to show that the processes she posits exist at all, and can compete with these others for influence.

Importantly, cognitive-developmental processes arise in the same form across the broad range of social interactions. They operate and evolve by inherent "principles" of cognitive construction, such as integration and differentiation. They form a holistic system for organizing moral experience and affording basic but general competence in facilitating moral judgment. Such cognitive-moral processes will use experience and learn from it. Perhaps they will encompass some reflective processes at the highest developmental levels. But they will not be determined by the peculiar shape of one's experience and socialization or the particular styles and discoveries of personal insight. Thus, for example, coming to believe in one's subservient roles and traits as a woman is not something we would expect to evolve in this way. This ideology is too particularized, too dependent on particular interpretations of fact and value, and on partisan social interests, to arise without being taught or "discovered" by intellect. It is also regressive, presumably, rather than developmental. In the same way, coming to adopt a distinctively feminist perspective or liberal ideology is not likely to be natural and basic to women's cognitive development.

Thus, to support the dominant roles of socialization and reflective coping in care, we will merely note their robust role in Gilligan's account and in her research. At the same time, we will cite the weakness of her grounds for conceiving care as cognitive-moral development. Let us begin with the reflective peculiarities of level 3, the ways care rests on certain reflective insights into particular sorts of experience, and into oneself.

Raising Consciousness

Gilligan first characterizes the transition to level 3 care in the responses of Sarah. Here Gilligan aims to show "how closely her transformed moral understanding is tied to changing self-concept" (Gilligan 1982a, 92). When asked to "describe yourself to yourself," Sarah answers quite self-consciously,

> I have been thinking about that a lot lately, and it comes up different than what my usual subconscious perception of myself is. Usually paying off some sort of debt, going around serving people who are not really worthy of my attention, because somewhere in life I think I got the impression that my needs are really secondary to other people's, and that if I feel, if I make any demands on other people to fulfill my needs, I'd feel guilty for it and submerge my own in favor of other people's, which later backfires on me, and I feel a great deal of resentment for other people that I am doing things for, which causes friction and the eventual deterioration of the relationship. And I start all over again. How would I describe myself to myself? Pretty frustrated and a lot angrier than I admit, a lot more aggressive than I admit. (92–93)

Notice that the process of actual self-reflection (and even the awareness of that process) figures into what Gilligan sees as transformation in Sarah's level of care. As Sarah also notes, "I am suddenly beginning to think . . . the things I believe and the kind of person I am are not so bad. . . . I am a lot more worthwhile than my past actions have led other people to believe . . . you realize that that is a very usual way for people to live—doing what you want to do because you feel your wants and your needs are important" (93–94). At earlier levels, women could self-reflect when asked, but they do not report actually doing so "a lot lately."

Notice also that this process of self-reflection uncovers socialization into an explicitly sexist "service orientation," into "going around serving people," as a respondent puts it (92). "Somewhere in life I think I got the impression that my needs are really secondary to other people's." "I am beginning to think that all these virtues aren't really getting me anywhere" (93). It also uncovers the "cycle of repetition" and "psychology of passivity" rationalized previously—"And I start all over again." Sarah's usual subconscious perception of herself did not reveal these psychological phenomena.[4]

Sarah's explicit process of consciousness-raising regarding her approach to sexist relationships is especially clear in the following passages from Gilligan:

> For Sarah, facing a second abortion, the first step in taking control is to end the relationship in which she has considered herself "reduced to a nonentity," but to do so in a responsible way. Recogniz-

ing hurt as the inevitable concomitant of rejection, she strives to minimize that hurt by dealing with her lover's needs "as best I can without compromising my own. That's a big point for me, because the thing in my life to this point has been compromising, and I am not willing to do that anymore." (95)

As Gilligan concludes from this case, in chapter 3,

Thus, release from the intimidation of inequality finally allows women to express a judgment that had previously been withheld. What women then enunciate is not a new morality, but a morality disentangled from the constraints that formerly confused its perception and impeded its articulation. (95)

Yet later, picking up the case again, Gilligan notes that in becoming "tired of always bowing to other people's standards," Sarah "draws on the Quaker tradition" in which "your first duty is to your inner voice. . . . [W]hen the inner voice replaces outer ones as the arbiter of moral truth, it frees her from the *coercion* of others" (118). As Gilligan continues,

Reiterating with more confidence and clarity her discovery of an inner voice, she says that her decisions previously "were based elsewhere, I'm not really sure where." . . . [T]he integration of this insight into Sarah's life, the completion of the transition precipitated by the crisis, entailed a long and painful process that lasted for most of a year. Through this experience, she became more reflective: "I see the way I am and watch the way I make choices, the things I do." And she is now committed to building her life on a "strong foundation" of "surprisingly old wisdoms" with respect to her work and her relationships. (122)

Sarah moves on to level 3 once she starts "watching herself" and "listening" to the "inner voice" she has "discovered after a long and painful process in which she became more reflective." These sorts of reflective responses are offered by Gilligan's other level 3 respondents as well, such as Diane:

It is part of a self-critical view, part of saying, "How am I spending my time and in what sense am I working?" When I am dealing with moral issues, I am sort of saying to myself constantly, "Are you taking care of all the things that you think are important, and in what ways are you wasting yourself and wasting those issues?"
The only way I know is to try to be as awake as possible, to try to know the range of what you feel, to try to consider all that's

involved, to be as aware as you can be of what's going on, as conscious as you can of where you're walking. (99)

Gilligan shows how heavily level 3 care relies on reflection by stressing the contextualism of level 3 thought. This is gauged by Perry's levels of intellectual judgment. In the transition to level 3, Gilligan tells us, women start breaking down their absolute equations between selfish and bad, altruistic and good, and start making judgments relative to situational contexts. They tentatively seek out the shades of moral gray in moral reality, as they perceive it (102–4, 166). At level 3, this contextualism reaches fruition.

Perry's levels of intellectual development arose primarily from the reflective struggle of college students to deal with conflicts between the theories and belief systems they were exposed to in class. They chart reflective or metacognitive orientations and the way they change. These are orientations to our beliefs, values, and ethical systems themselves, rather than to moral problems and social interactions. When Gilligan asks women for self-descriptions relative to moral choice and gets the sort of responses cited above, she is getting at such metacognition. The same is true when she asks respondents to define morality itself and elicits responses such as "trying to uncover a right path to live, and always in my mind is that the world is full of real and recognizable trouble and is heading for some kind of doom" (99).

By contrast, classic moral development approaches focus on first-order questions of what to do about this or that problem. They encompass only that reflection which we can assume will evolve inherently in anyone as a normal part of trying to deal with sociomoral problems in a basically competent way. For the most part, reflective processes (and their insights) seem determined by particular types of education, exposure to ideologies and culture-specific styles of thinking, as well as the luck of discovery. At level 3, as noted, these processes are intermixed.

Social Learning and Moral Ideology

To distinguish the phenomenon of moral development from socialization and personal experience, researchers have evolved a variety of empirical and interpretive methods. Their research interviews feature a standard variety of moral dilemmas accompanied by challenging probe questions. Together these are designed to assure the existence of stable cognitive systems underlying the gamut of moral beliefs and ideologies, and expressed in them. By testing the limits of moral competence, these research probes uncover the stability of these systems, including their resistance to strong situational pulls from the environment, on the one hand, and also their capacity to address varied moral situations consistently, on the other. Such cognitive competence would differ from the particular skills or *beliefs* we show in performing particular kinds of tasks. Cognitive systems which show such general competence and stability, which take a holistic organizational form, are unlikely to be determined by the varying schedules of situational reinforcement. These include reflective self-reinforcement. Yet moral ideologies and skills, by contrast, seem to arise primarily in this way.

Cognitive developmental researchers also measure the transformation of cognitive systems at regular intervals to chart the mechanisms of change. In this way, they can better distinguish inherently constructional processes from shaping due to socialization, personal experience, or reflection.

By contrast, Gilligan's research uncovered care using open-ended interviews. Here respondents emitted only those dilemmas they found personally salient. Alternatively, a single, real-life dilemma was used, such as abortion. This approach does not focus on general moral competence.[5] Rather than challenging care responses to see if stable cognitive systems lay beneath, Gilligan's interview "follow[s] the language and logic of the person's thought," only "asking questions in order to clarify the meaning of particular responses" (1982a, 2). This may very well clarify moral ideology or socialization rather than cognitive-moral competence.

Gilligan's largest study (s = 144) was cross-sectional. It did not chart the evolution of care longitudinally at regular intervals. Her other two studies (s = 25, s = 21) involved only a single follow-up interview (1982a, 2–3). On this basis, Gilligan gained little empirical sense of what prompted change in care when change occurred. Gilligan never actually observed women go through the levels of care, as noted. But even more important, her writings do not illustrate the holistic structure or functioning of care levels in any *one* respondent. Rather Gilligan reconstructs the care sequence of development *conceptually* in her book, by glimpsing a small interval of development in eight respondents (108). Care at each level, and as a general orientation, is presented as a reconstructed composite of responses across respondents.

Furthermore, Gilligan's abortion study, so key to defining care levels, pulled for unusual responses. As noted, it utilized a dilemma which all involved considered a desperate personal crisis for respondents (108). In fact, Gilligan's developmental analysis of these responses was termed "magnification of crisis." This indicates Gilligan's stated belief that care development is a form of "response to crisis" in particular (107). As Gilligan sees it, we will move up care levels only if we have sufficient self-confidence and sense of control over our lives when facing crisis. Where we meet rejection and hurt with vulnerability and despair, we will likely regress (76–78, 82, 123–26). It is unclear how much these psychological states or processes involve cognitive systems at all, much less morally competent and self-constructional ones. In any event, these sorts of processes are highly vulnerable to socialization influences and peculiarities of personal experience. Gilligan does not try to distinguish aspects of cognition that succumb to this vulnerability from those which do not. This is especially problematic in the abortion context where ideological positions on the issue are so prominent in social experience.

On the contrary, "No claims are made about the origins of the differences described" in Gilligan's account, differences in moral theme or self/other perspective or gender. Rather, the account acknowledges the shaping influence on care of social status and power, traditional gender stereotypes, sexual politics, and bad experiences in love relationships. Feelings of loneliness and depression play a role too (2–3).

Finally, Gilligan reports great changes in care during a mere one-year interval. Out of twenty-one respondents in the abortion study, eight developed and four "got worse" between pretest and post-test (108). Such a degree of change is unheard of where the inherent, constructional processes of cognitive development are at work (e.g., integration, differentiation, equilibration). Yet while change of this sort would be expected in moral ideology or reflective beliefs, especially during personal crises, Gilligan never poses such interpretations of her results. She also does not try to distinguish functionally regressive change in care performance from regression in the cognitive-developmental organization of care competence.

Against these observations of socialization and personal reflection in care stand Gilligan's few remarks on how women "construct" care levels, on how one level is a more "differentiated and comprehensive" transformation of the level before (73, 76, 78). These are key cognitive-developmental catchwords. The "care as liberation" hypothesis acknowledges that Gilligan has uncovered some strands of cognitive structure in care. However, there is no indication in her account that these strands are sizable or that existing theories of development cannot encompass them under other moral themes. Gilligan's remarks are so sparse, when seen in relation to any standard cognitive-developmental account, that they are best viewed as suggesting a different sort of account. Otherwise, they bear serious deficiencies.[6]

Conclusion

"Care as liberation" is meant to be a working hypothesis. Its degree of support is to be compared with Gilligan's "different voice" interpretation of what her observations indicate. In providing this support, I have attempted to illustrate care's primary concern with women confronting sexism, and the primary role of socialization, personal reflection, and coping involved. I hope it is obvious how much this discussion and the "care as liberation" hypothesis extend the feminist potential of care, and of Gilligan's voice.

Notes

1. Gilligan's sweeping criticisms of Piaget, Erikson and especially Kohlberg have reduced the credibility of care unnecessarily. See Gilligan 1982a, 12–22, 31, 45, 59, 66, 99, 104; Kohlberg 1984, 338–70; and Broughton 1983b, reprinted as chapter 9 in this volume.
2. The hypothesis borrows explicitly from "radical therapy" notions of "abstraction" and "personalization" in the ideological rationalization process. Some observers may find them questionable. However, these powerful notions might also have been derived from Gilligan's own consideration of how "abstraction" and "impersonality" enter patriarchal morality. Likewise the slave morality or "resentment" phenomenon can be identified in ideologically neutral terms.
3. Again, while some women learn the lessons of sexist abuse at levels 1 and 2 and face the inadequacies of their coping strategies and rationalizations, they mistakenly personalize responsibility for failure. As they evolve a more balanced and selective approach to care coping, they rationalize its lingering limitations through the ideology of selective generalization and equalization of (slavish) care. Thus, care at level 3 still constitutes service orientation, service to others generally, but now not to the extent that oneself is left out.
4. I believe we would term these realizations especially insightful—psychologically and interpersonally insightful—and recognize that they are tailored to the issue of sexism primarily. We should not expect "the average woman" across cultures to come up with such distinctive ways of thinking simply because she takes a relational perspective and is therefore concerned with not hurting others.
5. Gilligan used Kohlberg dilemmas in some studies, but primarily for purposes of comparing justice reasoning with the alternative care orientation her interviews uncovered. Gilligan criticized Kohlberg's dilemmas and probe questions for discriminating against care orientation. See Gilligan 1982a, 100; Gilligan & Belenky 1979.
6. Since Gilligan did not observe development over a significant length of time in these studies, she could only conceptualize how each level of care *might* have been constructed from another, not how they actually appeared to be. Such a constructional analysis might easily be provided of any two conceptually related ideologies, one of which is more conceptually sophisticated than the other. In addition, Gilligan does not actually explicate the difference between levels and transitions, showing how the latter stabilize into holistic equilibrated systems. She does not actually trace each key component of care from one level to the next, showing how it is transformed and reintegrated with each other (and with new cognitive differentiations) to form a functioning whole. Even the three defining features of care—its moral theme of helping and not hurting, its relational perspective, and its notions of responsibility to others—are not depicted at all three levels. Level 1 seems to lack all of them. The remaining two level sequences might just as well be conceived as a bimodal phenomenon, rather than a developmental sequence. Finally, key features of care that distinguish each level pop in or out of the care "sequence" without clearly being transformed, differen-

tiated, or reintegrated in cognitive organization. Among these are, (1) "survival orientation," which disappears at level 3; (2) the "concern for good," of level 2, which is later *replaced* by the "concern for truth"; and (3) the need to be "honest with oneself" in level 2–3 transition which does not appear to evolve from, or evolve into, any concern like it. (For a more detailed analysis of these points see Puka 1990.) The greatest deficiencies in Gilligan's account, however, were noted earlier. Gilligan's approach to research and interpretation simply does not provide for crucial distinctions between socialization, consciousness-raising, and cognitive development.

17

Beyond Gender Difference to a Theory of Care

Joan C. Tronto

The work of Carol Gilligan and her associates, which describes "an ethic of care" that complements an understanding of morality as concerned with justice, has been cited frequently as proof of the existence of a "women's morality." [1] Gilligan has asserted from the first that she does not regard the ethic of care as a category of gender difference [Gilligan 1982a, 2; 1986c, 327 (reprinted as chapter 15 in this volume)]. Nonetheless, her work is widely understood as showing that women are different from men, as evidenced in the *Signs* forum on *In a Different Voice*. For example, Linda Kerber wrote, "But by emphasizing the biological basis of distinctive behavior . . . Gilligan permits her readers to conclude that women's alleged affinity for 'relationships of care' is both biologically natural and a good thing" [1986, 309 (reprinted as chapter 7 in this volume)]. Catherine Greeno and Eleanor Maccoby wrongly assert, "The fact remains, however, that Gilligan claims that the views expressed by women in her book represent a *different* voice—different, that is, from men" [1986, 315 (reprinted as chapter 13 in this volume)]. Zella Luria also notes that the book seems to belie Gilligan's later assertions that she is not calling for distinctive psychologies for men and women [1986, 318 (reprinted as chapter 14 in this volume)]. Carol Stack seems to accept Gilligan's work as representing "a female model of moral development" [1986, 324 (reprinted as chapter 8)].

Gilligan's point is a subtle one. On the one hand, she wants to say her argument goes no further than the claim that the moral domain must be extended to include justice and care. On the other hand, she also notes that "the focus on care . . . is characteristically a female phenomenon in the advantaged populations that have been studied" (1986c, 330).

In considering the issue of gender difference and morality, I shall use Gilligan's theory as the primary way to understand the nature of "women's morality." Although other writers might also be identified with women's morality (Noddings 1984; Ruddick 1980, 1983, 1984b), none has been so widely read and so widely interpreted as an advocate of this concept as Gilligan.[2] I do not mean to misrepresent Gilligan's work. The equation of Gilligan's work with women's morality is a cultural phenomenon, and not of Gilligan's making. Nonetheless, the contemporary discussion about Gilligan's work sets the context for discussions of women and morality.

This essay argues that although an ethic of care could be an important intellectual concern for feminists, the debate around this concern should be centered not in discussions of gender difference but in discourse about the ethic's adequacy as a moral theory. My argument is threefold. The equation of "care" with "female" is questionable because the evidence to support the link between gender difference and different moral perspectives is inadequate. It is a strategically dangerous position for feminists because the simple assertion of gender difference in a social context that identifies the male as normal contains an implication of the inferiority of the distinctly female. It is philosophically stultifying because, if feminists think of the ethic of care as categorized by gender difference, they are likely to become trapped trying to defend women's morality rather than looking critically at the philosophical promises and problems of an ethic of care.

A Critique of the Gender-Difference Perspective

Carol Gilligan originally devised her ethic of care when she sought to address problems she saw in Lawrence Kohlberg's psychology of moral development.[3] Her argument provides a psychological and developmental account of why women's moral statements are often expressed in terms of caring, but her approach leaves many questions unexplored.[4] In suggesting that an ethic of care is gender related, Gilligan precludes the possibility that care is an ethic created in modern society by the condition of subordination. If the ethic of care is separated from a concern with gender, a much broader range of options emerges. These are options that question the place of caring in society and moral life, as well as questioning the adequacy of Kohlberg's cognitive-developmental model.[5]

Lawrence Kohlberg's cognitive-developmental theory is today the most widely accepted theory of moral development (e.g., Kurtines & Gewirtz 1984). According to this theory, individuals develop morally as their cognitive abilities to understand the nature of moral relations deepen. Kohlberg claims that the process of moral development proceeds through set, hierarchically arranged stages that correspond to different levels of moral reasoning.

An associate of Kohlberg's, Gilligan was disturbed by an early finding that girls generally were at lower stages of moral development than boys (1982a, 18). This finding led her to examine Kohlberg's work for possible gender bias. She discovered that, in general, men and women follow different paths to moral development, that there exists a morally "different voice" from the one that Kohlberg identified as definitive of mature moral judgment.[6] Fully elaborated, Gilligan described this "different voice" as expressing an ethic of care that is different from the ethic of justice that stands at the pinnacle of Kohlberg's moral hierarchy. As Gilligan explained the ethic of care:

> In this conception, the moral problem arises from conflicting responsibilities rather than from competing rights and requires for its resolution a mode of thinking that is contextual and narrative rather than formal and abstract. This conception of morality as concerned with the activity of care centers moral development around the understanding of responsibility and relationships, just as the conception of morality as fairness ties moral development to the understanding of rights and rules. (Gilligan 1982a, 19)

In this passage, Gilligan identifies three fundamental characteristics that differentiate the ethic of care from the ethic of justice. First, the ethic of care revolves around different moral concepts than Kohlberg's ethic of justice, that is, responsibility and relationships rather than rights and rules. Second, this morality is tied to concrete circumstances rather than being formal and abstract. Third, this morality is best expressed not as a set of principles but as an activity, the "activity of care." In Gilligan's different voice, morality is not grounded in universal, abstract principles but in the daily experiences and moral problems of real people in their everyday lives.

Gilligan and her associates found this ethic of care to be gender related. Research by Nona Lyons tied the two different moral perspectives to two notions of the self: those who viewed the self as "separated" from others and therefore "objective" were more likely to voice a morality of justice, while those who viewed the self as "connected" to others were more likely to express a morality of care. Since men are usually "separate/objective" in their self/other perceptions, and women more often view themselves in terms of a "connected" self, the difference between justice and care is gender related. Further, men usually express themselves only in the moral voice of justice, though women are more likely to use both forms of moral expression (Lyons 1983).

Lyons and Gilligan do not attempt to explain *why* the males and females interviewed developed different notions of the self. One possibility is that caring "is the constitutive activity through which women achieve their femininity and against which masculinity takes shape." Such psychological theories of gender difference provide the strongest evidence for thinking of an ethic of care as an intrinsically female characteristic.[7] Yet Gilligan's own work hints at another possible explanation of the origins of caring. In her description of women in the abortion study she and Mary Belenky conducted, Gilligan wrote:

> What begins to emerge is a sense of vulnerability that impedes these women from taking a stand, what George Eliot regards as the girl's "susceptibility" to adverse judgment of others, which stems from her lack of power and consequent inability to do something in the world. . . . The women's reluctance to judge stems . . . from their uncertainty about their right to make moral statements or, perhaps, the price for them that such judgment seems to entail. . . .
>
> When women feel excluded from direct participation in society, they see themselves as subject to a consensus or judgment made and enforced by the men on whose protection and support they depend and by whose names they are known. . . . The conflict between self and other thus constitutes the central moral problem for women. . . . The conflict between compassion and autonomy, between virtue and power. . . .[8]

This passage suggests that whatever psychological dimensions there might be to explain women's moral differences, there may also be a social cause: women's different moral expression might be a function of their subordinate or tentative social position. Alternatively, the psychological causes may be intermediate causes, resting in turn on the social conditions of secondary status. These possibilities suggest that Gilligan's work may be vulnerable to the same kind of criticism that she raised against Kohlberg. Gilligan's samples may lead her to draw a wrong conclusion about the nature of the moral voice that she has identified. For if moral difference is a function of social position rather than gender, then the morality Gilligan has identified with women might be better identified with subordinate or minority status.

There is little doubt that class status affects the level of justice reasoning (Colby et al. 1983, 70). A study that compared moral cognitive-development levels of whites, blacks, and Chicanos discovered that white children were ahead of the minority children (Cortese 1982a, 1982b). Would a study of these groups indicate that, as Gilligan found to be true for women, their moral views were not underdeveloped but simply not captured by Kohlberg's categories?[9]

To my knowledge, no one has examined minority group members using Gilligan's methodology to see if they fit the morality of care better than they fit Kohlberg's categories. Gilligan's abortion study, like Kohlberg's work, is limited in that it focuses solely on the privileged.[10] Yet circumstantial evidence strongly suggests that the moral views of minority group members in the United States are much more likely to be characterized by an ethic of care than by an ethic of justice. For example, Robert Coles' (1977) discussions with Chicano, Eskimo, and Indian children revealed frequent criticisms of Anglos for their inattention to proper moral concerns and for their lack of care for others and for the earth. Similarly, in his depiction of core black culture, John Langston Gwaltney (1980) reveals that blacks frequently express similar moral concerns. Core black culture, according to Gwaltney, emphasizes basic respect for others, a commitment to honesty, generosity motivated by the knowledge that you might need help someday, and respect for the choices of others. In the case histories that Gwaltney recorded, one person after another invoked these virtues and contrasted them to the views of the white majority, who were characterized as greedy, cheap, and self-involved, and as people who lie when it proves advantageous. Is this morality less coherent because it is not expressed abstractly? As Gwaltney succinctly put it, "Black Americans are, of course, capable of the same kind of abstract thinking that is practiced by all human cultures, but sane people in a conquest environment are necessarily preoccupied with the realities of social existence" (Gwaltney 1980, xxix).

Gerald Jackson also has identified characteristics of West African and Afro-American patterns of thought that are closely reminiscent of Gilligan's different voice, except that they are part of a large, coherent account of the place of humans in the cosmos. In contrast to the "analytical, logical, cognitive, rational, step by step" thinking of Europeans and Euro-Americans, African thought relies on "syncretistic reasoning, intuitive, holistic, affective" patterns of thought in which "comprehension [comes] through sympathy."[11] Indeed, Wade Nobles relates this different, connected pattern of thought to the fact that black Americans do not seem to have the same self-concept as whites. Nobles characterizes this view of the self, which stresses "a sense of 'cooperation,' 'interdependence,' and 'collective responsibility,'" as the "extended self." The parallel to Lyons' argument is striking.[12]

The possibility of a social and not just a psychological cause for Gilligan's different voice greatly broadens the implications of and possible interpretation of research on an ethic of care. One possible implication is that Kohlberg's theory of proper moral development is correct, so that the failure of women and minority groups to develop properly is just a reflection of a regrettably unequal social order. According to this explanation, social forces retard the moral development of women and minorities. A second interpretation rejects the view of women and minorities as passively affected by society. One could claim that women and minorities proudly cling to their moral views, even if they are considered "lesser" moral views by the society, as a way of asserting their distinctiveness.

A third possibility differs from the previous two in its rejection of the assumption that from the start Kohlberg's justice reasoning is somehow superior to an ethic of care. By stressing the positive qualities of an ethic of care, this approach would turn Kohlberg's "naturalistic" moral psychology on its head (Kohlberg 1971). While white women and minority men and women occupy vastly different positions in the social order, they disproportionately occupy the caretaking roles in our society. Thus, these groups, in terms of having an ethic of care, are advantaged by their social roles. It may be that, in order for an ethic of care to develop, individuals need to experience caring for others and being cared for by others. From this perspective, the daily experience of caring provides these groups with the opportunity to develop this moral sense. The dearth of caretaking experiences makes privileged males morally deprived. Their experiences mislead them to think that moral beliefs can be expressed in abstract, universalistic terms as if they were purely cognitive questions, like mathematical formulas.[13] This interpretation fits best with Lyons' finding that women, more often than men, are capable of using both types of moral reasoning.

Is Women's Morality Inferior?

Even if an ethic of care could primarily be understood as a gender difference, however, the unsituated fact of moral difference between men and women is dangerous because it ignores the broader intellectual context within which "facts" about gender difference are generally received. Despite decades of questioning, we still live in a society where "man" stands for human and where the norm is equated with the male (Gilligan 1982a; Nicholson 1983; Harding & Hintikka 1983, introduction). Gender difference, therefore, is a concept that concerns deviation from the normal. Given the conservative nature of our perceptions of knowledge,[14] evidence of a gender difference in and of itself is not likely to lead to the widespread questioning of established categories, such as Kohlberg's (see Barber 1983; cf. Nails 1983). Instead, it is likely to lead to the denigration of the "deviation" associated with the female.

Kohlberg's response to Gilligan is instructive. He has decided that although Gilligan has identified a morally different voice, this voice is of limited application.[15] Kohlberg distinguishes "two senses of the word *moral*":

> The first sense of the word *moral* corresponds to . . . "the moral point of view" [that] stresses attributes of impartiality, universalizability, and the effort and willingness to come to agreement or consensus with other human beings in general about what is right. It is this notion of a "moral point of view" which is most clearly embodied psychologically in the Kohlberg stage model of justice reasoning.

> There is a second sense of the word *moral,* which is captured by Gilligan's focus upon the elements of caring and responsibility, most vividly evident in relations of special obligation to family and friends. (Kohlberg et al. 1983, 229)

Kohlberg's example of the second type of moral concern is a woman's description of her decision to divorce (Kohlberg et al. 1983, 230–31). Although Kohlberg does not deny that such decisions involve moral choice, he believes it is clear that these concerns are parochial and private rather than universal and socially significant. If we accept Kohlberg's explanation that there are two different types of moral concerns, and if the two are connected to gender, the pattern is a familiar one: what is male is important, broad, and public; what is female is narrow, special, and insignificant. Feminist scholars have stressed the need to reject a simplistic evaluation of the "public/private split," with its implicit devaluation of the female.[16] Accordingly, then, the concept of women's morality should be disassociated from the private because the public and the private are not separate-but-equal moral realms.[17]

The contours of public morality in large part determine the shape of private morality. Indeed, it is in the public realm that the boundaries of the private are drawn. To use Kohlberg's example, if the universal, consensual norms of society did not permit divorce, then the woman who expressed her personal moral dilemma about divorce would have faced no moral dilemma at all; the boundaries about what would be right and wrong would be fixed, and she would know that choosing divorce would be wrong.

This last point raises a troublesome possibility. Perhaps women's morality is just a collection of "moral leftovers," of questions that gain significance only because they are left somewhat open-ended by the commandments and boundaries of public morality. Gilligan has noted that the ethic of care is a relational ethic, that it is tied to who one is, to what position one occupies in society. Such concerns have been considered of a secondary importance in the moral life of any community. In other words, the requirements of justice have traditionally set the boundaries of care.

As long as women's morality is viewed as different and more particular than mainstream moral thought, it inevitably will be treated as a secondary form of moral thinking. This is true because, as the etymology suggests, that which is private is deprived in at least one sense: insofar as the boundaries of the private (in this case, private morality as expressed by care) are set by the categories and definitions of the public (in this case, public morality, i.e., the ethic of justice), that which is relegated to the private is not judged on its own terms. Private morality is not perceived as independent of the "more important" public realm. It is by nature dependent and secondary.

Thinkers who advocate a women's morality have almost always assumed that it is a necessary corrective, not an alternative, to prevailing moral views.[18] By so doing, they have made it relatively easy for critics to dismiss women's morality as secondary and irrelevant to broader moral and political concerns.[19] To argue that women's morality is a corrective to prevailing modes of morality is to make a functionalist argument. To the extent that women's moral difference is viewed as functional to the improvement of the morality of society as a whole, it remains secondary.[20] If, armed with Gilligan's findings and similar work, the best feminists can do is to claim that letting women assert their morality in more important parts of public life will improve life (see, e.g., Rossi 1983, 731; Kleeman 1984, 3), or that public life is unimportant and women cultivate morality in the domestic realm (see, e.g., Tenenbaum 1982), then they are doomed to failure. Such arguments, all of which take the form "we can be useful to you," ignore the fact that privileged men are the adjudicators of what is useful, of what is important, and, therefore, of what stands most in need of correction. Rather than presenting an alternative moral theory, then, privatized women's morality is a supplemental moral theory. And when and how that different moral voice gets heard is beyond the power of the "different" to decide. In this way, as has happened before, women's moral voice, the ethic of care, is easily dismissed.

In arguing that there is a strategic problem with women's morality, I do mean to imply that strategy overshadows truth. If women were morally different from men, then strategy would not allow us to dismiss this fact. Yet the facts are not so simple, and it is thus legitimate to see if the direction in which the facts are likely to lead requires that we place them in a different intellectual context. I have tried to show that the consequences of a simplistic embrace of the ethic of care as specifically women's morality are potentially harmful. This is not to say that an ethic of care is morally undesirable but that its premises must be understood within the context of moral theory, rather than as the given facts of a gender-based psychological theory.

A Contextual Theory of Care

If an ethic of care is to be taken seriously as a moral position, then its advocates need to explore the assumptions on which such a moral position is founded. Unless the full social and philosophical context for an ethic of care is specified, the ethic of care can be dismissed as a parochial concern of some misguided women. In making this claim, I differ from some recent feminist theorists who have eschewed full-scale theory construction and have instead focused on the practical implications of an ethic of care. Several writers, for example, have focused on the question of peace as exemplary of the way in which care can inform our treatment of a crucial political issue.[21] Their approach, however, ignores the context in which questions of war and peace appear. Out of the context of any broader political and social theory, the question of peace can easily be dismissed for failing to consider other values (e.g., defense or honor), which others may view as broader or more important.[22] Only when care is assessed in its relative importance to other values can it begin to serve as a critical standpoint from which to evaluate public life. Such an assessment will require a full-fledged moral and political theory of care.

In addition to defining the concept of care, I suggest three sets of concerns that begin to address "care" at the theoretical level.[23]

The Metaethical Question

One reason why, from the standpoint of an ethic of justice, care seems to be such an inadequate moral position is that an ethic of care necessarily rests on a different set of premises about what a good moral theory is. As Alasdair MacIntyre (1966, 190) noted, the prevailing contemporary notion of what counts as a moral theory is derived from Kant.[24] According to this view, a moral theory consists of a set of moral principles rationally chosen after consideration of competing principles. William Frankena refers to this as "the moral point of view": it is universalizable, impartial, and concerned with describing what is right, and we would expect chosen moral principles to embody these standard notions of morality.[25]

An alternative model for moral theories is contextual metaethical theory.[26] Such theories consist of presumptions about the nature of morality that are different from Kantian-inspired metaethics. In any contextual moral theory, morality must be situated concretely, that is, for particular actors in a particular society. It cannot be understood by the recitation of principles. By this account, morality is embedded in the norms of a given society. Furthermore, contextual moral theory directs attention away from the morality of single acts to the broader moral capacities of actors. To be moral is to possess a moral character, or, as Aristotle put it, virtue is a disposition (Aristotle 1976, 91–92). Thus, morality cannot be determined by posing hypothetical moral dilemmas or by asserting moral principles. Rather, one's moral imagination, character, and actions must respond to the complexity of a given situation. Among prominent examples of contextual morality, I would include Aristotle's moral theory, the "moral sentiments" views of the Scottish Enlightenment, and some contemporary writers on morality.[27]

As a result of a starting concern with character, any contextual moral theory must embody a complex portrait of the self. Theories that are suspicious of nonrational moral motives often explain moral action as the result of rising above selfish passions. Noncontextual moral philosophers rely on rational tests to check self-interested inclinations. Hence the rational and the moral become identified.[28] In contrast, advocates of contextual moral theories often stress moral sensitivity and moral imagination as keys to understanding mature moral life. Rather than positing some ideal rational human being, contextual morality stands or falls on its ability to describe the ways in which individuals progress morally to exhibit concern for others.

As a fully developed moral theory, the ethic of care will take the form of a contextual moral theory. Perhaps the most important characteristic of an ethic of care is that, within it, moral situations are defined not in terms of rights and responsibilities but in terms of relationships of care. The morally mature person understands the balance between caring for the self and caring for others.[29] The perspective of care requires that conflict be worked out without damage to the continuing relationships. Moral problems can be expressed in terms of accommodating the needs of the self and of others, of balancing competition and cooperation, and of maintaining the social web of relations in which one finds oneself.

Quite obviously, if such caretaking is the quintessential moral task, the context within which conflicting demands occur will be an important factor in determining the morally correct act. To resort to abstract, universal principles is to go outside of the web of relationships. Thus, despite Kohlberg's dismissal of care as secondary to and dependent on justice reasoning, from a different metaethical perspective, care may set the boundaries of when justice concerns are appropriate.[30]

If feminists recognize a moral tradition that is non-Kantian, they will be able to ground an ethic of care more securely in philosophical theory. Yet there are some serious problems with all contextual moralities, and specifically with an ethic of care. Consequently, as the following analysis will show, an ethic of care requires more elaboration before feminists can decide whether to embrace it as the appropriate moral theory for feminism.

Conventionalism and the Limits of Care

Universalistic moral theories presume that they apply to all cases; contextual moral theories must specify when and how they apply.[31] Advocates of an ethic of care face, as Gilligan puts it, "the moral problem of inclusion that hinges on the capacity to assume responsibility for care."[32] It is easy to imagine that there will be some people or concerns about which we do not care. However, we might ask if our lack of care frees us from moral responsibility.[33]

This question arises because we do not care for everyone equally. We care more for those who are emotionally, physically, and even culturally closer to us.[34] Thus, an ethic of care could become a defense of caring only for one's own family, friends, group, nation. From this perspective, caring could become a justification for any set of conventional relationships. Any advocate of an ethic of care will need to address the questions, "What are the appropriate boundaries of our caring?" and more important, "How far should the boundaries of caring be expanded?"

Furthermore, in focusing on the preservation of existing relationships, the perspective of care has a conservative quality. If the preservation of a web of relationships is the starting premise of an ethic of care, then there is little basis for critical reflection on whether those relationships are good, healthy, or worthy of preservation. Surely, as we judge our own relationships, we are likely to favor them and relationships like them. It is from unreflective tastes, though, that hatreds of difference can grow. One of the reasons why impartiality is such an appealing universal moral characteristic is that in theory it can prevent the kind of special pleading in which we all otherwise engage. Yet it may be possible to avoid the need for special pleading while at the same time stopping short of universal moral principles; if so, an ethic of care might be viable (Winch 1972).

The possibility that an ethic of care might lead to the reinforcement of existing social patterns also raises the question of relativism. It is difficult to imagine how an ethic of care could avoid the charge that it would embody different moral positions in different societies and at different times. Philosophers do not agree about the seriousness of this type of relativism, however, and contextual moral theories may entail only a milder form of relativism, one that Dorothy Emmet calls "soft relativism." Viewed from the respective of "soft relativism," cultural variation in certain moral principles does not preclude the discussion of moral issues across cultures (Emmet 1977, chap. 5, esp. 91–92). The only way an ethic of care could entirely bypass the charge of relativism would be to posit some caring relationship, for example, the relationship of parent and child, as universal. This path, however, seems fraught with even greater difficulties for feminist scholars and prejudges in an unacceptably narrow way who "caretakers" should be.

Insofar as the difficulty with justice reasoning is that it ignores the importance of context, the expansion of a care ethic suggests a much more adequate moral theory. Yet, how to make sure that the web of relationships is spun widely enough so that some are not beyond its reach remains a central question. Whatever the weaknesses of Kantian universalism, its premise of the equal moral worth and dignity of all humans is attractive because it avoids this problem.

Past contextual moral theories usually have addressed the issue by resorting to some abstract impartial observer. This solution is also inadequate, however, since the impartial observer usually places the same limitations on caring as do conventional moral thinkers.[35] The only other way to resolve this problem is to specify how social institutions might be arranged to expand these conventional understandings of the boundaries of care. Thus, the legitimacy of an ethic of care will depend on the adequacy of the social and political theory of which it is a part.

Politics and Care

In the final analysis, successful advocacy of an ethic of care requires the exposition of a social and political theory that is compatible with the broadest levels of care. All moral theories fit better with some rather than other social and political institutions. Proponents of an ethic of care must specify which social and political institutions they understand to be the context for moral actors. It perhaps should give us pause that some of the most compelling visions of polities of care are utopian.[36]

Among the questions a convincing theory of care needs to address are the myriad questions crucial to any social and political theory. Where does caring come from? Is it learned in the family? If so, does an ethic of care mandate something about the need for, or the nature of, families? Who determines who can be a member of the caring society? What should be the role of the market in a caring society? Who should bear the responsibility for education? How much inequality is acceptable before individuals become indifferent to those who are too different in status? How well do current institutions and theories support the ethic of care?

Finally, we need to think about how an ethic of care might be situated in the context of existing political and social theory. An ethic of care constitutes a view of self, relationships, and social order that may be incompatible with the emphasis on individual rights that is so predominant in Western, liberal, democratic societies. Yet, as it is currently formulated by political theorists, the debate between advocates of rights and advocates of community does not offer a clear alternative to feminists who might advocate an ethic of care. As onerous as rights may seem when viewed from the standpoint of our desires for connected, extended selves, they do serve at least somewhat to protect oppressed individuals. While current yearnings for greater community seem to manifest a view of the self that would allow for more caring, there is nothing inherent in community that keeps it from being oppressive toward women and others.[37] Unless feminists assume responsibility for situating the ethic of care in the context of the rights/community discussions, the end result may be that caring can be used to justify positions that feminists would find unacceptable.[38]

Toward a Theory of Care

I have suggested that feminists should no longer celebrate an ethic of care as a factor of gender difference that points to women's superiority but that they must now begin the arduous task of constructing a full theory of care.

Taken together, the arguments in this chapter suggest that the direction for future feminist moral thinking must be broader and more theoretical. In order to demonstrate this final claim let me consider a less drastic response to the question, "What might the ethic of care mean?"

One could assert that an ethic of care is just a set of sensibilities that every morally mature person should develop, alongside the sensibilities of justice morality. Rather than rethinking the nature of moral philosophy, then, we need to change the educational or familial institutions that are responsible for making the differences between justice and care gender specific. We should endorse the development of two equal moralities for everyone and leave it to individuals to decide when to apply either morality.

There are two problems with this alternative. First, such a response ignores the evidence about the origins of the current gender differences. Whether the cause of the gender difference in morality is a psychological artifact of femininity, a cultural product of caretaking activity, or a positional result of social subordination, it is difficult to imagine how any of these causes or some combination of them could affect all individuals equally.

In the second place, expressing such an ideal ignores the tendency, in reality, to accommodate two desirable moralities by falling back into a rigid gender division. If there are two desirable moralities and two genders, what is wrong with viewing one as predominantly male and one as predominantly female? Having separate but, supposedly, equal spheres allows the two different moralities to flourish and delineates their boundaries clearly.

The most promising alternative, I have suggested, is to face squarely the difficult task of discussing the ethic of care in terms of moral and political theory. This task would include looking critically at the notion of a women's morality advanced by interpretations of research on morality and gender differences, and by situating such interpretations in the context of research on morality and class, racial, and ethnic differences as well. It would also mean recognizing the limitations of a gender specific moral theory in our culture. Finally, it would entail exploring the promises, as well as the problems, involved in thinking about the ethic of care as an alternative moral theory, rather than simply as a complement to traditional moral theories based on justice reasoning.

Although this task will be a difficult one, there is much to gain from it. Attentive to the place of caring both in concrete daily experience and in our patterns of moral thought, we might be better prepared to forge a society in which care can flourish.

Notes

1. See Gilligan 1977, 1979, 1980, 1982a, 1983, 1986c. Among collaborative works and works by associates, see Gilligan & Belenky 1980; Gilligan, Langdale & Lyons 1982; Pollak & Gilligan 1982, 1983, 1985; Lyons 1983; Murphy & Gilligan 1980.

2. See as evidence the *Ms.* article in which Gilligan is proclaimed the magazine's "Woman of the Year": Van Gelder 1984. A quick perusal of the entries in the *Social Science Citation Index* will reveal how widely, and in what diverse scholarly fields, Gilligan's work is being cited. In her survey of developments in psychology of women for 1983–1984, Watstein noted, "The very name *Gilligan* has become a buzzword in both academic and feminist circles" (1984,178).

3. See Kohlberg, Levine & Hewer 1984. One extensive bibliography is Leming 1983.

4. Gilligan (1983, 36) herself noted the way in which theories are confined by the questions they seek to address.

5. Nicholson (1983, 515, reprinted as chapter 6 in this volume) made a similar point when she warned against overgeneralizing gender differences.

6. Some scholars have challenged Gilligan's claim of gender difference. Broughton (1983b, reprinted as chapter 9 in this volume), reviewing the interviews, found both men and women exhibiting both modes of moral expression. Nails (1983) also believes that Gilligan has exaggerated the extent of gender difference in her findings. Benton et al. (1983) report a failed attempt to replicate Gilligan's findings about violence. Other methodological criticisms are raised by Greeno & Maccoby (1986, reprinted as chapter 13 in this volume) and Luria (1986, reprinted as chapter 14 in this volume). Auerbach et al. observe that since Gilligan leaves out considerations such as class and religion, "Gilligan attributes all the differences she does encounter to gender" (1985, 157). Kohlberg's own position on gender difference has changed since his initial finding: he now finds no significant gender difference. His challenge to Gilligan's finding rests on Lawrence Walker's extensive review of the literature (1984, reprinted as chapter 11 in this volume), also cited by Greeno & Maccoby, and Luria. Most studies in Walker's review reported no gender differences; those that did find differences found them among women who have been more isolated from "role-taking" opportunities in society, which is how Kohlberg has always explained gender difference (Kohlberg, Levine & Hewer 1983, 347). Insofar as Walker reviewed "justice-reasoning" tests, Gilligan is willing to concede that there are no gender differences, but, since justice reasoning is only one part of morality, his finding does not address the issue of gender difference in moral reasoning (Gilligan 1986c, 328). It is perhaps interesting to note that this dispute follows a pattern that should be familiar to social scientists: different methodologies tend to produce different results. Here two groups of investigators are looking at related but different phenomena. Each group claims, using its method, that the findings of the other group are invalid.

7. Graham (1983, 17) draws this conclusion from her examination of the works

of Horney, Miller, and Chodorow. Greeno & Maccoby (1977) also review the basis for psychological gender differences.

8. Gilligan 1977, 486, 487, 490. For further support of this finding, see Golding & Laidlaw 1979–1980, 102.

9. In asking this question I certainly do not mean to imply that the type of moral reasoning found among privileged American women should be substituted for the morality found among privileged American men as a universal model for moral development. Kohlberg's work has often been criticized for being an ideological embodiment of liberal values. See, e.g., Sullivan 1977. However, if we knew *why* privileged women, lower-class children, and minority group members differ from privileged males in Kohlberg's model, we would know a great deal more about the limits of this model as well as about the psychosocial origins of care itself. See Stack 1986 (reprinted as chapter 8 in this volume).

10. The abortion sample consisted of interviews conducted with women from various social and ethnic backgrounds, but no analysis of this material has been done from the standpoint of racial or class differences. See Gilligan & Belenky 1980. The other sample that has been used to generate most of the findings of Gilligan and her associates was that used for the longitudinal study by Murphy & Gilligan (1980). Those subjects were initially chosen because they took a course in moral development at college. Thus, the sample is already limited by the opportunity, interest, and ability of individuals who go to college. I know of no analysis that considers the racial, ethnic, and class composition of these samples. For a related criticism of the samples, see Luria 1986 (reprinted as chapter 14 in this volume).

11. Jackson, cited in Richards 1978. See also Jackson 1982.

12. Nobles 1976, 19. Incidentally, we can raise the same questions about the origins of care among black Americans as we can among women. Jackson and Nobles provide a cultural explanation that describes blacks as morally different from whites because of their African roots; this idea parallels the notion that women care because culturally that is what being a woman is about. Other authors have suggested a more positional cause: Ockerman 1979 suggests that social subordination produces the psychological response of greater group solidarity. Zimmerman 1982 explains the different tasks for psychological development that black women face as a result of racial discrimination.

13. "Justice 'operations' of reciprocity and equality in interaction parallel logical operations of relations of equality and reciprocity in the nonmoral cognitive domain" (Kohlberg 1984, 306).

14. See the description of "normal science" in Kuhn 1970. Knowledge is conservative in that we tend to conceive new knowledge in existing frameworks; unless knowledge contains a challenge to the context in which it will likely be placed, it reinforces existing perceptions. Since gender differences are currently perceived in terms of a male norm, we can expect that newly identified gender differences will be perceived in the same way. Of course, Code is correct when she writes, "To assert a difference . . . is not, inevitably, to evaluate. That is an additional step: one which no epistemically responsible person, male or female,

should take without careful consideration. This is a fundamental cognitive imperative" (1983, 546–47). But the worlds of power and knowledge are intertwined; we do not live in a world that adheres to Code's ideal of the epistemically responsible community.

15. Kohlberg (& Levine & Hewer 1984) denies that his stages of moral development do reflect a gender difference. Kohlberg believes that Gilligan's most important contribution is her identification of "responsibility" as a separate moral dimension. See Kohlberg 1982, 513.

16. See Rosaldo 1980. Imray & Middleton 1983 suggest that the problem is not in the public/private dichotomy itself but in our failure to understand that what is essential in the public/private split is not "activity" or "sphere" but power.

17. A different perspective on the problem of public/private life is presented in Elshtain 1982. For a response to Elshtain, see Dietz 1985.

18. Gilligan 1983 seems to suggest that care is such a complementary moral theory.

19. A good example of this phenomenon is the fate of Jane Addams. Addams was enormously popular for her good works during the first two decades of this century. When the United States entered World War I, though, and she continued to maintain a steadfast belief that moral values, including pacifism, should guide political action, she was vilified as a traitor. Although Addams was honored with the Nobel Prize for Peace in 1931, her reputation and political influence never recovered their prewar levels. See Davis 1977. An argument similar to the one I make here is found in Stoper & Johnson 1977. I should note that my criticism of the misuse of this argument is not directed against Gilligan herself. Auerbach et al. 1985 raise a different objection to the political implications of Gilligan's work. While I have emphasized how the women's morality argument can be turned to conservative purposes (a point they make on 159), they also assert that "the problem with [Gilligan's] book is not that its politics are bad, but that it lacks a politics altogether" (160). Gilligan hinted at a response to this criticism when she alluded to the need for both moralities to play a part in "public as well as private life" (Gilligan 1986c, 326; reprinted as chapter 15 in this volume). Yet she has not made clear what that interaction might mean.

20. Several authors have made arguments similar to this one. See especially Walker 1983; Stacy 1983. My use of the language of functionalism is inspired here by my reading of Okin 1978.

21. See Ruddick 1983, 1984b. Elshtain (1983, 1985) often seems to support a similar position, but in her most recent essays, she is critical of a simplistic "beautiful souls" argument on the part of women. Nevertheless, she has not yet provided any full theoretical alternative to naive pacifism except to demur about statism.

22. Consider, e.g., how ephemeral the tremendous wave of interwar pacifism proved to be. See Brock 1970.

23. Noddings (1984) distinguishes between the "one-caring" and the "cared-for." Caring, she claims, is not of itself a virtue but rather the occasion for the exercise of virtues.

24. Indeed, Gilligan has been criticized for not presenting a Kantian form of ethical

theory. See Nunner-Winkler 1984 (reprinted as chapter 10 in this volume). For a critique of Kant that follows some of the directions found in an ethic of care, see Elshtain 1981.

25. See Frankena 1973. Kohlberg recites Frankena's argument in the quotation cited in the text above following the number for n. 16.

26. Contextual moral theories can be teleological, deontological, axiological, or aretaic. The common theme in contextual moral theories is that they eschew a formal and absolute resolution of moral questions. The reader may suspect that I am coining a new phrase only to weaken the position of my opponents. After all, even Kohlberg believes that his theory is situation specific and not universalistic. Indeed, perhaps only the Kantian perfect duties can be described as an unqualifiedly nonsituated morality. If that is the case, then my argument for introducing contextual morality grows stronger because it requires that moral philosophers drop the convenient fiction that their work stops once they have clarified the moral rules. Contextual moral theories involve a shift of the essential moral questions away from the question, "What are the best principles?" to the question, "How will individuals best be equipped to act morally?" Many moral philosophers are beginning to claim the need to return to a contextual ethical theory. A good recent collection of essays that shows both the diversity and core concerns of this emerging perspective can be found in MacIntyre & Hauerwas 1983.

27. Among traditional moral theorists, I have in mind especially David Hume and Adam Smith. Among contemporary moral philosophers, a succinct statement of a contextual moral position can be found in Kekes 1984.

28. Rawls' 1971 description of the "original position" is probably the best-known example of this approach. Kohlberg's description of reciprocity ultimately hinges on an application of rationality as well. See his "Justice as Reversibility" (1981, 198).

29. Gilligan describes the stages of care in 1983, 41–45.

30. This inversion of Kohlberg's position is recommended to us by the logical requirements of making an ethic of care into a full-fledged moral theory. How the caring person would know when to invoke the more remote criteria of justice is obviously a crucial question.

31. "We have been told nothing about morality until we are told what features of situations context-sensitive people pick out as morally salient, what weightings they put on these different features, and so on" (Flanagan & Adler 1983, 591–92). A similar point is made by Dancy 1983.

32. Gilligan 1983, 44. Aristotle (1946, 47; 1262b [2.4.8]) insisted that to try to extend the bounds of familial love to everyone simply destroys family bonds.

33. Thus, David Hume (1978; book 3, part 2, 494–95) understood justice, an artificial passion, as a necessary complement to the natural passion, benevolence. Hume argued that if benevolence were sufficiently strong, there would be no need of justice. Yet the limited range of benevolence made it an insufficient basis for moral life in human society.

34. This point was illustrated graphically by the Scottish Enlightenment thinker Francis Hutcheson, who drew an analogy between the relative strength of our

closest and furthest emotional ties and the ties of gravity (1726/1971, 1: 198–99). Perhaps some individuals, the saints among us, can resist the greater pull of those closest to us. A provocative account of moral saints is Wolf 1982.

35. For example, Adam Smith (1976, 3.1.2, 110) posited the existence of an "impartial spectator." Brandt (1979, 225–28) is a recent moral philosopher who advocated an "ideal observer" theory, but he has since repudiated it because it provided no way to prevent the ideal observer from invoking what would seem to him to be harmless preferences that might seriously constrict others' choices. (He uses as one example the preference against homosexuality.)

36. Consider Charlotte Perkins Gilman 1979; Piercy 1976. Khanna (1984) draws a parallel between Gilligan's ethic of care and Piercy's novel.

37. See, e.g., Sandel; 1981. It seems doubtful that Sandel's vision holds any more promise for women than Rawls' theory that feminists need to be somewhat suspicious of invocations of community. See Barry's 1984 review of Sandel; and Gutmann 1985.

38. Consider the argument made by Hardwig 1984, "Should Women Think in Terms of Rights?" Hardwig answers this question negatively; among his reasons is that "rights" imply a particular atomistic view of the self. To use rights arguments, he claims, is to adopt this understanding of the self. Women would have to surrender their sense of their connected, female nature if they used rights arguments. Hence, they should not. Alas, Hardwig does not explain how women can convince men who do think in terms of rights to take them seriously.

18

Beyond Caring:
The De-Moralization of Gender

Marilyn Friedman

Carol Gilligan heard a "distinct moral language" in the voices of women who were subjects in her studies of moral reasoning (Gilligan 1982a, 73).[1] Though herself a developmental psychologist, Gilligan has put her mark on contemporary feminist moral philosophy by daring to claim the competence of this voice and the worth of its message. Her book, *In a Different Voice*, which one theorist has aptly described as a bestseller (Haug 1984, 44), explored the concern with care and relationships which Gilligan discerned in the moral reasoning of women and contrasted it with the orientation toward justice and rights which she found to typify the moral reasoning of men.

According to Gilligan (1982a), the standard (or "male") moral voice articulated in moral psychology derives moral judgments about particular cases from abstract, universalized moral rules and principles which are substantively concerned with justice and rights. For justice reasoners: the major moral imperative enjoins respect for the rights of others (100); the concept of duty is limited to reciprocal noninterference (147); the motivating vision is one of the equal worth of self and other (63); and one important underlying presupposition is a highly individuated conception of persons.

By contrast, the other (or "female") moral voice which Gilligan heard in her studies eschews abstract rules and principles. This moral voice derives moral judgments from the contextual detail of situations grasped as specific and unique (100). The substantive concern for this moral voice is care and responsibility, particularly as these arise in the context of interpersonal relationships (19). Moral judgments, for care reasoners, are tied to feelings of

Reprinted by permission from M. Hanen and K. Nielsen, eds., *Science, Morality, and Feminist Theory*: 87–110. Copyright © 1987 by *Canadian Journal of Philosophy*.

empathy and compassion (69); the major moral imperatives center around caring, not hurting others, and avoiding selfishness (90); and the motivating vision of this ethic is "that everyone will be responded to and included, that no one will be left alone or hurt" (63).

While these two voices are not necessarily contradictory in all respects, they seem, at the very least, to be different in their orientation. Gilligan's writings about the differences have stimulated extensive feminist reconsideration of various ethical themes.[2] In this paper, I use Gilligan's work as a springboard for extending certain of those themes in new directions. My discussion has three parts. In the first part, I will address the unresolved question of whether or not a gender difference in moral reasoning is empirically confirmed. I will propose that even if actual statistical differences in the moral reasoning of women and men cannot be confirmed, there is nevertheless a real difference in the moral norms and values culturally associated with each gender. The genders are "moralized" in distinctive ways. Moral norms about appropriate conduct, characteristic virtues, and typical vices are incorporated into our conceptions of femininity and masculinity, female and male. The result is a dichotomy which exemplifies what may be called a "division of moral labor"[3] between the genders.

In the second part of the paper, I will explore a different reason why actual women and men may not show a divergence of reasoning along the care-justice dichotomy, namely, that the notions of care and justice overlap more than Gilligan, among others, has realized. I will suggest, in particular, that morally adequate care involves considerations of justice. Thus, the concerns captured by these two moral categories do not define necessarily distinct moral perspectives, in practice.

Third, and finally, I propose that, even if care and justice do not define distinct moral perspectives, nevertheless, these concepts do point to other important differences in moral orientation. One such difference has to do with the nature of relationship to other selves, and the underlying form of moral commitment which is the central focus of that relationship and of the resulting moral thought. In short, the so-called "care" perspective emphasizes responsiveness to particular persons, in their uniqueness, and commitment to them as such. By contrast, the so-called "justice" perspective emphasizes adherence to moral rules, values and principles, and an abstractive treatment of individuals, based on the selected categories which they instantiate.

Let us turn first to the issue of gender difference.

The Gender Difference Controversy

Gilligan has advanced at least two different positions about the care and the justice perspectives. One is that the care perspective is distinct from the moral perspective which is centered on justice and rights. Following Gilligan [1986c, 326 (reprinted as chapter 15 in this volume)], I will call this the "different voice" hypothesis about moral reasoning. Gilligan's other hypothesis is that the care perspective is typically, or characteristically, a *woman's* moral voice, while the justice perspective is typically, or characteristically a *man's* moral voice. Let's call this the "gender difference" hypothesis about moral reasoning.

The truth of Gilligan's gender difference hypothesis has been questioned by a number of critics who cite what seems to be disconfirming empirical evidence.[4] This evidence includes studies by the psychologist Norma Haan (1978), who has discerned two distinct moral voices among her research subjects, but has found them to be utilized to approximately the same extent by both females and males.[5]

In an attempt to dismiss the research-based objections to her gender difference hypothesis, Gilligan [1986c, 326 (reprinted as chapter 15 in this volume)] now asserts that her aim was not to disclose a statistical gender difference in moral reasoning, but rather simply to disclose and interpret the differences in the two perspectives. Psychologist John Broughton [1983b, 636 (reprinted as chapter 9 in this volume)] has argued that if the gender difference is not maintained, then Gilligan's whole explanatory framework is undermined. However, Broughton is wrong. The different voice hypothesis has a significance for moral psychology and moral philosophy which would survive the demise of the gender difference hypothesis. At least part of its significance lies in revealing the lopsided obsession of contemporary theories of morality, in both disciplines, with universal and impartial conceptions of justice and rights and the relative disregard of *particular,* interpersonal relationships based on partiality and affective ties.[6] (However, the different voice hypothesis is itself also suspect if it is made to depend on a dissociation of justice from care, a position which I shall challenge in the second part of this paper.)

But *what about* that supposed empirical disconfirmation of the gender difference hypothesis? Researchers who otherwise accept the disconfirming evidence have nevertheless noticed that many women readers of Gilligan's book find it to "resonate ... thoroughly with their own experience" [Greeno & Maccoby 1986, 314–15 (reprinted as chapter 13 in this volume)]. Gilligan [1986c, 325 (reprinted as chapter 15 in this volume)] notes that it was precisely one of her purposes to expose the gap between women's experience and the findings of psychological research, and, we may suppose, to critique the latter in light of the former.

These unsystematic, anecdotal observations that females and males do differ in ways examined by Gilligan's research should lead us either: (1) to question, and examine carefully, the methods of that empirical research which does not reveal such differences; or (2) to suspect that a gender difference exists but in some form which is not, strictly speaking, a matter of statistical differences in the moral reasoning of women and men. Gilligan has herself expressed the first of these alternatives. I would like to explore the second possibility.

Suppose that there were a gender difference of a sort, but one which was not a simple matter of differences among the form or substance of women's and men's moral reasonings. A plausible account might take this form. Among the white middle classes of such Western industrial societies as Canada and the United States, women and men are associated with different moral norms and values at the level of the stereotypes, symbols, and myths which contribute to the social construction of gender. One might say that morality is "gendered" and that the genders are "moralized." Our very conceptions of femininity and masculinity, female and male, incorporate norms about appropriate behavior, characteristic virtues, and typical vices.

Morality, I suggest, is fragmented into a "division of moral labor" along the lines of gender, the rationale for which is rooted in historic developments pertaining to family, state, and economy. The tasks of governing, regulating social order, and managing other "public" institutions have been monopolized by men as their privileged domain, and the tasks of sustaining privatized personal relationships have been imposed on, or left to, women.[7] The genders have thus been conceived in terms of special and distinctive moral projects. Justice and rights have structured male moral norms, values, and virtues, while care and responsiveness have defined female moral norms, values, and virtues. The division of moral labor has had the dual function both of preparing us each for our respective socially defined domains and of rendering us incompetent to manage the affairs of the realm from which we have been excluded. That justice is symbolized in our culture by the figure of a woman is a remarkable irony; her blindfold hides more than the scales she holds.

To say that the genders are moralized is to say that specific moral ideals, values, virtues, and practices are culturally conceived as the special projects or domains of specific genders. These conceptions would determine which commitments and behaviors were to be considered normal, appropriate, and expected of each gender, which commitments and behaviors were to be considered remarkable or heroic, and which commitments and behaviors were to be considered deviant, improper, outrageous, and intolerable. Men who fail to respond to the cry of a baby, fail to express tender emotions, or fail to show compassion in the face of the grief and sorrow of others, are likely to be tolerated, perhaps even benignly, while women who act similarly can expect to be reproached for their selfish indifference. However, women are seldom required to devote themselves to service to their country or to struggles for human rights. Women are seldom expected to display any of the special virtues associated with national or political life. At the same time, women still carry the burden of an excessively restrictive and oppressive sexual ethic; sexual aggressiveness and promiscuity are vices for which women in all social groups are roundly condemned, even while many of their male counterparts win tributes for such "virility."

Social science provides ample literature to show that gender differences are alive and well at the level of popular perception. Both men and women, on average, still conceive women and men in a moralized fashion. For example, expectations and perceptions of women's greater empathy and altruism are expressed by both women and men (cf. Eisenberg & Lennon 1983). The gender stereotypes of women center around qualities which some authors call "communal." These include: a concern for the welfare of others; the predominance of caring and nurturant traits; and, to a lesser extent, interpersonal sensitivity, emotional expressiveness, and a gentle personal style.[8]

By contrast, men are stereotyped according to what are referred to as "agentic" norms.[9] These norms center primarily around assertive and controlling tendencies. The paradigmatic behaviors are self-assertion, including forceful dominance, and independence from other people. Also encompassed by these norms are patterns of self-confidence, personal efficacy, and a direct, adventurous personal style.

If reality failed to accord with myth and symbol, if actual women and men did not fit the traits and dispositions expected of them, this might not necessarily undermine the myths and symbols, since perception could be selective and disconfirming experience reduced to the status of "occasional exceptions" and "abnormal, deviant cases." "Reality" would be misperceived in the image of cultural myth, as reinforced by the homogenizing tendencies of mass media and mass culture, and the popular imagination would have little foothold for the recognition that women and men were not as they were mythically conceived to be.

If I am right, then Gilligan has discerned the *symbolically* female moral voice, and has disentangled it from the *symbolically* male moral voice. The moralization of gender is more a matter of how we *think* we reason than of how we actually reason, more a matter of the moral concerns we *attribute* to women and men than of true statistical differences between women's and men's moral reasoning. Gilligan's findings resonate with the experiences of many people because those experiences are shaped, in part, by cultural myths and stereotypes of gender which even feminist theorizing may not dispel. Thus, both women and men in our culture *expect* women and men to exhibit this moral dichotomy, and, on my hypothesis, it is this expectation which has shaped both Gilligan's observations and the plausibility which we attribute to them. Or, to put it somewhat differently, *whatever* moral matters men concern themselves with are categorized, estimably, as matters of "justice and rights," whereas the moral concerns of women are assigned to the devalued categories of "care and personal relationships."

It is important to ask why, if these beliefs are so vividly held, they might, nevertheless, still not have produced a reality in conformity with them.[10] How could those critics who challenge Gilligan's gender hypothesis be right to suggest that women and men show no significant differences in moral reasoning, if women and men are culturally educated, trained, pressured, expected, and perceived to be so radically different?[11]

Philosophy is not, by itself, capable of answering this question adequately. My admittedly *partial* answer to it depends upon showing that the care/justice dichotomy is rationally implausible and that the two concepts are conceptually compatible. This conceptual compatibility creates the empirical possibility that the two moral concerns will be intermingled in practice. That they are actually intermingled in the moral reasoning of real women and men is, of course, not determined simply by their conceptual compatibility, but requires as well the wisdom and insight of those women and men who comprehend the relevance of both concepts to their experiences.[12] Philosophy does not account for the actual emergence of wisdom. That the genders do not, in reality, divide along those moral lines is made *possible*, though not inevitable, by the conceptual limitations of both a concept of care dissociated from considerations of justice and a concept of justice dissociated from considerations of care. Support for this partial explanation requires reconceptualization of care and justice—the topic of the next part of my discussion.

Surpassing the Care/Justice Dichotomy

I have suggested that if women and men do not show statistical differences in moral reasoning along the lines of a care/justice dichotomy, this should not be thought surprising since the concepts of care and justice are mutually compatible. People who treat each other justly can also care about each other. Conversely, personal relationships are arenas in which people have rights to certain forms of treatment, and in which fairness can be reflected in ongoing interpersonal mutuality. It is this latter insight—the relevance of justice to close personal relationships—which I will emphasize here.

Justice, at the most general level, is a matter of giving people their due, of treating them appropriately. Justice is relevant to personal relationships and to care precisely to the extent that considerations of justice itself determine appropriate ways to treat friends or intimates. Justice as it bears on relationships among friends or family, or on other close personal ties, might not involve duties which are universalizable, in the sense of being owed to all persons simply in virtue of shared moral personhood. But this does not entail the irrelevance of justice among friends or intimates.

Moral thinking has not always dissociated the domain of justice from that of close personal relationships. The earliest Greek code of justice placed friendship at the forefront of conditions for the relation of justice, and construed the rules of justice as being coextensive with the limits of friendship. The reader will recall that one the first definitions of justice which Plato sought to contest, in the *Republic,* is that of "helping one's friends and harming one's enemies." [13] Although the ancient Greek model of justice among friends reserved that moral privilege for freeborn Greek males, the conception is, nevertheless, instructive for its readiness to link the notion of justice to relationships based on affection and loyalty. This provides an important contrast to modern notions of justice which are often deliberately constructed so as to avoid presumptions of mutual concern on the parts of those to whom the conception is to apply.

As is well known, John Rawls, for one, requires that the parties to the original position in which justice is to be negotiated be mutually disinterested (1971, 13, passim). Each party is assumed, first and foremost, to be concerned for the advancement of her own interests, and to care about the interests of others only to the extent that her own interests require it. This postulate of mutual disinterestedness is intended by Rawls to ensure that the principles of justice do not depend on what he calls "strong assumptions," such as "extensive ties of natural sentiment" (1971, 129). Rawls is seeking principles of justice which apply to everyone in all their social interrelationships, *whether or not* characterized by affection and a concern for each other's well-being. While such an account promises to disclose duties of justice owed to all other parties to the social contract, it may fail to uncover *special* duties of justice which arise in close personal relationships the foundation of which is affection or kinship, rather than contract. The methodological device of assuming mutual disinterest might blind us to the role of justice among mutually interested and/or intimate parties.

Gilligan herself has suggested that mature reasoning about care incorporates considerations of justice and rights. But Gilligan's conception of what this means is highly limited. It appears to involve simply the recognition "that self and other are equal," a notion which serves to override the problematic tendency of the ethic of care to become *self-sacrificing* care in women's practices. However, important as it may be, this notion hardly does justice to justice.

There are several ways in which justice pertains to close personal relationships. The first two ways which I will mention are largely appropriate only among friends, relatives, or intimates who are of comparable development in their realization of moral personhood, for example, who are both mature responsible adults. The third sort of relevance of justice to close relationships, which I will discuss shortly, pertains to families, in which adults often interrelate with children—a more challenging domain for the application of justice. But first the easier task.

One sort of role for justice in close relationships among people of comparable moral personhood may be discerned by considering that a personal relationship is a miniature social system, which provides valued mutual intimacy, support, and concern for those who are involved. The maintenance of a relationship requires effort by the participants. One intimate may bear a much greater burden for sustaining a relationship than the other participant(s) and may derive less support, concern, and so forth than she deserves for her efforts. Justice sets a constraint on such relationships by calling for an appropriate sharing, among the participants, of the benefits and burdens which constitute their relationship.

Marilyn Frye, for example, has discussed what amounts to a pattern of *violation* of this requirement of justice in heterosexual relationships. She has argued (1983, 9) that women of all races, social classes, and societies can be defined as a coherent group in terms of a distinctive function which is culturally assigned to them. This function is, in Frye's words, "the service of men and men's interests as men define them." This service work includes personal service (satisfaction of routine bodily needs, such as hunger, and other mundane tasks), sexual and reproductive service, and ego service. Says Frye: "at every race/class level and even across race/class lines men do not serve women as women serve men" (1983, 10). Frye is, of course, generalizing over society and culture, and the sweep of her generalization encompasses both ongoing close personal relationships as well as other relationships which are not close or are not carried on beyond specific transactions, for example, that of prostitute to client. By excluding those latter cases for the time being, and applying Frye's analysis to familial and other close ties between women and men, we may discern the sort of one-sided relational exploitation often masquerading in the guise of love or care, which constitutes this first sort of injustice.

Justice is relevant to close personal relationships among comparable moral persons in a second way as well. The trust and intimacy which characterize special relationships create special vulnerabilities to harm. Commonly recognized harms, such as physical injury and sexual assault, become more feasible; and special relationships, in corrupt, abusive, or degenerate forms, make possible certain uncommon emotional harms not even possible in impersonal relationships. When someone is harmed in a personal relationship, she is owed a rectification of some sort, a righting of the wrong which has been done her. The notion of justice emerges, once again, as a relevant moral notion.

Thus, in a close relationship among persons of comparable moral personhood, care may degenerate into the injustices of exploitation, or oppression. Many such problems have been given wide public scrutiny recently as a result of feminist analysis of various aspects of family life and sexual relationships. Woman battering, acquaintance rape, and sexual harassment are but a few of the many recently publicized injustices of "personal" life. The notion of distributive or corrective injustice seems almost too mild to capture these indignities, involving, as they do, violation of bodily integrity and an assumption of the right to assault and injure. But to call these harms injustices is certainly not to rule out impassioned moral criticism in other terms as well.

The two requirements of justice which I have just discussed exemplify the standard distinction between distributive and corrective justice. They illustrate the role of justice in personal relationships regarded in abstraction from a social context. Personal relationships may also be regarded in the context of their various institutional settings, such as marriage and family. Here justice emerges again as a relevant ideal, its role being to define appropriate institutions to structure interactions among family members, other household cohabitants, and intimates in general. The family, for example,[14] is a miniature society, exhibiting all the major facets of large-scale social life: decision-making affecting the whole unit; executive action; judgments of guilt and innocence; reward and punishment; allocation of responsibilities and privileges, of burdens and benefits; and monumental influences on the life-chances of both its maturing and its matured members. Any of these features *alone* would invoke the relevance of justice; together, they make the case overwhelming.

Women's historically paradigmatic role of mothering has provided a multitude of insights which can be reconstructed as insights about the importance of justice in family relationships, especially those relationships involving remarkable disparities in maturity, capability, and power.[15] In these familial relationships, one party grows into moral personhood over time, gradually acquiring the capacity to be a responsible moral agent. Considerations of justice pertain to the mothering of children in numerous ways. For one thing, there may be siblings to deal with, whose demands and conflicts create the context for parental arbitration and the need for a fair allotment of responsibilities and privileges. Then there are decisions to be made, involving the well-being of all persons in the family unit, whose immature members become increasingly capable over time of participating in such administrative affairs. Of special importance in the practice of raising children are the duties to nurture and to promote growth and maturation. These duties may be seen as counterparts to the welfare rights viewed by many as a matter of social justice.[16] Motherhood continually presents its practitioners with moral problems best seen in terms of a complex framework which integrates justice with care, even though the politico-legal discourse of justice has not shaped its domestic expression.[17]

I have been discussing the relevance of justice to close personal relationships. A few words about my companion thesis—the relevance of care to the public domain—is also in order.[18] In its more noble manifestation, care in the public realm would show itself, perhaps, in foreign aid, welfare programs, famine or disaster relief, or other social programs designed to relieve suffering and attend to human needs. If untempered by justice in the public domain, care degenerates precipitously. The infamous "boss" of Chicago's old-time Democratic machine, Mayor Richard J. Daley, was legendary for his nepotism and political partisanship; he cared extravagantly for his relatives. friends, and political cronies (Royko 1971).

In recounting the moral reasoning of one of her research subjects, Gilligan once wrote that the "justice" perspective fails "to take into account the reality of relationships" (1982a, 147). What she meant is that the "justice" perspective emphasizes a self's various rights to noninterference by others. Gilligan worried that if this is all that a concern for justice involved, then such a perspective would disregard the moral value of positive interaction, connection, and commitment among persons.

However, Gilligan's interpretation of justice is far too limited. For one thing, it fails to recognize positive rights, such as welfare rights, which may be endorsed from a "justice" perspective. But beyond this minor point, a more important problem is Gilligan's failure to acknowledge the potential for *violence and harm* in human interrelationships and human community.[19] The concept of justice, in general, arises out of relational conditions in which most human beings have the capacity, and many have the inclination, to treat each other badly.

Thus, notions of distributive justice are impelled by the realization that people who together comprise a social system may not share fairly in the benefits and burdens of their social cooperation. Conceptions of rectificatory, or corrective, justice are founded on the concern that when harms are done, action should be taken either to restore those harmed as fully as possible to their previous state, or to prevent further similar harm, or both. And the specific rights which people are variously thought to have are just so many manifestations of our interest in identifying ways in which people deserve protection against harm by others. The complex reality of social life encompasses the human potential for helping, caring for, and nurturing others *as well as* the potential for harming, exploiting, and oppressing others. Thus, Gilligan is wrong to think that the justice perspective completely neglects "the reality of relationships." Rather, it arises from a more complex, and more realistic, estimate of the nature of human interrelationship.

In light of these reflections, it seems wise both to reconsider the seeming dichotomy of care and justice, and to question the moral adequacy of either orientation dissociated from the other. Our aim would be to advance "beyond caring," that is, beyond *mere* caring dissociated from a concern for justice. In addition, we would do well to progress beyond gender stereotypes which assign distinct and different moral roles to women and men. Our ultimate goal should be a nongendered, nondichotomized, moral framework in which all moral concerns could be expressed. We might, with intentional irony, call this project, "de-moralizing the genders."

Commitments to Particular Persons

Even though care and justice do not define mutually exclusive moral frameworks, it is still too early to dispose of the "different voice hypothesis." I believe that there is something to be said for the thesis that there are different moral orientations, even if the concepts of care and justice do not capture the relevant differences and even if the differences do not correlate statistically with gender differences.

My suggestion is that one important distinction has to do with the nature and focus of what may be called "primary moral commitments." Let us begin with the observation that, from the so-called "care standpoint," responsiveness to other persons in their wholeness and their particularity is of singular importance. This idea, in turn, points toward a notion of moral commitment which takes *particular persons* as its primary focus.[20] A form of moral commitment which contrasts with this is one which involves a focus on general and abstract rules, values, or principles. It is no mere coincidence, I believe, that Gilligan found the so-called "justice" perspective to feature an emphasis on *rules* (e.g., 1982a, 73).

In the second part of this paper, I argued that the concepts of justice and care are mutually compatible and, to at least some extent, mutually dependent. Based on my analysis, the "justice perspective" might be said to rest, at bottom, on the assumption that the best way to *care* for persons is to respect their rights, and to accord them their due, both in distribution of the burdens and benefits of social cooperation, and in the rectification of wrongs done. But to uphold these principles, it is not necessary to respond with emotion, feeling, passion, or compassion to other persons. Upholding justice does not require the full range of mutual responsiveness which is possible between persons.

By contrast, the so-called "ethic of care" stresses an ongoing responsiveness. This ethic is, after all, the stereotypic moral norm for women in the domestic role of sustaining a family in the face of the harsh realities of a competitive marketplace and an indifferent polis. The domestic realm has been idealized as the realm in which people, as specific individuals, were to have been nurtured, cherished, and succored. The "care" perspective discussed by Gilligan is a limited one; it is not really about care in all its complexity, for, as I have argued, that notion *includes* just treatment. But it *is* about the nature of relationships to particular persons grasped as such. The key issue is the sensitivity and responsiveness to another person's emotional states, individuating differences, specific uniqueness, and whole particularity. The "care" orientation focuses on whole persons and deemphasizes adherence to moral rules.

Thus, the important conception which I am extracting from the so-called "care" perspective is that of commitment to particular persons. What is the nature of this form of moral commitment? Commitment to a specific person, such as a lover, child, or friend, takes as its primary focus the needs, wants, attitudes, judgments, behavior, and overall way of being of that particular person. It is specific to that individual and is not generalizable to others. We show a commitment to someone whenever we attend to her needs, enjoy her successes, defer to her judgment, and find inspiration in her values and goals simply because they are *hers*. If it is *who she is,* and not her actions or traits subsumed under general rules, which matters as one's motivating guide, then one's responsiveness to her reflects a person-oriented, rather than a rule-based, moral commitment.

Thus, the different perspectives which Gilligan called "care" and "justice" do point toward substantive differences in human interrelationship and commitment. Both orientations take account of relationships in some way; both may legitimately incorporate a concern for justice and for care, and both aim to avoid harm to others and (at the highest stages) to the self. But from the standpoint of "care," self and other are conceptualized in their *particularity* rather than as instances for the application of generalized moral notions. This difference ramifies into what appears to be a major difference in the organization and focus of moral thought.

This analysis requires a subtle expansion. Like care and justice, commitments to particular persons and commitments to values, rules, and principles are not mutually exclusive within the entire panorama of one person's moral concerns. Doubtless, they are intermingled in most people's moral outlooks. Pat likes and admires Mary because of Mary's resilience in the face of tragedy, her intelligent courage, and her good-humored audacity. Pat thereby shows a commitment *in general* to resilience, courage, and good-humored audacity as traits of human personality.

However, in Mary, these traits coalesce in a unique manner: perhaps no one will stand by a friend in deep trouble quite so steadfastly as Mary; perhaps no one petitions the university president as effectively as Mary. The traits which Pat likes, in general, converge to make *Mary,* in Pat's eyes, an especially admirable human individual, a sort of moral exemplar. In virtue of Pat's loyalty to her, Mary may come to play a role in Pat's life which exceeds, in its weightiness, the sum total of the values which Pat sees in Mary's virtues, taken individually and in abstraction from any particular human personality.

Pat is someone with commitments both to moral abstractions and to particular persons. Pat is, in short, like most of us. When we reason morally, we can take up a stance which makes either of these forms of commitment the focal point of our attention. The choice of which stance to adopt at a given time is probably, like other moral alternatives, most poignant and difficult in situations of moral ambiguity or uncertainty when we don't know how to proceed. In such situations, one can turn *either* to the guidance of principled commitments to values, forms of conduct, or human virtues, *or* one can turn to the guidance which inheres in the example set by a trusted friend or associate—the example of how *she* interprets those same moral ambiguities, or how *she* resolves those same moral uncertainties.

Of course, the commitment to a particular person is evident in more situations than simply those of moral irresolution. But the experience of moral irresolution may make clearer the different sorts of moral commitment which structure our thinking. Following cherished values will lead one out of one's moral uncertainties in a very different way than following someone else's example.

Thus, the insight that each person needs some others in her life who recognize, respect, and cherish her particularity in its richness and wholeness is the distinctive motivating vision of the "care" perspective.[21] The sort of respect for persons which grows out of this vision is not the abstract respect which is owed to all persons in virtue of their common humanity, but a respect for individual worth, merit, need, or, even, idiosyncrasy. It is a form of respect which involves admiration and cherishing, when the distinctive qualities are valued intrinsically, and which, at the least, involves toleration when the distinctive qualities are not valued intrinsically.

Indeed, there is an apparent irony in the notion of personhood which underlies some philosophers' conceptions of the universalized moral duties owed to all persons. The rational nature which Kant, for example, takes to give each person dignity and to make each of absolute value and, therefore, irreplaceable,[22] is no more than an abstract rational nature in virtue of which we are all alike. But if we are all alike in this respect, it is hard to understand why we would be irreplaceable. Our common rational nature would seem to make us indistinguishable and, therefore, mutually interchangeable. Specific identity would be a matter of indifference, so far as absolute value is concerned. Yet it would seem that only in *virtue* of our distinctive particularity could we each be truly irreplaceable.

Of course, our particularity does not *exclude* a common nature, conceptualized at a level of suitable generality. We still deserve equal respect in virtue of our common humanity. But we are also *more* than abstractly and equivalently human. It is this "more" to which we commit ourselves when we care for others in their particularity.

Thus, as I interpret it, there is at least one important difference in moral reasoning brought to our attention by Gilligan's "care" and "justice" frameworks. This difference hinges on the primary form of moral commitment which structures moral thought and the resulting nature of the response to other persons. For so-called "care" reasoners, recognition of, and commitment to, persons in their particularity is an overriding moral concern.[23]

Unlike the concepts of justice and care, which admit of a mutual integration, it is less clear that these two distinct forms of moral commitment can jointly comprise the focus of one's moral attention, in any single case. Nor can we respond to all other persons equally well in either way. The only integration possible here may be to seek the more intimate, responsive, committed relationships with people who are known closely, or known in contexts in which differential needs are important and can be known with some reliability, and to settle for rule-based equal respect toward that vast number of others whom one cannot know in any particularity.

At any rate, to tie together the varied threads of this discussion, we may conclude that nothing intrinsic to gender demands a division of moral norms which assigns particularized, personalized commitments to women and universalized, rule-based commitments to men. We need nothing less than to "de-moralize" the genders, advance beyond the dissociation of justice from care, and enlarge the symbolic access of each gender to all available conceptual and social resources for the sustenance and enrichment of our collective moral life.

Notes

1. More recently, further works by Gilligan on related issues have also appeared [1983, 1986b, 1986c (reprinted as chapter 15 in this volume)].
2. These sources include: Flanagan & Adler 1983; Noddings 1984; Card 1985 [cf. 1990—Ed.]; Friedman 1985, 1986, 1987; Meyers & Kittay 1987; Kerber 1986 (reprinted as chapter 7 in this volume); Greeno & Maccoby 1986 (reprinted as chapter 13 in this volume); Luria 1986 (reprinted as chapter 14 in this volume); Stack 1986 (reprinted as chapter 8 in this volume); Flanagan & Jackson 1987 (reprinted as chapter 5 in this volume). An analysis of this issue from an ambiguously feminist standpoint is to be found in Broughton 1983b (reprinted as chapter 9 in this volume). For a helpful review of some of these issues, cf. Grimshaw 1986, esp. chaps. 7 and 8.
3. This term is used by Held (1984b) to refer, in general, to the division of moral labor among the multitude of professions, activities, and practices in culture and society, though not specifically to gender roles; cf. chap. 3. Held is aware that gender roles are part of the division of moral labor, but she mentions this topic only in passing (29).
4. Research on the "gender difference" hypothesis is very mixed. The studies which appear to show gender differences in moral reasoning for one or more age levels include: Haan, Brewster-Smith & Block 1968; Fishkin, Keniston & Mackinnon 1973; Haan 1975; Holstein 1976a (showing gender differences in middle adulthood but not for other age categories; see references below);

Langdale 1983; Johnston 1985. The last two sources are cited by Gilligan 1986c, 330 (reprinted as chapter 15 in this volume).

Among the studies which show no gender differences in moral reasoning at one or more age levels are: Turiel 1976; Holstein 1976a (showing no differences in childhood or adolescence but showing differentiation in middle adulthood); Haan et al. 1976; Berkowitz et al. 1980; and Brabeck 1983 (reprinted as chapter 3 in this volume).

L. Walker (1984, reprinted as chapter 11 in this volume) surveyed all the research to date and claimed that rather than showing a gender-based difference in moral reasoning, it showed differences based on occupation and education. This "meta-analysis" has itself recently been disputed: Haan 1985; Baumrind 1986 (reprinted as chapter 12 in this volume). The last two sources are cited by Gilligan 1986c, 330 (reprinted as chapter 15 in this volume).

5. Also cf. Haan 1975; and Nunner-Winkler 1984 (reprinted as chapter 10 in this volume).

6. Gilligan's work arose largely as a critical reaction to the studies of moral reasoning carried on by L. Kohlberg and his research associates. For the reaction by those scholars to Gilligan's work and their assessment of its importance to moral psychology, see Kohlberg 1982; and Kohlberg et al. 1983.

In philosophy, themes related to Gilligan's concerns have been raised by, among others: Stocker 1976; Williams 1981; Blum 1980; MacIntyre 1981a, esp. chap. 15; Stocker 1981; Flanagan 1982; Slote 1982; and Sommers 1986.

7. For a discussion of this historical development, cf. Nicholson 1983 (reprinted as chapter 6 in this volume), and 1986, esp. chaps. 3 and 4.

8. Cf. Eagly 1986. Also cf. Eagly & Steffen 1984.

9. The stereotypes of men are not obviously connected with justice and rights, but they are connected with the excessive individualism which Gilligan takes to underlie the justice orientation; cf. Eagly 1986, 8.

10. Eagly (1986, passim) argues both that people do show a tendency to conform to shared and known expectations, on the parts of others, about their behavior, and that a division of labor which leads people to develop different skills also contributes to differential development. It follows from Eagly's view that if the genders are stereotypically "moralized," they would then be likely to develop so as to conform to those different expectations.

11. Eagly & Steffen (1984, passim) have found that stereotypic beliefs that women are more "communal" and less "agentic" than men, and that men are more "agentic" and less "communal" than women, are based more deeply on occupational role stereotypes than on gender stereotypes. In this respect, Eagly & Steffen force us to question whether the gender categorization which pervades Gilligan's analysis really captures the fundamental differentiation among persons. I do not address this question in this paper.

12. In correspondence, Marcia Baron has suggested that a factor accounting for the actual emergence of "mixed" perspectives on the parts of women and men may have to do with the instability of the distinction between public and private realms to which the justice/care dichotomy corresponds. Men have always been recognized to participate in both realms and, in practice, many women have participated, out of choice or necessity, in such segments of the public world as that of paid labor. The result is a blurring of the experiential segrega-

tion which otherwise might have served to reinforce distinct moral orientations.

13. Book I, 322–35. A thorough discussion of the Greek conception of justice in the context of friendship can be found in Hutter 1978.

14. For an important discussion of the relevance of justice to the family, cf. Okin 1987.

15. For insightful discussions of the distinctive modes of thought to which mothering gives rise, cf. Ruddick 1980, 1984b; also Held 1984a.

16. This point was suggested to me by L. Sumner.

17. Broughton 1983b (reprinted as chapter 9 in this volume), also discusses the concern for justice and rights which appears in women's moral reasoning as well as the concern for care and relationships featured in men's moral reasoning (esp. 603–22). For a historical discussion of male theorists who have failed to hear the concern for justice in women's voices, cf. Pateman 1980.

18. This discussion owes a debt to Cancian's (1986) warning that we should not narrow our conception of love to the recognized ways in which women love, which researchers find to center around the expression of feelings and verbal disclosure. Such a conception ignores forms of love which are stereotyped as characteristically male, including instrumental help and the sharing of activities.

19. Card (1985 [cf. 1990—Ed.]) has critiqued Gilligan's work for ignoring, in particular, the dismaying harms to which women have historically been subjected in heterosexual relationships, including, but by no means limited to, marriage.

20. Discussion in the third part of my paper draws upon the insights of Card 1985 [cf. 1990—Ed.] and Benhabib 1987.

21. This part of my discussion owes a debt to Card.

22. Cf. Kant 1959, 46–47, 53–54.

23. For a helpful discussion on this topic, cf. M. Walker 1987.

References

Addelson, K. 1987. "Moral Passages." In Kittay and Meyers, *Women:* 87–110.

Adelson, J. and M. Doehrman. 1980. "The Psychodynamic Approach to Adolescence." In *Handbook of Adolescent Psychology.* J. Adelson, ed. New York: Wiley.

Adler, J. 1987. "Moral Development and the Personal Point of View." In Kittay and Meyers, *Women:* 205–34.

Adler, J. 1989. "Particularity, Gilligan, and the Two-Levels View." *Ethics* 100: 149–56.

Alker, H., and P. Poppen. 1973. "Personality and Ideology in University Students." *Journal of Personality* 41: 653–71.

Andolsen, B., et al., eds. 1985. *Women's Consciousness, Women's Conscience.* San Francisco: Harper & Row.

Anscombe, G. 1958. "Modern Moral Philosophy." *Philosophy* 33: 1–19.

Arbuthnot, J. 1975. "Modification of Moral Judgment through Role Playing." *Developmental Psychology* 11: 319–24.

Arbuthnot, J. 1983. "Attributions of Responsibility by Simulated Jurors." *Psychological Reports* 52: 287–98.

Aristotle. 1946. *The Politics of Aristotle.* Trans. E. Barker. New York: Oxford University Press.

Aristotle. 1976. *Nichomachean Ethics.* Trans. J. Thomson and H. Tredennick. Harmondsworth: Penguin.

Attanucci, J. 1984. "Mothers in Their Own Terms." Doctoral dissertation, Harvard Graduate School of Education.

Auerbach, J., et al. 1985. "On Gilligan's *In a Different Voice.* " *Feminist Studies* 11: 149–61.

Bachofen, J. 1967. *Myth, Religion and Mother Right.* New York: Bollingen Foundation.

Baier, A. 1982. "Caring about Caring." *Synthese* 53, no. 2: 291ff. Also, 1989. In *Postures*.

Baier, A. 1985a. "What Do Women Want in a Moral Theory?" *Nous* 19, no. 1: 53–63. (Reprinted in this collection.)

Baier, A. 1985b. *Postures of the Mind*. Minneapolis: University of Minnesota Press.

Baier, A. 1986a. "The Moral Perils of Intimacy." In *Pragmatism's Freud*: 93–101. J. Smith and W. Kerrigan, eds. Baltimore: Johns Hopkins University Press.

Baier, A. 1986b. "Trust and Antitrust." *Ethics* 96: 231–60.

Baier, A. 1987a. "Hume, the Women's Moral Theorist?" In Kittay and Meyers, *Women*: 37–55.

Baier, A. 1987b. "The Need for More than Justice." In Hanen and Nielsen, *Science*: 41–56.

Bakan, D. 1966. *The Duality of Human Existence*. Boston: Beacon.

Barber, B. 1983. "Beyond the Feminist Mystique." *New Republic*. 11 July 1983: 26–32.

Baron, M. 1984. "The Alleged Repugnance of Acting from Duty." *Journal of Philosophy* 81: 197–220.

Barry, B. 1984. "Review of Sandel [1981]." *Ethics* 94: 523–25.

Bar-Yam, M., L. Kohlberg, and A. Naame. 1980. "Moral Reasoning of Students in Different Cultural, Social, and Educational Settings." *American Journal of Education* 88: 345–62.

Basseches, M. 1980. "Dialectical Schemata." *Human Development* 23: 400–421.

Baumrind, D. 1978. "A Dialectical Materialist's Perspective on Knowing Social Reality." In *New Directions for Child Development*. Vol. 2: 61–82. W. Damon, ed. San Francisco: Jossey-Bass.

Baumrind, D. 1982. "Are Androgynous Individuals More Effective Persons and Parents?" *Child Development* 53: 44–75.

Baumrind, D. 1986. "Sex Differences in Moral Reasoning." *Child Development* 57: 511–21. (Reprinted in this collection.)

Bear, G., and H. Richards. 1981. "Moral Reasoning and Conduct Problems in the Classroom." *Journal of Educational Psychology* 73: 664–70.

Beauvoir, S. de. 1953. *The Second Sex*. London: Jonathan Cape.

Beauvoir, S. de. 1948; 1976. *The Ethics of Ambiguity*. B. Frechtman, trans. New York: Citadel.

Belenky, M., et al. 1987. *Women's Ways of Knowing*. New York: Basic Books.

Bem, Daryl, and D. Funder. 1978. "Predicting More of the People More of the Time." *Psychology Review* 85: 485–501.

Bem, S. 1974. "The Measurement of Psychological Androgyny." *Journal of Consulting and Clinical Psychology* 42: 155–62.

Benhabib, S. 1987. "The Generalized and the Concrete Other." In Kittay and Meyers, *Women*: 154–77.

Benjamin, J. 1980. "The Bonds of Love." *Feminist Studies* 6: 144–74.

Benjamin, J. 1987. "The Oedipal Riddle." In *Critical Theories of Psychological Development*. J. Broughton, ed. New York: Plenum.

Benton, C., et al. 1983. "Is Hostility Linked with Affiliation among Males and with Achievement in Females?" *Journal of Personality and Social Psychology* 45: 1167–71.

Berkowitz, M., et al. 1980. "The Relation of Moral Judgment Stage Disparity to Developmental Effects of Peer Dialogues." *Merrill-Palmer Quarterly* 26: 341–57.

Berkowitz, M., F. Oser, and W. Althof. 1987. "The Development of Sociomoral Discourse." In Kurtines and Gewirtz, *Moral Development:* 322–52.

Bernstein, B. 1975. *Class, Codes and Control.* Vol. 3. London: Routledge & Kegan Paul.

Bettleheim, B. 1943. "Individual and Mass Behavior in Extreme Situations." *Journal of Abnormal and Social Psychology* 38: 417–52.

Biaggio, A. 1976. "A Developmental Study of Moral Judgment of Brazilian Children and Adolescents." *Interamerican Journal of Psychology* 10: 71–78.

Bielby, D. and D. Papalia. 1975. "Moral Development and Perceptual Role-Taking." *International Journal of Aging and Human Development* 6: 293–308.

Bishop, S. 1987. "Connections and Guilt." *Hypatia* 2, no. 1: 7–23.

Blasi, A. 1976. "Vico, Developmental Psychology, and Human Nature." *Social Research* 43: 672–97.

Blasi, A. 1981. "Moral Cognition and Moral Action." In *Moralisches Urteil in Gruppen*. F. Oser, ed. Frankfurt: Suhrkamp.

Blasi, A., and J. Broughton. In press. "Universality in the Development of Moral Judgment." *Moral Development: Theory and Research*. L. Kohlberg and A. Colby, eds. New York: Cambridge University Press.

Blatt, M., and L. Kohlberg. 1975. "The Effects of Classroom Moral Discussion upon Children's Level of Moral Judgment." *Journal of Moral Education* 4: 129–61.

Block, J., and J. Block. 1980. "Studying Situational Dimensions." In *The Situation*. D. Magnusson, ed. Hillsdale, N.J.: Lawrence Erlbaum.

Blum, L. 1980. *Friendship, Altruism and Morality*. London: Routledge & Kegan Paul.

Blum, L. 1982. "Kant and Hegel's Moral Rationalism." *Canadian Journal of Philosophy* 12: 287–302.

Blum, L. 1986. "Iris Murdoch and the Domain of the Moral." *Philosophical Studies* 50: 343–67.

Blum, L. 1987. "Particularity and Responsiveness." In Kagan and Lamb, *Emergence:* 307–37.

Blum, L. 1988. "Gilligan and Kohlberg." *Ethics* 98: 472–91. (Reprinted in this collection.)

Blum, L. 1990. "Vocation, Friendship, and Community." In Flanagan and Rorty, *Identity:* 173–97.

Blum, L., et al. 1976. "Altruism and Women's Oppression." In *Women and Philosophy:* 222–47. C. Gould and M. Wartofsky, eds. New York: Putnam.

Bograd, M. 1988. "Power, Gender, and the Family." In *Feminist Psychotherapies:* 118–33. M. Dutton-Douglas and L. Walker, eds. Norwood, N.J.: Ablex.

Bowlby, J. 1969. *Attachment.* New York: Basic Books.

Boyd, D. 1979. "An Interpretation of Principled Morality." *Journal of Moral Education* 8: 110–23.

Boyd, D. 1983. "Careful Justice or Just Caring: A Response to Gilligan." In *Philosophy of Education 1982: Proceedings of the Philosophy of Education Society:* 63–69. Normal: Illinois State University Press.

Brabeck, M. 1983. "Moral Judgment." *Developmental Review* 3: 274–91. (Reprinted in this collection.)

Brabeck, M., ed. 1989. *Who Cares?.* New York: Praeger.

Brandt, R. 1979. *A Theory of the Good and the Right.* Oxford: Oxford University Press.

Bridenthal, R., et al. 1984. *When Biology Became Destiny: Women in Weimar and Nazi Germany.* New York: Monthly Review.

Brock, P. 1970. *Twentieth Century Pacifism.* New York: Van Nostrand.

Broughton, J. 1978a. "The Development of Concepts of Self, Mind, Reality and Knowledge." In *New Directions for Child Development,* Vol. 1: 75–100. W. Damon, ed. San Francisco: Jossey-Bass.

Broughton, J. 1978b. "Dialectics and Moral Ideology." In *Readings in Moral Education.* P. Scharf, ed. Minneapolis: Winston.

Broughton, J. 1981. "The Divided Self in Adolescence." *Human Development* 24: 13–32.

Broughton, J. 1982. "Is Adult Development Good for Us?" Paper read at Conference on Adult Development and Education, Teachers College, Columbia University Press.

Broughton, J. 1983a. "The Cognitive-Development Theory of Adolescent Self and Identity." In *Developmental Approaches to the Self.* B. Lee and G. Noam, eds. New York: Plenum.

Broughton, J. 1983b. "Women's Rationality and Men's Virtues." *Social Research* 50, no. 3: 597–642. (Reprinted in this collection.)

Broughton, J. 1984. "Not Beyond Formal Operations, But Beyond Piaget." In *Beyond Formal Operations:* 395–411. M. Commons et al., eds. New York: Praeger.

Broughton, J., and M. Zahaykevich. 1977. "Review of J. Loevinger's *Ego Development.*" *Telos* 32: 246–53.

Broughton, J., and M. Zahaykevich. 1980. "Personality and Ideology in Ego Development." In *La Dialectique dans les sciences sociales.* J. Gabel and V. Trinh Van Thao, eds. Paris: Anthropos.

Broverman, D., et al. 1970. "Sex-Role Stereotypes and Clinical Judgments of Mental Health." *Journal of Consulting and Clinical Psychology* 34: 1–7.

Buck, L., et al. 1981. "Relationship between Parental Moral Judgment and Socialization." *Youth and Society* 13: 91–116.

Buck-Morss, S. 1975. "Socio-Economic Basis in Piaget's Theory and Its Implications for Cross-Culture Studies." *Human Development* 18: 35–49.

Bush, D., and B. Balik. 1977. "Factors Contributing to Moral Stage Change in Adolescence and Adulthood." *Social Science Forum* 1: 14–24.

Bussey, K., and B. Maughan. 1982. "Gender Differences in Moral Reasoning." *Journal of Personality and Social Psychology* 42: 701–6.

Calhoun, C. 1988. "Justice, Care, Gender Bias." *Journal of Philosophy* 85: 451–63.

Cancian, F. 1986. "The Feminization of Love." *Signs* 11: 692–709.

Cannon, K. 1988. *Black Womanist Ethics*. Atlanta: Scholars.

Card, C. 1985. "Virtues and Moral Luck." Working Series I, No. 4. Institute for Legal Studies, University of Wisconsin, Madison, Law School.

Card, C. 1990. "Gender and Moral Luck." In Flanagan and Rorty, *Identity*: 199–218.

Card, C., ed. 1991. *Feminist Ethics*. Lawrence: University Press of Kansas.

Carlson, R. 1971. "Sex Differences in Ego Functioning." *Journal of Consulting and Clinical Psychology* 37: 267–77.

Carroll, J., and J. Rest. 1982. "Moral Development." In *Handbook of Developmental Psychology*. B. Wolman and G. Stricker, eds. Englewood Cliffs, N.J.: Prentice-Hall.

Cattell, R. 1965. *The Scientific Analysis of Personality*. Baltimore: Penguin.

Cavell, S. 1979. *The Claim of Reason*. Oxford: Oxford University Press.

Chasseguet-Smirgel, J. 1976. "Freud and Female Sexuality." *International Journal of Psychoanalysis* 57: 275–86.

Chodorow, N. 1978. *The Reproduction of Mothering*. Berkeley: University of California Press.

Chodorow, N. 1979. "Feminism and Difference." *Socialist Review* 46: 54–69.

Chodorow, N. 1986. "Toward a Relational Individualism." In Heller et al., *Reconstructing*: 197–207.

Cocks, J. "Wordless Emotions." Unpublished.

Code, L. 1983. "Responsibility and the Epistemic Community." *Social Research* 50, no. 3: 537–54.

Code, L., S. Mullett, and C. Overall, eds. 1988. *Feminist Perspectives: Philosophical Essays on Method and Morals*. Toronto: University of Toronto Press.

Cohen, J. 1977. *Statistical Power Analysis for the Behavioral Sciences*. Rev. ed. New York: Academic.

Colby, A. 1978. "Evolution of a Moral-Developmental Theory." In *New Directions for Child Development*. Vol. 2: 89–104. W. Damon, ed. San Francisco: Jossey-Bass.

Colby, A. 1979. "Standard Form Scoring Manual." Unpublished. Center for Moral Education, Harvard University.

Colby, A., and W. Damon. 1983. "Listening to a Different Voice: A Review of Gilligan's *In a Different Voice.*" *Merrill-Palmer Quarterly* 29: 473–82.

Colby, A., L. Kohlberg, J. Gibbs, D. Candee, et al. 1984. *Assessing Moral Stages: A Manual.* New York: Cambridge University Press.

Colby, A., L. Kohlberg, J. Gibbs, and M. Lieberman. 1983. "A Longitudinal Study of Moral Judgment." *Monographs of the Society for Research in Child Development* 48, 1–2, serial no. 200: 1–96.

Coles, R. 1977. *Eskimos, Chicanos, Indians.* Boston: Little, Brown.

Collins, P. 1990. *Black Feminist Thought.* Cambridge: Unwin Hyman.

Conarton, S., and L. Silverman. 1988. "Feminine Development Through the Life Cycle." In *Feminist Psychotherapies:* 37–67. M. Dutton-Douglas and L. Walker, eds. Norwood, N.J.: Ablex.

Connolly, J., and M. McCarrey. 1978. "The Relationship between Levels of Moral Judgment Maturity and Locus of Control." *Canadian Journal of Behavioral Science* 10: 162–75.

Cooper, H., and R. Rosenthal. 1980. "Statistical Versus Traditional Procedures for Summarizing Research Findings." *Psychological Bulletin* 87: 442–49.

Cortese, A. 1982a. "A Comparative Analysis of Cognition and Moral Judgment in Chicano, Black, and Anglo Children." Paper read at American Sociological Association.

Cortese, A. 1982b. "Moral Development in Chicano and Anglo Children." *Hispanic Journal of Behavioral Science* 4, no. 3: 353–66.

Cortese, A. 1984. "Standard Issue Scoring of Moral Reasoning: A Critique." *Merrill-Palmer Quarterly* 30:227–46.

Daly, M. 1978. *Gyn/Ecology: The Metaethics of Radical Feminism.* Boston: Beacon.

Dancy, J. 1983. "Ethical Particularism and Morally Relevant Properties." *Mind* 92, no. 368: 530–47.

Darwall, S. 1983. *Impartial Reason.* Ithaca: Cornell University Press.

D'Augelli, J., and H. Cross. 1975. "Relationship of Sex Guilt and Moral Reasoning to Premarital Sex in College Women and in Couples." *Journal of Consulting and Clinical Psychology* 43: 40–47.

Davidson, F. 1976. "Ability to Respect Persons Compared to Ethnic Prejudice in Childhood." *Journal of Personality and Social Psychology* 34: 1256–67.

Davis, A. 1977. *American Heroine.* New York: Oxford University Press.

Davis, L. 1985. "Female and Male Voices in Social Work." *Social Work* 30, no. 2: 106–13.

Deaux, K. 1976. *The Behavior of Men and Women.* Monterey, Cal.: Brooks/Cole.

Dietz, M. 1985. "Citizenship with a Feminist Face." *Political Theory* 13, no. 1: 19–37.

Dill, B. 1983. " 'On the Hem of Life.' " In Swerdlow and Lessinger, *Class:* 173–88.

DuBois, E. 1980. "Politics and Culture in Women's History." *Feminist Studies* 6: 28–36.

DuBois, E., M. Dunlap, C. Gilligan, C. MacKinnon, and C. Menkel-Meadow, conversants. 1985. "Feminist Discourse, Moral Values and the Law—A Conversation." *Buffalo Law Review* 34: 11–87.

Dugan, D. 1987. "Masculine and Feminine Voices: Making Ethical Decisions in the Care of the Dying." *Journal of Medical Humanities and Bioethics* 3, no. 2: 129–40.

Dulit, L. 1983. "From Piaget through Kohlberg to Gilligan." Paper read at the American Association of Adolescent Psychiatry.

Dworkin, R. 1977. *Taking Rights Seriously.* Cambridge: Harvard University Press.

Eagly, A. 1986. "Sex Differences and Social Roles." Paper read at Experimental Social Psychology meeting.

Eagly, A., and V. Steffen. 1984. "Gender Stereotypes Stem from the Distribution of Women and Men into Social Roles." *Journal of Personality and Social Psychology* 46: 735–54.

Edwards, C. 1978. "Social Experience and Moral Judgment in East African Young Adults." *Journal of Genetic Psychology* 133: 19–29.

Ehrenreich, B., and D. English. 1979. *For Her Own Good.* New York: Anchor/Doubleday.

Eisenberg, N., and R. Lennon. 1983. "Sex Differences in Empathy and Related Capacities." *Psychological Bulletin* 94: 100–131.

Eisenberg, N., et al. 1989. "Gender Differences in Empathy and Prosocial Moral Reasoning." In Brabeck, *Who Cares?:* 127–53.

Elkind, D. 1969. "Conservation and Concept Formation." In *Studies in Cognitive Development.* D. Elkind and J. Flavell, eds. New York: Oxford University Press.

Elshtain, J. 1981. "Kant, Politics, and Persons." *Polity* 14, no. 2: 205–21.

Elshtain, J. 1982. "Antigone's Daughters." *Democracy* 2, no. 2: 46–59.

Elshtain, J. 1983. "On Beautiful Souls, Just Warriors and Feminist Consciousness." In *Women and Men's Wars:* 341–49. J. Stiehm, ed. Oxford: Pergamon.

Elshtain, J. 1985. "Reflections on War and Political Discourse." *Political Theory* 13, no. 1: 39–57.

Emler, N. 1983. "Moral Character." In *Morality in the Making:* 47–71. H. Weinreich-Haste and D. Locke, eds. New York: Wiley.

Emmet, D. 1966. *Rules, Roles and Relations.* New York: St. Martin's.

Erikson, E. 1958. *Young Man Luther.* New York: Norton.

Erikson, E. 1969. *Gandhi's Truth.* New York: Norton.

Erickson, L., et al. 1978. "Sex Differences in Moral Judgment during Childhood and Young Adulthood." Paper read at Society for Research in Child Development.

Eugene, T. 1989. "Sometimes I Feel Like a Motherless Child: The Call and Response for a Liberational Ethic of Care by Black Feminists." In Brabeck, *Who Cares?:* 45–62.

Evans, C. 1982. "Moral Stage Development and Knowledge of Kohlberg's Theory." *Journal of Experimental Education* 51: 14–17.

Ferguson, A. 1987. "A Feminist Aspect Theory of the Self." In Hanen and Nielsen, *Science:* 339–54. Also, 1989. In Garry and Pearsall, *Women, Knowledge:* 93–107.

Fisher, B., and J. Tronto. 1990. "Toward a Feminist Theory of Caring." In *Circles of Care:* 35–62. E. Abel and M. Nelson, eds. Albany: State University of New York Press.

Fishkin, J., K. Keniston, and C. MacKinnon. 1973. "Moral Reasoning and Political Ideology." *Journal of Personality and Social Psychology* 27: 109–19.

Flanagan, O. 1982. "Virtue, Sex and Gender." *Ethics* 92: 499–512.

Flanagan, O. 1984. *The Science of the Mind.* Cambridge: MIT Press.

Flanagan, O. 1991. *Varieties of Moral Personality.* Cambridge: Harvard University Press.

Flanagan, O., and J. Adler. 1983. "Impartiality and Particularity." *Social Research* 50: 576–96.

Flanagan, O., and K. Jackson. 1987. "Justice, Care, and Gender." *Ethics* 97: 622–37. (Reprinted in this collection.)

Flanagan, O., and A. Rorty, eds. 1990. *Identity, Character, and Morality.* Cambridge: MIT Press.

Flavell, J., and E. Markham, eds. 1983. *Cognitive Development.* In *Handbook of Child Psychology: Formerly Carmichael's Manual of Child Psychology.* Vol. 3. 4th ed. P. Mussen, gen. ed. New York: Wiley.

Flax, J. 1980. "Mother-Daughter Relationships." In *Future of Difference.* H. Eisenstein and A. Jardine, eds. Boston: Hall.

Fowler, J. 1981. *Stages of Faith.* New York: Harper & Row.

Frankena, W. 1973. *Ethics.* 2d ed. Englewood Cliffs, N.J.: Prentice-Hall.

Frankfurt, H. 1982. "What We Care About." *Synthese* 53, no. 2: 257–72.

Freedman, E. 1979. "Separation as Strategy." *Feminist Studies* 5: 512–29.

Freeman, S., and J. Giebink. 1979. "Moral Judgment as a Function of Age, Sex and Stimulus." *Journal of Psychology* 102: 43–47.

Freud, A. 1946. *The Ego Mechanisms of Defense.* New York: International University Press.

Freud, S. 1914; 1963. *The History of the Psychoanalytic Movement.* New York: Collier.

Freud, Sigmund. 1914. "On Narcissism: An Introduction." In *General Psychological Theory.* New York: Collier.

Freud, S. 1925; 1961. "Some Psychological Consequences of the Anatomical Distinction between the Sexes." In *Standard Edition.* Vol. 19. J. Strachey, ed. London: Hogarth.

Freud, S. 1931; 1961. "Female Sexuality." In *Standard Edition.* Vol. 21. J. Strachey, ed. London: Hogarth.

Friedman, M. 1985. "Abraham, Socrates, and Heinz: Where are the Women?" In *Moral Dilemmas:* 25–42. C. Harding, ed. Chicago: Precedent. Also, 1986. *Care and Context in Moral Reasoning.* Bath, England: University of Bath Press. Also, 1987. "Care and Context in Moral Reasoning." In Kittay and Meyers, *Women:* 190–204.

Friedman, M. 1987. "Beyond Caring." In Hanen and Nielsen, *Science:* 87–110. (Reprinted in this collection.)

Friedman, M. 1989. "Friendship and Moral Growth." *Journal of Value Inquiry* 23: 3–13.

Froman, T., and L. Hubert. 1980. "Application of Prediction Analysis to Developmental Priority." *Psychological Bulletin* 87: 136–46.

Froming, W. 1978. "The Relationship of Moral Judgment, Self-Awareness, and Sex to Compliance Behavior." *Journal of Research in Personality* 12: 396–409.

Frye, M. 1983. *The Politics of Reality.* Trumansberg, N.Y.: Crossing Press.

Garry, A., and M. Pearsall, eds. 1989. *Women, Knowledge, and Reality.* Boston: Unwin Hyman.

Garwood, S., et al. 1980. "Effect of Protagonist's Sex on Assessing Gender Differences in Moral Reasoning." *Developmental Psychology* 16: 677–78.

Gert, B. 1973. *The Moral Rules.* New York: Harper & Row.

Getzels, J., and P. Jackson. 1962. *Creativity and Intelligence.* New York: Wiley.

Gibbs, J., K. Arnold, H. Ahlborn, and F. Cheesman. 1984. "Facilitation of Sociomoral Reasoning in Delinquents." *Journal of Consulting and Clinical Psychology* 52: 37–45.

Gibbs, J., K. Arnold, and J. Burkhart. 1984. "Sex Differences in the Expression of Moral Judgment." *Child Development* 55: 1040–43.

Gibbs, J., K. Widaman, and A. Colby. 1982. "Construction and Validation of a Simplified, Group-administerable Equivalent to the Moral Judgment Interview." *Child Development* 53: 895–910.

Gilligan, C. 1977. "Concepts of the Self and of Morality." *Harvard Educational Review* 47: 481–517. Repr., 1986, as "In a Different Voice." In Pearsall, *Women and Values:* 309–39.

Gilligan, C. 1979. "Women's Place in Man's Life Cycle." *Harvard Educational Review* 49: 431–46.

Gilligan, C. 1980. "Justice and Responsibility." In *Toward Moral and Religious Maturity.* C. Brusselmans et al., eds. Morristown, N.J.: Silver Burdett.

Gilligan, C. 1981. "Are Women More Moral than Men?" *Ms.,* December 1981: 66.

Gilligan, C. 1982a. *In a Different Voice: Psychological Theory and Women's Development.* Cambridge: Harvard University Press.

Gilligan, C. 1982b. "New Maps of Development: New Visions of Maturity." *American Journal of Orthopsychiatry* 52: 199–212.

Gilligan, C. 1982c. "Why Should a Woman Be More Like a Man?" *Psychology Today,* June: 68–77.

Gilligan, C. 1983. "Do the Social Sciences Have an Adequate Theory of Moral Development?" In Haan, et al., *Social Science:* 33–51.

Gilligan, C. 1984. "The Conquistador and the Dark Continent." *Daedulus* 113: 75–95.

Gilligan, C. 1986a. "Remapping Development." In *Value Presuppositions in Theories of Human Development:* 37–53. L. Cirillo and S. Wapner, eds. Hillsdale: Eilbaum.

Gilligan, C. 1986b. "Remapping the Moral Domain." In Heller et al., *Reconstructing:* 237–50. Also, 1988. In Gilligan et al., *Mapping:* 3–19.

Gilligan, C. 1986c. "Reply." *Signs* 11: 324–33. (Reprinted in this collection.)

Gilligan, C. 1987a. "Exit-Voice/Dilemmas in Adolescent Development." In *Development, Democracy and the Art of Trespassing.* A. Goxley et al., eds. Notre Dame: University of Notre Dame Press.

Gilligan, C. 1987b. "Moral Orientation and Moral Development." In Kittay and Meyers, *Women:* 19–33.

Gilligan, C., and J. Attanucci. 1988. "Two Moral Orientations." *Merrill-Palmer Quarterly* 34: 223–37. Also, 1988. In Gilligan et al., *Mapping:* 73–86.

Gilligan, C., and M. Belenky. 1978. "A Naturalistic Study of Abortion Decisions." In *New Directions for Child Development.* Vol. 7: W. Damon, ed. San Francisco: Jossey-Bass.

Gilligan, C., and M. Belenky. 1980. "A Naturalistic Study of Abortion Decisions." In *Clinical-Developmental Psychology:* 69–90. R. Selman and R. Yando, eds. San Francisco: Jossey-Bass.

Gilligan, C., L. Kohlberg, et al. 1971. "Moral Reasoning about Sexual Dilemmas." In *Technical Report of the Commission on Obscenity and Pornography.* Vol. 1 (no. 5256-0010). Washington, D.C.: U.S. Government Printing Office.

Gilligan, C., S. Langdale, and N. Lyons. 1982. "The Contribution of Women's Thought to Developmental Theory." Washington, D.C.: National Institute of Education.

Gilligan, C., S. Langdale, N. Lyons, and J. Murphy. 1982. "The Contribution of Women's Thought to Developmental Theory." Unpublished. Center for Moral Education, Harvard University.

Gilligan, C., N. Lyons, and J. Hanmer, eds. 1989. *Making Connections.* Troy, N.Y.: Emma Willard School.

Gilligan, C., and J. Murphy. 1979. "Development from Adolescence to Adulthood." In *Intellectual Development beyond Childhood:* 85–99. D. Kuhn, ed. San Francisco: Jossey-Bass.

Gilligan, C., J. Ward, and J. Taylor, eds. 1988. *Mapping the Moral Domain.* Cambridge: Harvard University Press.

Gilligan, C., and G. Wiggins. 1987. "The Origins of Morality in Early Childhood Relationships." In Kagan and Lamb, *Emergence:* 277–306. Also, 1988. In Gilligan et al., *Mapping:* 111–37.

Gilligan, C., among others. 1985. "Feminist Discourse, Moral Values and the Law—A Conversation." *Buffalo Law Review* 34: 11–87.

Gilman, C. 1979. *Herland*. New York: Pantheon.

Gleser, G., and D. Ihilevich. 1969. "An Objective Instrument for Measuring Defense Mechanisms." *Journal of Consulting and Clinical Psychology* 33: 51–60.

Golden, R. 1983. "The Development of Levels of Reflective Consciousness in Upper Middle-Class High School Students." Doctoral dissertation. Teachers College, Columbia University.

Golding, G., and T. Laidlaw. 1979–80. "Women and Moral Development: A Need to Care." *Interchange* 10, no. 2: 95–103.

Graham, H. 1983. "Caring: A Labour of Love." In *A Labour of Love: Women, Work and Caring*: 13–30. J. Finch and D. Groves, eds. London: Routledge & Kegan Paul.

Greeno, C., and E. Maccoby. 1986. "How Different is the 'Different Voice'?" *Signs* 11: 310–16. (Reprinted in this collection.)

Griffin, S. 1978. *Woman and Nature*. New York: Harper & Row.

Grimshaw, J. 1986. *Philosophy and Feminist Thinking*. Minneapolis: University of Minnesota Press.

Guilford, J. 1957. "A Revised Structure of Intellect." *Reports from the Psychological Laboratory*, no. 19. University of Southern California Press.

Guttman, A. 1985. "Communitarian Critics of Liberalism." *Philosophy and Public Affairs* 14: 308–21.

Guttman, D. 1965. "Women and the Conception of Ego-Strength." *Merrill-Palmer Quarterly* 11: 229–40.

Guttman, J., et al. 1978. "Developmental Trends of the Relativistic-Realistic Dimension of Moral Judgment in Adolescence." *Psychological Reports* 42: 1279–84.

Gwaltney, J. 1980. *Drylongso: A Self-Portrait of Black America*. New York: Random House.

Haan, N. 1971. "Moral Redefinition in Families as the Critical Aspect of the Generational Gap." *Youth and Society* 2: 259–83.

Haan, N. 1974. "Changes in Young Adults after Peace Corps Experiences." *Journal of Youth and Adolescence* 3: 177–94.

Haan, N. 1975. "Hypothetical and Actual Moral Reasoning in a Situation of Civil Disobedience." *Journal of Personality and Social Psychology* 32: 255–70.

Haan, Norma. 1977. *Coping and Defending*. New York: Academic Press.

Haan, N. 1978. "Two Moralities in Action Contexts." *Journal of Personality and Social Psychology* 36: 286–305.

Haan, N. 1982. "Can Research on Morality be 'Scientific'?" *American Psychologist* 37, 10: 1096–1104.

Haan, N. 1983. "An Interactional Morality of Everyday Life." In N. Haan, R. Bellah, et al., *Social Science*: 218–51.

Haan, N. 1985. "With Regard to Walker [1984] on Sex 'Differences' in Moral Reasoning." Unpublished. Institute of Human Development, University of California, Berkeley.

Haan, N., E. Aerts, and B. Cooper. 1985. *On Moral Grounds*. New York: New York University Press.

Haan, N., R. Bellah, P. Rabinow, and W. Sullivan, eds. 1983. *Social Science as Moral Inquiry*. New York: Columbia University Press.

Haan, N., M. Brewster Smith, and J. Block. 1968. "Moral Reasoning in Young Adults." *Journal of Personality and Social Psychology* 10: 183–201.

Haan, N., J. Langer, and L. Kohlberg. 1976. "Family Moral Patterns." *Child Development* 47: 1204–6.

Haan, N., J. Stroud, and C. Holstein. 1973. "Moral and Ego Stages in Relationship to Ego Processes." *Journal of Personality* 41: 596–612.

Haan, N., R. Weiss, and V. Johnson. 1982. "The Role of Logic in Moral Reasoning and Development." *Developmental Psychology* 18: 245–56.

Habermas, J. 1975. "Moral Development and Ego Identity." *Telos* 24: 41–55.

Hacking, I. 1984. "Winner Take Less," a review of *The Evolution of Cooperation* by R. Axelrod. *New York Review of Books* 30, no. 11, 28 June 1984.

Haier, R. 1977. "Moral Reasoning and Moral Character." *Psychological Reports* 40: 215–26.

Hampshire, S. 1959. *Thought and Action*. New York: Viking.

Hampshire, S. 1978. "Public and Private Morality." In *Public and Private Morality*. S. Hampshire, ed. New York: Cambridge University Press.

Hampson, R. 1981. "Helping Behavior in Children." *Developmental Review* 1: 93–112.

Hanen, M., and K. Nielsen, eds. 1987. *Science, Morality and Feminist Theory*. Calgary: University of Calgary Press.

Harding, S., and M. Hintikka, eds. 1983. Introduction. *Discovering Reality*. Dordrecht: Reidel.

Hardwig, J. 1984. "Should Women Think in Terms of Rights?" *Ethics* 94: 441–55.

Hare, R. 1952. *The Language of Morals*. London: Oxford University Press.

Hare, R. 1963. *Freedom and Reason*. New York: Oxford University Press.

Harkness, S., et al. 1981. "Social Roles and Moral Reasoning." *Developmental Psychology* 17: 595–603.

Hartshorne, H., et al. 1928. *Studies in the Nature of Character*. Vol. 2. New York: Macmillan

Haste, H. 1983. "Morality, Social Meaning and Rhetoric." In *Moral Development and Education*. J. Gewirtz and W. Kurtines, eds. New York: Wiley.

Hauerwas, S. 1977. *Truthfulness and Tragedy*. Notre Dame: University of Notre Dame Press.

Haug, F. 1984. "Morals Also Have Two Genders." R. Livingstone, trans. *New Left Review* 143.

Held, V. 1984a. "The Obligations of Mothers and Fathers." In Trebilcot, *Mothering:* 7–20.

Held, V. 1984b. *Rights and Goods.* New York: Free Press/Macmillan.

Heller, T., et al., eds. 1986. *Reconstructing Individualism.* Stanford: Stanford University Press.

Herman, B. 1983. "Integrity and Impartiality." *Monist* 66: 233–50.

Herman, B. 1985. "The Practice of Moral Judgment." *Journal of Philosophy* 82: 413–36.

Hildebrand, D., et al. 1977. *Prediction Analysis of Cross Classifications.* New York: Wiley.

Hoagland, S. 1988. *Lesbian Ethics.* Palo Alto: Institute of Lesbian Studies.

Hoffman, M. 1977. "Sex Differences in Empathy and Related Behaviors." *Psychological Bulletin* 84: 712–22.

Hoffman, S. 1977. "Intelligence and Development of Moral Judgment in Children." *Journal of Genetic Psychology* 130: 27–34.

Hollingshead, A., and F. Redlich. 1958. *Social Class and Mental Illness.* New York: Wiley.

Holstein, C. 1972. "The Relation of Children's Moral Judgment Level to That of Their Parents and to Communication Patterns in the Family." In *Readings in Child Development and Relationships:* 484–94. R. Smart and M. Smart, eds. New York: Macmillan.

Holstein, C. 1976a. "Development of Moral Judgement: A Longitudinal Study of Males and Females." *Child Development* 47: 51–61.

Holstein, C., 1976b. "Irreversible, Stepwise Sequence in the Development of Moral Judgment." *Child Development* 47: 51–61.

Hooks, B. 1981. *Ain't I a Woman: Black Women and Feminism.* Boston: South End.

Houston, B. 1987. "Rescuing Womanly Virtues." In Hanen and Neisen, *Science:* 237–62.

Houston, B. 1988. "Gilligan and the Politics of a Distinctive Women's Morality." In Code et al., *Feminist Perspectives:* 168–89.

Houston, B. 1989. "Prolegomena to Future Caring." In Brabeck, *Who Cares?:* 84–100.

Hudgins, W., & N. Prentice. 1973. "Moral Judgment in Delinquent and Nondelinquent Adolescents and Their Mothers." *Journal of Abnormal Psychology* 82: 145–52.

Hudson, L. 1968. "Personality and Scientific Attitude." *Nature* 198: 913–14.

Hudson, S. 1986. *Human Character and Morality.* London: Routledge & Kegan Paul.

Hull, G., P. Scott, and B. Smith, eds. 1982. *But Some of Us Are Brave: Black Women's Studies.* Old Westbury, N.Y.: Feminist Press.

Hume, D. 1740; 1880, 1978. *Treatise on Human Nature.* Selby-Bigge edition. Oxford: Oxford University Press.

Hurtado, A. 1989. "Relating to Privilege." *Signs* 14: 833–55.

Hutcheson, F., 1726; 1971. *Collected Works*. B. Fabian, ed. Hildesheim: George Olms.

Hutter, H. 1978. *Politics as Friendship*. Waterloo, Ont.: Wilfrid Laurier University Press.

Imray, L., and A. Middleton. 1983. "Public and Private." In *The Public and the Private:* 12–27. Eva Gamarnikov et al., eds. London: Heinemann.

Jack, D. 1984. "Clinical Depression in Women." Doctoral dissertation, Harvard Graduate School of Education.

Jacklin, C. 1981. "Methodological Issues in the Study of Sex-Related Differences." *Developmental Review* 1: 226–73.

Jackson, G. 1978. "Black Psychology as an Emerging Point of View." Cited by A. Richards in *Sourcebook on the Teaching of Black Psychology* 2: 175–77. R. Jones, ed. Association of Black Psychologists.

Jackson, G. 1982. "Black Psychology." *Journal of Black Studies* 12, no. 3: 241–360.

Jaggar, A. 1991. "Feminist Ethics: Projects, Problems, Prospects." In Card, *Feminist Ethics:* 78–104.

James, W. 1907. *Pragmatism*. New York: New American Library.

Janeway, E. 1971. *Man's World Women's Place*. New York: Morrow.

Jennings, W., and L. Kohlberg. 1983. "Effects of Just Community Programs on the Moral Level and Institutional Perception of Youthful Offenders." *Journal of Moral Education* 12.

Jennings, W., et al. 1983. "Moral Development Theory and Practice for Youthful and Adult Offenders." In *Personality, Theory, Moral Development and Criminal Behavior*. W. Laufer and J. Kay, eds. Lexington, Mass.: Lexington Books.

Johnston, K. 1985. "Two Moral Orientations—Two Problem-Solving Strategies." Doctoral dissertation, Harvard Graduate School of Education.

Joint Center for Political Studies. 1982. *Blacks on the Move*. Washington, D.C.

Jones, H. 1939. "The Adolescent Growth Study, I," and "The Adolescent Growth Study, II." *Journal of Consulting Psychology* 3: 155–59, 177–80.

Jordan, J., and J. Surrey. 1986. *The Self-in-Relation*. Hillsdale, N.Y.: Analytic Press.

Josselson, J. 1987. *Finding Herself: Pathways through Identity Development in Women*. San Francisco: Jossey-Bass.

Kagan, J., and S. Lamb, eds. 1987. *The Emergence of Morality in Young Children*. Chicago: University of Chicago Press.

Kahn, J. 1982. "Moral Reasoning in Irish Children and Adolescents as Measured by the Defining Issues Test." *Irish Journal of Psychology* 5: 96–108.

Kant, I. 1797; 1977. *Die Metaphysik der Sitten*. Frankfurt: Suhrkampf.

Kant, I. 1959. *Groundwork of the Metaphysics of Morals*. L. Beck, trans. Indianapolis: Bobbs-Merrill.

Kavanagh, H. 1977. "Moral Education." *Journal of Moral Education* 6: 121–30.

Keasey, C. 1971. "Social Participation as a Factor in the Moral Development of Preadolescents." *Developmental Psychology* 86: 157–58.

Keasey, C. 1972. "The Lack of Sex Differences in the Moral Judgment of Preadolescents." *Journal of Social Psychology* 86: 157–58.

Kegan, R. 1982. *The Evolving Self*. Cambridge: Harvard University Press.

Kekes, J. 1984. "Moral Sensitivity." *Philosophy* 59, no. 227: 3–19.

Keller, E. 1978. "Gender and Science." *Psychoanalysis and Contemporary Thought* 1: 409–33.

Keniston, K. 1968. *Young Radicals*. New York: Harcourt, Brace & World.

Kerber, L. 1986. "Some Cautionary Words for Historians." *Signs* 11: 304–10. (Reprinted in this collection.)

Khanna, L. 1984. "Frontiers of Imagination: Feminist Worlds." *Women's Studies International Forum* 7, no. 2: 97–102.

Kittay, E., and D. Meyers, eds. 1987. *Women and Moral Theory*. Totowa, N.J.: Rowman & Littlefield.

Kleeman, K. 1984. *Learning to Lead*. Public Leadership Education Network.

Klein, M. 1971. *Love, Guilt and Reparation and Other Essays, 1921–1945*. London: Hogarth.

Kohlberg, L. 1966. "A Cognitive-Developmental Analysis of Children's Sex-Role Concepts and Attitudes." In Maccoby, *Development*.

Kohlberg, L. 1969. "Stage and Sequence." In *Handbook of Socialization Theory and Research*. D. Goslin, ed. Chicago: Rand McNally.

Kohlberg, L. 1971. "From Is to Ought." In *Cognitive Development and Genetic Epistemology*: 151–235. T. Mischel, ed. New York: Academic. Also, Kohlberg 1981: 101–89.

Kohlberg, L. 1973a. "The Claim to Moral Adequacy of a Highest Stage of Moral Judgment." *Journal of Philosophy* 70: 630–46.

Kohlberg, L. 1973b. "Continuities in Childhood and Adult Moral Development Revisited." In *Life-Span Developmental Psychology*. P. Baltes and K. Schaie, eds. New York: Academic Press.

Kohlberg, L. 1976. "Moral Stages and Moralization." In *Moral Development and Behavior*: 31–53. T. Lickona, ed. New York: Holt, Rinehart & Winston.

Kohlberg, L. 1978. "Moral Education Reappraised." *Humanist* 38, No. 6: 13–15.

Kohlberg, L. 1980. "The Future of Liberalism as the Dominant Ideology of the West." In *Moral Development and Politics*. R. Wilson and G. Schochet, eds. New York: Praeger.

Kohlberg, L. 1981. *Essays on Moral Development*. Vol. 1: *The Philosophy of Moral Development*. San Francisco: Harper & Row.

Kohlberg, L. 1982. "A Reply to Owen Flanagan and Some Comments on the Puka-Goodpaster Exchange." *Ethics* 92: 513–28.

Kohlberg, L. 1984. *Essays on Moral Development*. Vol. 2: *The Psychology of Moral Development*. New York: Harper & Row.

Kohlberg, L., and R. de Vries. 1971. "Relations between Piaget and Psychometric Assessments of Intelligence." In *Current Topics in Early Childhood Education.* Vol. 1. L. Katz, ed. Norwood: Ablex.

Kohlberg, L., and D. Elfenbein. 1981. "Capital Punishment, Moral Development, and the Constitution." In Kohlberg 1981.

Kohlberg, L., and R. Kramer. 1969. "Continuities and Discontinuities in Childhood and Adult Moral Development." *Human Development* 12: 93–120.

Kohlberg, L., et al. 1975. *Corrections Manual.* Cambridge: Moral Education Research Foundation.

Kohlberg, L., C. Levine, and A. Hewer. 1983. *Moral Stages: A Current Formulation and a Response to Critics.* New York: Karger.

Kohlberg, L., and C. Power. 1981. "Moral Development, Religious Thinking and the Question of a Seventh Stage." In Kohlberg 1981.

Kraditor, A. 1965. *The Ideas of the Woman Suffrage Movement, 1890–1920.* New York: Columbia University Press.

Krebs, D. 1970. "Altruism." *Psychological Bulletin* 73: 258–302.

Krebs, D., and J. Gillmore, 1982. "The Relationship among the First Stages of Cognitive Development, Role-Taking Abilities, and Moral Development." *Child Development* 53: 877–86.

Krebs, R. 1967. "Some Relationships between Moral Judgment, Attention, and Resistance to Temptation." Doctoral dissertation, University of Chicago.

Kuhn, D. 1972. "Role-Taking Abilities Underlying the Development of Moral Judgment." Unpublished. Graduate School of Education, Harvard University.

Kuhn, D., et al. 1977. "The Development of Formal Operations in Logical and Moral Judgment." *Genetic Psychology Monographs* 95: 97–188.

Kuhn, T. 1970. *The Structure of Scientific Revolutions.* 2d. ed. Chicago: University of Chicago Press.

Kurtines, W., and J. Gewirtz, eds. 1987. *Moral Development through Social Interaction.* New York: Wiley.

Laing, R. 1960. *The Divided Self.* Harmondsworth: Penguin.

Langdale, S. 1983. "Moral Orientations and Moral Development." Doctoral dissertation, Harvard Graduate School of Education.

Lanser, S., and E. Beck. 1979. "Why Are There No Great Women Critics?" In Sherman and Beck, *Prism.*

Larrabee, M. 1991. "The Care Ethics Debate: A Selected Bibliography." *American Philosophical Association Newsletter on Feminism and Philosophy:* 102–9.

Lasch, C. 1976. "Planned Obsolescence: Review of Sheehy's *Passages.*" *New York Review of Books,* October 1976: 7–8.

Lasch, C. 1977. *Haven in a Heartless World.* New York: Basic Books.

Lauritzen, P. 1989. "A Feminist Ethic and the New Romanticism." *Hypatia* 4: 28–44.

Lavoie, C. 1974. "Cognitive Determinants of Resistance to Deviation in Seven-, Nine-, and Eleven-Year Old Children of Low and High Maturity of Moral Judgment." *Developmental Psychology* 10: 393–403.

Leacock, E. 1977. "Women in Egalitarian Societies." In *Becoming Visible*. R. Bridenthal and C. Koonz, eds. Boston: Houghton Mifflin.

LeFurgy, W., and G. Woloshin. 1969. "Immediate and Long-Term Effects of Experimentally Induced Social Influence in the Modification of Adolescents' Moral Judgments." *Journal of Personality and Social Psychology* 12: 104–10.

Leming, J. 1978. "Intrapersonal Variations in Stage of Moral Reasoning among Adolescents as a Function of Situational Context." *Journal of Youth and Adolescence* 7: 405–16.

Leming, J. 1983. *Foundations of Moral Education: An Annotated Bibliography.* Westport, Conn.: Greenwood.

Leonardo, M. di. 1984. *The Varieties of Ethnic Experience*. Ithaca: Cornell University Press.

Lerner, G. 1969. "The Lady and the Mill Girl: Changes in the Status of Women in the Age of Jackson." *Midcontinent American Studies Journal* 10: 1–15.

Levi, E. 1948. *Introduction to Legal Reasoning.* Chicago: University of Chicago Press.

Levine, C. 1976. "Role-Taking Standpoint and Adolescent Usage of Kohlberg's Conventional Stages of Moral Reasoning." *Journal of Personality and Social Psychology* 34: 41–46.

Levinson, D. 1978. *The Seasons of a Man's Life.* New York: Ballantine.

Lloyd, G. 1984. *The Man of Reasoning.* Minneapolis: University of Minnesota Press.

Lockwood, A. 1975. "Stage of Moral Development and Students' Reasoning on Public Policy Issues." *Journal of Moral Education* 5: 51–61.

Lugones, M. 1987. "Playfulness, 'World'-Traveling, and Loving Perception." *Hypatia* 2, no. 2: 3–19. Also, 1989. In Garry and Pearsall, *Women, Knowledge:* 275–90.

Lugones, M. 1991. "On the Logic of Pluralist Feminism." In Card, *Feminist Ethics:* 35–44.

Luker, K. 1984. *Abortion and the Politics of Motherhood.* Berkeley: University of California Press.

Luria, Z. 1986. "A Methodological Critique." *Signs* 11: 316–21. (Reprinted in this collection.)

Lykes, B. 1989. "The Caring Self." In Brabeck, *Who Cares?:* 164–79.

Lyons, N. 1982. "Conceptions of Self and Morality and Modes of Moral Choice." Doctoral dissertation, Harvard Graduate School of Education.

Lyons, N. 1983. "Two Perspectives." *Harvard Educational Review* 53: 125–44. Also, 1988. In Gilligan, et al., *Mapping:* 21–48.

Lyons, N. 1987. "Ways of Knowing, Learning, and Making Moral Choices." *Journal of Moral Education* 16. Also, 1989. In Brabeck, *Who Cares?:* 103–26.

Maccoby, E. 1966. "Sex Differences in Intellectual Functioning." In *Development of Sex Differences*. E. Maccoby, ed. Stanford: Stanford University Press.

Maccoby, E. 1985. "Social Groupings in Childhood." In *Development of Antisocial and Prosocial Behavior*. D. Olwens et al., eds. San Diego: Academic Press.

Maccoby, E., and C. Jacklin. 1974. *The Psychology of Sex Differences*. Stanford: Stanford University Press.

MacIntyre, A. 1966. *A Short History of Ethics*. New York: Macmillan.

MacIntyre, A. 1981. *After Virtue*. Notre Dame: University of Notre Dame Press. Also, 1984, 2d ed.

MacIntyre, A. 1982. "How Moral Agents Become Ghosts." *Synthese* 53: 292–312.

MacIntyre, A., and S. Hauerwas, eds. 1983. *Revisions*. Notre Dame: University of Notre Dame Press.

MacKinnon, D. 1962. "The Nature and Nurture of Creative Talent." *American Psychologist* 17: 484–95.

Magnusson, D., and N. Endler, eds. 1977. *Personality at the Crossroads*. Hillsdale, N.J.: Lawrence Erlbaum.

Mahler, M., F. Pine, and A. Bergman. 1975. *The Psychological Birth of the Human Infant*. New York: Basic Books.

Maqsud, M. 1980a. "Locus of Control and Stages of Moral Reasoning." *Psychological Reports* 46: 1243–48.

Maqsud, M. 1980b. "Relationships between Personal Control, Moral Reasoning, and Socioeconomic Status of Nigerian Hausa Adolescents." *Journal of Youth and Adolescence* 9: 281–88.

McClelland, D. 1975. *Power: The Inner Experience*. New York: Irvington, Halsted-Wiley.

McMillan, C. 1982. *Women, Reason and Nature*. Princeton: Princeton University Press.

Menkel-Meadow, C. 1985. "Portia in a Different Voice." *Berkeley Women's Law Journal* 1, no. 1: 39–63.

Mercer, R., E. Nichols, and G. Doyle. 1989. *Transitions in a Woman's Life*. New York: Springer.

Meyer, A. Letters to the *New York Tribune*. 30 March 1908, 16 January 1938.

Michaels, M. 1986. "Morality without Distinction." *Philosophical Forum* 17: 175–87.

Miller, J. 1976. *Toward a New Psychology of Women*. Boston: Beacon.

Miller, R. 1985. "Ways of Moral Learning." *Philosophical Review* 94: 507–56.

Millett, K. 1970. *Sexual Politics*. New York: Doubleday.

Mitchell, J., and J. Rose. 1982. *Feminine Sexuality*. New York: Norton.

Modgil, S., and C. Modgil. 1976. *Piagetian Research*. Vol. 3. Slough: NFER.

Moody-Adams, M. 1991. "Gender and the Complexity of Moral Voices." In Card, *Feminist Ethics:* 195–212.

Morgan, K. 1988. "Women and Moral Madness." In Code et al., *Feminist Perspectives:* 146–67.

Morgan, M. 1973. *Total Woman*. Old Tappen, N.J.: Revell.

Mullett, S. 1987. "Only Connect." In Hanen and Nielsen, *Science:* 309–38.

Mullett, S. 1988. "Shifting Perspective." In Code, et al., *Feminist Perspectives:* 109–26.

Murdoch, I. 1970. *The Sovereignty of the Good*. London: Routledge & Kegan Paul.

Murphy, J., and C. Gilligan. 1980. "Moral Development in Late Adolescence and Adulthood." *Human Development* 23, no. 2: 77–104.

Mussen, P., and N. Eisenberg-Berg. 1977. *Roots of Caring, Sharing, and Helping*. San Francisco: Freeman.

Nagel, T. 1986. *The View from Nowhere*. New York: Oxford University Press.

Nails, D. 1983. "Social-Scientific Sexism: Gilligan's Mismeasure of Man." *Social Research* 50, no. 3: 643–64.

Nassi, A. 1981. "Survivors of the Sixties." *American Psychologist* 36: 753–61.

Nicholson, L. 1980. "Women and Schooling." *Educational Theory* 30.

Nicholson, L. 1983. "Women, Morality and History." *Social Research* 50: 514–36. (Reprinted in this collection.)

Nicholson, L. 1986. *Gender and History*. New York: Columbia University Press.

Niemark, E. 1975. "Intellectual Development during Adolescence." In *Review of Child Development*. Vol. 4. F. Horowitz, ed. Chicago: University of Chicago Press.

Noam, G., et al. 1983. "Steps toward a Model of the Self." In *Developmental Approaches to the Self*. B. Lee and G. Noam, eds. New York: Plenum.

Nobles, W. 1976. "Extended Self: Rethinking the So-called Negro Self-Concept." *Journal of Black Psychology* 2, no. 2: 15–24.

Noddings, N. 1984. *Caring: A Feminine Approach to Ethics and Moral Education*. Berkeley: University of California Press.

Nunner-Winkler, G. 1984. "Two Moralities?" In *Morality, Moral Behavior and Moral Development:* 348–61. W. Kurtines and J. Gewirtz, eds. New York: Wiley. (Reprinted in this collection.)

Nunner-Winkler, G., ed. 1991. *Weibliche Moral: Die Kontroverse um eine geschlechtsspezifische Ethik*. New York: Campus.

Ockerman, J. 1979. *Self-Esteem and Social Anchorage of Adolescent White, Black and Mexican-American Students*. Palo Alto: R & E Research.

Offer, D. 1969. *The Psychological World of the Teenager*. New York: Basic Books.

Okin, S. 1978. *Women in Western Political Thought*. Princeton: Princeton University Press.

Okin, S. 1987. "Justice and Gender." *Philosophy and Public Affairs* 16: 42–72.

Okin, S. 1989. "Reasoning and Feeling in Thinking about Justice." *Ethics* 99: 229–49.

O'Leary, V. 1977. *Toward Understanding Women*. Belmont, Cal.: Wadsworth.

O'Neill, O. 1975. *Acting on Principle*. New York: Columbia University Press.

O'Neill, O. 1984. "Kant after Virtue." *Inquiry* 26: 387–405.

Orchowsky, S., and R. Jenkins. 1979. "Sex Biases in the Measurement of Moral Judgment." *Psychological Reports* 44: 1040.

Ortner, S., and H. Whitehead, eds. 1981. *Sexual Meanings*. New York: Cambridge University Press.

Parikh, B. 1980. "Development of Moral Judgment and its Relation to Family Environmental Factors in Indian and American Families." *Child Development* 51: 1030–39.

Parsons, K. 1979. "Moral Revolution." In Sherman and Beck, *Prism*.

Parson, T. 1964. *The Social System*. New York: Free Press.

Parsons, T., and R. Bales. 1985. *Family, Socialization and Interaction Process*. Glencoe, Ill.: Free Press.

Pateman, C. 1980. "The Disorder of Women." *Ethics* 91: 20–34.

Pearsall, M., ed. 1986. *Women and Values*. Belmont, Cal.: Wadsworth.

Perry, W. 1968. *Forms of Intellectual and Ethical Development in the College Years*. New York: Holt, Rhinehart & Winston.

Petchesky, R. 1983. "Reproduction and Class Divisions among Women." In Swerdlow and Lessinger, *Class:* 157–243.

Piaget, J. 1932; 1965. *The Moral Judgment of the Child*. New York: Free Press.

Piercy, M. 1976. *Woman on the Edge of Time*. New York: Fawcett Crest.

Polanyi, K. 1957. *The Great Transformation*. Boston: Beacon.

Pollak, S., and C. Gilligan. 1982. "Images of Violence in Thematic Apperception Test Stories." *Journal of Personality and Social Psychology* 42: 159–67.

Pollak, S., and C. Gilligan. 1983. "Differing about Differences." *Journal of Personality and Social Psychology* 45: 1172–75.

Pollak, S., and C. Gilligan. 1985. "Killing the Messenger." *Journal of Personality and Social Psychology* 48: 374–75.

Prakash, M. 1984. "Review of C. Gilligan's *In a Different Voice*." *Educational Studies* 15: 194.

Prawat, R. 1976. "Mapping the Affective Domain in Young Adolescents." *Journal of Educational Psychology* 68: 566–72.

Puka, B. 1982. "An Interdisciplinary Treatment of Kohlberg." *Ethics* 92: 468–490.

Puka, B. 1988. "Ethical Caring." In *Inquiry into Values*. S. Lee, ed. New York: Mellen.

Puka, B. 1990. "The Liberation of Caring." *Hypatia* 5: 58–82. (Reprinted in this collection.)

Puka, B. 1991. "Interpretive Experiments." *Human Development* 34: 61–80.

Quinn, N. 1982. "Occupational Segregation and Cultural Beliefs about Women." Washington, D.C.: National Academy of Sciences Committee on Women's Employment and Related Issues.

Rawls, J. 1971. *A Theory of Justice*. Cambridge: Harvard University Press.

Rawls, J. 1985. "Justice as Fairness." *Philosophy and Public Affairs* 14: 223–51.

Redmore, C., et al. 1970. "Measuring Ego Development." Supplement to J. Loevinger et al., *Measuring Ego Development*. Vol. 2. San Francisco: Jossey-Bass.

Reid, B. 1984. "An Anthropological Reinterpretation of Kohlberg's Stages of Moral Development." *Human Development* 27: 56–74.

Rest, J. 1979. *Development in Judging Moral Issues*. Minneapolis: University of Minnesota Press.

Rest, J. 1983. "Morality." In Flavell and Markman, *Cognitive Development*: 556–629.

Rich, A. 1976. *Of Woman Born*. New York: Norton.

Riesman, D. 1950. *The Lonely Crowd*. New Haven: Yale University Press.

Roberts, A., and P. Donston. 1980. "Effect of a Conflict Manipulation on Children's Moral Judgments." *Psychological Reports* 46: 1305–06.

Rosaldo, M. 1980. "The Use and Abuse of Anthropology." *Signs* 5: 389–417.

Rosaldo, M., and L. Lamphere, eds. 1974. *Woman, Culture, and Society*. Stanford: Stanford University Press.

Rose, S. 1991. "The Contribution of Alice Miller to Feminist Therapy and Theory." *Women and Therapy* 11, no. 2: 41–53.

Rosenthal, R. 1978. "Combining Results of Independent Studies." *Psychological Bulletin* 85: 185–93.

Rosenthal, R. 1979. "The 'File-Drawer Problem' and Tolerance for Null Results." *Psychological Bulletin* 86: 638–41.

Rosenthal, R. 1984. *Meta-analytic Procedures for Social Research*. Beverly Hills: Sage.

Ross, W. 1930. *The Right and the Good*. Cambridge: Cambridge University Press.

Rossi, A. 1977. "A Biosocial Perspective on Parenting." *Daedalus* 106: 1–31.

Rossi, A. 1983. "Beyond the Gender Gap." *Social Science Quarterly* 64: 718–33.

Royko, M. 1971. *Boss: Richard J. Daley of Chicago*. New York: New American Library.

Rubin, Z., and S. Schenker. 1978. "Friendship, Proximity, and Self-Disclosure." *Journal of Personality* 46: 1–22.

Ruddick, S. 1980. "Maternal Thinking." *Feminist Studies* 6: 342–67. Reprinted 1984a. In Trebilcot, *Mothering*: 213–30. Reprinted, condensed, 1986. In Pearsall, *Women and Values*: 340–51.

Ruddick, S., 1983. "Pacifying the Forces." *Signs* 8: 471–89.

Ruddick, S. 1984b. "Preservative Love and Military Destruction." In Trebilcot, *Mothering*: 231–62.

Ruddick, S. 1989. *Maternal Thinking: Toward a Politics of Peace*. Boston: Beacon.

Rustin, M. 1982. "A Socialist Consideration of Kleinian Psychoanalysis." *New Left Review* 131: 71–96.

Sagi, A., and Z. Eisikovitz. 1981. "Juvenile Delinquency and Moral Development." *Criminal Justice and Behavior* 8: 79–93.

Saltzstein, H., et al. 1972. "Moral Judgment Level and Conformity Behavior." *Developmental Psychology* 7: 327–36.

Sampson, E. 1981. "Cognitive Psychology as Ideology." *American Psychologist* 36: 730–43.

Sandel, M. 1982. *Liberalism and the Limits of Justice*. Cambridge: Cambridge University Press.

Sanford, N. 1955. "The Dynamics of Identification." *Psychological Review* 51.

Sawin, D., et al. 1979. "Empathy and Altruism." Unpublished. Department of Psychology, University of Texas at Austin.

Saxton, M. 1981. "Are Women More Moral than Men?" *Ms.*, December 1981: 63–66.

Schneewind, J. 1986. "The Uses of Autonomy in Ethical Theory." In Heller et al., *Reconstructing*: 64–75.

Schweder, R. 1982. "Liberalism as Destiny." Review of Kohlberg 1981. *Contemporary Psychology* 27: 421–24.

Selman, S. 1971. "The Relation of Role-Taking to the Development of Moral Judgment in Children." *Child Development* 42: 79–91.

Sen, A., and B. Williams, eds. 1982. *Utilitarianism and Beyond*. Cambridge: Cambridge University Press.

Shantz, C. 1983. "Social Cognition." In Flavell and Markham, *Cognitive Development*: 495–555.

Sher, G. 1987. "Other Voices, Other Rooms?" In Kittay and Meyers, *Women*: 178–89.

Sherif, C. 1979. "Bias in Psychology." In Sherman and Beck, *Prism*.

Sherman, J., and E. Beck, eds. 1979. *Prism of Sex*. Madison: University of Wisconsin Press.

Shigetomi, C., et al. 1981. "Sex Differences in Children's Altruistic Behavior and Reputations for Helpfulness." *Developmental Psychology* 17, no. 4: 434–37.

Sidgwick, H. 1893, 1907; 1981. *Methods of Ethics*. Indianapolis: Hackett.

Siegel, S. 1956. *Nonparametric Statistics for the Behavioral Sciences*. New York: McGraw-Hill.

Simon, A., and L. Ward. 1972. "Age, Sex, History Grades and Moral Judgments in Comprehensive School Pupils." *Educational Research* 14: 191–94.

Simon, A., and L. Ward. 1973. "Variables Influencing Pupils' Responses on the Kohlberg Schema of Moral Development." *Journal of Moral Education* 2: 282–86.

Simpson, E. 1974. "Moral Development Research." *Human Development* 17: 81–106.

Slote, M. 1982. "Morality Not a System of Imperatives." *American Philosophical Quarterly* 19: 331–40.

Slote, M. 1985. "Morality and the Practical." In his *Common-Sense Morality and Consequentialism*. London: Routledge & Kegan Paul.

Small, L. 1974. "Effects of Discrimination Training on Stage of Moral Judgment." *Personality and Social Psychology Bulletin* 1: 423–25.

Smith, A. 1976. *The Theory of Moral Sentiments*. Oxford: Oxford University Press.

Smith, R. 1985. "Feminism and the Moral Subject." In Andolsen et al., *Women's Consciousness*: 235–50.

Smith-Rosenberg, C. 1975. "The Female World of Love and Ritual." *Signs* 1: 1–20.

Snarey, J. 1985. "Cross-Cultural Universality of Social-Moral Development." *Psychological Bulletin* 97: 202–32.

Snarey, J., et al., 1985. "Development of Social-Moral Reasoning among Kibbutz Adolescents." *Developmental Psychologist* 21: 3–17.

Sohn-Rethel, A. 1978 *Intellectual and Manual Labour*. London: Macmillan.

Sommers, C. 1986. "Filial Morality." *Journal of Philosophy* 83: 439–56.

Speicher-Dubin, B. 1982. "Relationships between Parent Moral Judgment, Child Moral Judgment, and Family Interaction." Doctoral dissertation, Harvard Graduate School of Education.

Spelman, E. 1991. "The Virtue of Feeling and the Feeling of Virtue." In Card, *Feminist Ethics*: 213–32.

Spence, J., et al. 1975. "Ratings of Self and Peers on Sex Role Attributes and Their Relation to Self-Esteem and Conceptions of Masculinity and Femininity." *Journal of Personality and Social Psychology* 32: 29–39.

Stacy, J. 1983. "The New Conservative Feminism." *Feminist Studies* 9, no. 3: 559–83.

Stack, C. 1974. *All Our Kin: Strategies for Survival in a Black Community*. New York: Harper & Row.

Stack, C., 1986. "The Culture of Gender: Women and Men of Color." *Signs* 11: 321–24. (Reprinted in this collection.)

Stack, C., and R. Hall, eds. 1982. *Holding On to the Land and the Lord*. Athens: University of Georgia Press.

Steiner-Adair, C. 1984. "The Body Politic." Doctoral dissertation, Harvard Graduate School of Education.

Steward, J. 1979. "Modes of Moral Thought." *Journal of Moral Education* 8: 124–34.

Stocker, M. 1976. "The Schizophrenia of Modern Ethical Theories." *Journal of Philosophy* 63: 453–66.

Stocker, M. 1981. "Values and Purposes." *Journal of Philosophy* 78: 747–65.

Stoper, E., and R. Johnson. 1977. "The Weaker Sex and the Better Half." *Polity* 10, no. 2: 192–217.

Strom, E. 1943. *Vocational Interests of Men and Women.* Stanford: Stanford University Press.

Sullivan, E. 1974. "A Study of Kohlberg's Structural Theory of Moral Development." *Human Development* 20: 353–76.

Sullivan, E. 1977. *Kohlberg's Structuralism.* Toronto: Ontario Institute for Studies in Education.

Sullivan, E., et al. 1970. "A Developmental Study of the Relationship between Conceptual, Ego, and Moral Development." *Child Development* 41: 399–411.

Swerdlow, A., and H. Lessinger, eds. 1983. *Class, Race, and Sex.* Boston: G. K. Hall.

Tavris, C., and C. Offir. 1977. *The Longest War.* New York: Harcourt Brace Jovanovich.

Taylor, C. 1982. "The Diversity of Goods." In Sen and Williams, *Utilitarianism.*

Taylor, J., and T. Achenback. 1975. "Moral and Cognitive Development in Retarded and Nonretarded Children." *American Journal of Mental Deficiency* 80: 43–50.

Tenenbaum, S. 1982. "Women through the Prism of Political Thought." *Polity* 15, no. 1: 90–102.

Timm, J. 1980. "Group Care of Children and the Development of Moral Judgment." *Child Welfare* 59: 323–33.

Trebilcot, J., ed. 1984. *Mothering: Essays in Feminist Theory.* Totowa, N.J.: Rowman & Allanheld.

Tronto, J. 1987. "Beyond Gender Difference to a Theory of Care." *Signs* 12: 644–61. (Reprinted in this collection.)

Tronto, J. 1989. "Women and Caring." In Jaggar and Bordo, *Gender/Body/Knowledge:* 172–87. New Brunswick: Rutgers University Press.

Turiel, E. 1972. "A Comparative Analysis of Moral Knowledge and Moral Judgment in Males and Females." Unpublished.

Turiel, E. 1976. "A Comparative Analysis of Moral Knowledge and Moral Judgment in Males and Females." *Journal of Personality* 44: 195–208.

Unger, R. 1975. *Knowledge and Politics.* New York: Free Press.

Vaillant, G. 1977. *Adaptation to Life.* Boston: Little, Brown.

Van Gelder, L. 1984. "Carol Gilligan." *Ms.* 12, January: 37–40, 100.

Walker, J. 1983. "In a Diffident Voice: Cryptoseparatist Analysis of Female Moral Development." *Social Research* 50: 665–95.

Walker, L. 1980. "Cognitive and Perspective-Taking Prerequisites for Moral Development." *Child Development* 51: 131–39.

Walker, L. 1982. "The Sequentiality of Kohlberg's Stages of Moral Development." *Child Development* 53: 1330–36.

Walker, L. 1983a. "Social Experiences and Moral Development in Adulthood." Paper read at the Society for Research in Child Development.

Walker, L. 1983b. "Sources of Cognitive Conflict for Stage Transition in Moral Development." *Developmental Psychology* 19: 103–10.

Walker, L. 1984. "Sex Differences in the Development of Moral Reasoning: A Critical Review." *Child Development* 55: 667–91. (Reprinted in this collection.)

Walker, L. 1986. "Sex Differences in the Development of Moral Reasoning: A Rejoinder to Baumrind." *Child Development* 57: 522–27.

Walker, L. 1989. "A Longitudinal Study of Moral Reasoning." *Child Development* 60: 157–66.

Walker, L., B. DeVries, and S. Bichard. 1984. "The Hierarchical Nature of Stages of Moral Development." *Developmental Psychology* 20: 960–66.

Walker, L., B. DeVries, and S. Trevethan. 1987. "Moral Stages and Moral Orientations in Real-Life and Hypothetical Dilemmas." *Child Development* 58: 842–58.

Walker, M. 1987. "Moral Particularism." Paper read at American Philosophical Association, Pacific meeting.

Walker, M. 1989. "Moral Understandings: Alternative 'Epistemology' for a Feminist Ethics." *Hypatia* 4: 15–28.

Walzer, M. 1983. *Spheres of Justice*. Oxford: Blackwell.

Waterman, A. 1981. "Individualism and Interdependence." *American Psychologist* 36: 762–73.

Watstein, S. 1984. "Psychology." In *The Women's Annual*. Vol. 4: *1983–1984:* 167–186. S. Pritchard, ed. Boston: G. K. Hall.

Weiner, B., et al., 1983. "Compounding the Errors." *Journal of Personality and Social Psychology* 45: 1176–78.

Weisbroth, S. 1970. "Moral Judgment, Sex, and Parental Identification in Adults." *Developmental Psychology* 2: 396–402.

Weiss, R. 1983. "The Relation between Moral Judgment, Identity Status and Cognitive Development in Community College Women." Doctoral dissertation, Teachers College, Columbia University.

Welter, B. 1966. "The Cult of True Womenhood: 1820–1860." *American Quarterly* 18: 151–74.

Whitbeck, C. 1976. "Theories of Sex Difference." In *Women and Philosophy*. C. Gould and M. Wartofsky, eds. New York: Putnam.

Whitbeck, C. 1983. "A Different Reality." In *Beyond Domination:* 64–88. C. Gould, ed. Totowa, N.J.: Rowman & Allanheld.

Whitbeck, C. 1984. "The Maternal Instinct." In Trebilcot, *Mothering:* 185–91.

White, C. 1975. "Moral Development in Bahamian School Children." *Developmental Psychology* 11: 535–36.

Willard, A. 1985. "Self, Situation and Script." Doctoral dissertation, Harvard Graduate School of Education.

Williams, B. 1973. "A Critique of Utilitarianism." In *Utilitarianism*. B. Williams and J. Smart, eds. Cambridge: Cambridge University Press.

Williams, B. 1976. "Morality and the Emotions." In his *Problems of the Self*. Cambridge: Cambridge University Press.

Williams, B. 1982. "Persons, Character and Morality." In his *Moral Luck*. New York: Cambridge University Press.

Williams, B. 1985. *Ethics and the Limits of Philosophy*. Cambridge: Harvard University Press.

Winch, P. 1972. *Ethics and Action*. London: Routledge & Kegan Paul.

Winnicott, D. 1965. "Ego Distortion in Terms of True and False Self." In his *Maturational Processes and the Facilitating Environment*. New York:International Universities Press.

Witkin, H., et al. 1962. *Psychological Differentiation*. New York: Wiley.

Wolf, S. 1982. "Moral Saints." *Journal of Philosophy* 89: 419–39.

Youniss, J. 1987. "Social Construction and Moral Development." In Kurtines and Gewirtz, *Moral Development:* 131–48.

Zahaykevich, M. 1982. "A Study of the Psychological Development of Soviet Human Rights Activists." Doctoral dissertation, Teachers College, Columbia University.

Zimmerman, V. 1982. "The Black Woman Growing Up." In *The Woman Patient*. Vol. 2: 77–92. C. Nadelson and M. Notman, eds. New York: Plenum.

Index

Abandonment, 90, 218, 223, 229

Abortion, 134; and different construals, 73; decisions on, 103, 115, 130, 160, 197, 203 n. 1, 209, 223, 227; as individual's concern, 151; and life choices, 121; obligatory, 24–25; and Supreme Court, 3

Abortion study. *See* Gilligan: abortion study; Interview subject

Absolutes, 46–47, 121. *See also* Universal; Standard(s)

Abstraction, 90; of dilemmas, 148; ethic of care as, 47; formalistic vs. mathematical, 93; moral, 269; not opposite of care, 203; and rationalization, 238 n. 2. *See also* Reasoning

Addams, Jane, 255 n. 19

Adler, Jonathan, 7, 70, 74, 256 n. 31, 271 n. 2

Adolescence: individuation in, 15; and moral decisions, 153–55, 162–71; and moral relativism, 46; and preferred moral construal, 73; sex differences in, 41, 102, 194, 272 n. 4

Adult(s), 15, 41, 127; and adulthood, 14–15, 22, 162, 171, 194

Affect. *See* Emotion; Feeling

African, 190, 244, 254 n. 12

African-American moral development, 110

African-American women, 8, 12

Afro-American life, 244. *See also* Blacks

Alienation, 14, 191, 219

Altruism: related to connection, 76; related to ethic of care, 39; research on, 43–44,

195–196, 262; at risk, 227, 229; and self-interest, 216; and Southeast Asia, 123

Ambiguity, 114, 131, 269

Androcentricity, 157, 193, 194

Androgyny, 137, 138

Anscombe, Elizabeth (G. E. M.), 19, 69

Anzaldua, G., 14

Aristotelian views, 22, 69, 70, 74, 75

Aristotle, 69, 87, 128, 129, 248, 256 n. 32

Attachment, 36, 72, 76, 77, 92, 121, 160. *See also* Connection; Self: connected

Attanucci, Jane, 10, 14, 214 n. 3

Auerbach, J., 14, 253 n. 6, 255 n. 19

Autonomy: and childhood experience, 76–77; in conflict with compassion, 243; different sense of, 52; illusory, 115; and men, 109; mythic need for, 46; need to protect, 90; and women 121. *See also* Self: autonomous

Bachofen, J., 45

Bad faith, 27

Baier, Annette, 6, 12, 28, 30, 68 n. 25, 75, 77–78

Bakan, David 114, 133

Baumrind, Diane, 9–10, 80, 163, 165, 172, 173 n. a, 178, 189, 211, 272 n. 4

Beauvoir, Simone de, 12, 128

Behavior, prosocial. *See* Prosocial behavior(s)

Belenky, Mary, 166, 169, 232; and abortion study, 115, 210, 243, 253 n. 1, 254 n. 10

Bem, Sandra, 178, 195, 203